NEW DIRECTIONS IN LATINO AMERICAN CULTURES
Also Edited by Licia Fiol-Matta & José Quiroga

Forthcoming Titles

New Concepts in Latino American Cultures
A Series Edited by Licia Fiol-Matta & José Quiroga

Violence without Guilt

Ethical Narratives from the Global South

Hermann Herlinghaus

palgrave
macmillan

Cover Image: Marta Moramay Cuevas, *Memory in Blue*
© Marta Cuevas, 2002

First published in 2009 by
PALGRAVE MACMILLAN®
in the United States—a division of St. Martin's Press LLC,
175 Fifth Avenue, New York, NY 10010.

Where this book is distributed in the UK, Europe and the rest of the world,
this is by Palgrave Macmillan, a division of Macmillan Publishers Limited,
registered in England, company number 785998, of Houndmills,
Basingstoke, Hampshire RG21 6XS.

Palgrave Macmillan is the global academic imprint of the above companies
and has companies and representatives throughout the world.

Palgrave® and Macmillan® are registered trademarks in the United States, the
United Kingdom, Europe and other countries.

ISBN-13: 978–0–230–60818–4 (Paperback)
ISBN-10: 0–230–60818–3 (Paperback)
ISBN-13: 978–0–230–60817–7 (Hardcover)
ISBN-10: 0–230–60817–5 (Hardcover)

Library of Congress Cataloging-in-Publication Data

Herlinghaus, Hermann.
    Violence without guilt : ethical narratives from the global south /
Hermann Herlinghaus.
        p. cm.—(New directions in Latino American cultures)
    Includes bibliographical references and index.
    ISBN 0–230–60817–5
        1. Latin American literature—20th century—History and criticism.
    2. Latin American literature—21st century—History and criticism.
    3. Violence in literature. 4. Violence in popular culture—Latin America.
    5. Violence—Social aspects—Latin America. 6. Violence—Philosophy.
    I. Title.

PQ7081.H42 2008
700'.4552—dc22   2008021596

A catalogue record of the book is available from the British Library.

Design by Newgen Imaging Systems (P) Ltd., Chennai, India.

First edition: January 2009

10 9 8 7 6 5 4 3 2 1

Printed in the United States of America.

CONTENTS

PART III COLOMBIAN MARGINALITIES AND THE CULTURE OF EXCEPTION

PART IV AFFECTIVE POLITICS AND THE IMAGE

A Note on Translations

English quotations of corrido lyrics cited from Spanish-language editions, as well as extracts from foreign-language editions are my translations. Quotations cited from published English translations are the work of those translators unless otherwise indicated. Full information on sources is given in the bibliography.

H. H.

PART I

A Modern War on Affect

CHAPTER 1

From Walter Benjamin's Early Writings to the Perils of Global Modernity

REAPPROACHING BENJAMIN, LOCATING EMERGING NARRATIVES

This book owes more to Walter Benjamin than I had originally foreseen. Several of his early writings on violence and religiosity have inspired me to cut a wide swath through conceptual phenomena that belong to some of the most compelling experiential and narrative figurations of today's world. To begin with, there has been a shift in critical attention traversing relevant current debates, the implications of which scholars have barely started to explore. In the wake of Giorgio Agamben's *Homo Sacer* (1998), a perspective came to the fore that allows casting doubt on deconstruction's having uttered the definitive word in the discussion of Benjamin's concept of violence.[1] Agamben's innovative move consisted in addressing the crucial link, in the work of the German Jewish philosopher, between "violence" and *blosses Leben* (bare life), whereas previous studies had widely overlooked the conceptual importance of *blosses Leben* in Benjamin's early political thinking. "Bare life" is the term used in *Critique of Violence* (1921) when, throughout the final pages of the essay, the author raises intricate issues related to "guilt," "expiation," and "law." Regarding "bare life" and "guilt," probably thus far the two most perplexing notions of the early Benjamin, Agamben, in his reformulation of the theory of sovereignty, views them as originary juridical concepts.[2] However, the "historical index" that can afford Benjamin's thought-images with particular scenarios of "legibility"[3] has been so drastically challenged, that the original purpose of tracing a philosophy of history of violence[4] poses further questions today. It resonates, for example, in the emergence of inhabitual aesthetic projects at the margins of both the established political-juridical markers of ethical thinking, and the perception of ethics as a unique act of understanding in the way it has been supposed to emanate from the self-constitutive realms of literature and the arts.[5] Ingraining violence into the core of modernity and violence as a feature of everyday experience cannot be addressed without forcing reflection anew, pushing it toward what have remained underestimated spheres of analysis: the contradictory dynamics of secularization[6] and the resultant affective undergrounds and paradoxes that exist within heterogeneous modernity. We can start to bring out the vibrancy that resonates in Benjamin's concept of bare life if we extend the horizon beyond juridical thought and ontological abstraction, as well as beyond European epistemology, and approach *blosses Leben* as a conceptual, historicizing tool that, far from being an archaic relic, helps cast a sharper light on unequal contemporary globalization and those ominous terrains where life itself is at stake.

The second, and indeed tenacious, inspiration for this text emerged from my acquaintance with narrative territories that have displaced influential ramifications of scholarly work in Latin American literary studies and hemispheric border studies, as well as in comparative literature. These territories confront us with a kind of demand, to use Paul Bové's term, that we question the literary critical constructs of state formations.[7] Let me introduce an example that I call *transnational narconarratives.* The epithet *narco* stands as a symptom whose possible meanings warrant further reflection. Attempting a first assessment, narconarratives designate a multiplicity of dramas expressed in antagonistic languages and articulated, in Latin America and along the hemispheric border, through fantasies that revolve around the depravity and deterritorialization of individual and communitarian life worlds caused by various factors. Among these factors, the deterioration of traditional, social, and democratic civic relationships,[8] new scales in the mobility and spatial experience of common people, together with the drastic increase of urban informal economies,[9] and the rise of the transnational narcotics economy appear as surface indicators.[10] Narconarratives are marked by varied kinds of rhetorical strategies and affective aesthetics through which they defy the harshness and "unreality" of a "society of spectacle,"[11] to use Guy Debord's term, in which Latin American countries have been living the tectonics of neoliberal adjustment since the 1970s. It is not drug consumption and its artistic representations, a wide panorama of which have already been produced in modern literature and film, which is at issue in the first place. Nor do I point to depictions of violence linked to the latest firsthand avatars of the narcotics trade, as they are often displayed by some media. My approach is heuristic, different, for example from Pérez Ramírez' typological description that holds that "narcoliterature" has well-defined profiles.[12] What mark this dynamic, untheorized realm of narrative production in Latin America today are pervasive images and configurations of shattered life, precarious life—human existences that are massively endangered by privation, urban, and occupational marginality,[13] and illicit global flows,[14] all of which reproduce innumerable forms of intertwined violence and unnatural death. At the same time, these narratives disclose images of deviance and projects of survival that are ethically affirmative in paradoxical, often shocking ways. Today, literary criticism and cultural analysis are interpellated by narrative formations and concept-figures whose strangely nonsecular contours do not equal backwardness, and whose partly nonmetropolitan constituencies can afford revealing insights into the shadow zones of global struggles. There is a fundamental question that is still considered either too trivial or too threatening to be pursued in depth. If lettered high reflexivity has a stake in exploring the inner bonds between "qualified life"[15] and the genuine anxieties of those who can best lay claim to it, should reflection not explore, with equal attention in the narratives that have gone very far in addressing "the unspeakable abyss of humanity," the "interruption[s] of civility?"[16] These narratives should not be dismissed as aberrations from a norm that is supposed to hold upright—by the sheer force of projection—its moral and epistemological promise. Throughout Latin America, the faces of endangered life and of bodies that are vulnerable and exposed to destruction, together with the fantasies of those that neoliberal freedom leaves behind, are not the exception but a daily presence about which a transnational group of narratives can provide firsthand insights.

Let me illustrate the problem with a paradox that Benjamin pointed out when he questioned Kurt Hiller's postulate that "higher even than the happiness and justice of existence stands existence itself."[17] Benjamin's polemic with post-World War I pacifism pointed to an epistemic issue that Hiller, in his claims for a pacifistic state,[18] had not recognized: the modern state's central implication in the Western political and philosophical tradition that ties violence to the category of means and ends, and thus to instrumentality.[19] Hiller's insistence on the unmediated sacredness of human life[20] had a blinding effect regarding a vicious circle of violence: "All violence as a means is either law-positing or law-preserving."[21] Therefore, Benjamin criticized Hiller's claim as a dogma, the belief of a left political variant of vitalism that life and death be the "very cosmic affair"[22] of the human being. On the one hand, the dogma of bare life's sacredness overshadowed the question of justice and social change. But at the core of his argument, Benjamin questioned what appeared as an abstract, religiously tuned vitalism, responding that "however sacred man is . . . , there is no sacredness in his condition, in his bodily life vulnerable to injury by his fellow men."[23] This renders life at its precarious ends a complex notion, calling for a revision of the concept beyond its cosmological mythification as well as beneath the Western certainties of qualified life. Judith Butler, in a somewhat different vein, speaks of the dramatically increased vulnerability of today's globe and of the threats that can severely dislocate the privileges of the First World. She suggests that we take "precarious life"—life's exposedness to injury and aggression—as a vantage point for an internationalist ethical thinking.[24] This implies that we ask anew—how do the mechanisms for "distributing vulnerability" work, nationally and globally? How do we become acutely aware of "differential forms of allocation that make some populations more subject to arbitrary violence than others?"[25] Where is the limit at which "graduated citizenship," as a "differential mode of treatment of populations"[26] according to their status within globalized space, to use Aihwa Ong's expression, turns into a postdevelopmental form of bio- and geopolitical oppression? Or more drastically, how can we address the experiences of what Mike Davis calls a "surplus humanity," the new "informal working class, without legal recognition or rights"[27] that, on the one hand, defies Negri's and Hardt's unifying tele-ology of the multitude[28] but, on the other, shows astonishing potentials of communitarian survival and response to destitution and the abortion of hope? To take another example, does a recently suggested concept of "weak citizenship" not point in a similar direction, in that the modern citizen is more and more exposed to a "thinned, unobstructed social texture" that is itself embedded in an "impoverished and hygienized public realm?"[29] Bare life still cannot be understood as a self-evident category. We might retain the basic attribute of "precarious." Bare life can be understood as precari-ous, to the extent that it is prevented from delivering an intelligible lin-guistic utterance[30] that could account for existence exposed to violent or latent death, together with exploitation, intimidation, and exhaustion.[31] The peculiar semantic of the concept has only started to receive the attention of scholars. To reapproach Benjamin's term *blosses Leben* requires that we develop interpretive strategies from an end other than that of abstract onto-logical speculations, or of inertias that tend to take the normative construct-edness of modern society as the self-fulfilling impulse of transcendental will. Endangered human existence has begun to acquire unprecedented shapes of global immanence, and its distribution follows avenues that are as arbitrary as they are paved with cynical common sense, trying to reason away the heightened vulnerability of the world or to close up permeable borders by escalating sovereign rule.

The realms of Latin American literature and cinema were traversed, during the 1990s, by discontinuous, singular, and sometimes extreme imag-inaries and aesthetic configurations. These emerge, for example, from the amazing wave of narcocorrido culture that spreads along the Mexican-U.S. border; the Colombian chronicles and novels about the fantasies of ado-lescent killers unheard of a few decades ago—the *sicarios*; and a remark-able, yet offensively unfamiliar series of new films from Argentina, Brazil, Peru, Venezuela, Mexico, and Colombia, whose images draw on spatial-political formations of bare life as they spread across the twilight zones of late modernity. Rather than aberrant transnational artistic representations, these narratives are themselves part of a change in aesthetic and conceptual sensibilities. They can be perceived to be singular figurations of the ubiquity of violence in terms of experience. The way violence is becoming immanent is the aesthetic sign of narratives and images that explore dimensions that modern tragedy has never taken interest in and which reach beyond, as well, melodrama's more democratic wagers. We regard the loss of an aesthetically normative pathos regarding terror and life's destruction, the erosion of tragic norms, and the infection of literature by figures of stunning sobriety to be symptoms that will allow us to embrace, across varied spaces and contexts, a heterogeneous group of literary, musical, and cinematic expressions.

The writing of this book, as it evolved, led me to what seemed to be, at first glance, disconcerting genealogical relationships of modernity, violence, and affective experience that are often traversed by elements of religious imagination. The questions that struck me reached beyond narconarratives and into wider territories of cultural figurality, marked by representations of survival and exception, of global experience outside cosmopolitan ground, and by new narrative investments in the spheres of the sacred and the profane, all of which combined to erode my expectations for a conciliatory space in which aesthetic and ethical prolegomena could still meet. There was no way to move ahead, except by paying attention to *life* not primarily as a politico-juridical notion or as the fragmented object of the biosciences, but as a rhetorical-practical concept located at the juncture where human bodies and the peculiar energies that tie imagination to action can be perceived as the most intensely politicized matter. How can analysis go beyond a ready-made catalogue of assumptions that had previously taken charge of the concept of life by relieving us from its tremendous closeness, or to borrow from Foucault's remarks on Canguilhem—by eschewing its pathological as well as its destructive aspects?[32] Life's closeness is not a question that can be reduced to what is at hand—its empirical and timely data. It is linked, in the case of our study, to insights that examining its anthropological and ethical charge under extreme circumstances and its relationship to knowledges that defy symbolic hierarchies will help provide.

This led me back to Benjamin. I am thinking of a less well known Benjamin, one whose early writings seem scattered and uncertain, especially since part of them has not survived.[33] This philosopher keeps confronting his readers with paradoxes that arose from his desire to unravel two of modernity's most controversial issues: violence and religiosity. My study of new narrative formations in Latin America started gravitating toward relationships between violence and guilt, and the way it became possible to see them at the moment when bare life is changed from an obsolete or opaque notion into a first-rate conceptual tool. This might, at first glance, seem to be a move toward Agamben, who champions a juridical concept that is linked to a genealogy of sovereignty reaching back to Roman origins. However, I believe the particular way Benjamin addresses religiosity cannot be reduced to a state of indistinction between life and the virtuality of violent death as it is generated by the implements of sovereign power (the state of exception). How can a vantage point for examining the concept of bare life be located, one that will shed light on another dimension of life under the exception—which is not solely owing to a sovereign decision under particular circumstances of conflict, or to the paradoxical "form of the law"?[34] Figures of exception and alternate empowerment are of interest, ingrained as they are in existential spaces that have been globalized at the edge of cosmopolitan freedom and civic nationhood. How can bare life be readdressed regarding the enforced neoliberal adjustment to which Latin America has been subjected, while taking cultural analysis beyond statistical evidence, sociological critique, and static representations of an "altogether-other"?[35] Where can the particular force of comprehension and of transgression inherent in the narratives we will explore, be located?

I am not suggesting that Benjamin reemerges as someone whose interest in the margins of modernity would warrant, today, a geographical-historical extrapolation of his thinking to the peripheries. Things are more intricate as long as they have anything incredible or paradoxical to offer. An appreciation of Benjamin's early concern for violence and modern affective topographies, however, will have to ask after highly unusual indexes for "legibility."[36] It has to include the scarce references through which the philosopher, during his lifetime, moved closer to Latin America—as a latent, and as John Kraniauskas thinks, repressed space[37]—than has been imagined. Only in this way can the prevailing attribution of Benjamin's intellectual world to the legacies of Europe be contrasted with new insights into the untimely dimension of his search.

Finally, my interest in narrative domains that are emerging from the globalized peripheries today implies a shift of perspective, away from previous studies that have worked along the lines of equating *cultures of violence* and "cultures of fear."[38] What comes into focus, instead, are spheres of imagination sustained by unanticipated relationships among violence, guilt, and expiation, together with demands for elementary solidarity and dignity that are sometimes supported by figures of violent action itself. Turning the reflection on violence toward the problematic of guilt and what will become pertinent as resistances directed against particular conditions of culpability means following an uncommon path. In Benjamin, these concepts lie hidden in his thoughts on a genealogy of emerging law and of "capitalism as religion." On a related yet very different level, "guilt" and its contestation will be shown to play a central yet often concealed role in what I call a *modern war on affect.*

A War on Intoxication: Affective Marginalities and the Examination of Experience

Modern Western history revolves around a deep split in the secret in which truth's dependence on untruth is ethnically and geographically divided between north and south.

—*Michael Taussig*

Before addressing several aspects of Benjamin's posthumous work, I will argue that a *war on affect,* understood as an intrinsically modern phenomenon, can be thought of as a conceptual and historical blueprint for engaging globalization. Let me start by proposing a paradoxical concept: *affective marginalities.* Its social and geopolitical perception is less difficult to picture than it is to recognize its properly affective mold. Marginalization abounds at numerous levels—in relationship to the increase of poverty; to the attacks on the equality of women that legal cynicism jeopardizes[39] or which morality and market fetishism tend to reaccommodate into "decent" divisions of labor; the decreasing availability of legal protection for vast groups of individuals and communities throughout the world; the precarious stance of the laboring classes within global networks of production and exchange; the offenses to the rights to the integrity of the human body and to the freedom of gender identity, as well as to the acceptance of cultural and ethnic differences; the seizure on the conditions of sustainability of living environments and natural resources, not to speak of the "right to political association and 'good' governance."[40] Niklas Luhmann's systemic logic of inclusion/exclusion[41] acquires an involuntary radicality today. A vision has started to loom up among large segments of the middle classes, growing into an uncanny hallucination. It has to do with life's being taken over by labor in the elementary sense, at the point at which "no man-exerted violence, except the violence used in torture, can match the natural force with which necessity itself compels."[42] The tendency of either exhaustion or marginalization of formerly secure sectors carries a disturbing effect, for it threatens to hollow out the features on which a late liberalist image of the cosmopolitan citizen[43] has been built. On the other hand, the onslaught of neoliberalism has provoked a recent reevaluation of the practices of primitive or original accumulation, especially regarding the assault on livelihood at the point where it affects local and peripheral regions and vast heterogeneities of peoples. This means that the assumption that "accumulation based upon predation, fraud, and violence"[44] belonged to an early phase of capitalism that is no longer relevant has proven false.[45] Central assumptions of Benjamin's *Critique of Violence* have to be read anew. By applying and reapplying perplexing mechanisms of domination, which Benjamin once called the dialectics of "law-positing" and "law-preserving violence,"[46] forces that today champion "economic universalism backed by military coercion"[47] have turned bare life into a looming presence.

Jacques Rancière has placed the terrain of social and political struggles in a direct relationship with what he calls the organization and "distribution of the sensible."[48] Modes of subjectivation are highly dependent on "aesthetico-political fields" that delimit the horizons of a given order or hierarchy of the sayable, desirable, and performable and that which remains secret or excluded.[49] These axioms can indicate a useful heuristic trace. We are approaching a concept-figure of *affective* marginalities by asking not for the sociological object—predefined social groups or reified discourses of presumed collective identities—, but rather for the theater of social emotions[50] and the regulation of their aesthetic coordinates. In other words, globalization can on the one hand be perceived, as does Arjun Appadurai, in terms of " 'disjunctures' between various kinds of flows—of images, ideologies, goods, people, and wealth."[51] On the other hand, the affective (dis)charge that underlies the main conflicts in the present world speaks of the existence of flows and "aesthetic" condensations that are less differentiated. At this point, the logic of marginalization is more difficult to picture. Let me take the example of a hemispheric "war on drugs," and by putting it in perspective, help reveal genealogical links between modernity, violence, and a global distribution of the sensible. My aim is to trace a tentative map, in which the junctures of modernity and intoxication, globalization, and narcotics management can disclose astonishing scenarios for analysis.

There is a complex matrix of marginalization that is related to the advent of a transatlantic modern world[52] and to the strategies used to establish global control over the forces of intoxication.[53] *Rausch* (intoxication) is the German word that I am taking from Benjamin's essay on surrealism and placing within an extended horizon of arguments, since this concept can have a powerful bearing on the distribution of a "sensible order that parcels out places and forms of participation in a common world."[54] Taking a closer look at intoxication as a philosophical problematic that exceeds narcotics, can help expand our insights, to paraphrase Nietzsche, into the production of modernity's "troubled soul" and the particular role the concept of guilt has come to play for the affective constitution of a globalized world. Our perspective seeks to connect, by virtue of "dialectical imaging," a philosophical interest in the question of experience and an historical look into the conflicts that have unfolded around the production and distribution of psychoactive substances and their role in the formative processes of modernity. As will be argued, the international narcotics economy stretches back into the Western history of colonization and modernization. Its trajectories are puzzling and its forces merciless. To begin by addressing the obvious yet not necessarily understandable—in the Western hemisphere, the contemporary conundrum of a trans- and multinational narcotics economy has become virtually indistinguishable from the issue of the drug war[55] and its discourse of purification. Since 1914, the United States has been engaged in a fight in which one legal drug after another has "fallen from grace."[56] In the early 1970s, "raids" were transformed into a major "war" that was escalated under the administrations of Presidents Reagan and the first Bush in the 1980s and early 1990s.[57] A main target of transnational belligerent actions, separate from the domestic fronts, has been Latin America, especially the countries of Bolivia, Peru, Mexico, and Colombia, as well as Panama. Among the symptomatic values of the narcotics war is its self-fulfilling driving force.[58] This scenario has to be placed in the context that Agamben calls, using Hannah Arendt's expression, the assumption of a "global civil war,"[59] a war that has extended the "no-man's-land between public law and political fact," disturbing "the structure and meaning of the traditional distinction between constitutional forms."[60] My concern is not to engage this war from the perspective of juridical theory. However, it is intriguing to note that when Agamben discusses the "state of exception's" becoming a leading paradigm in contemporary politics, he does not mention the phenomenon of the hemispheric narcotics crusade, nor has the issue been addressed in Hardt and Negri's *Empire*, or in other major political-philosophical studies. Hasn't the drug war become a sensitive arena where, in addition to economic struggles, fantasies related to original sin, guilty territories and populations, and geopolitical punishment are being restaged and played out anew? This leads up to the question of the affective forces that this war has brought to serve a large-scale redefinition of the "exceptions" to the rule. At issue today is the alloying of the idea of containment—the normative construction of the individual subject's omnipotence over its emotions, corporeal, and energetic existence[61]—with the principles of righteousness and truth, the prosperity of transnational capital, and national as well as international security.

The narcotics conflict contributes distinct features of sensibility to a malleable "state of exception" of global scope. It has been orchestrated by political discourse and the mass media since the 1980s, on the grounds of ideological patterns and symbolic devices whose denominator has been its high emotional charge. The specter of the uncontained subject, sustained by a pharmacological discourse that equates intoxication, addiction, and degeneration or destruction has itself become part of an uncontained campaign.[62] What ushered in the military strikes against areas of coca cultivation in Latin America was not the kind of strategy that Žižek called "secretly doing the 'necessary but dirty thing', that is, by violating the explicit ruling ideology,"[63] but rather by carrying out a kind of sacred battle. To put it succinctly—the drug war has received a deciding push for legitimation from its construction as a large-scale cultic venture. It has become addicted to itself. Many systematic studies have produced evidence of its failure to solve the drug problem.[64] Nevertheless, a politics of foundationalist assumptions, together with a repertoire of images and symbols for rendering evident guilty territories and bodies, have succeeded in "crowd[ing] out the possibility of reason, care, and collective responsibility."[65]

Behind an imperial horror of the human body[66] as a site that is susceptible to intoxication and transgression lingers the picture of a divisive economy of production, appropriation, and interdiction of what was classified, in the twentieth century, as illicit drugs versus the "ethical medicines of the pharmaceutical market and the drugs of the grey market"[67] (alcohol, tobacco, and caffeine). In the Western hemisphere, this conflict is closely related to what Richard DeGrandpre calls America's "cult of pharmacology," which is promoted by the pharmaceutical industry, modern biological psychiatry, the biomedical sciences, the drug enforcement agencies, and the judicial system. It constitutes a large-scale venture comparable, in its drive to fuse economic, political, and cultural mechanisms of othering into one single movement, to what Said has discussed under the rubric of "orientalism."[68] The power of the cult consists in classifying drugs as either "angels" or "demons."[69] The policing of contamination, administered from the global North, is confronted with—and enabled by—the struggle for survival by considerable populations of South American countries under the present circumstances of hemispheric design.[70] Bearing in mind the fact that the largest amount of drug consumption, legal and illegal, occurs in the developed countries, led by the United States, we can confer a compelling logic to the following words: "The dialectics of intoxication are indeed curious. Is not perhaps all ecstasy in *one* world humiliating sobriety in the world complementary to it?"[71] We are tempted to take these words—by Benjamin referred to a "curious experience of love"— out of their context, so that they can convey, by means of juxtaposition, a condensed concept-figure of a global-local dynamic of *humiliating sobriety* and *ecstasy*. "Ecstasy" might refer to the state that follows drug consumption. Yet it can also point to regulatory devices that help turning emotional containment into the central aspect of the moral self, as it is democratically applied to the full-fledged modern citizen. For example, low-level ecstasy is constantly reproduced by a "society of spectacle"[72] as a means of taming intoxication or by the incorporation of numerous legal drugs, literally, into the organism of society versus the stigmatization of illicit ones. Such mechanisms are susceptible to what DeGrandpre describes as the "placebo-text" principle,[73] that is to say, the effects that public perception, normative values, and socioeconomic and geographical conditions exert on the ways of how psychoactive "commodities" are used or misused. There is one paradox that seems to lie at the heart of the Western conundrum of ecstasy and humiliating sobriety. Doesn't a universal, that is to say, market-driven, demand for "happiness" accompany "the widespread unhappiness in our society"[74] as Arendt foresaw in 1958? Isn't the lack of a language for articulating general unhappiness part of the same dilemma—the phenomenon that advanced societies have increasing difficulties in publicly scrutinizing the questions related to drug consumption and, more generally, to psychic-corporeal dilemmas whose discursive opacity marks the very conditions of their economic pervasiveness and sociocultural ingrainment?

Viewed from these vantage points, my concept of *affective marginalities* can designate a heterogeneous range of phenomena. Affective marginalities are shaped by the global-local dynamics of *ecstasy and humiliating sobriety*,[75] yet their status varies according to the site and the role they play within this dynamics. At the point at which modernity is perceived in terms of intoxication, the production of marginality turns into a foremost question for both social and affective regulation and control. As taught in Christian epistemology, purity is not a matter whose resolution resides in the corporeal and material world. It presupposes a referent that establishes a sacred sphere that is kept separate from profane desires. It will be seen, when we discuss Benjamin's thoughts about *capitalist religiosity*, that the policing of intoxication feeds into a larger strategy of sacralization. Not by chance has the imaginary that fuels drug war propaganda been charged with elements of a sacred war.[76] There is an implicit verdict of "profane crime" inscribed in the discourse that excited this war: what is feared are (profaning)[77] forces or developments that are capable of contradicting the cultic view of drugs. The discourse stigmatizes those at the source of the "evil" who produce and distribute the proscribed substances from isolated zones of the cosmopolitan *polis*, that is to say, from the Andean highlands and Colombian valleys, for example. Therefore, these regions have been facing the threat of destruction of their agricultural soils by biochemical warfare. The threat is contrasted by the peasants' struggle to escape bare life that keeps generating such dramatic forms of labor.[78] This situation feeds into the deteriorating conditions of life of other sectors—both urban and semi-urban—in Latin America, people whose integration into the new informal working class is not unlikely to push them into the spheres of low-level narcotics trade. At the other end of this gamut are the consumers of illicit narcotics, deep in the heart of the global North, where drug crime, transgressive social and sexual behaviors, and stock repertoires of health fetishism are cover stories, behind which much larger repositories of intoxication have spread. These are bound to the psychosocial streams of energies that are regulated by both taboos and politics of allowance. There are, therefore, at least two overlapping yet distinct domains of marginalization—the one in the South, and the one in the North, strangely interrelated, under certain conditions, prospering within similar geographies as well. These spheres are targets and catalysts of different forms of violence related to both civilian biopolitical regulation and neoliberalism's godlike powers that are supported by coercive measures like the war. Affective marginalities, constitutively linked to the global distribution of the sensible, are therefore highly asymmetrical and heterogeneous.

The formation of the "modern/colonial world system"[79] has been accompanied by longer-lasting production cycles of marginalities, whose nerve centers, especially in relation to the history of narcotics, remain to be addressed. Before we argue that the "psychoactive revolution" has allowed narcotics to become a central matter of transatlantic exchange, industrialization, and psychological modernization, a glance at the troubled contours of modern subjectivity is, once again, necessary. Teresa Brennan has suggested that we address the concept of affect to trace an alternative map to contrast prevailing assumptions of psychoanalysis or "metapsychology."[80] She discusses an origin of affect that is social and environmental and bound to culturally available images and narratives, rather than autonomously induced by the individual psyche.[81] Speaking in basic terms, "the impulses [. . .] described in psychoanalysis might not originate in the individual psyche, but in the broader social order."[82] Fear and depression are collectively induced emotions before they can become individual feelings.[83] In the numerous historical and psychic mechanisms of repression of affectively "uncontained" cultural formations, Brennan locates the cornerstones of a Western, subject-centered identity that is based on "forming boundaries by projection."[84] Projection, rather than a distinctly individual mechanism, has serious anthropological-political implications. The modern Self has historically over time begun to project outside of "itself" those emotions that are deemed to be unwanted affects such as fear, anxiety, and depression to be rewritten as narrations of barbarism, but which, as Taussig has so eloquently shown,[85] must be controlled and thus reappropriated once they are turned into the features of alterity. Projection thus designates relationships whose internalization would be better served by Nietzsche's term "genealogy of morality" than one of the individual repression of desire. These insights, turning psychoanalysis upside-down, are not new but have often been displaced by the methods that the "human sciences" use to construct their objects.[86] We may recall Norman Brown's almost forgotten decentering of Freud, which suggested a critical syncretism of psychoanalysis, anthropology, and history. "The repressed unconscious which produces neurosis is not an individual unconscious but a collective one. . . . the theory of neurosis must embrace a theory of history; and conversely a theory of history must embrace a theory of neurosis."[87]

These insights will resonate, in the third part of this chapter, in accord with Benjamin's perplexing use of *guilt* as a "world-historical category."

Similar to Brown's hypothesis is Brennan's main premise, guided by the question of how "emotional containment" has been built, via psychorepressive politics, into the moral foundations of modern societies. Containment finds its seed in what Brennan calls the "interactive energetic economy"[88] or affective economy. It refers to the idea that there are movements, palpable yet not visible, in which natural and social spaces are conjoined by their energies. In other words, emotions and feelings are not naturally but rather artificially contained, yet what is socially and politically constructed is still linked, in one way or another, to biological and physical flows. In terms of energies, "there is no secure distinction between the 'individual' and the 'environment.'"[89] This distinction is artificial, and thus the invention of the self-contained subject—the individual qua modern citizen who is sovereign over the transgressive forces of nature and history—has served to establish a dualistic world with corresponding hierarchies of self and other. The concept of "othering" has become widely acknowledged at the junctures of psychoanalysis, postcolonial theory, and ethics. However, its relationship with forces that undermine the dual model of the individual and the social which is linked to an "economy" that bends human energies to norm and order, remains open to debate. There is reason to presume that a modern history of affective policing that relates to a genealogy of an increasing sense of guilt caused by repression/projection,[90] not only associates the conflicts at the heart of expanding Christianity, its crises and reformations since St. Paul's far-reaching dictum, "Faith is what saves us, not works."[91] It can also, in often paradoxical ways, furnish insights into the motives and forces that have been driving the machinery of the transatlantic world-system and, at its respectable metropolitan ends, the construction of the modern subject and its "bad conscience."[92]

Accentuating these relationships helps us to sketch out a more general marker. *Affective marginalities* become thinkable, but not as fundamentally uncontained agents, that is, the nonsubjects of Western culture who would find a heroic specter in Nietzsche's Dionysus figure. Rather, what acquire sharper contours are mechanisms of subjectification characterized by the condition of "carrying a burden." This predicament may originate by virtue of interiorization or by force of incrimination, or by both. In one important sense, affective marginalities can be considered those that "carry the negative affects for the other,"[93] acting as potential or imagined trespassers that allow governing desires and anxieties to incur in projection and thus occupy a morally safe place. Those carrying the burden are, as we will argue in the following text, profane actors in sacred territories, or subjects and communities that are being positioned at the low end of the class spectrum and ethnic scale, or the geopolitical map, or serving as targets of moral stigmatization in several other regards.[94] This obviously holds, although in different registers, for those in the South who make their living by trading illicit drugs, and those others, predominantly inhabiting the North or having access to the life styles of the centers, who indulge in the pleasures of illicit consumption. However, what we call the "war on affect" has to be viewed as a long-standing, "cold-war" constellation—a battle on numerous fronts in which, so far, triumph has gone to the strategies and bound energies that succeeded, over the centuries during which modernity achieves its global ascent, in creating evidence of the ever-increasing danger of intoxication. In this fight, the *discourse of containment* has become a central weapon, loyal to the Platonic principle that the capacity to rule "one's self" provides the "supreme criterion of fitness for ruling others."[95]

Genealogically speaking, the dialectics of ecstasy and humiliating sobriety offer revealing turning points. How is the contemporary hemispheric drug war to be placed within the *war on affect*, and where can formative tensions be located that will account for the relationship between the two? The war on affect acquires its transatlantic contours regarding what David Courtwright terms a gigantic "psychoactive revolution."[96] The expression refers to the production, exchange, and consumption of psychoactive substances as they have ranged at the core of Western expansion and colonization, to eventually become an enabling condition of modernity as a whole. Historically at issue, beyond the repression of "affectively uncontained cultures" to which Brennan refers, was the fight over the organization of strategic relationships between containment and transgression. A *narcotics fetishism* characterized the transatlantic politics of the world's governing elites from about the mid-seventeenth to the late nineteenth century, when they were concerned with manufacturing and taxing drugs, not with their suppression.[97] Profit-driven globalization of psychoactive plants and their derivatives, many of which came from the New World, would, across the centuries, transform habits and arouse fantasies of millions of people and influence the environment: wine, spirits, tobacco, coffee, opiates, cannabis, coca, and others. Narcotics were indispensable commodities and psychoactive agents, destined to second the practices of colonization, just as they were, eventually, to become fuels of industrial civilization. In short, the role of psychoactives ranked in close proximity to the introduction of colonial dominion and labor exploitation, together with the installation of the transatlantic trade networks and their crucial commodity chains (e.g., sugar, tobacco, and silver) beginning in the sixteenth century.[98] Fernando Ortiz has brilliantly narrativized the transcultural formations that unfolded from the tensions between dependent agrarian economies and the peripheral self-fashioning that has accompanied the dynamics and dramatic fantasies of nation-building in Latin America.[99] At the other extreme, the consumption of psychoactives as exotic goods would rank at the center of socioeconomic prosperity in Western Europe and the United States, with tobacco, alcohol, and caffeine, as well as opium and cannabis becoming the daily habits of masses of middle-class consumers—those that came to represent the modern individual in his or her exposure to the experiences of urbanization and industrialization.

The fact that certain plant-derived drugs were, during the twentieth century, declared objects of restriction and prohibition (such as opium and cocaine), while others (e.g., the more pernicious tobacco and alcohol) have been admitted, sanctioned, and celebrated remains one of the most controversial issues. The great about-face in the treatment of drugs, the large-scale criminalization of the nonmedical sale, and the use of narcotics, especially opiates and marijuana, occurred during the 1910s and 1920s.[100] We can call this movement the *second modernization of narcotics*. The gravity of establishing restrictive, and increasingly coercive, international and national control systems for certain drugs—yet not for others—should be considered against the background of the *first modernization of drugs* that took place centuries earlier. In other words, there was a world-historical "psychoactive revolution" during which massive consumption was both imposed and democratized, depending on the geoeconomic location and the social status of producers and consumers. In relationship to the history of sexuality, Foucault has observed two ruptures that together set the framework of the "great repressive cycle."[101] One took place during the seventeenth century with the advent of modern prohibitions; the other occurred in the twentieth century when "mechanisms of repression were seen as beginning to loosen their grip."[102] This large cycle regarding sexuality corresponds, inversely, to the historical movement from the psychoactive revolution to narcotics prohibition. After the about-face leading, from the dawning of the twentieth century onward, to selective narcotics prohibition on an international scale, during the 1970s and 1980s new forms of transnational warfare were set up to ward off, and simultaneously to control, narcotics' central role in the context of advanced, neoliberal globalization.

It appears as a striking issue that both the loosening and the sophistication of sexual repression have been paralleled, over the centuries, by a coercive movement toward the criminalization of narcotics and the biopolitical policing of its consumption and use. If there were a coherent discourse among the rationalizers of industrial progress in favor of selective prohibition, it has been linked to the nexus of sociomedical regulation and labor efficiency. Restricting and controlling the psychoactive revolution was dictated by the need to develop an increasingly sophisticated, capital-intensive work force in industrial and postindustrial contexts,[103] while downsizing the massive exploitation and narcotic numbing of pre- or early industrial labor in which opium, coca, nicotine, and alcohol were crucial ingredients for securing the functioning of the labor treadmill.[104] To use the terms of biopolitical critique, similar rationales for dominance and control of the biopolitical body, which under certain historical circumstances promoted narcotics, called for their selective proscription under the changing conditions of the twentieth century. Finally, the late twentieth-century hemispheric war on drugs, directed, in its external logic, against coca-growing communities in South America, has propelled the dialectic of psychoactive progress and control into a new phase, one that entails harsh strategies and sophisticated logistics to take hold of the uneven, chaotic geographic dynamics that accompanied the rise of neoliberalism over the last decades.

I would now like to suggest the expression of *(in)comparable intoxications* to demarcate a common ground for historico-cultural and philosophical reflection. These intoxications refer, on the one hand, to the previously described psychoactive revolution (and its long aftermath) during the formation of the transatlantic world and, on the other, to the concept of "anthropological materialism," designed by Benjamin as a movement toward an alternative theory of experience.[105] Because of its ambiguity, its placebo effects, and its mental and physiological stimuli, intoxication pertains to experience, probably to a greater degree than to any other philosophical concept. Intoxication dispels the dichotomies of good and evil under which it is commonly subsumed. A few more markers have to be sketched out to signal the unusual epistemological status of "intoxication." For Benjamin, both the sacred and the profane world were susceptible to intoxication within that conflict in which modern culture was constituted as concrete totality of experience: the realm where the regulation of the collective psyche was staged as a sublimely Western achievement. What cannot be pursued in detail here still deserves a condensed aside: it is necessary to recall that Benjamin's thoughts on surrealism, as Karlheinz Barck has emphasized, were not primarily dedicated to literature and the arts but to extraliterary affairs raging at the heart of history.[106] We need to relativize, at the same time, a prevailing tendency of interpretation that has focused Benjamin's critique of surrealism on the concept of "profane illumination."[107]

The essay "Surrealism" was published in 1929, a crucial moment in the "second modernization of narcotics," at a time when its author was struck by the powers that tended to repress historical perception and memory into the spheres of an opaque imagination—the dreamworlds with which capitalism was inundating everyday life.[108] If Benjamin was acting, "not as a historian of Surrealism, but as the theorist of Surrealist experience *as* historical experience,"[109] what was it that made the Surrealist project so compelling to him if not its attack against the forces that ruled over the modern subject—the administrators of containment who seemed to have summoned old and new magical powers into one single plan? Had "religious illumination" even in the shape of its massively fetishized and mediatized surrogates, made its way back into the contemporary everyday? We are not dealing with a traditional notion of religiosity here. If, according to Horkheimer and Adorno, a "dialectic of enlightenment,"[110] had succeeded in implementing abstract, instrumental reason but, at the same time, had covered social life with a mist of sacred illusions, what was—"anthropologically" speaking—the actual terrain of conflict? Against the commonplace assumption that a secularized, industrialized world had become the great other of religion, Benjamin emphasized that in a "bitter, passionate revolt against Catholicism...Rimbaud, Lautréamont, and Apollinaire" had brought surrealism to life, thus taking religious illumination as a lesson whose powers should not be discarded but inverted.[111] Illumination when succumbing to "theology" had to do, as Benjamin insinuated a few years later in his writings on hashish, with that "despotism" of digressive feeling that was capable of fusing everyday space into a most intense sensation of givenness, a sort of theological space "submerged in that of cheap fiction."[112] In contrast, it should be thinkable to derive from intoxication deviant and creative potentials, a project that went beyond the surrealism essay, and whose "furthest boundary" Benjamin was "still unable to survey."[113] A reflexive recovery, not only of illumination but of intoxication in terms of experience versus "the religious lesson" of what Auerbach had termed the ordered magic of Christianity[114] seemed to be the crux. Critical energies had to be sought after in a terrain where conventional Marxists had not deemed them possible—at the juncture of the "physiologically-human, the animalistic-human,"[115] and the need to reassess transgression as an inherently political question. The fact that most interpreters of the surrealism essay have given preference to "profane illumination" has cut short the theorizing about intoxication, as though the summoning of profane spirits for conscious awakening would naturally dissolve the theoretical challenges of the dubious sphere—*Rausch*. In a letter that Benjamin wrote to Scholem in July 1932, he spoke of his intention to write "a truly exceptional book about Hashish."[116] After his reflections on surrealism, intoxication kept vibrating as a site that his imagistic search for the aporias of experience had just started to mark off. In other words, if Benjamin's preference of illumination over intoxication—as a part of his writings does suggest[117]—could be so neatly assumed, why then his eventual insistence on writing the book on hashish?

To keep paying attention to "intoxication" helps to relate the dialectics of ecstasy and humiliating sobriety to those geographical and cultural territories that the essay on surrealism had left unaddressed. In fact, we are touching on an antidialectic, in that intoxication can be shown, as well, to potentially destabilize the idea of a European identity principle of "Being-in-Itself."[118] "Myslovice–Baunschweig–Marseilles. The Story of a Hashish Trance" is a kind of modern fairy tale in which Benjamin tells the travel adventures of the German painter "Scherlinger," who becomes irrevocably contaminated when moving into alien space. The first-person narrator, in his intention to meet intoxication face-to-face, ventures into the marginal zones of Marseilles. These are districts that represent a "town in a state of emergency," a terrain where battles of modernization are "continuously being fought out"[119] between town and country, center and periphery. Few passages in Benjamin provide a similarly intense mirage of globalized space as this text suggests, a territory in which substances such as hashish and opium are treated as part of a daily diet against fatigue and as a common article of transnational exchange, and where the flaneur and the destitute are suddenly being fused into one single person. The narrator, to yield to the magic force of these territories, renounces the self-centered cosmopolitanism of the European traveler: "I was probably closer in spirit to those Arabs [doing exhausting labor and dealing in drugs] than to the tourists."[120] As his state of intoxication advances, he can watch himself from a close yet abysmal distance, visualizing his own transformation into an African prophet, someone whose "supercilious" smile is that of "a man about to see through the world and its destinies and for whom nothing remains a mystery anymore, either in objects or in names."[121] We have come across an image space that is innately non-Hegelian but at the same time exceeds the surrealist workshop—one from which, for the intoxicated subject, the return to Central-European ratiocination is impossible. The subject's transformation into a (self)image of Sardanapolus "loosens"[122] the privilege of discourse that European universalism has kept over both objects and names.

In a similar vein, a few dream-images in "One-Way Street" elicit contours of a modernity haunted by transatlantic specters. This is the case with the fragment "Mexican Embassy," which resounds of Benjamin's early acquaintance with the work of Bernardino de Sahagún.[123] A first-person narrator—Benjamin "dreaming"—reports a place where "a religious order had survived from the time of the first missionaries." There he witnesses a ceremony that unites Mass and ancient rite: "toward a wooden bust of God the Father...a priest raised a Mexican fetish. At this, the divine head turned thrice in denial from right to left." The accompanying epigraph is taken from Baudelaire: "I never pass by a wooden fetish, a gilded Buddha, a Mexican idol without reflecting: perhaps it is the true God."[124] In other words, has secular modernity never been identical to "Itself"? Here we might resume the particular "historical index" of a modern war on affect—our mapping of those constellations from which Benjamin's images can be shown to acquire particular readability. What is the troubling issue of "Mexican Embassy" if not the presence of religious images on a plane where the criteria for distinguishing truth and identity from transgression and barbarism have become inverted? What could be more deceptive than alien epistemic spaces that can be recognized, in a certain light, as the ominous territory of modernity itself? If modernity "has never been modern"—to recall a range of arguments on the crisis of secularization that we later find in Löwith, Blumenberg, and Latour and up to Agamben, as well as in Latin American authors like Morandé, Martín-Barbero, and Rozitchner, what would a critical examination of experience imply when it is placed within the history of both the psychoactive revolution and its eventual repression? Might not the transatlantic war on intoxication, the production of affective marginalities, and the enigmatic call of "Mexican Embassy" for reviewing the (in)comparable scenarios of intoxication place Benjamin's thoughts on an anthropological materialism in global perspective?

"Capitalism as Religion": Guilt and the Success Story of Containment

My rereading of Benjamin's early thoughts on violence and religion has been inspired by my dialogue with emerging Latin American narratives. The interpretation of their imaginary worlds must touch on the genealogical spectrum of modernity and affective experience, especially when guilt and images of vigorous release or escape from culpability are set forth by aesthetic projects from today's global South. For the remaining part of this theoretical mapping, we will engage two texts of Benjamin, one of which was part of a complex that the philosopher had envisioned as three major essays on "politics."[125] Of these, only "Critique of Violence" has survived. "Capitalism as Religion" (1921), on the other hand, belongs to a group of short texts whose critical discussion is more recent, due to its fragmentary shape and posthumous publication.

Regarding "Critique of Violence" the discussions that have taken place since the late-1980s have engendered two marked tendencies. One arose within the framework of "critical legal studies," when Derrida positioned his reading of the essay at center stage during the first conference on "Deconstruction and the Possibility of Justice" held in New York, in 1989.[126] The other consists of the text's more recent recovery by Italian political philosopher Agamben. By alluding to, rather than reassessing, these different positions, I will draw on Benjamin's point of departure to shed light on specific affinities and contrasts between this essay and "Capitalism as Religion." My goal is to revisit the concept of "guilt" in both texts. Toward the end of *Critique of Violence*, Benjamin recapitulates:

> The critique of violence is the philosophy of its history—the "philosophy" of this history because only the idea of its *beginnings* [my translation and emphasis] makes possible a critical, discriminating, and decisive approach to its temporal data. A gaze directed only at what is close at hand can at most perceive a dialectical rising and falling in the law-positing and law-preserving forms of violence.[127]

What ensues in Benjamin's text is the controversial remark about "divine violence." Whereas Derrida insisted on arguing that *Critique of Violence* has a "too messianico-Marxist or archeo-eschatological" stance,[128] Agamben, in *Homo Sacer*, suggests a shift of attention. As has been repeatedly observed, a Jewish image of "divine violence" helps Benjamin figure the *interruption* of the cycle by which an alienating law is both constituted (posited) and perpetuated (preserved); he uses the German word "Entsetzung": de-position (of law).[129] However, we think that some doubt must be expressed about a reading that finds a violent divinity to be the main figure of the text. There is another notion "whose decisive function in the economy of the essay has until now remained unthought."[130] This about-face is far-reaching. Among the several difficult concepts in the essay, Agamben deems *bare life* to be the central one. He reads divine violence, in turn, from the viewpoint of the "state of exception," and situates it semantically "in a zone in which it is no longer possible to distinguish between exception and rule."[131] Yet, I will argue that by doing so, Agamben has curtailed the problem of an *affective* genealogy of bare life.

Regarding the paragraph cited earlier, I would like to discuss the idea of *Ausgang* under the aspect of the "beginnings" of a possible speculative history of violence, translated in the English edition of 1996 as "development," and read as "consummation" in various studies."[132] This assumption will help us, on a different plane, to think about the *beginnings* of a modern war on affect. Let me suggest a semantics of beginnings by referring to Said's reflection on this concept in Vico. "A philosopher who tries to understand an institution like law uses a conceptual language far removed from the distant and murky circumstances from which the law originally derived."[133] These may have been circumstances for whose understanding rational description would be "by definition a less accurate, more indefinite means than is imagery."[134] "Sympathetic imagination," "the body," and affective experiences such as "fear" are expressions that Said relates to Vico's way of approaching the "childhood" of human institutions. In Benjamin, the beginnings, as a vantage point for tracing a genealogy of violence can be perceived by thought images in which we find "bare natural life's being guilty."[135] This image seems to refer to both the Christian original sin and ancient mythology. No criterion of logical conclusion could sustain its force. As Said remarked about Vico, "a beginning is at once never given and always indefinite or devined and yet always asserted at considerable expense."[136]

What the image conveys is the nexus between "bare life" and a religious energy called "guilt": it seems to insinuate a threshold situation in which transcendence—either mythic or divine—seizes on the human body to the extent that it becomes a mark of immanence—as *blosses Leben*. If bare life is the "innocent bearer of guilt," there is a projection at work, implying that the (Christian vision of the) "dissolution" of the (Greco-Roman) law is enabled and sustained by grace (a Pauline reading). *Guilt*, more than any other complex affective state except for fear, stands for a collectively induced emotion, an assemblage. The mechanism of projection that generates guilt constructs obedience on the basis of expiation, irrespective of the deeds of the subdued party. *Sühne* (expiation) is the condition of "fate"[137] in the early times of human institutions, where unhappiness is defined as the innocent state of guiltiness—tied to original sin—which requires atonement. Guilt therefore arises as a necessary condition of identity before God. Similar to a perception in Kafka's "Before the Law"[138] humans are guilty *in advance*, without knowing how to explain or to avoid this immanent state. Curiously, in the 1977 edition of Benjamin's *Gesammelte Schriften*, the expression "dissolution" (*Auflösung*) of legal violence, readable in St. Paul's logic of "discharge from" (see the *Schriften* edition of 1955) appears as *Auslösung*—either "instigation" or "redemption." The 1996 English edition, in turn, corresponds with *Schriften*:

> …the dissolution of legal violence stems from bare natural life's being guilty, which consigns the living, innocent and unhappy, to an atonement that expiates the guilt of bare life—and presumably also frees the guilty, not from guilt, however, but from law.[139]

The apparent error in the 1977 German original might illustrate, ex post facto, the complexity inherent in Benjamin's criticism of the law, especially when it comes to what I perceive to be affective graftings onto consciousness in which law is involved. On the one hand, the Pauline meaning might have been appealing, to use one of Taubes' ideas, in connection to a Jewish "potential of liberation."[140] On the other, Benjamin's emphasis on "mythic" as law-positing force has genealogical implications, pointing to a logic by which its initial powers can turn "natural guilt"—the being guilty of mere life before God—into a form of foundational yet immanent violence, to be built upon. In that sense, Benjamin's approach may resonate with Vico's findings about the early period of Greek history when Athens was an aristocracy, and "the heroes, meaning the nobles, claimed to have a nature of divine origin."[141] The "living, innocent and unhappy," and yet guilty, were those who were granted "only the benefits of natural liberty," without civil rights. In other words, the problem of the original construction, or appropriation of guilt through the sphere of law is inherent in Benjamin's early thinking.[142] If "law-positing" force finds a main conceptual figure in "mythic violence," then we can assume that law, as does religion, reinvents transcendence by making it immanent to define a practical—psycho-physiological—canon of obedience and fulfillment. Historically speaking, the Christian invention of grace, connected to the "institution of atonement that is open 'through faith' to everyone" had undermined the Greco-Roman and—in part—Jewish systems of honor and shame backed by the laws of these traditions.[143] However, the universal guilt implanted by St. Paul's project of "liberation" would eventually inaugurate a more sophisticated canon of violence where religion and affectivity as identity markers of culture were concerned. This leads up to the problematic of "Capitalism as Religion."

To resume a genealogical link between guilt and law: At the root of law, there resides a law-positing violence that is "mythic," "sets boundaries," "brings at once guilt and retribution," "threatens," and is "bloody."[144] That way, the grounds are being laid for an eventual formation of law-preserving structures that, in turn, will enable an increasingly complex matrix of obedience, especially in the process in which ruling law creates authority through convention. It is here that the guilt of "bare natural life" mutates into the more ordered containment that befalls the "subject of the law."[145] Derrida points out, referring to Pascal and citing Montaigne, "Lawes are now maintained in credit, not because they are just, but because they are lawes. It is the mystical foundation of their authority; they have no other...Whosoever obeyeth them because they are just, obeyes them not justly the way as he ought."[146] What follows from this is an intricate dimension of containment. It embraces the powers that make foundational violence invisible (mythic violence becomes mystical), or create the illusion that "law-positing" force is held under control. Law-preserving force ensures the "mystical" spell of authority whose real power resides in its capacity to guarantee affective attachment. What becomes palpable in Benjamin is a daunting map that spans violence, law, and the underestimated concept of guilt, into which I have now introduced the idea of affective containment.

Let me recapitulate that, in his perplexing scheme, Benjamin argues that "mythic violence" sacrifices life to the law, whereas "divine" violence acts in the service of life and survival, although it might allow "sacrifice." Violent death can take place in both contexts, yet there is a distinction between them. Mythic violence eternalizes guilt, whereas "pure" or divine violence supposedly breaks the guilt cycle, all of which makes a bold imagery of expiation the crucial concern of the final passages of the text. Hence the different meanings of "Sühne" and "Entsühnung" that are not entirely evident in the English word "expiation." Benjamin's concept of *Ent-Sühnung* implies the active (and "in exceptional cases" violent)[147] breaking of the malediction of guilt that mythic violence has established. *Ex-piation* can be thought of as potential liberation from a state of rule (mythic violence eventually turned into law) that has placed guilt above knowledge and free will. Our reading causes a shifting of attention. What seems to matter first is Benjamin's attempt to undermine the tormenting, unspeakable predicament of guilt—that condition by which culpability becomes immanent in life and culture. When dealing with "Capitalism as Religion," written in the same year as *Critique of Violence*, we will show how Benjamin takes up the phenomenon of projection to place objectified guilt in a contemporary framework, but without maintaining the figure of divine violence. Guilt and divine violence can thus be supposed to open up to asymmetric registers. To the extent that we have discussed parts of Benjamin's reflection in relationship to the notion of a modern war on affect, it is not a longing for the coming of superior "justice" that is at issue. I assume, rather, from reading both texts together and asking for a global "historical index," that there is a central concern about a state of affairs to be finally associated with capitalism, in which containment and projection have succeeded in making guilt immanent to human life on the planet.

Life and *guilt* surface as markers of inhospitable reflexivity. How can the problematics of immanent guilt, together with Benjamin's desire for its suspension, offer a broader framework for understanding? The constellations, in which archaic and early Christian cultural imaginaries once met the origins of Western law, provide one possible archaeological scenario for rethinking modernity's tormenting roots. "Capitalism as Religion" suggests a bold shift of critical mapping: can we visualize the extension of the thought figure of bare life—the "marked bearer of guilt"—into a framework that is capable of embracing the dynamics of historical and contemporary capitalism? This question has acquired an unforeseeable timeliness. Only a few years ago, Benjamin's posthumous fragment began to evoke strong resonances, starting in Italy and Germany. Regarding the late ascent of this text, Dirk Baecker notes:

> The question of whether capitalism can be understood as a religion addresses, in contemporary times, a situation in which one would scarcely hesitate to give an affirmative answer. Since the socialist alternative is no longer available, and thus the character of society has ceased to be the object of ideology-based political decisions, today's society believes in capitalism. It believes that capitalism is its destiny....Society feels at home with capitalism, as it felt at home in earlier times with those spirits and gods who could be worshipped, yet whose moods and intentions would always remain surprising and unfathomable.[148]

There are several possible approaches to the concept of religion that Benjamin pursued when he wrote, "capitalism serves essentially to allay the same anxieties, torments, and disturbances to which the so-called religions offered answers."[149] At first, what comes to mind is religiosity without either dogma or observance. Toward the end of the fragment, one reads that for understanding capitalism, it is helpful "to realize that, to begin with, the first heathens certainly did not believe that religion served a 'higher,' 'moral' interest but that it was severely practical. In other words, original paganism did not achieve any greater clarity about its 'ideal' or 'transcendental' nature than modern capitalism does today."[150] Nevertheless, a central issue is Christianity, and Benjamin does not distinguish between Roman Catholicism and Protestant religion here. He presumed that there has been a historical dynamic during which Christianity has exchanged its "genuinely theological-ethical contents" for "pragmatic-cultic" practices.[151] Only under that condition could Christianity finally metamorphose into the "history of its parasite"—capitalism.[152]

Among the surprising features of the text is its refusal to enter into any kind of universal polemic between Christian and pagan arguments. Nor does it pay attention to specific contents of Christian teachings or of capitalist ideologies. In this diagnosis that draws on theological notions, it is a political anthropology "in reverse" that makes Benjamin's fragment compelling. Whereas Max Weber, competing with the Marxist determinism that proclaimed that religion would succumb to enlightened modernity, had formulated, in 1920, his thesis about the Protestant work ethic as the enabling condition of the capitalist economy,[153] Benjamin goes still further by attributing to capitalism an essentially religious structure. He provides three characteristics in the form of concise assumptions. "In the first place, capitalism is a purely cultic religion, perhaps the most extreme that ever existed. In capitalism, things have a meaning only in their relationship to the cult; capitalism has no specific body of dogma, no theology."[154] This is the cult that imbues daily routines with their dependence on capital as god: it turns utilitarianism religious. As the second feature, Benjamin, in an allusion to Bloch, speaks of the permanent duration of the cult. "Capitalism is the celebration of a cult *sans trêve et sans merci*[155] (without truce and without mercy). There are no weekdays. There is no day that is not a feast day, in the terrible sense that all its sacred pomp is unfolded before us; each day commands the utter fealty of each worshipper."[156] The time of capital is the time of a "dead now," with surplus value acting as eternal revenant.[157] That which guarantees endless duration is the ongoing "sacred" state that can be perceived as the cult of the commodity, with consumption all-pervasive. There is no single day that is not a feast day of commodity fetishism. Agamben recently pointed out the special character of sacralization which, in advanced capitalism, tendentially separates everything from "itself" by imposing exchange value and "exhibition-value" over use value: "spectacle and consumption are the two sides of a single impossibility of using."[158] What follows is that exchange value and its fetishes have enabled a unique state of religious intoxication—this idea traverses the visual and anthropological concerns of Benjamin's entire *Arcades Project*, crystallized for example in the notion of "phantasmagoria."[159] The third and most severe characteristic that constitutes the basis of capitalism's cultic condition reads: "the cult makes guilt pervasive. Capitalism is probably the first instance of a cult that creates guilt, not atonement."[160]

The concept of "guilt," after indicating an uncommon way of reading into, and out of "Critique of Violence" and its assumptions regarding the mythic forces of violence converted into law, suddenly reappears as the defining feature of the capitalist mode of subjection. This posture regarding the Janus face of secularization is genuine. It marks the frightening intimacy of modernity and capitalism, where subjection through guilt and, as we will see debt, might finally appear as the most efficient mechanism by which the so-called modern subject is both formed and controlled.[161] Throughout the twentieth century, from the standpoint of renewed eschatology in the light of threatening "progress," a Christian attitude has reaffirmed the notion of fear, whereas hope and conviction have been found in the expectations of the Enlightenment and its heirs. Benjamin, for his part, acknowledges guilt as capitalism's—and perhaps modernity's—very own destructive matrix. Following his hypothesis of a cult that creates guilt, Benjamin continues:

> . . . this religious system is caught up in the headlong rush of a larger movement. A vast sense of guilt that is unable to find relief seizes on the cult, not to atone for this guilt but to make it universal, to hammer it into the conscious mind, so as once and for all to include God in this system of guilt. . . . Capitalism is entirely without precedent, in that it is a religion which offers not the reform of existence but its complete destruction.[162]

This argument has abandoned the image of divine violence. Instead, Benjamin pictures an immanent God: "God's transcendence is at an end. But he is not dead; he has been incorporated into human existence." God himself has become guilty to such an extent that his "maturity" must be kept secret.[163] A terrible shadow seems to be cast on Negri's Spinozian vision of "this naked and powerful community"—the multitude of the poor—, which by laying claim to the radical immanence of its existence can "construct the world under the sign of the common."[164] According to Benjamin, the ontological exposedness of the "collective" to a secret god results in despair, disseminated not by dogma and transcendental illumination, but by the forces that have taken hold of the "carnal world to which our bodies chain us"[165]—immanence. This is the dimension that Negri and Hardt have preferred not to engage in when postulating a materialist teleology of the multitude.[166] Benjamin's argument entails a double displacement. Christian dogma has conceived of guilt as sine qua non, a state grounded in a timeless transcendental predicament. Capitalist society, in turn, handles guilt in a different way—fusing it with indebtedness to an extent that it becomes a central ingredient of life's and nature's organization by the market. Here it is necessary to point out the double meaning of the German word *Schuld*, which is pivotal for grasping the argument. The word means both "guilt" in its traditional sense of Latin *culpa*, and "debt" as financial or economic liability. If one "saw the spirit of capitalism as a form of secularized Calvinism, one could see debt (*Schuld*) as secularized sin, a version of guilt (*Schuld*) that is carried to all corners of the globe and to all corners of the soul by money."[167] Thus there are innumerous historical relationships between guilt and debt, part of whose efficiency may consist, in the end, in sustaining the status of that public secrecy[168] that binds religious morality and utilitarianism together. Benjamin's argument is astute because guilt is retraced to the point at which sacralization, inhering in an ever-expanding market, is propelled into contemporary dimensions. It creates, hypothetically speaking, a secret juncture of economic, juridical, and psychological constraints—a properly modern, that is flexible, matrix of "public unconscious." In an early philosophico-historical fragment, Benjamin writes that there is one way of vouching for the "one-meaningness of what is happening" in world-historical terms: to understand "guilt" as the "highest category of world history."[169] This assumption could never rely on a totality that, according to a rational theory of history, obeys cause-and-effect relationships. However, there is a different totality: " . . . one state of the world is always only guilt(y) in regard to any later state." Guilt appears as ubiquitous, omnipresent.

A sense of guilt as the capitalist-religious "state of the world," aludes, on the one hand, to an emotional structure that is evocative of Christianity's "dark workshop, its machine for manufacturing guilt,"[170] yet without any specific dogma. On the other, God's becoming guilty by being incorporated into human existence—the withering away of his transcendent role—amounts to a psycho-economic ontology. Hamacher observes that it was not Weber but Marx who provided insights into this complex relationship. Indeed, Marx' chapter, "So-called Primitive Accumulation," together with section VII of *Das Kapital* can be read, as well, as a treatise on the superior economic obsession with debt.[171] "Primitive" or "original" accumulation generates immense resources for the establishment of the capitalist credit system, with the production of guilt (in this case, of debt) becoming a universal state of affairs. Capital's success story starts with its being an "original sin," for which no expiation can exist: "conquest, enslavement, robbery, murder, in short, force"[172] being used under the laws of those in power. Only in this manner can the magical formula of the productivity of capital be instated throughout the world. "This primitive accumulation plays approximately the same role in political economy as original sin does in theology."[173]

"The guilt of money is a form of eternal guilt that weighs on people. The terrible fact is that humans in the capitalist age are unable to achieve atonement."[174] Money becomes the universal equivalent, and its increasing capacity to conceal the endless chain of debt that it creates in the service of capital's exponential reproduction appears as godlike power, the power of the fallen God who is finally included in the system of guilt. *Ent-Sühnung*, which surfaced in "Critique" as a liberating figure that insinuates the suspension of the spiral of guilt, now appears to be itself drowned by the capitalist cult, one that makes guilt universal and even threatens to destroy the existence of the "planet Human." Through its economic movement, capitalism seems to fulfill a supernatural logic that appears to be even stronger than the mythic capacity of law-preserving violence. An analogy might suggest that guilt, once generalized as "becoming culpable," that is debt with its fetishistic over-tones and religious undertones appears as a widely tolerated state of desire and despair. Authors like George Sorel, Gustav Landauer, Adam Müller, and others, listed by Benjamin at the end of "Capitalism," have all insisted on the role of money as a god that not only generates debt but carries an increasing burden of guilt itself.[175] Thus, "god capital" reproduces itself from never-ending credit, to the extent that today "credit moneys can roam the world as fast as information can move."[176] Once "original accumulation," that is the separation between the means of production and free laborers, has been achieved, exchange value can dominate use value, and commodities become the central mystical force. To find an analogy, Marx wrote, to the fantas-magoric character of the commodity, "we must take flight into the misty realm of religion."[177] Commodity fetishism stands out, in the end, as the accomplished form of containment—economic debt becomes immanent in life and society as a natural, sensuous-suprasensible,[178] and even desired state of guilt. Boundless consumption has come to adumbrate the most powerful manifestation of individual and social desire, accounting for a paradoxical kind of containment, which ever more drastically subordinates the *use value* of things (and of life) to the dynamics imposed by exchange value. In the sphere of social fantasies as emotional projection, the desire to consume is paralleled by an overall sense of depression in view of the increasing diffi-culty in making "profane" use of the world.[179]

Against the background of contemporary landscapes of interdependence and inequality, new light is shed on Benjamin's fragment. Saskia Sassen has eloquently asked for recognizing "forms of violence [that are] less visible than crashes of planes into buildings...," calling attention to the "debt trap" that has turned Third World countries into hyperdependent nations.[180] Owing to today's conditions of "global immanence,"[181] the indebtedness of peripheral countries functions as an empirical economic fact, and a tension of planetar-ian scope. It also works as a projection, especially for those living on the wealthier sides of the globe. It is supposed to serve the magical balance of wealth and inequality, and thus contribute to holding First world and Third world populations in check. However, a state of culpability "that is unable to find relief," implemented by the magic of the capitalist cult, makes social life appear to be "entified" in an ontology of guilt, creating affective (im)balances throughout the world. Applying a more timely wording for the spiral of universal economic indebtedness and the geopolitical strategies on which it draws, and which it nurtures, there can be no atonement for the exhaustion of life energies on the globe, the erosion of communitarian expe-rience, together with the proliferation of precarious life, and the destruction of resources and ecological environments, whose preservation should be the birthright of future generations.

What guides the ensuing reflections is the call to bring Benjamin's thoughts to bear on heterogeneous imaginaries of our contemporary world. The narrative spaces that I address in the next chapters as global localizations are to be understood in their peculiar relationships to a war on affect that succeeds in concealing the conditions of both psychic repression and economic oppression, demanding that specific attention be given to the nonrepresentative territories of the West. The literatures and musical and cinematic narratives that interest me do not engage exclusively in socioeconomic marginalization in Latin America and across hemispheric border spaces that signals the tip of the iceberg. Beneath the waters, there is submission turned into psychic reality—affective marginalization—at whose center lies the matter of life itself—its corporality and its immanent expressions. Life is pervaded, in diverse ways, by a nonindividual, dreary consciousness about which Nietzsche once asked, "How then did that other 'dismal thing', the consciousness of guilt, the whole 'bad conscience', come into the world?"[182] Could this have happened by virtue of "reason, solemnity, mastering of emotion, this really dismal thing called reflection, all these privileges and splendours man has: what a price had to be paid for them! How much blood and horror lies at the basis of all 'good things'!"[183] An associated question starts to resonate forebodingly: How can "that stroke of midday and of great decision that makes the will free again" be imagined; who could make the "will free" and "give earth its purpose and man his hope again?"[184] To free the will of guilt is, within rather non-Nietzschean configurations, the deviant affective and still reflective purpose of the narrative projects that I will discuss. At stake are propositions that have come to contest the capital—the sin—that continues to pay "interest on the hell of the unconscious."[185]

My arguments differ substantially from what Franco deems to be a tendency in contemporary criticism toward "semireligious language" and a "Benjaminian weak messianism."[186] Nevertheless, I will argue that the idea that capitalism has turned into the ominous, all pervasive religion of the contemporary era helps open an unhospitable realm for cultural analysis and ethical critique. Post-secular narratives advancing imaginaries that are related to violence, and resistance against particular conditions of culpability, together with claims for solidarity and dignity, can be read as profanations within and against dismal spaces of dependency and inertia that advanced capitalist modernity has spread throughout the world. They are presenting new resistances to the *war on affect*—that sacred modern battle about which I have provided this first genealogical map.

PART II

The Narcocorrido: A Phenomenological and Philosophical Look into Transnational Storytelling

CHAPTER 2

When Narcocorridos Were Born

A PARADOX OF GLOBAL ARCHAISM

The cultural landscapes that have emerged along with advanced globalization in the Western Hemisphere are nothing less than disconcerting. One of their most startling phenomena today is called the *narcocorrido*: an archaic and, one might think, even "primitive" form of balladry. Its music intervenes into public consciousness, however, and serves as an affective force of border identity that seems to rely on epic adventures derived from today's cross-border drug traffic. When using the term "landscapes," we think of culture as a world of shaped matter in its visual, spatial, corporal, and auditory expressions, without necessarily belonging to the discursive universe. The presence of narcocorridos is linked to an imagination that has been emerging out of the conflicts marking U.S.-Mexican border history for more than one hundred and fifty years. The written versions of these songs do not stem from the specialized formats of writing culture but are sustained by pervasive affective repertoires. Since the late 1970s, these drug ballads have been stigmatized and adored throughout huge areas on both sides of the border, becoming transnational narratives of a new type, yet looking surprisingly localist in tone and style.

Music specialists and academics interested in popular culture know the traditional *corrido* as an antique ballad form with a singular epic history that was brought to the New World by the *conquistadores*, appropriated by indigenous people, and since then has reemerged within an astonishing variety of contexts—colonization, independence, revolution, and border conflict.[1] According to Américo Paredes, this ancient genre entered a time of "decadence," from which it has not recuperated, only after 1930.[2] For Elijah Wald, in contrast, the corrido, despite its archaic features, is far from belonging to the past. This medieval narrative form that had reemerged in the border region between Mexico and the United States, especially after the Mexican-American War of 1848, achieving tremendous popularity during the Mexican Revolution (1910–1917) and living an aftermath as bootlegger ballads during Prohibition, has experienced a new upturn that is attributed to the so-called phenomenon of *narcocorridos*.

Wald attributes to this tendency a vertiginous logic. It embraces a development that bridges a period (the 1970s and 1980s) when the corrido begins to take on a new role as "deterritorializing" narrative, epically foregrounding drug traffic and undocumented migration, without yet being a style of transnational scope and a time during which, only a few years later, the narcocorrido has evolved into a new wave of international, "down-to-earth" pop, revealing striking indications of a postnational culture in the Americas.

> The narcocorrido is...a medieval ballad style whose Robin Hoods now arm themselves with automatic weapons and fly shipments of cocaine in 747s. Since the rise of Los Tigres in the early 1970s, the narcocorrido has been taken up by thousands of bands and singers, first in Mexico and the United States, but now as far afield as Colombia and wherever the Latin American drug traffic thrives. Many corridistas (corrido singers and composers) are still rural artists whose popularity scarcely extends beyond their home villages. Others have become international stars...They are carrying on an archaic folk tradition in a world of beepers, cell phones, and high-powered SUVs, at once as old-fashioned as Appalachian ballad singers and as contemporary as gangsta rappers.[3]

Paradoxes abound. A glance into the music market of the United States reveals that, toward the end of the twentieth century, and contrary to the assumption that Afro-Caribbean styles dominate the Hispanic/Latin boom, Mexican-based music accounts for approximately two-thirds of Latin record sales.[4] Indeed, who would have expected that old Mexican country music would come to the forefront of one of the most dynamic cultural phenomena of the turn of the century. In the guise of ongoing and even increasing mass migration from the South to the North, and of drug traffic's global ascent, we are dealing with a visible "new wave" and, at the same time, with the complex undercurrents of an orally based tradition of rural descent, which has nowadays acquired strong transnational visibility. This music is sung and performed entirely in everyday Spanish, and it has been increasingly welcomed in the Mexican border states and by considerable parts of the Latino public in the United States, gaining in popularity in Central and South America as well. During the seventies, their lyrics started generating an apotheosis of adventure stories that speak of the avatars of drug traffic and migration in new ways, making these corridos familiar to a variety of audiences, many of which had perceived drug violence and deadly adventures as relatively remote from their own lives.[5]

The historicality of Mexican corridos has been explored in generic, but rarely in intercultural terms. Under the influence of Mendoza's historical study, the Spanish *romancero* tradition has been described as the root of the Mexican corrido.[6] Although Mendoza pays special attention to the *romance andaluz* (Andalusian romances) as the ancient genre that seems to have the most resonance in modern Mexican corridos, he observes that the "corridas andaluzas" had already assimilated, alongside the older *relatos caballerescos* (stories of knights), the more timely adventures of the *pícaro*—the astute, trickster-like popular hero who would become so highly influential in early modern Spanish literature. But how can we know today if, in fact, those early romances preserved in manuscripts had not already been pervaded by the rhythms and stock repertoires of still older ballads that left no textual records at all, so that romances themselves have come to influence more recent ballads but without marking the beginning of a tradition,[7] or better still, of a particular mode of *performing narration*. It is here that an intertextual interest would have to turn to intercultural histories whose traces lay hidden within unstable repertoires, probably to a much higher degree than within the records left by the archived traditions.[8] We are concerned with narrative antecedents that are more heterogeneous and paradoxical than any established literary or written archives can account for. Regarding the romanceros, their lyrics tend to obey, on the one hand, a simple and stable metric structure based on "the invariable form of a musical phrase consisting of four parts."[9] On the other, the primary meaning of the word romance points—according to Menéndez-Pidal—toward "vulgar language" as opposed to the Latin written by the clerics,[10] suggesting that the obsessively speech-act related dimension of this language must have been at least as important as its formal end results, the written texts. Both elements, the metric matrix and the oral dimension, point toward more ancient cultural practices but, above all, toward intercultural predispositions lacking the stability of modern genres. As far as the thematic aspect is concerned, Mendoza refers to the centrality of events "powerfully affecting the sensibilities of the multitudes (noisy crimes, violent deaths, stories of bandits, catastrophes, train wrecks, wars, battles, adventures, humoristic stories, simple songs of love, of sadness, and satires)."[11] The enumeration is multifold, assisted by a terminological variety that circumscribes the expressive forms that corridos have taken on in Mexico: *romance, tragedia, ejemplo, versos, coplas, relación*, and so on.[12] Although metrically and rhythmically restricted, traditional corridos are regarded as playful, cheerful, vivid, and jittery, and simultaneously as lacking in emotion.

Menéndez-Pidal's formulation helps us address what will be considered, in the course of our study, as a paradoxical condition of corridos. The narration of common events that pertain to epic expectations and empower the fantasies of ordinary ("vulgar") people has become possible by a "vague format," as opposed to the media of classified scripture. At issue is an epistemological situation in which clear literary explanations are likely to be absent. As further discussed in the following chapter, corridos pertain to an ancient yet perplexing praxis where narrating is performed as "acting" and is connected to an imagination capable of shaping figurative modes of space and life, modes of longing and belonging—belonging within and despite the deprivations of social life within which a "low genre" like the corrido has flourished. Part of the logic of this format consists in animating human senses and passions with mimetic intensity, mostly devoid of the refining control of educated or institutionalized taste. As far as the "vague format" is concerned today, it may help us understand that the point made by narcocorridos is not just a matter of plotting abominable events. These transnational corridos draw on a living repertoire of affective dispositions to which they have given a fabulous vitality. In other words, the referential traits of narcocorridos that deal with drug traffic are not the only—and sometimes not even the most important—clue for their interpretation. Questions have to be formulated differently. Rather than representing a Manichaean genre that—involuntarily—feeds an official canon of good and evil, narcocorridos lend emphasis to the question of the peculiar conditions under which a conventional and even archaic narrative musical style has become connected with contemporary dynamics of technology, migration, and ever-increasing economic and social inequality between and in the Americas.

We are confronted with an unseemly, deviant revival of corridos that, as a tradition, have been enjoying academic recognition in the Western Hemisphere for several decades (and much longer in Spain). The problem here is not only that new corridos move beyond the traits of an older tradition, but that they are also in contrast with the norms through which this tradition has been previously addressed and constructed as an object of study. Understanding new corridos will require different interpretive notions, but it may be that these corridos help cast new light on the older narrative-performative style as well. Moreover, there is a peculiar concern brought forward by these corridos, a claim for an alternate global presence without first possessing a metropolitan background. That is to say, a dimension for study arises—narcocorridos as "global localizations"—whose historical and phenomenological backgrounds call for the problematization of a notion of cosmopolitanism that is deeply ingrained in the epistemology of modern citizenship.[13] The global presence of corridos and their "non-modern" heroes is linked to the avatars of cross-border drug traffic and, at the same time, to the ascent and ethical prowess of an expressive form that formerly belonged to the periphery. What are the implications for research and scholarship, especially relating to the status and local/transnational contours of today's border culture?

Authors in the fields of U.S.-Latino and Chicano border studies have addressed corridos as agencies of dissident cultural expression, spontaneous democracy, and alternative memories. Saldívar writes, "The nature of the corrido is social and revolutionary, drawing heavily on the deepest levels of what Fredric Jameson has called 'the political unconscious.' "[14] Corridos have been interpreted as agencies of orally transmitted and socially empowering consciousness, as well as sites of subaltern opposition, thereby becoming one of the paradigms of Chicano cultural critique.[15] Does the phenomenon of the "global corrido" challenge these assumptions? Or does it perhaps provide new insights into the realm of alternative border culture? Can the rapid rise in popularity of narcocorridos since the seventies, on both sides of the hemispheric border, be understood without reformulating these problems and coming to terms with what indeed seems to be a striking contrast between the timely and the untimely? Indecent times require that we ask terrible questions. It may be useful to remember that the corrido tradition has unfolded deep in the shadows of a Western canon that bears the stamp of Christianity, the Renaissance, the Enlightenment, "Progress," and Neoliberalism; and a balance is not entirely unlikely, according to which corridos would finally succumb to uncontrolled violence and the spell of the narcotics industry. How can this kind of conclusion be meaningfully contested? One of the necessities guiding our study is that of remapping the epistemological and affective scenarios in which identities are lived and performed. This inquiry will lead into a postnational hemispheric framework—the highly charged areas in which the spatial-symbolic contact zones between Mexico's northern regions and U.S. Latino cultural territories, as well as areas reaching into the U.S. mainstream, are being reshaped once again. As for the emergence of narcocorridos, these zones reach from Culiacán to Los Angeles and beyond, on both sides of the border. If no conventional cultural-geographic design exists for what have been areas of informal exchange and illegal cross-border traffic for more than a century, then the narcocorrido phenomenon can help trace a map that will allow us to understand this anachronistic space. For an interpretive strategy must be found for accessing that which either remains invisible or is put under quarantine by officialist pronouncements.

An incipient line of study can be derived from ethnographic approaches to the uneven maps of globalization, communication, and everyday culture. Wald, a musician and writer, focuses his inquiry into the Mexican-American narcocorrido on testimonies of metier and milieu offered by the unrecognized composers of drug ballads at the local level in the Mexican border states of Sonora, Chihuahua, and Baja California, as well as in Sinaloa. Wald's book, *Narcocorrido*, is somewhat paralleled by an investigation from the Mexican side, *Jefe de Jefes. Corridos y narcocultura en México*, by José Manuel Valenzuela. Valenzuela pays attention to the texts and thematics of the narcocorridos of the border, reading them against the background of Mexican nationalism and high culturalism and trying to decipher the enigma of the narcocorrido by looking at explicit narrative representation. Wald explores the vigorous spread of the musical style on both sides of the border, and he starts by relating the composers' life experiences as they evolved far away from the metropolitan centers, which their music nevertheless compels. Our own study will conceptualize a constitutive anachronism: local Mexican traditions and narratives have radically outgrown their provincial framework and entered the global stage, yet they sidestep the metropolitan and nationalist norm. What seems to account for a growing pervasiveness of corrido music, along and beyond border regions, is its intercultural ubiquity, its proclivity to technological changes, together with—to contrast Heidegger—an "inauthentic" ontological imagination regarding life and violence. It is symptomatic that there exists a narrative matrix that can be adapted to the needs of different genres and media formats, as well as to varied segments of the public. Yet already, in the oral traditions of epic storytelling, an intercultural pattern can be observed that does not necessarily imply a change of media or genre. It is related, above all, to an openness to intermedial imagination, a tendency toward incorporating heterogeneous elements into one and the same narrative praxis.[16] Without pursuing these leads, it would be difficult to understand how the corridos have come to infiltrate social fantasies on a major scale.

To develop a phenomenological framework, we have to acknowledge that these ballads are not immune to reification; on the contrary, they have had a huge influence in the transnational music business for more than a decade. However, it can be shown that they inhabit differential spaces regarding the market as well as to the symbolic order of society. In addition to acquiring an industrial format and being produced as musical CDs and DVDs, these ballads continue to draw on (narrative) registers emerging from the materiality of social life, especially from the moral dispossession of a growing part of the Mexican population, by both the state and the neoliberal economy. Narcocorridos and, even more broadly, the rise of a postnational narcoculture in the Americas are considerably shaped by the absence or decay of public and legal networks of social integration and economic support within wide areas of rural Mexico, as well as in the dark zones of cross-border migration. During the 1970s, 1980s, and 1990s, the distribution of narcocorridos was informal and based on secondhand technology, at least as much as it had come to embrace the most advanced technological formats of the music market.[17] Approaching the ballads from these assumptions will provide clues for reviewing the work of composers and singers. One could argue that, at first sight, corrido composers glorify the deeds and risky adventures of today's drug traffickers, thus serving the mythification of a doubtful cause. Yet the problem escapes such easy judgment.

A considerable number of narcocorridos appear to be related to human and logistical situations that have emerged from the conditions of globally enforced inequalities, often linked to poverty and violence.[18] According to Astorga and Valenzuela, the ballads constitute a kind of "oral retranslation of the visible."[19] What the tales narrate have already been published by the press and circulated through radio and television. Drug ballads transmit "appreciations of traffickers and the trade of illicit drugs which, in general, conflict with dominant visions expressed in governmental and related circles."[20] They have found their listeners not only among poor peasants and migrants, but also among urban youth and adults belonging to diverse social strata and ways of life. It is worthwhile insisting on the intercultural rhetoricity of the ballads. They foreground appropriation and renarration, serving as irritations and interceptions of discourses in which border conflicts and imminent issues related to the drug business find their official depictions. Narcocorridos can thus be described as postscripts of normative discourses on drugs and violence, activating imagination at the point where primary public depictions exhaust their explanatory or scandalizing potentials. Once we take *renarration*[21] and its uncertain discursive place seriously, we can realize that corridos are not just story generators for an insane music market. A central question here is how they deal with issues that are quite explicit at the referential level of the ballad texts but which cannot be accessed in their aesthetic density by merely considering that level: corridos provide—as we will show—affective retranslations of adventures and stories that seem trivial and coarse. At issue are particular affective dispositifs regarding violence and survival that escape the usual representational paradigms. Only by posing the problematic in this way will we be able to pay attention to the question as to why and how narcotraffic from the South to the North has found a sometimes dramatic, and often stoically reiterative, magnification through the rebirth of a ballad style that traditionally belonged to the ways the dispossessed dream and survive.

Los Tigres del Norte and the Suspension of Melodrama

Let us start by taking a closer look at narcoballads before we include migration corridos in our considerations. "Narcocorridos" is not an academic term but probably emerged as a spontaneous description of the new style that arose during the seventies, when Los Tigres del Norte introduced the most conflictive and violent issues of transnational border life into the "country music" of northern Mexico. The group has given a global presence to rural musical performance without recurring to metropolitan standards of style and taste.[22] From the perspective of the late-1990s, Wald comments that Los Tigres' polka- and waltz-like ballads have not attracted trendsetting intellectuals and agents in the Anglo-cultural realms. However, their music sells in the millions, and "their concerts pack halls throughout the North American continent."[23] There is no doubt that countless other groups drew on the success of Los Tigres, eventually producing mixtures and adaptations that would "modernize" the old-fashioned groove. This became particularly visible after the music pervaded, during the early 1990s, the Los Angeles Mexican cultural environments, including huge immigrant suburbs. Vigorously self-affirmative subcultural tendencies emerged when narcocorridos became intertwined with rap culture and its impact among Los Angeles Mexican-American working-class youth. Younger narcocorrido bands appropriated manners and gestures that made "violence" an energetic factor of the spectacle itself—the most telling example, that of Chalino Sánchez.[24] In addition, throughout Latin America, subaltern musical projects are found that turn violence into a central element of the performance. Here we have the key example of MV Bill (Brazil) with records such as *Traficando informação* (Trafficking Information, 1999) or *Declaração de guerra* (Declaration of War, 2002). In these cases, there is an aesthetics that pursues a critical stance via "affective aggression." The synaesthetic strategy of Los Tigres, however, is different, and we will start out from a thorny hypothesis: although their drug ballads relate the fatal avatars of narcotics traffic, violence does not lie at their aesthetic core, nor can these songs be subsumed under the rubric of celebrating abominable actions and events.

The name *narcocorridos* does not reflect such complexity. Nevertheless, it leads us right into the controversial point of the matter—the evolution of narcotraffic into a common business with deep effects on social imaginary in several Mexican states and huge border regions of the United States, as well as in a country like Colombia. It is necessary to emphasize that narcocorridos are composed in Spanish, and they function in Spanish. In this respect they differ from the major segment of narrative expressions of "Latino culture" whose filmic, literary, and theatrical language is English, although they often carry a bilingual tone. One of the corridos that signaled the rise of this new wave that would start attracting the attention of the *norteño* (country) music world during the early 1970s, and spread the news across the border, is called *La Banda del Carro Rojo*, written by Paulino Vargas. It was first performed by Los Tigres del Norte in 1975. Featuring a collective hero—the actor is "La Banda," the Gang—the corrido provides a travel narrative of its own kind. We cite from the text version provided by Luis Astorga:

> It is said that they came from the south in a red car,
> They were carrying one hundred kilos of cocaine,
> They were headed for Chicago,
> That's what the snitch said who had squealed on them.
>
> They'd already gotten past the customs stop,
> The one in El Paso, Texas
> But right there in San Antonio, they were waiting for them,
> They were the Texas rangers, the guys who run that county,
> A siren cried out, an immigrant shouted.
> They were ordered to stop the car so it could be checked out
> And that they don't resist, or they'd be killed.
> An M16 blasted, as it roared in the air,
> The light of a patrol car could be seen flying through the air;
> That's how the battle began where that massacre happened.
> Lino Quintana said, "This had to happen,
> My buddies have died, and I'm sorry, Sheriff,
> but I don't know how to sing."
>
> Of the seven who died, only the crosses on their graves are left,
> Four were in the red car, the other three were from the government,
> But don't worry about them, they'll all go to hell with Lino.
> It's said that they came from Candil, others,
> That they were from Altar,
> There are even many out there who say they were from Parral,
> The truth was never known, no one came to claim the bodies.[25]

A climate of fatalism and despair emanates from the text of the song. Its main dispositif is that of a memory tale. There is a sober verisimilitude to the plot, as if the "real-politik" of cross-border traffic, in its way of owning up to brutal facts and coarse emotions, were dragged into the open. However, the language is not coarse, but set into a sparse ballad verse, capable of conveying a memorable story with little means.

"It is said," links *La Banda's* story to a detached voice, one that rests on shared knowledge about the topic being tied to an impersonal narrator. It is somehow difficult to make an explicit statement just on the grounds of focalization. We might, for example, apply the German term "erlebte Rede" (experienced/lived speech), yet the dimension of immanent commonality reaches beyond the formal traits of an impersonal perspective. Kittredge gave an account of the perplexing status inscribed in this perspectivation when commenting on English and Scottish popular ballads, and his assessment sounds all too familiar when related to our example. The narrator "merely tells what happened and what people said, and he confines the dialogue to its simplest and most inevitable elements. The story exists for its own sake. If it were possible to conceive a tale as telling "itself," without the instrumentality of a conscious speaker, the ballad would be such a tale."[26]

By the end of the first stanza of *La Banda*, a proleptic element has already been introduced, alluding to the story's drama by anticipating its fatal outcome: "that's what the squealer said who had informed on them." The anticipatory device is a de-dramatizing one. The whole issue seems monstrously trivial, centering on an anonymous group of traffickers that moves a load of cocaine from the Mexican side of the border into Texas. After an initial anticipation of defeat, the action unfolds bluntly and almost in fragments, bearing the marks of an outcome that has already been ensured by the act of treason. As part of an indirect narrative reference, rather than of the action itself, the laconic reference to treachery contrasts with a mainstream convention of deploying violence, especially in films, where dramatic stress is placed on tricky suspense and arbitrary affects. Given that betrayal is followed by stoic and even fatalistic perseverance and the destruction of numerous lives, it can be perceived as a pattern of guilt, whose incidence seems to be as normal as that of violent death.

The only individual who momentarily occupies a speaking position is Lino Quintana, a man whose name is rescued from an anonymous group of low-level traffickers who come from everywhere and nowhere ("no one came to claim the bodies"). The construction of the memory of *La Banda's* action is as terse as it is drastic, gaining expressive weight through impersonal focalization. The San Antonio police who intercept the traffickers are treated equally, as players in the same game, and one should not worry about them when "together with Lino, they go to hell." As far as the moral is concerned, there is only one, lending the story an almost ontological tone: men who act as local outlaws in risky endeavors are more memorable than the man who denounces them to the authorities of centralized state power. Finally, the initial impersonal focus reappears through an implied chorus of voices, invisible public opinion testifying to what appears to be shared knowledge: "It's said that they came from *Candil*, others, that they were from *Altar*." The names of the *traficantes'* home villages are uncertain; however, they seem to share an aura of territorial memory. A follow-up story to "La Banda" is entitled *La Muerte del Soplón* ("The Death of the Squealer"). In it, Lino Quintana's valiant lover takes the initiative of vengeance in her hands and kills the traitor. There have been other follow-up stories and a movie entitled *La Banda del Carro Rojo* (1976) in which Los Tigres were featured "live," long before they became internationally famous.

Composer Paulino Vargas from Durango, the son of an accordion player, grew up in a mountain village close to *el Espinazo del Diablo* (the Devil's Backbone)—the road that leads from Durango to Mazatlán. According to an interview given to Wald, he feels indebted to the generation of corrido masters who lived through the Mexican Revolution. He was an illiterate who only learned to read and write when he married a school teacher. *La Banda del Carro Rojo* was inspired by a real event that was reported by the local press, and Vargas holds that an authentic corridista must be like a good reporter, only adding a bit of *morbo* to a factual narrative. It becomes clear that Vargas' notion of what is "real" is rather flexible, oscillating between fact and verisimilitude. The *Corrido de Lamberto Qintero*, which became the title song of a popular film, is one of his creations, as is the tragic tale of an illegal migrant worker, *La Tumba del Mojado* (The Wetback's Grave). "Paulino seems to feel a special sympathy for the poor adventurers who make their way across the border by stealth, whether they are simple farm workers or carry a couple of kilos of heroin."[27]

Another corrido of his, *Los Super Capos* (The Super Drug Lords) deals with anticocaine politics of the United States, and attributes to its leaders politically ambiguous and economically ruthless behavior throughout the world, while drugs abound in the streets at home.[28] *Los Super Capos* can be read, together with other songs, as a social commentary on the "war on drugs," especially the escalation of U.S. drug enforcement actions imposed on Latin America during the 1980s.[29] Valenzuela also shows that numerous narcocorridos address the role of the United States—"the country of confidence"—not only in the control of drug trade but also in the traffic itself. In the corrido *La Banda de la Suburban*, sung by "Los Tucanes de Tijuana," we find the following passage:

> Into the American Union
> Drugs enter easily
> It's the country of confidence
> They'll sell there for sure.[30]

Another song, *El Avión de la Muerte* (The Death Plane) is related to the events of "Operation Condor"—one of the major initiatives in the "war on drugs" that began in the second half of the 1970s and that aimed at destroying production and distribution sites of marijuana and opium in northern Mexico.[31] According to John McDowell, the corrido is based on an authentic story whose hero, Atilano, a drug trafficker, "was captured, tortured, and then forced to fly his private plane under heavy guard to Sinaloa for further questioning. During the flight, he crashed his plane into a military escort plane, killing everyone aboard both planes.'"[32] In view of the concerted action of the U.S. and Mexican armed forces, as well as their secret police, the corrido makes its point by praising Atilano as a victimized yet honorable person. Ongoing references to a situation of transnational law enforcement that is officially called "war" constitute a mark of deviant corrido lyrics.[33] In María Celia Toro's words, "It is ironic that Mexico's current antidrug policy is largely determined by U.S. antidrug policy."[34] Border corridos of the 1980s and 1990s, sung by Los Tigres del Norte, are suspicious of coercive campaigns that reflect geopolitical domination from the North, offering sometimes sarcastic, sometimes stoic accounts of the belligerent measures directed against smaller traffickers and other losers in the battles of large-scale antidrug enforcement. This enforcement has, for several reasons, not reduced but instead tendentially fostered, reorganized, and further centralized the drug trade between both countries.[35]

When Paulino Vargas, the ballad writer from Durango, speaks about his motives for renarrating stories of the drug trade, he foregrounds an ethical stance. In his eyes, justice is a crucial matter, yet he is skeptical about a notion of morality that is predicated on big power and an abstract body politic. His revamping of the stories of illicit drug traffic is far from showing bad faith. On the one hand, he has written about prominent figures like the Colombian drug lord Pablo Escobar. However, most of his protagonists have been like Lino Quintana and Lamberto Quintero, "local characters who would have remained unknown outside the sierran crime world had he not made them into legends."[36] Vargas insists that the protagonists of his songs are not the root of the problem. Referring to the reality of rural Mexico he explains:

> Most of us...don't even finish high school, so they can't get credit even if they have some land to plant. [...] They're suffering, and they fight because they have to. They know a little bit about how to move some inebriants, and more or less where they can sell them, but, for example, the problems you find in Tijuana and Juárez [the border drug capitals], which are like a daily news item—and bad news, sad to say—there is too much money involved there for those to be stupid people. How do you explain the fact that a huge airplane or truck gets by, with all the laws and all the controls on the roads and the airspace?[37]

Wald, for his part, argues that the responsibility for the drug trade lies not with the local poor "growing or carrying the dope, but with those giving the orders, in whichever country." He continues, summarizing the view of Vargas, "it is the rich and powerful who control both the illegal traffic and the borders...if Mexico is supplying drugs to the United States, the United States is the source for most of the guns being smuggled into Mexico.[38]

A refined take on narcocorridos might result in feelings of doubt if not contempt. Why is it important, then, to interview the composers who turn local tales, as well as media reports on drug traffic, into sometimes lucrative storytelling projects? Authors like Wald, Astorga, and Valenzuela are aware of the contradictory complexity of the matter. After careful investigation, they argue that on the Mexican side, most composers of drug corridos are not hypocritical businessmen but voices that articulate questions of survival and the stoic self-affirmation of ordinary people within informal business, in the face of an uneven and violent geopolitical situation.

La Banda del Carro Rojo has provided us with a first impression of the character of stories that are told in song. Its subject relates to a situation so obvious "as to be matter of general experience, or a recent occurrence which has been taken up by the mouth of common fame."[39] The story exhibits a sobriety that borders on fatalism; there is simplicity of metrical structure, as well as an impersonal focus as far as authorship is concerned. We will now take a look at the lyrics of *Contrabando y Traición* (Contraband and Betrayal), composed at the beginning of the 1970s. Similar to *La Banda del Carro Rojo*, its narrative is laconically straightforward, yet it introduces an element of vigorous feminine empowerment into the imagination of a ruthless metier. The lyrics are by Angel González, the "father of the narcocorrido."[40] This song, and the way it was established among the public by Los Tigres, is considered to be another pathbreaking case of the narcoballad type, one that would prefigure the emergence of myriad follow-ups and other ballad groups during the years and decades to come. The lyrics are as follows:

> They left San Ysidro, coming from Tijuana,
> The tires of the car were full of bad grass,
> They were Emilio Varela and Camelia the Texan.
>
> As they passed by San Clemente,
> they were stopped by the migration cops,
> They asked them for their documents,
> they asked them, "Where are you from?"
> She was from San Antonio, a woman with heart,
>
> If a woman loves a man, for him she'll give her life,
> But you have to be careful if this woman is wounded,
> treason and smuggling are things that are not shared.
>
> They got to Los Angeles, they went to Hollywood,
> In a dark alleyway, they changed the four tires,
> There they turned over the weed, and right there they were paid.
>
> Emilio said to Camelia, "Today is our goodby,
> With your part you can remake your life,
> I'm off to San Francisco with the love of my life."
>
> Seven gun shots rang out, Camelia killed Emilio,
> The police just found a gun thrown away,
> About the money and Camelia, nothing more was ever known.[41]

The record was released in 1972, performed by the still unknown Los Tigres del Norte. The lyrics show a reduction of the plot to a few peripeties and an unhappy outcome. At this point, we anticipate the feature of *para-tactical narration*: a partial but notable "unconnectedness" of clauses that is formally owing to a lack of conjunctions, leading to a loose and even contingent linking of the events by the plot. In other words, the plot is advanced without a refined connecting structure and is devoid of explanatory narrative devices. We will address the specific potential that parataxis offers for montage, together with a rhetorico-cultural appropriation of space in the next chapter.

Distinct from the previous ballad example, in this song, Emilio and Camelia's border crossing and drug deal are successful, thanks to the "bad grass" (marijuana) in the car tires. But suddenly the situation between them turns melodramatic and violent, when Emilio decides to pursue his own romance after the deal is completed. It should be noted that the melodramatic turn, in its drastic aspect, does not culminate in any kind of hyperbolic expression. To the contrary, the Texan woman is a person of deeds instead of sorrowful or hysterical gestures: "Seven gun shots rang out, Camelia killed Emilio." Although melodrama has been common in Mexican culture throughout the twentieth century, its de-emotionalized combination with the narcoworld was striking. It seemed as though a vigorous María Felix had traveled across space and time, finding a comeback as a laconically violent woman in the imagination of the border underworld.

The composer, González, whose grandfather was an accordionist, still lives in the village of Basuchil in Chihuahua. He is described as a man in his sixties who gets along, in respectable modesty, in a relatively peaceful rural setting: "I prefer it to the big city; it's calmer, for example, for my son, cleaner and safer with regard to drugs and all of that."[42] Words that may seem cynical bear a claim for decency. They reflect a common rural view that cultivating and shipping drugs to the North is marked by dramatic economic and social need, not by a consumerist stance that can afford to buy drugs. González tells Wald that the plot's violent conversion to melodrama was his invention, and he sounds like he wants justice for those women who have been depicted in melodrama and traditional corridos as devout to submission or as unsteady and compulsive:

I am a feminist, five hundred percent. Maybe you don't know what that means. A feminist is a man who knows what a woman is worth, who knows that woman is the greatest. Why is woman the greatest? Because woman is half the world, and what's more she's the mother of the other half. In my songs, I always have the woman come out ahead. "Contrabando y Traición" was the first song like that.[43]

What González may have overlooked in his pleasantly paternalist statement—although addressed in his song—is the increasingly active role of women at the lower and middle levels of the global drug trade. Camelia's violent action to get justice for her desire for love was not borrowed from the narcobusiness. Nonetheless, the anticipatory intuition of the composer was correct. The effect of introducing a woman's self-empowerment into a male-centered corrido tradition increasingly gained influence on new border imaginaries, tackling an issue that would be appropriated by numerous other narratives in Mexican and Colombian music, prose, and film toward the end of the 1980s, during the 1990s, and thereafter: marginal women's consciously becoming actors in the drug trade or conversely, subjects of violence.[44] The narrative panorama of this phenomenon is varied and resists generalization. Los Tigres themselves would eventually diversify their repertoire, incorporating a new type of female figure, and this demarcation between male-bonding images related to a tough milieu, and the rise of women's audacity and cunning as values, would demand further attention. Elmer Mendoza, in his first narconovel, *Cada respiro que tomas* (Every Breath You Take, 1991), presents "Camelia la Tejana" as a figure who has acquired legendary status in popular consciousness across the northern Mexican states and who is associated with bold, enigmatic female characters in "real life."[45] *Mujeres del fuego*, by Alonso Salazar (Women of Fire, 1993) presents testimonies of women who—sometimes against their own will—have assumed protagonic roles in the "macrodrama of violence"[46] in Colombia. An example of a literary and filmic imagination inspired by ballad heroines who become global players, *La Reina del Sur*, is a corrido performed by Los Tigres that was later turned into a central plot by Arturo Pérez-Reverte (Spain) when he wrote a novel of the same name, *The Queen of the South* (2002).[47] Jorge Franco's novel *Rosario Tijeras* (Colombia, 1999), turned into a film in 2005 and the movies *María llena eres de gracia* (*Maria Full of Grace*, Joshua Marston, Colombia 2005) and *Sin dejar huella* (Without a Trace, María Novaro, Mexico 2001) are other cases. More recently, Gustavo Bolívar Moreno's novel *Sin tetas no hay paraíso* (Without Boobs There Is No Paradise, 2005) became a bestseller and was adapted as a telenovela by the same title. In addition to exploring the involvement of marginal female subjects in the local-global topographies of violent survival, there are other literary antecedents reframing femininity within what Mary Pat Brady calls contemporary "narcospatialities"[48]— Laura Restrepo's *Leopardo al sol* (Leopard in the Sun, 1993) and *Delirio* (2004), and Mary Helen Ponce's "The Marijuana Party" provide intriguing cases among a larger number of contemporary novels and short stories. Is there any reason to be sardonic like Carlos Monsiváis who, for example, labels the sociological equivalent of "Camelia la Tejana" as "just" deterritorialized prostitutes?[49] This would certainly foreclose the question if we are not, perhaps, facing genealogical traits of affective agency at an opposite end of the normalizing norms of heterosexual subjectification of women. We will deal more specifically with this topic when discussing Salazar's *We Were Not Born to Life* (chapter 5) and Víctor Gaviria's film *The Rose Seller* (chapter 7).

Now we can return to the *Contrabando* song. Because of its ballad mode, the individual motives of the person called Camelia are overwritten by an inherent mimetic fascination that derives from the testimony of her actions, which is capable of appealing to common sense in a variety of ways. Wald gives the story a certain Hollywood flair. Usually the women in corridos are supposed to be victims or docile lovers, "not dashing bad girls in the tradition of *Bonnie and Clyde*. Camelia la Tejana was something out of a flashy modern action film."[50] Valenzuela thinks differently: "In more recent corridos, women are abandoning a presence exclusively within the walls of the house."[51] According to this Mexican analyst, corridos rely on social stereotypes, and they can also take on a compensatory paternalistic function, for example, when women's proactive role in society is disqualified by its relationship to the distortions of today's drug business. In this case, the corrido would appear as a morally corrective tale: the undaunted woman is drawn into a bad world where she encounters her unavoidably negative fate.

It is necessary to think in yet another direction. As we will see, *Contrabando y Traición* touches on imagination by way of recognition: its cultural construction is a mimetic one. Although it operates with specific references and moral messages, its main function is the repetitive appropriation of "believable" legends.[52] These legends offer a forum for the dissemination of collective longings, especially those lacking a legitimate place within a larger symbolic order. Instead of giving an autonomous account of reality, as "realistic literature" was once supposed to do, corridos are dedicated to the continuous recounting of "real events." The spirit of retelling permits the linkage of diverse corridos to each other, even if they do not share explicit similarities. This mimetic affluence is revealed—as the discussion of the Camelia story will show—by a dominance of the hero over the author as self-consciously distancing agency, embracing the fascinating power of ordinary yet vigorous protagonists who attack rules and order, whether or not their actions are invented. In fact, the impersonality of ballads, as far as an author is concerned, seems to be grounded in an attraction that accounts for innumerable follow-up stories that tend to emerge out of the most appealing ones. The peculiar skill of González and Vargas could not be well explained by a romantic attribution that the composers belong to the people, but we can provisionally use Kittredge's expression, "sympathetic company."[53] It points to the composer's sense of narrative as cultural dispositifs, a dense and shifting sphere that Taussig calls "implicit social knowledge"[54]—acquired through practice to at least the same extent as through conscious learning.

The phenomenon of what will attain the informal public scope of legendary narratives, moving people through an "acting imagination," can be illustrated by the open-ended tale of "Camelia La Tejana" and its follow-ups. In *Contrabando y Traición*, a melodramatic plot cut short by a stoic violent gesture helped create a female version of "el bandolero social." Camelia's behavior appears, however, as an unusual kind of social protest, which becomes effective at the point where the heroine's fight for her own emotional justice meets an emerging desire for a less traditional model of femininity.[55] A few years after the release and success of the story of Camelia and Emilio, Angel González and Estanislao Rivera created the corrido, *Ya encontraron a Camelia* (They Finally Found Camelia). Its text starts by summarizing the outcome of the first "Contrabando" tale.

> I didn't know Emilio very well, the guy Camelia killed
> In a dark alleyway, without anyone knowing,
> But those smugglers, they never forgive anything.[56]

The first story is thus continued by showing that Camelia became an object of revenge. Emilio's gang sets out to find Camelia's tracks to hold her accountable for the act she committed and the money she took. The search for the woman extends throughout the double territory of the United States and Mexico. No visible border stops the actions that conform this global plot of revenge. The squealer, a common figure in the drug dealers' milieu, now reappears as a woman:

> A friend of hers said, "Fellows, I don't know anything.
> But they say she was seen near Guadalajara,
> invoking Emilio Varela, and they say she even cried."[57]

At this point, melodramatic desire infiltrates the ballad mode: Camelia's commitment to the dream of love has moved away from utilitarian behavior and even from an interest in survival.

> The gang, without waiting, sped toward Jalisco
> They looked for her in cantinas, until they finally found her
> Camelia was already sentenced, and they took her away.
> They gave her to the bosses. The mission was over.
> "If you give back the money, we'll spare your life."
> "Without Emilio Varela, why would I want to live?"
> Several shots were heard. Camelia fell immediately.
> Now she's resting with the love of her life.
> Treason and contraband put an end to many lives.[58]

The follow-up story to *Contrabando y Traición* shows that the woman looses interest in the practices of the drug trade when she is overcome by a wave of nostalgia. In its tragic consequence of a happy ending in reverse, the story finds a contradictory closure. Being quite atypical, as far as the resolute woman acting within the drug world is concerned, it turns melodramatic and thus recuperates a symbolical reintegration of the woman into hierarchic masculine fantasies. Touching upon melodrama's and narcocorrido's mutual competition, the conceptual situation becomes tricky. At the referential level of the follow-up versions, we can attribute to melodrama the final triumph over Camelia's radically self-determined behavior. However, *Ya encontraron a Camelia* only remotely achieved the public resonance of the *Contrabando* song. Although its text provides a reintegration of the heroine into the strain of unconditional love, its affective sobriety, and even laconism at the musical and rhythmic levels (when sung by Los Tigres) sharply limits the melodramatic tone.

Another follow-up story, continuing the saga of Camelia is called *El Hijo de Camelia* (Camelia's Son) written by Manuel Contreras and performed by Los Tigres in 1977. Once more, the issue at stake is revenge, and this time we find Camelia's grown-up son traversing, almost mythically, the northern border regions to find and eliminate the Varela gang that had slain his mother. The son has taken on patriarchal gender authority, now striving for justice in the name of his family:

> In a black-colored car with plates from Ciudad Juárez
> It seems mysterious, as it goes up and down the streets
> The car and the person driving it, no one knows where he's from.

His clothes are simple, a jacket and jeans
A scarf around his neck, cowboy boots and "sombrero"
He looked like a brave man, you can see it in his eyes.[59]

The story has moved in an archetypical direction, and the pattern of the avenger of the murder of his mother breathes some sacred energy into the tale. The corrido concludes as follows:

They say he met up with the gang from Tijuana,
Leaving five dead men and fleeing to Guadalajara
He sped so quickly in his car, nothing ever happened to him.
He's been seen everywhere, speeding along the highways,
Looking for those delinquents, Varela's buddies,
He continues to get revenge for his mother,
His mother who was Camelia.[60]

Revenge is a continuous motif in contemporary corrido narratives. Shared patterns of desire breed a variety of peripeties. Looking at the sparse details of the story, we realize that Camelia was, according to the Contreras version that gives her an adult son, a mature woman. Her Texan heritage and the Mexican origin of her lover point toward the hemispheric framework of the marijuana business. Camelia's and Emilio's respective origins address an encounter that is anything but peaceful. Inter-American territories have become a coercive zone. It is a space in which physical hazards and repression abound, so that in the end, the story of the self-criminalization of love is as credible as legends come.

What makes melodrama and narcocorrido similar to one another is their precarious status in the sphere of language and representation, although the first tends to be overtly dramatic, whereas the second prefers a restrained dramatic intensity, just as it favors an anonymous narrator over dialogic exuberance and individual theatrical passion. If discursive sophistication has become the way in which modern literature talks meaningfully about the topics of love, justice, criminality, and punishment, then narcocorridos and melodramas can easily be ruled out as illegitimate. In the case we are discussing—and this seems to hold for other examples of corridos as well,—the narcocorrido leads melodrama into crisis, constituting a major change regarding the narrative and affective blueprints of cultural imagination in Latin America. But whereas an aesthetic posture that tends to include compulsive performance, excessive suffering and heightened dramatization becomes minimized under the impact of a new laconism, melodrama's preference for ordinary heroes finds itself well respected by Los Tigres del Norte.

It should have become clear by now that we do not subscribe to a simplistic view that narcocorridos are agents of violence and of fear, "leaving a feeling of impotency in a society that closes its eyes to the obvious, or that only dares to make comments in private spheres."[61] Instead, it may well be that these corridos form part of a repertoire through which a climate of moral exclusion and social incrimination is interpellated in deviant ways. If these songs give public resonance to cross-border drug traffic and its protagonists, their ballad status shows an unequivocal duality. On the one hand, banditry, betrayal, and coarse drama abound. On the other, there is an implicit desire for disavowal. Poverty-stricken traffickers in corridos have renounced moral accountability in exchange for illicit action in view of the absence of a democratic social contract in the Western Hemisphere.

Jesús Malverde: On the Hidden Core of Enacted Narration

Faith in Malverde was always strongest among Sinaloa's poor and highland residents, the classes from which Mexico's drug traffickers emerged.

—*Sam Quiñones*

One of the most potent yet enigmatic figures of the corrido world is Jesús Malverde who, having become the patron saint of drug traffickers, is also the symbolic hero of an annual festival and other events that take place in Culiacán, the capital of the Pacific coast state of Sinaloa. The fact that a regional imaginary has produced its own "narco saint" outside the canonic discourses of religion and politics, as well as Sinaloa's reputation as a suspect area, suggests that we take a closer look at this region. According to Astorga, in national public opinion, Sinaloa rises as "a very rich state, very agricultural and it's sad to say, a land where the *pistolero* and his woman is the couple that walks arm in arm along the streets."[62] In Wald's ethnographic journey, this northern state appears to receive special consideration as a narcocultural environment sui generis. Since the 1980s, artists and researchers from Sinaloa, including Elmer Mendoza, Óscar Liera, Astorga, and others have started to articulate a genuine, cultural-studies oriented interest in the relationships between the status of illicit drugs in global exchange and the emergence of social mythologies focused on and around the figure of the *narcotraficante*. The decade before was the time when a new type of narrative emerged, first in the realms of nontextual imagination and embodied expression like the corrido—the "sociodisea"[63] (the social odyssey) of drug trafficking and its ordinary heroes.

Culiacán and its upland surroundings that, together with Chihuahua and Durango, have hosted drug plantations for many decades may appear as one of the world's most gruesome regions, a major target of "Operation Condor" in the late 1970s and of other military campaigns, during which fields were sprayed, plants destroyed, and thousands of villages abandoned by their inhabitants. Astorga informs his readers that those Mexican agricultural states were drawn into uneven international exchange throughout the twentieth century.[64] When global capital begun its biopolitical control and large-scale reorganization of the Latin American regions where drug plants were cultivated—the 1970s and 1980s—, it had already been "illuminated" by the dreamlike dimensions of profit that lay hidden in the shifting grounds of the transnational economics of drugs. The uncanny history of intoxication that ties the hemispheric Americas together is still to be written. What acquires sharper contours today, especially from the analysis of a cultural phenomenon such as the "social odyssey" of drug trafficking, is the chasm between societies that consume drugs while waging a contradictory "war on drugs," and those poorer countries and regions whose truncated economies have become tragically dependent on the cultivation of dangerous crops. When Astorga comments on the criminalization of drug traffic and antidrug enforcement in Mexico, he observes that "diminishing the activity doesn't appear to be the order of the day."[65] So he asks if perhaps antidrug enforcement is contingent on the events and actions that occasion it. One of the issues at question is the emergence of a system of production of wealth in which the large-scale manipulation of transactions linked to the different logistics of drug traffic and marketing have tied Mexico and the United States together into a semilegal, industry-like dynamic. Revealingly, the "war on drugs" has become a functional part of this dynamic. The diversity of spheres interconnected within this system—its enormous operative capacities, reaching from local cultivation to international distribution, from political to legal corruption and invisibilization—suggests the existence of an economy as well as an institutionality of "narcoliberalism." Thus, analysis has to move beyond what is declared thinkable by the discourses that produce the officialist version of the matter, often overlooking its complexity.[66] Drug traffic confronts the analyst with a silent system, not only because it foregrounds violence and brute economic rationality but also because of the singular intensity of its symbolic reign. It is within this controversial range of conflicts that an understanding of narcocorridos helps by actively entering the limits of the thinkable.

We have previously commented on two vanguard examples of "sociodiseas," narcocorridos that, without displaying a metropolitan style, have circulated far beyond the place where they originated. Taking a closer look at Sinaloa, the "hotbed of the drug business," and its capital Culiacán will help us explore the legendary rise of an acclaimed hero—Jesús Malverde. This does not mean that we are establishing a framework of local community in which ballads can be seen to share in the stability of existing social relationships.[67] We are, rather, interested in understanding the bearing that local images and stories can have on an imagination that has been disseminated broadly across the hemisphere.

Wald observes that drug ballads in Sinaloa "are simply called 'corridos'; it would be tautological to append the 'narco' prefix, since in Sinaloa there is no other corrido theme."[68] However, we will attempt to show that drug ballads in Sinaloa are not just that, but that they can also reveal a thematical and epistemological "other." If the name Sinaloa has become a synonym for drugs and violence in Mexico, corridos allow us to question this image. Let us consider more closely the figure of Malverde, whose presence in the memory of entire regions (Sinaloa, Baja California, and some regions north of the border) feeds into social imaginaries of amazing ubiquity. There are numerous corridos dealing with Malverde, many of which are versions of a fairly basic tale. For example, *El Bandido Generoso* (The Generous Bandit) composed by Lino Valladares, resembles an ode-like legend of glory. It begins with heroic praise for the city of Culiacán and concludes with a sentimental farewell gesture of the narrator.

> Beautiful capital of Sinaloa, first of all I want to greet you,
> To tell you of the fame that you have, no other can equal you.
> In you there have been many brave men, and one achieved glory.
> Jesús Malverde, the generous bandit, who is up in heaven,
> together with God,
> He was a bandit but never a killer, when he stole it was for necessity,
> Because the little or much that he stole, he shared it generously.
> [...]
> Now I'll say goodbye, full of emotion.
> With your permission I'll leave now
> Only God knows what I'm feeling in my soul
> This corrido has to end.[69]

The presence of the first-person in the corrido conveys a celebratory rhetoric lacking the laconism that is characteristic of the previously described songs. *La Muerte de Malverde* (Malverde's Death) is the title of another commemorative corrido, attributed to composer Seferino Valladares, which delivers a more sober tale of the hero's life.[70] An impersonal voice gives resonance to a subliminal lament—the people's sorrow over the death (or murder) of a widely beloved man during the Porfirio Díaz dictatorship (1877–1911). The Malverde legend lives on in an endless array of ballads, all of which claim to be faithful renditions of the facts, however inventive they may be. Their narrative kernel condenses the message that Malverde was a thief who identified with the poor. After one of his companions betrays him, he dies under mysterious circumstances. Finally, the government authorities order that his corpse be hung from a tree as warning to the public. Furthermore, the messages refer to a shrine and the subsequent veneration of the hero as a martyr. The numerous ballads draw on a pattern that enlists Malverde in a wider pantheon of Latin American saints, while they tell their listeners about the existence of the shrine where active devotions can be practiced. How are the elements of the stories composed? This happens in such a manner that no explanation takes place.[71] The ballads often start in medias res, and they have a tendency to narrate sad facts that have already occurred in the form of scenic flashbacks, rather than indulging in the dramatization of the recounted affairs.[72]

The construction of social legends at the margin of (although not independent from) symbolic institutions such as the state works through a process of mimetic transformation of the "real event" into a recognizable plot. Narratological analysis has been accustomed to interpreting the end product (the text); however, we are—instead—concerned with *narratives in action*. Numerous versions of the tale are available, yet the genealogy of the legend is difficult to establish. Its authority resides in the ongoing process of retelling, not in the value of the original or in a claim for individual authorship. "The narrator's only claim to competence for telling the story is the fact that he has heard it himself."[73]

Wald mentions several facts from an oral history, related to him in 1999 by Carlos García from Culiacán who, by then, was a man in his seventies. García's account of the Malverde tale is on the basis of the memories of elderly people he himself had heard speaking during the 1930s and 1940s. His version of the story lacks the element of betrayal as well as the Manichaean image of its hero, providing us with a more lively and ambivalent picture of Malverde. His real name was probably Jesús Juárez Maso.[74] According to García's oral testimony, Jesús was a resourceful, good-looking boy who grew up as an orphan in old Culiacán. Without a family, he got involved in shady dealings and became a crook. "He would steal, and then he would go to the cantinas and buy drinks for all his friends. [...] And one day, at a get-together, he boasted that he was going to steal the governor's sword."[75] The time came, it is said, when the governor's sword was, in fact, stolen, or the theft was simulated, and the politician put a reward on Jesús's head. Since he had many friends in the marginal neighborhoods, the police were unable to catch him. Years later, Jesús died of a disease. When his friends asked for permission to bury him, the Porfirista governor, Francisco Cañedo, ordered instead that his body be publicly hung by the road to intimidate lawbreakers. The latter act—that Foucault would have called the "excessive revenge of the sovereign"[76]—probably happened in 1909. This date is more or less agreed on, so that the punishment of the dead body carries a political message in Culiacán's public memory.[77]

The history that unfolds between the castigation of the corpse—a horrific sacrifice in reverse—, and Jesús Juárez Maso's becoming "El Narcosantón" (the big Drug Saint) is hard to specify. It is linked to the emergence of a particular kind of "narrational knowledge,"[78] one whose status in relationship to established discursive orders is heterogeneous. Such schooling, "like knowledge of one's mother tongue, need not be attended by or incarnated in any given corpus of information."[79] More than that, the imminent social knowledge about Malverde is a subaltern narrative carving in the "mother tongue." It appeals either to those who have suffered from the dictatorial Porfirista State's monopoly of violence, or to those who are compelled, for different reasons, to keep an alternate memory alive. With this kind of knowledge, not being attached to a referentially solid corpus of information does not mean that it is sustained by the timeless power of myth. Social legends, as long as their permeation of life and culture lasts, are embodied narratives: their textual part triggers a psychoactive other that manifests itself through tacit proliferation, making enactment in space and time their primary mode of being.

According to Eligio González, self-ordained chaplain and builder of the shrine, it was popular gossip that created the name "Malverde," referring to the green plants (plantas verdes) where he used to hide from the rural police.[80]

Malverde was first known as "El Bandido Generoso" and even "El Angel de los Pobres" (the Angel of the Poor). Wald, after paying the Malverde shrine and its chaplain a visit, says that the drug traffickers, at least those at the lower and most risky end of the business chain, belong to exactly the same class of poor people.[81] Eligio is introduced to the reader as a musician and composer. During the process in which the shrine was becoming a gathering place, he wrote a cassette-long series of ballads and was finally converted into a corrido protagonist himself. His previous experience of illumination reads as follows: Eligio was still a bus driver when he was severely wounded in a robbery on April 23, 1973. The place where he miraculously was able to recover was the site of Malverde's modest grave, located in old Culiacán, close to the rail yards. The grave was already being frequented by people who left stones to receive the saint's help. As soon as Eligio recovered, he dedicated himself to giving the grave a more visible presence. Later he recalls that the spot became a battle ground when, in the early 1980s, the local government wanted to bulldoze the area to construct the new state capitol building. The state's arbitrary actions caused protests and marches of the faithful, and legend has it that the earth-moving machinery kept breaking down and the workers became frightened.[82] Finally, bowing to a combination of pressures, among which the role of the drug business is as probable as it is unclear, the local authorities donated a piece of barren ground behind the capitol building for a shrine. The shrine was built between 1986 and 1987. Its construction speaks to the existence of well-heeled donors who might be familiar to the readers of the Mexican "nota roja" (scandal sheets).

> Eligio does not deny that the drug world has made his chapel its own, but says that the narcos only make up a small fraction of Malverde's constituency. The saint is available to anyone who needs his assistance, and people travel from all over Sinaloa and beyond…For example, I struck up a conversation with a twenty-two-year-old woman from Guamúchil who had taken the bus to Culiacán just to light two candles at the saint's shrine before making her first trip to the United States, where she had been promised a job in a poultry-processing plant.[83]

The Malverde saint "is available to anyone who needs his assistance," a wager that speaks to the power of nonspecialized imagination. It works through energies that corridos have helped to keep vibrant and alive. For the emergence of what today is called *narcoculture*, there had to exist crossover fantasies giving the ballad-based storytelling about the ordinary traffickers coming out of Sinaloa and its neighboring states a wider affective scope. Malverde was labeled the "Narcosaint" in an arbitrary manner. According to Astorga and Quiñones, the "drug smugglers, due to their social origin, had inherited the belief in Malverde. But the media gave it a kind of yellow slant. They were really the ones who made Malverde into the drug smuggler's saint, forgetting how old the belief in him really was."[84] In her study *Northward Bound*, María Herrera-Sobek remarks that "until economic conditions improve in Mexico (and other Latin American countries), immigration, both legal and 'illegal,' will continue to be a fact of life."[85] Today, the trade in illicit drugs is an intrinsic part of a global economic and geopolitical situation in which "each country plays a role relevant to its resources, political structure, and domestic demand."[86] This has led to an experience that is as disturbing as it is ostensible: the context of mass migration overlaps the social conditioning of the lives of those who work in the dark zones of low-level drug traffic, serving as a disposable army on the global labor market. It becomes thus necessary to destigmatize narcocorridos and their separation from law and order. Rather, what is called for is a perspective that allows us to situate *narcocorridos* and *migration corridos* under the same angle of problematization. I therefore suggest the notion of *global corridos* to embrace both types that have given the ancient ballads a transnational presence throughout the hemisphere.

There are a number of corridos whose protagonists are members of the notoriously powerful *narcotraficantes'* guild, not a few of whom have been eager to pay composers for a story on their behalf. This makes it difficult not to recognize in certain ballads an aggressively paternalist vein. Yet the boasting gesture of drug lords paying for songs in praise of themselves has almost disappeared during recent times. What keeps narcocorridos alive is their proclivity for common heroes whose affective appeal is more ambiguous than the word "bravery." It relates to their unbound stoicism, an attitude detached from normative morals, even if this means, in the case of those heroes, the odds of violent death are higher than those of desired luck. What comes to mind is the Deleuzian figure of an ethics without morality.[87] To put it in the words of Monsiváis: "These born-to-die, joking with destiny, give unlimited value to the present. The corrido announces: *They go along, talking/ that one day they'll kill me./ I am not afraid of snakes./ I know how to lose and win./ I have a goat's horn/ for him who wants to come in.*"[88] In the chapel in Culiacán, Malverde's bust is placed in the company of Saint Judas Thaddaeus and the Virgin of Guadalupe.[89] At this place, the custom of hailing popular sainthood seems to have reached an excessive point. But an extreme dramatism applies, as well, to the lives of many of those who have come to seek their particular share of aid. There is no visible hierarchic norm that rules the relationship between sanctity and criminality. This makes the spot where the three holy ones are eying each other through the devotion of the visitors, all the more telling.

Wald, however, refers to his visit as if Malverde were the only saint in the chapel: Beer and whiskey bottles were placed alongside the votive candles, "and Malverde's followers like to join the saint in a drink and buy him a serenade from the *norteño* trio stationed at the entrance of the inner chapel."[90] The audience that forms when concerts are given in Malverde's honor is varied. As for those asking for encouragement and consolation from the saints, the supportive range is unlimited. The proximity between the precarious situation of the migrant on the one hand and the adventurous condition of the ordinary trafficker on the other is taken for granted at sites like the chapel. This closeness is culturally powerful, yet it does not amount to a deterministic phenomenon. Corridos enact narrative modes that can suddenly make the beliefs of needy people, the dreams of the migrants (especially the undocu-mented), and those of the ordinary traficantes indistinguishable.

> Goodby, dear countrymen
> They'll deport us soon
> But we're not bandits
> We came to do some trafficking in order to survive.
> (Song of the Deported).[91]

Among the more than twenty successful long-play CDs of *Los Tigres*, there is hardly one that does not include, along with a great variety of narcocor-ridos, ballads in which a migrant's drama is told. Not without sarcasm when alluding to the drug business, Monsiváis states, "In these years of crisis, a hero is anyone who can create jobs."[92] Valenzuela's remark about migration corridos applies to narcocorridos, as well, "one thing is certain in [all] the corridos about migration: the migrant is looking for work, and emigrat-ing is a way to earn a living."[93] Extreme conditions of need and insecurity, paired with endless stories of displacement in which the search for luck and the fatal outcome are tied together, have come to characterize the features of deviant imagination. People with dreams and practical projects for cross-ing the border ask the statues of Jesús Malverde, Our Lady of Guadalupe, and Saint Judas Thaddaeus for assistance. The convocation of saints at the Malverde shrine in Culiacán can be understood from the viewpoint of non-dogmatic religious practice. "More people come here than go to church."[94] The requested aid is of existential character and enables alternate morali-ties, at the same time that the veneration associates a postsecular, an almost profane form of polytheism. It looks as though the hemispheric border is figured as an area of initiation, rather than a zone of unbreakable taboo. Images of horror attached to border crossing are accepted as familiar by Malverde's worshippers. Could these visions serve as an exercise in redemp-tion, marking signposts alongside a road to salvation? Or is this knowledge about imminent danger and violence overcast by more atavistic longings, by which people cannot take moral responsibility without striving for their very own survival?

With unceasing regularity, concerts are given in Malverde's honor at the shrine.[95] One feels compelled to ask how diverse the audience addressed by these archaic songs actually is. The answer might be astonishing. Corrido bands play their monotonous yet enchanting, accordion-driven sound for hours and hours, while they offer a highly valued gift: the art of telling about a common hero's adventures as if the drama could "happen to you." The mechanism is paradoxical. A fantasmatic sensation unfolds, an experi-ence through which desires and fears are displaced and affectively assumed.[96] Listening to corridos can help deal with the horrors of life. In that way, the affection that is enabled by these songs bears an element of slyness. Global corridos will make us think, in a somewhat Spinozean manner, of a "singular mode of existence"—one whose power to affect people speaks from the borders of their daily corporeal existence. The obsessive need to renarrate plots that are widely known accounts for the imaginary suspense of longing in which many people join. Corridos help them act out a fantasy to correct the lack of geopolitical peace, and often just aim at existential decency. Can these songs be thought of as a "proliferating machine,"[97] a kind of sounding board on which an immanent drama is rhythmically and stoically affirmed? Could this drama be perceived in the terms of Benjamin's peculiar distinction between just life and bare life, in that rhythm and renarration are exercises in ethical praxis? Whatever the answer might be, it is linked to a participatory experience whose meaning "both displays itself in its consummation and withholds itself by its displacement to another story 'waiting to be told' just beyond the confines of 'the end.'"[98]

CHAPTER 3

Parataxes Unbound

TROPOSCAPES OF IMAGINATION AND THE FIGURAL ENGAGEMENT OF BORDER CROSSING

As scholars concerned with the disjunctures of globalization and the conflicts of contemporary culture have observed, a movement in critical notions "away from linear narratives of immigration, assimilation, and nationhood"[1] toward shifting and hazardous experiences of migration and border identities has taken place. The complex meanings of globalization as "denationalization" and reterritorialization are constituted both inside the nation and across its borders.[2] The phenomenon of *global ballads* (the close relationship between migration corridos and narcocorridos) has in its own particular way shaken stable criteria of space with its assumptions of insides and outsides of national states. These corridos seem to suggest a notion of heterogeneity that is bound to eccentric movement and reiterative intensity. José David Saldívar gives the example of Los Tigres del Norte being "one of the first undocumented bands to receive a Grammy Award for best regional Mexican-American recording" in 1988.[3] The crossover of the band from the traditional Sinaloan *norteño* (country) region into the mass-cultural geographies of the overdeveloped Silicon Valley region renders the spatial and conceptual paradox evident: border ballads of peripheral and rural provenance have established an aleatory yet strong presence, both in Mexico and in one of the most sophisticated territories of the postindustrial world. This passage became visible after 1975, starting with the long-lasting success of the corrido *Contrabando y Traición*. Los Tigres' narcocorridos, together with migration corridos, have become part of posttraditional and transnational narratives, signaling deep changes that had been taking place during the final decades of the twentieth century.

Referring to the conceptual challenges that globalization poses to cultural studies, Appadurai writes:

If globalization is characterized by disjunctive flows that generate acute problems of social well-being, one positive force that encourages an emancipatory politics of globalization is the role of the imagination in social life...The imagination is no longer a matter of individual genius, escapism from ordinary life, or just a dimension of aesthetics. It is a faculty that informs the daily lives of ordinary people in myriad ways...This view of the role of imagination as a popular, social, collective fact in the area of globalization recognizes its split character. On the one hand, it is in and through the imagination that modern citizens are disciplined and controlled...But it is also the faculty through which collective patterns of dissent and new designs for collective life emerge. As the imagination as a social force itself works across national lines to produce locality as a spatial fact and as a sensibility...we see the beginnings of social forms without either the predatory mobility of unregulated capital or the predatory stability of many states. Such social forms have barely been named by current social science, and even when named their dynamic qualities are frequently lost.[4]

One of the aims of the present chapter is to show how corridos, especially migration corridos and narcocorridos, have become agents of an alternate public imagination that not only resignifies but reappropriates space. What remains unmentioned in Appadurai's study, besides the figurative unfolding of imagination into heterogeneous forms of cultural praxis is a global network that is producing tremendous "disjunctive" effects on the life of entire regions and societies: the narcotics economy and its material, human, and symbolic movements in and across the Western Hemisphere.[5] However, narcoculture is not the root but rather one of the paradoxically vibrant consequences, of geopolitical developments. These realities have generated unwelcome scenarios along with the accumulation of "surplus power"[6] and sovereign adjustments, exercised for the benefit of omniscient control of the borderlands and the entire hemisphere. This leads us to ask how the question of violence can be understood when it enters the spatial-symbolic experiences of humans who are not a legitimate part of the subject formations that sustain sovereign rule. Shedding new light on the problematics of imagination is a necessary move in the direction of tracing a hermeneutics of globalization that can reach beyond its common explanations. Corridos express an ethical stance that engages and contests "predatory" forms of violence by means of embodied narration. What marks the strange ubiquity of these ballads, as distinct from mobile capital and the material and symbolic flows originated by established state structures, are their particular powers of rhetorical-spatial dissent. Corridos provide a salient case of imaginaries closely linked to human action, bodies, and thus identities, which do not hold a distinctive discursive position in society, being all too often named in representation or silenced by others.

The recuperation of another notion of imagination, different from the Western tradition initiated by Plato, leads into the relationships between "figurative action" and spatial as well as bodily practices that are both emphasized and repressed by the dynamics of globalization. It is less an emancipatory politics we are looking for, as envisaged by Appadurai, but rather the traces through which imagination displays its rhetorical and spatial materiality. In this framework, one of our guiding hypotheses holds that the struggle for the organization and control over space, as well as for alternative spatial strategies, has increasingly taken on the characteristics of a rhetorical struggle. It is a struggle, not only in functional and (infra)structural terms, but over the figurative power produced by the encoding and decoding of spaces through movements of bodies, all kinds of speech acts and, of course, technology-based forms of representation and circulation. Staging the phenomenon of posttraditional balladry, it is important to ask what is the role of these songs within the struggle over the borderlands? How can these narrative and performative practices be understood in terms of spatial figurations, to the extent that they shape social dispositifs, bodily subjectivities, and transnational desires, while they also provoke ideological and legal counterdiscourses? In other words, how can they be understood as constituting an imagination that is enabled by and itself enables constitutive spatial experiences? From here, it will be necessary to reflect on embodied imagination as a complex affective, rhetorical, and spatial category.

When David Harvey formulated the idea that globalization is about the sociospatial relations among millions of individuals, he suggested that the largely separated discursive categories of *globalization* and *the body* be integrated into a shared continuum to advance toward a "historical-geographical materialism."[7] When we start dealing with the hemispheric border, the relationship between globalization and "the body" becomes drastically discordant, as far as the well-known prolegomena of political modernity are concerned. The commonplaces of Western identity—citizenship, universal morality and "general will," the subject and the individual, civil society, human rights, equality before the law, and social justice—look like realities that have become increasingly precarious in the eyes of those who pay the drastic costs of globalization by exposing their bodies daily to conditions of unhomeliness. The transnational realm of exchange and flexible imperial regulation across the north-south divide is relying on an increasing number of "nonsovereign" citizens, millions of human beings who are the particular, corporal, and situational agents of labor and communication, succumbing to the deterritorializing and "informal" pressures of a neoliberal labor market and the promises of today's mass media. To use a more functional expression, we refer to Ong's term of "graduated citizenship" that circumscribes the differential treatment of populations within global spaces in which distinctions between exceptions and norm are flexibilized according to major geoeconomic and political interests.[8] Given that these people inhabit zones that are devoid of the civilian securities provided by stable nationhood, a sheer presence of moving and displaced bodies and their energies of imagination generates singular yet difficult to define forces of agency.

"Immigration" is the term that specialists and public servants use quite naturally to describe and administer a general state of affairs. Immigration and, above all, migration are the words that exhibit and, at the same time, metaphorize problems, tensions, and sensitivities that have closely accompanied the modern history of the hemispheric border.[9] As Samuel Huntington, an advocate of American identity defined as U.S. sovereignty over the hemisphere, has put it, during recent decades developments have unfolded that, "if continued, could change America into a culturally bifurcated Anglo-Hispanic society with two national languages. [...] The driving force [...] has been immigration from Latin America and especially from Mexico."[10] This formulation, dating to 2004, ranges close to governmental strategies that have taken control of the world to the point where they intend to establish a "total planetary regime of security."[11] Nevertheless, as other analysts argue, migration across the hemispheric border cannot be separated from its historical genealogy.[12] Today, Mexican immigration to the United States, although strongly influenced by economic promises, has not succumbed to a smoothly market-driven, social and cultural assimilation of its several postwar generations into the American mainstream. Two factors are especially worrisome in Huntington's eyes. First, "roughly two thirds of post-1975 Mexican emigrants, it has been estimated, entered the United States illegally."[13] Second, many Mexican and Hispanic immigrants do not dream in English. The author reproachfully holds that Hispanic immigrants do not dream "the American dream created by an Anglo-Protestant society."[14] This, however, is the programmatic condition he sets for sharing in America's values—to "dream in English." The plea foregrounds a purifying and normative view of what, in fact, has "never been modern" as far as the treatment and integration of Latin American neighbors since the Mexican-American War has been concerned. Huntington carefully passes over the paradox: if the zones of migration and border crossing have constituted regions of endemic crisis confronting any major attempt to generate homogenous cultural territories and unadulterated human bodies, it is this reality that has merged with U.S. border policy to become a long-standing training course for what today is called a flexible, and globally networking apparatus of scaling and control.[15]

There has always existed a double dimension of migratory flow and ebb, desired and controlled by what would have to be called a "cynical economy"[16] that has been at the heart of the geopolitical modernization of North America. In this way, we can explain the fact that "migrant populations from Mexico had historically been recognized and accepted as U.S. citizens after a period of work and acculturation, regardless of forms of U.S. immigration laws [...]."[17] A major change occurred between the late 1960s and 1976 when "the status of a large portion of long-established Mexican migrant flow [was converted] from legal to illegal."[18] This change of focus, which turned migrants into outlaws, could nevertheless continue to rely on a sufficient northward flow of Mexican and Central American labor. The change was that the experience of "nonsovereign" migrants (an extreme form of "graduated citizens"), being "accepted as U.S. citizens after a period of work and acculturation" transmuted into one that made access to citizenship an increasingly unlikely enterprise, or a goal that had to be pursued through the sometimes informal, and sometimes criminal networks that started to boom around this very situation. Border corridos have shown high sensitivity toward these changes, on the grounds that they have been commenting on "the adventures and travails of Mexicans immigrating to the United States" for more than one hundred and thirty years. According to Herrera-Sobek, the immigration process during the 1970s and 1980s, as reflected in Mexican corridos, has focused on three major themes:

> [. . .] the quest for a *mica*, or legal border-crossing card (also called a green card); the role of coyotes, or guides, who serve as mediators (for a fee they smuggle undocumented persons into the United States); and the conflict and tension between the migra, or border patrol, and the immigrant.[19]

The critic observes that the rise in corrido production during the 1970s and 1980s "parallels the drastic changes in immigration policy undertaken by the United States" since the 1960s.[20] Surprisingly, she concentrates on "immigration corridos" but leaves narcocorridos aside, precisely at the point where both become variants of social fantasies within the same enforced situation. In contrast, we suggest speaking of "global corridos" to show that both ballad variants are immersed in one and the same hemispheric context in which the flexibilization of global economic developments,[21] together with new strategies of enforcement and control, have been relying on massive reserve armies of labor, especially in Mexico and Central America. Monsiváis observes that the gestures and modes of behavior of low-level Mexican drug traffickers have tended, since the 1980s, to follow the pathway of the stories and experiences of migration on the grounds of the same or a similar framework of social conditions, territorial knowledge, and public legends.[22] The striving of migrating Mexicans for citizenship "on the other side" has been facing an exponentially increasing cost, as it has changed from an informal to an illegal experience during recent decades (the meanings remain slippery owing to their ambivalent usage throughout U.S.-Mexican border history). This cost translates into seriously endangered lives and an epidemic spread of what state forces call "uncontrolled violence," a reality whose terms remain ill-defined in official language. We therefore relate the rise of global border corridos to this very phenomenon: the need of the noncitizen to reestablish a space for both survival and sociosymbolic (self)recognition in times of harsh deterritorialization affecting significant segments of the Mexican, Central American, and other Latin American populations. The amazing level of popularity of the group Los Tigres del Norte for more than thirty years is due, according to Sam Quiñones, to their chronicling the "unarticulated and unpublicized" sort of "rebellion" that underlies Mexican working-class immigration to the United States.[23]

We understand the term "graduated citizen," somewhat differently from Ong, in polemical relation to the image of universal democratic citizenship, from which market-driven North American society has so benefited as it spread the American Dream to the "inauthentic" citizens of the peripheries. The market is often the only remaining yet pervasive universal symbol. This image has become all the more compelling, the more Latin American countries have themselves become modern societies—modern on the grounds of a heterogeneity that has led to a proliferation of strategies for "entering and leaving modernity"[24] at the same time. Migration is one of the prominent passages of this kind. But market universalism has not kept its promise to give people sovereignty over space. It translates rather into the tensions between aggravated peripheral and desired universal citizenship. Radical mobility and porous borders have turned into networks of despair, and new forms of control, as well as of violence. In this regard, to "enter and to leave modernity" has become an increasingly violent endeavor that reciprocates the character of hemispheric modernity as it has been unfolding since the Mexican-American War of 1848. In that war, Mexico lost half of its territory—regions that had been home to Hispanic culture for more than three centuries. Since this gigantic "law-making" act, hemispheric contemporaneity has unfolded as the eventual "modernization" of geopolitical inequality. It is unlikely, however, that analysis can devise a single transcendental thread connecting the ways by which border subjects and their practices of resistance are constituted. Viewed in terms of long-standing affective patterns, the described predicament is charged by modes of existence through which an imminent social imagination unfolds. In other words, analysis needs to recognize the figurative, that is the embodied drive that informs the fantasies that are linked to an innate mode of action in the first place: "northward bound." When using Herrera-Sobek's expression, we do not conceive of it as a metaphor. Corridos will instead evidence the paratactical character of *Northward Bound*, which is built on contiguities of body and space. Thus, cultural experience can be perceived as arising from immanent relationships to a violent hemispheric modernity.[25]

The unprecedented appeal of groups such as Los Tigres can now be explained on the basis of a double phenomenon. First, their impact relies on the renarration of experiences that draw on the historical immanence of informal or (in the eyes of many migrants) customary border crossing. Therefore, contemporary low-level drug trafficking is neither an isolated structural or juridical issue nor can it be reduced to a deterministic outcome of the narcotics industry. There is only a thin dividing line between migration ballads and narcocorridos. Second, that which seems still distinct within a referential frame of storytelling becomes almost indistinguishable once we start considering the affective side of the music. The public appeal of Los Tigres relates to aesthetic sensibilities that account for, as they are nurtured by, narco and migration ballads' mutually enabling relationship. Before exploring this second facet, an inquiry into the rhetorical-spatial language of corridos is necessary.

To resume a guiding hypothesis, contemporary cultural conflicts over the borderlands can be understood, to an important degree, as rhetorical conflicts consisting of a struggle over the figurative potentials displayed by speech acts and bodies, and entangled with numerous practices of movement and exchange. That corridos have been a deep-rooted aspect of the embodied side of displacement for many decades is a fact whose phenomenology has led us to work at the margins of the discursive orders. This premise requires a heightened sense of the figurative potential of spatial experience, not only as a way of foregrounding a "geographical" (Harvey) but at the same time "rhetorical materialism." A parenthesis has to be opened here. A materialistic view should also embrace the appropriation of corridos by artistically more established forms such as novels, testimonies, short stories and, of course, film. But despite the crossover of ballad plots into domains of writing culture and the media industry during the 1980s and 1990s, these ballads reproduce their collective vigor and sometimes become agencies of alternative consciousness, inasmuch as their presence remains aleatory, situational, and rhetorically ubiquitous. Ballads remain tied to a considerable degree to oral and embodied communication. At the same time, corridos as dissenting practices have merged with the symbolic power of several mass cultural formats (music, radio, and film) to such an extent that analysis must avoid a unifying take. Focusing on the extraordinary case of Los Tigres allows us to draw on a constitutive discrepancy. Is there a figural matrix to their corridos that cannot be unified by industrialized media formats and which pervades these narratives with peculiar persistency, so that imagination can draw in one way or another on media speech without being entirely governed by its logic?

The traditional borderlands corrido has undergone processes of contemporaneization and mass-mediated dissemination without losing what we perceive as its enabling atavistic gesture. It is a gesture of imagining and actively constructing a spatial presence, an ability to express desire and indignation, defiance and grief, by virtue of a mnemonic (renarrating) insistence and by the rhythmic codification of space. This enabling gesture confronts the world by means of "shaped behaviour,"[26] and it follows a desire that seeks territorialization under precarious and often violent circumstances. Let us thus assume that the primary rhetorical conditioning that shapes the corridos' presence is a spatial-corporeal one. Corridos suggest that we speak of "transversal migration"—a movement across space that is not identical to the lineal crossing of the border, but rather exposed to a variety of contingent factors that find themselves condensed in the semilegitimate economy of labor flow. This type of migration is informal according to normative criteria, however and especially regarding informality it relies on a long-standing tradition. This partially feeds into dynamics that pertain to the narcotics economy. Transnational labor migration has been of tremendous benefit for the economic growth of the North. Speaking in terms of U.S. employment needs, David Lorey observes that, according to several recent studies, differences between legal and illegal migrants have not been recorded as a major criterion of hiring practices and governmental statistical analysis.[27] Transversal migration can thus be seen as one of the most characteristic yet most paradoxical features of the hemispheric condition.

To provide a conceptual mold appropriate to the cultural antagonisms of border crossing, I suggest the term "troposcapes." In a primary sense, troposcapes can be understood as those shifting and fluctuating maps that are configured through particular kinds of speech acts. Regarding theoretical debates about "deterritorialization," we share Appadurai's approach to the concept of "ethnoscapes."[28] However, a "transnational anthropology" cannot leave aside assemblages of cultural rhetoric and tropological behavior by which space is reimagined and even reinhabited by the subjects of transversal migration. For an understanding of our subject matter, migration is a more compelling term than immigration. It has also been, in the realm of cultural studies of the border, the less theorized notion of the two. In a basic sense, the movement that shapes the transversal migrants' relationships to territory resembles the logics of speech acts.[29] It is not condensed in the end product (the accomplished linguistic work as an independent unit or the final arrival at a destination after a self-conscious displacement through space, as expressed in an influential image of the modern traveler)[30] but, rather, in an utterance whose character and outcome depend on the given performative risks and circumstances. Deploying a framework that is informed by De Certeau, migration can be understood as an interference at times more and at times less dissonant into the "literal meaning" of strategically organized and normatively connotated border space. And this, when translated into a "poetic tropology" (Vico),[31] is what much of the sorrowful, repetitious yet aleatory rhythm of border ballads is all about.

Transversal migration suggests associating the "speaking of the unheeded steps"[32] in a more dramatic way than that described in De Certeau's acclaimed metonymy, in which the author speaks of the "walking citizen," deprived of a stable territorial identity when facing the vertigo of urbanization. When comparing "walking" in late modern urban spaces with the character of a speech act, De Certeau wrote:

> At the most elementary level, it [the speech act] has a triple "enunciative" function: it is a process of *appropriation* of the topographical system on the part of the pedestrian (just as the speaker appropriates and takes on the language); it is a spatial acting-out of the place (just as the speech act is an acoustic acting-out of the language); and it implies *relations* among differentiated positions, that is, among pragmatic "contracts" in the form of movements.[33]

Now, what is it that makes the embodied speech acts of transversal migrants and their phatic relationship to space so symptomatic? In the case of the undocumented migrant, "appropriation," "realization," and especially "agreement" are marked by an abyss in the first place. *El corrido de los mojados* (The Wetbacks' Corrido), written by Luis Armenta, makes this type of aggravated speech-act situation evident. It synthesizes the wetbacks' symptomatic condition of having neither legality nor legitimate linguistic status.[34] The threat of deportation is constant, as is the continuous drive of many Mexicans to escape poverty and instability. De Certeau's notion of "pragmatic agreement" turns into a "pragmatic contest"—a race against immobilization and sometimes against death—since different territorial zones are fused into one continuous area of conflicting movements ("the stubborn gringo chases us out, and then we return"[35]). The "we"—the collective plural of the migrants—is contrasted with the third person singular of "el gringo" who appears typified as disciplinary authority, thus identifying a tactical situation against the background of strategic control that involves language as much as space. And, again and again, corridos keep replicating an atavistically sounding mission: the more they are kicked out, the more come in every month.[36]

When they deal with ordinary smugglers, corridos tend to deploy similar fables of cunning and self-asserting verse. The lyrics of *Juana La Patera* (Juana the Smuggler) speak of a "proud Mexican woman" who comes and goes, crossing the borderlands "as she pleases."[37] The use of the first person singular in this and other corridos does not cause an individualizing effect; it appears as though the "I" of the female smuggler or the migrant were the focalizing device of testifying to an imaginary companionship among border crossers. Another corrido says:

> The border cops caught me
> Let's say, three hundred times,
> But they never tamed me
> I taught them how to comply.[38]

Where the "gringo" ("la migra") represents indomitability over the control of space, the collective "I" holds on to a shared Sisyphus-like capability of reversing the spatial order, if necessary, 300 times. The paradox of the phenomenon is raised to the level of normality where it appears to respond to conflicting types of violence. The versatility of the migrant's behavior in rhetorical-spatial terms finds its reverse yet complementary side in the experience of violent living conditions, an exposure that is even more merciless than the impending threat of deportation. Otherwise migrants would not take the risk of a journey that inevitably converts them into "mojados" (wetbacks) and "ilegales" (illegals). This primary experience of violence lies in the dark zones of geopolitical and economic domination and, specifically, massive poverty.

> Don't condemn me
> For leaving my country like this
> It's the fault of poverty
> And of need.
>   (Corrido of the Deported).[39]

La Tumba del Mojado (The Wetback's Grave) calls up the image of the Río Grande tainted with the blood of undocumented migrants. The "Tortilla Curtain," a popular name for the border between Mexico and the United States, is viewed as nothing less than an offense to the Mexican people.[40]

Attention deserves what can be epitomized as an alternative geopolitical ethics. What is the distinctive affective force of these ballads? This question will be pursued in detail when we extend the discussion of corridos to intermedial aesthetic analysis (see the following chapter). We can say, so far, that the narratives performed by Los Tigres offer metonymical visions of a relentless desire for the actions of displacement, crossing, and thus transgression. The names of the ballad heroes (Camelia la Tejana, Emilio Varela, Lino Quintana, Juana la Patera, El Mojado, and many others) are contiguous with embodied and embodying speech acts that signal deviant interference into normatively organized border space. Metonymical construction precludes a generalizing, for example ideological, judgment. In other words, the alternative ethical stance is due to immanent modes of action and expression. The singular and yet uncountable migrants and small smugglers do not consider their crossing of the border as an illegal or unjust act. Such acts, especially in their proclivity to confront violence, cannot be described on the grounds of a Platonic, or Hegelian, or strategic higher purpose, either. They are implied, rather, in an existential (or life-asserting) perseverance in a sort of Spinozian way[41] by virtue of which the bodies of ballad heroes and heroines confront immanent hemispheric modernity. "Law-preserving" force that keeps the border safe has long been common, overshadowing the founding act of "law-positing" violence that dates back to the Mexican-American War. What it cannot do away with, however, is the ongoing affective situation: "la herida abierta"—the open wound.[42]

Corridos help us understand long-lasting cycles of customary rights by which migrants have asserted their desire and liberty to traverse border space as many times as necessary. Poverty and bare subsistence labor in the South and the existence of an "other" Latino world in the developed North are contiguous realities whose interstices have become culturally meaningful. In these in-between territories, figures and rhythms of insistence regarding the tactical appropriation of space abound. The movement between escaping poverty in vast regions of rural Mexico and immersion in coercively administered border spaces has generated a paradoxical language, for which corridos may well be viewed as the main fora: their rhythm is ingrained in repetitive movement, its content bears a host of dramatic plots, and one of its characteristic poetic tensions unfolds between endurance and cunning.[43] Global ballads do not simply represent an underlying reality; they function as vital and sometimes reflective gestures, acting within constellations that are themselves narratively conditioned, sharing the company of other fables and alternative knowledges. Thus, corridos narrate the cycle of transnational displacement and relocation (and sometimes integration) in a particular way. They translate the occupation of border space into a rhythmical and tropological mode, which we will soon explore as the *paratactical* engagement of space.

We can wonder whether our extension of the speech act to describe the spatial-rhetorical character of corridos applies to the older ballad tradition as well. The answer would presumably be yes, at least to the extent to which the latter has mediated the immigrant experiences of hardship and indefatigable dreams for more than a hundred years. Nevertheless, it makes sense to speak of *global corridos* only if we can access their logic of being cultural "power stations" in the contemporary world. A main assumption shows the affinity of global ballads to the avatars in the lives of immigrants and migrants throughout history, the way they crystallize around the figures of ordinary social heroes whose actions become legends. A second assumption can be recalled from our previous chapter. It is based on the fact that the composers of the songs like to poach media and information sources, extracting memorable occurrences and breathtaking plots for their own purposes. Hence, there should exist a socioanthropological matrix that helps to (re) incorporate the most timely material into the sober ballad style. All of this combines to mean that, in the social imagination of the borderlands, these ballads function as agents of renarration and reembodiment rather than as creations sui generis. The main case under consideration will continue to be the cultural style that has emerged from the work of Los Tigres del Norte. This group has, in a unique way, called upon and assembled the stories of ordinary rebels, acting in the dark zones of the border to create an endless musical repertoire that, since the 1970s, has been taken up by innumerable other groups. But above all, Los Tigres have reshaped an ancient tradition in affective terms and made it a timely art of archaicizing storytelling.

ERICH AUERBACH'S CONFLICT WITH THE ARCHAIC OTHER

How can we better understand the peculiar dimension of the corridos' storytelling in its relationship to experiential patterns? On the one hand, we are dealing with spatial networks shaped by acting humans (migrants) and, on the other, with narrative figures (corridos as legends and songs), both of which have an effect on social fantasies. These questions lead us into a brief epistemological journey that will bring to light submerged traces of the concept of figural imagination. We will offer an atypical reading of Auerbach's renowned study on mimesis, turning it against its distinct "modernist historicism" (White). Our hypothesis is that for Auerbach, the medieval ballad tradition resonates as a literary other that, although not explicitly named as such, constitutes an interesting undercurrent of his work. In *Mimesis: The Representation of Reality in Western Literature* (1946), the deployment of figural stylistic innovations "ever better adapted to the depiction of a reality as various in its forms as it is multiple in its meanings,"—starting out with classical antiquity and Biblical figuralism—supports the idea of fulfilling Western literature's "unique promise to represent reality realistically."[44] Although the notion of realism has vanished today under the influence of anti-Hegelian and non-Lukácsian concerns, Auerbach's peculiar interest in the tension between creatureliness (*Kreatürlichkeit*) and figural imagination has not ceased to present a major force field of debate.[45] Our study of the global ballad phenomenon will discuss a similar tension, although it is motivated by cultural diagnostics that can cut a swathe through any teleological perception of Western literature.

For Auerbach, there is an uncomfortable idea that keeps bothering his historicist sense. The concept in question is "parataxis," and the startling aspect for the philologist is its anachronistic status. Through parataxis, an archaic narrative figure resonates within the "rising" modern imagination, as the critic himself noticed when reflecting about the beginnings of Western literary forms and styles. In Auerbach's logic, paratactical narration, so persistent within medieval and early modern narrative, is eventually superceded by an increasingly complex and self-reflexive literary consciousness in which "hypotaxes" and other more reflexive devices take over. Our purpose is to lay out the irritating question: can parataxis be read as a stylistic (and cultural) factor that tends to threaten literature's modernist fulfillment? If there is one notion in the book *Mimesis* that seems to go astray whenever the author explores the figures through which reality is represented "realistically," this notion is parataxis. Auerbach situates the origins of the principle of paratactical style within Biblical and Medieval epics, especially when there is a lack of (classically shaped) syntactic connectives allowing for an understanding of cause and effect in the text (*hypotaxes*). This observation is not accidental. However, the strong presence of orally shaped narrative and musical forms such as popular balladry in medieval storytelling is a fact that the author does not problematize. He is, rather, concerned with those works whose trajectory (or promise) is supposed to lead up to a modern aesthetics. He thus submits inherent narrative forms and rhetorical devices to stylistic criteria in the first place, whereas other observers have related them to anthropological concerns.[46] This explains why the classical philologist engages otherness in a somewhat mysterious way. In relation to the epic poem *Chanson de Roland* (eleventh or twelfth century) we read:

> The poet explains nothing; and yet the things which happen are stated with a paratactical bluntness which says that everything must happen as it does happen, it could not be otherwise, and there is no need for explanatory connectives. This [...] refers not only to the events but also to the views and principles which form the basis of the actions of the persons concerned.[47]

"The poet explains nothing" signals a gesture of incorporation of (or seduction by) what could have appeared as "impure" narrative agency in the first place. The attributes devoted to the paratactical phenomenon that Auerbach sees as "manifestly unclassical," but also as nonmodern, are similar in different cases of written texts: predominance of "principle clauses, juxtaposed and opposed like blocks," absence of temporal and causal hypotaxes, impulsive tone, dramatic effectiveness, readiness to "absorb the sensorily realistic, even the ugly, the undignified, the physically base," "vivid sensory depiction of outward events, especially of the magical, the morbid, and the horrible." Auerbach refers, for example, to a verse in the *Chanson de Roland*, in which Sir Roland is appointed to a dangerous post by the king, a conspiracy that leads to his death. Yet, similarly to the ballad style, the horrible events do not offer either dramatic heightening or a wallowing in morbid details but rather an account that summons a violent experience or situation into a pulsating, almost fragmentary, and prosodic tale. A style of scenic and spatial immediacy, a "low style, such as would properly only be applicable to comedy, but which now reaches out far beyond its original domain...."[48] Using a different terminology, this style can be attributed to an *intermedial effectiveness*—a capacity to infiltrate more complex aesthetic and textual realms. However, if parataxis reaches beyond an alleged "original domain," it may also be worthwhile to think further about that very domain that is certainly not limited to "comedy" but may associate still less established forms of narration and embodiment. This is a step that the critic is less interested in, since he prefers not to engage oral culture as heterogeneous, that is, as not confined to its mediation by long-standing norms of a more discrete, learned, and less sensuous character than the nonliterary forms of imagination.

When Auerbach speaks of "parataxis" as a figure expressing unmediatedness and brutal sensuousness, which are also attracted to dramatic and violent experiences, it can be gathered that an association with the primitive is not far away. Shouldn't it be that the immanent presence of popular ballads within more established medieval styles of writing has played a part in the interpretive invention of a "primitive" and bloodthirsty reality? And is that which could be perceived as being the primitive—prone to paratactical expression—really something located outside or at an opposite end of the hypotactical mind? At issue is the concept of "mimetic faculty" at the point of its utmost tension—understood with Benjamin[49] as a faculty that separates and approximates both the textualized universe and cultural experience in its immediate, spatialized, ceaselessly embodying expressions. In other words, can "parataxis" be perceived as an anachronistic style to the extent that it emerges at the borders of central concepts such as literature, culture, and experience? Returning to Auerbach's formulations, we cannot help but be astounded by the pervasiveness of this style. The critic tells us that paratactical narration is capable of depicting extraordinary or marvelous things through a few sensuous details and with astonishing accuracy, and without expanding itself over time. Extreme economy in the deployment of aesthetic devices, an almost monotonous rhythm of presentation resembling an aleatory, unrelenting presence in space, and a profound impact by the means of narrative soberness—these are the elements that seem to account for the enigmas that parataxis has not ceased to contain.

As far as Auerbach's interest in early modern writing is concerned, his approach to the "low style" does not aim at a social hermeneutics, one that would link the figural expression of ugly directness, brute sensoriousness, and a scenic account of colliding forces to a nonphilological context of imagination. His main purpose is to name the Western literary evolution by which an archaic (paratactical) style would be subdued by refinement and complexity: "reason and ethics" shall triumph over "magic and sense."[50] *Mimesis* thus engages, in its initial chapters, the linguistic and stylistic appropriation of a nonhomogeneous, supposedly horrifying and irrational world by the Judaeo-Christian tradition. One of Auerbach's remarks about St. Augustine's *Confessions* seems to praise the violence inscribed in Christian indoctrination itself—in a discourse that has been cunningly coercive: Western civilization appears as superior to other cultures, even in its way of deploying "magic" and "bloodlust":

> ...in the fight against magical intoxication, Christianity commands other weapons than those of the rational and individualistic ideal of antique culture; it is, after all, itself a movement from the depths, from the depths of the multitude as from the depths of immediate emotion; it can fight the enemy with his own weapons. Its magic is no less a magic than its bloodlust, and it is stronger because it is a more ordered, a more human magic.[51]

Christianity, in its fight against its enemies, has commanded a profound consciousness of the role of language, and hence of style and figuration, as battlefields. It has lessons to teach as far as the use of violence, coupled with its simultaneous domestication, is concerned. Aesthetically, we are dealing with a kind of montage, so that St. Augustine's discourse is described as displaying a "mixed style," and therefore considered superior.[52] Behind stylistic blending lurks a rhetorical struggle whose battleground is the contaminated materiality of culture. The above citation confers a far-reaching insight: heterogeneity is recognized as the actual field of conflict. This is why Christianity's fight with the forces of imagination must actively include the principle of "montage." This makes it understandable how Western civilizing reason, schooled by Christian epistemology in masking its colonial impetus, reveals its actual character the moment we recognize it as "*rhetorical* reason."[53] Modern *rhetorical* reason, as I have argued elsewhere, is strategically aware of heterogeneity and makes it work for its own purpose, although the enterprise is only successful when the move is cautiously hidden beneath a surface of dualism and homogeneity. At issue is, to recall Sloterdijks expression, a critique of "cynical reason"[54] as a powerful epistemic matrix of the Western intellect. In an intense although enigmatic way, the concept of paratactical narration fits in the middle of these conflicts. It appears like a subtext pertaining to the corporeal materiality of culture at the point where its rhythm can pervade different forms of narrating and writing (ballads, chronicles, religious treatises, etc.). There is evidence, even when seemingly so banal that it has barely been noticed, that one of the main historical sources of paratactical figuration can be discerned in medieval ballads, as well as in romances. Auerbach realizes that parataxis, in its enigmatic status, connects with what appear to be the most immediate, embodied, and thus active forces of imagination, lying hidden within the narrative and figurative potentials of a wider consciousness that awaits domestication ("the depths of the multitude").

Returning to the rhetorical practice of cunning in St. Augustine, using well-measured doses of paratactical expression can presumably call up the primitive forces of violence and disorder and make them "obey" the "more human" violence of the Christian enterprise. Auerbach shows how St. Augustine, in his *Confessions* and other writings, had developed a stylistic project that seemed to embody the struggle with "magical intoxication" from "within"—in the very realm of the soul: "the enemy is known," striving for "the triumph of magic and sense over reason and ethics," but "the soul's counterforces are mobilized to meet him."[55] These are words in which Plato's "allegory of the cave" resonates.[56] We are reminded of the nerve centers of the Western concept of imagination, at the point at which cunning reason is becoming the ordering force of modernity, whose strategic aim is the successful linkage of transcendental and instrumental criteria. The interaction of both is expected to rule over contaminated imagination where paratactical compulsions are supposed to loom large. This is why St. Augustine in Auerbach's reading, far from trusting the "weapon of individualistic, aristocratic, moderate, and rational self-discipline"[57] that was inherited from enlightened classical narratives, knew he needed the spells of magical powers, together with the less visible deployment of violence (hidden in educated and legitimate discourse), to lead Christian doctrine to success. It is here—in the cunning move of monotheism toward instrumental yet secretly heterogeneous concepts of knowledge and truth—, that the complex problematics of modern imagination was set on their course. Minor narratives of the ballad type were taken as "mimetic lessons" that could help to build flexible variants of hegemonic narratives. Simultaneously, these minor tales would be relegated to the cultural underground, especially those that did not share in the adoration of aristocratic heroes and epic deeds of the sublime sort. The battle for imagination has ever since remained a contradictory field. After all, the disciplinary project stretching from Christianity to transcendental rationalism and global neoliberalism has not been able, in the course of the centuries, to completely subdue the embodied, impure forces of imagination.

Dealing with the reemergence of paratactical narratives throughout today's scenarios of globalization can contribute to an understanding of the history of rhetorical realities as political ones. A Spinozan expression would have it that depraved experience obtains its energies from the "sea of existential imagination"[58] without superior and transcendental traits; a world in which bodies, desires, and cultural dispositives can gather into formative as well as disintegrative forces of reality. According to Negri, the most compelling singularity of plural existence lays grounded in the experiences of poverty and indignation. His view is guided by the abstract idea that the poor "can construct the world under the sign of the common,"[59] a teleology of the multitude that is difficult to share. In turn, our approach to parataxis as a figure that signals radical impurity aims at observing that "poverty and indignation" cannot be abstracted from a spatialized and corporalized existence but have to be scrutinized from there. This is the case, as we will discuss, as far as the imagination of the nonsovereign subjects of transnational diaspora and its relations to the global corrido phenomenon is concerned.

While we shed new light on the phenomenon of "paratactical bluntness" in narration, where "everything must happen as it does happen," as opposed to hypotaxis as stylistic device of the ordering mind, we will retain an open interpretive horizon. At this point in our reflection, where the aesthetic and the social, the anthropological and the spatial aspects have come ominously close to each other, the corrido in its mutable yet atavistic bluntness can be situated within wider comparative concerns. The following series of questions, offered by Hayden White in *The Content of the Form*, calls for attention in this regard:

> Does the world really present itself to perception in the form of well-made stories, with central subjects, proper beginnings, middles, and ends, and a coherence that permits us to see "the end" in every beginning? Or does it present itself more in the forms that the annals and chronicle [largely consisting of paratactical constructions; HH] suggest, either as mere sequence without beginning or end or as sequences of beginnings that only terminate and never conclude? And does the world, even the social world, ever really come to us as already narrativized, already "speaking itself" from beyond the horizon of our capacity to make scientific sense of it? Or is the fiction of such a world, capable of speaking itself and of displaying itself as a form of a story, necessary for the establishment of that moral authority without which the notion of a specifically social reality would be unthinkable?[60]

White does not touch on the dimension of space when dealing with the question of narrative as the figural experience of life and history. Spatiality starts with the embodiment of human speech and action. A remarkable sentence comes to mind that was once expounded by Vico under the rubric of "Corollaries Concerning Poetic Tropes, Monsters, and Metamorphoses":

> ...as rational metaphysics teaches that man becomes all things by understanding them (*homo intelligendo fit omnia*)...imaginative metaphysics shows that man becomes all things by *not* understanding them (*homo non intelligendo fit omnia*); and perhaps the latter proposition is truer than the former, for when man understands he extends his mind and takes in the things, but when he does *not understand* he makes the things out of himself and becomes them by transforming himself into them.[61]

At least two observations allow Vico some timely credit here. On the one hand, the abstraction of space by rationalist, historicist, and humanist modernity has not succeeded in shaking off the local, corporeal, and affective grounds of imagination. On the other, a "philology of human actions," as conceived by Vico, foregrounds a notion of poetry different from a sublime or an autonomous one. This is why the notion of "poetic tropes" can be easily misunderstood. To speak of a "poetics of space" (Bachelard)[62] is not the same as to experience a becoming space, that is to say the transmuting of an embodied imagination into one that (in the case of border ballads) actively refigures the experience of space. We will later discuss how this kind of affectivity is not devoid of a reflexive quality, as Vico had maintained. In any event, there is one more aspect to "not understanding," once we perceive it as a figural mark of human action—not of a speech that deals with space, but of speech acts whose condition is bound to spatial intervention itself. "Not understanding" would imply, in the cases of migration corridos, that the fixed meaning of space (the "literal" or "strategic" meaning that in De Certeau's terms lies codified within a geographical system)[63] is undone by the rhetorical, bodily work of the migrants. Paraphrasing White's wording, the lesson taught by ballads is found in the way they undermine coherent geographical narratives "with central subjects, proper beginnings, middles and ends." Migration corridos are an active part of the adventures of border crossers in that they function as "sequence(s) without beginnings or end," or "sequences of beginnings that only terminate and never conclude." The footpaths of migrants follow a design that hollows out the linguistic framework of hierarchized space. It is oriented toward by-ways and short cuts that circumvent the system, and it is guided by legends, rumors, and an atavistic existential rhythm—all of which associate the figure of parataxis. Even if migrants were to command the language of the geopolitical system, they would barely be tolerated as legitimate subjects of enunciation. For it is strategic language that, in a biopolitical order of control, is defined by its capacities to abstract and to exclude.

There is hardly a phenomenon that resembles more intensely the submission of human bodies to geo-biopolitical rationalization than the exposedness of migrating border crossers to the rules of territories that are not their own. The condition of the transient's "not knowing" is not primarily a question of schooling (although it may carry the burden of poor education). It is a matter of surviving by tactically reorganizing a strategically codified space. The *ethical subjects* of contemporary globalized space are not the tourists who inhabit, to an increasing degree, the euphemistically praised open borders as Marc Augé would still have it.[64] The persons who, by virtue of their tactical agility, their corporal and logistic creativity, pay the costs that help the machinery of "open" borders function are the migrants of today's world. In the Western Hemisphere, it is not an exaggeration to say that masses of underemployed people in Colombia, Central America, and Mexico, who—by the use of their bodies—have become disposable creatures in the game of global labor trafficking and narcotics trade, are paying that price. Parataxes, when thus readdressed by a hermeneutic of embodied imagination, render account of experiences whose aesthetics can only be understood against Auerbach's vision of figural fulfillment.[65] Parataxes help associate the recalcitrance of social drama, its obtuse materiality, its distance from the symbolic reign, at the point at which precarious meaning comes accompanied by a surplus of rhythmic insistence and the vitality of stoic remembrance, which "the storyteller" keeps upright at all costs. Parataxes seem to associate, today, a conceptual space where Auerbach's contrast between *figura* and *creatura* is suddenly effaced, in that the paratactical dramas condensed by global ballads are situated at the threshold of extreme biopolitical conditioning of life. These dramas can be perceived, defamiliarizing Eric Santner's comments on Benjamin, Kafka, Celan, and Rosenzweig, to name "the 'essential disruption' that renders man 'creaturely'...[at] the threshold where life becomes a matter of politics and politics comes to inform the very matter and materiality of life."[66]

PARATACTICAL DRAMA AND THE EFFACEMENT
OF TRAGEDY: CASUALTIES OF GLOBALIZATION

Unruly narrative and embodied knowledges, to the extent that they have enabled the emergence of global corridos, help to inhabit as well as to recharge space through an acting imagination. A widespread condition of spatial inequality is at stake, one that is predetermined by colliding yet interacting forms of violence: dispossession by impoverishment is nurtured and, in turn, nurtures a mobility of massive scale that benefits a "cynical economy," and the relationship between them is administered by imperial rule. There is no doubt that the ballads address these issues in an obsessive way; however, it has become apparent that the manner in which they treat violence escapes easy judgment.

Throughout major trajectories of Western literatures, as well as throughout a good part of the philosophical discourse of modernity, violence has been encoded by tragic narratives. "The experience of the tragic is the experience of the borders of reason."[67] Constructing a tragedy is a way of giving legitimacy to the actions of a distinct individual whose project is bound to fail and who, in that very course of events, is often destroyed him or herself. Tragedy in its metaphysical assumptions, such as those laid out by Hegel, has circled around the "unique aspiration" of the subject who violently ends up losing the vantage point of a rational individual.[68] However, both a poetic discourse of modernity and philosophical thinking have bemoaned the vanishing of the tragic, the one as a gain, and the other as blinded optimism. From a contemporary vantage point, it seems that tragedy is returning. Terry Eagleton, while recently discovering a potentially tragic spirit regarding the life stories of every individual exposed to inhumane society, writes, "Tragic heroes and heroines are now to be found loitering on every street corner...To alchemize the base metals of daily lives into the pure gold of tragedy, one may have to take these men and women and push them to the very limit of their endurance."[69] Yet, the problem seems to lie in an epistemic assumption of "purity," or unique truth. The "gold of tragedy" has been built on the power of the aesthetic sublime in the first place, which has tended to preclude the unnamed street heroes—not to speak of poor migrants—from its privileges. What if the "base metals of daily lives" were incompatible with an authentically tragic ecstasy or were to bury the "pure gold" under a world of "humiliating sobriety" in which the modernizing circle of violence in Western history, culminating in neoliberal globalization, has already underminded any tragic norms? We should remember that tragedy, by articulating aesthetic perception relating to an extreme experience is centered on conflicts that unfold within an elect subject—leading this ennobled individual, in a situation of cataclysm, toward a sentiment of singular intensity. The problem of justice is crystallized in the utmost suffering of the hero as that kind of truth that pushes the idea of reason to its limits. Tragic violence thus appears as the ultimate attack that can be carried out against the self-determined subject.

Hasn't the "sovereignty" of the rational subject become porous and double-faced, especially in view of unholy manifestations—in contemporary history—of Hegel's famous dictum that "the state consists in the march of God in the world, and its basis is the power of reason actualizing itself as will."[70] But the question has to be led further—what about those other "ultimate" human beings who cannot claim a tragic distinction, since they have never been in conditions to question the moral order of the state from within or from a position of eternal quest? These are people whose situation is not tragically significant at all, who have been converted into disposable parts of "sad collisions" where human praxis confronts, according to a distinction made by Hegel, the impact of mere "situational" powers. Tragedy is therefore not the right word for the exposed people of capitalism's peripheries an increasing part of whom are bound to move into the globalized network of fluctuating labor. Here, their presence has become indispensable because mobility and disposability are the rule and economic well-being the *exception*. The violent experiences that these human beings encounter would be, to paraphrase Hegel again, not more than the "effects of external casualties and relative conditionings." For the tragic hero's predicament is the conscious, often self-reflective exaltation of his fiasco. Dealing with today's particular conditions of homelessness and uprootedness, within which violence has become inherent—simply a "sad" circumstance—, narcocorridos and migration corridos function as never-ending dramas without "that sense of reconciliation that the tragedy affords by the glimpse of eternal justice."[71]

It is worth thinking about aesthetic differences. Corridos display metonymic plots in that agents stand for actions, and it is with their bodies, coupled with the paratactical rhythm of the songs, that the heroes and heroines draw memorable figurations in space. The reading of these figures—a reading of that which "was never written"[72]—implies affective participation that is devoid of psychological depth but which can recognize experience by means of paratactical involvement. In tragedy, bodies are besieged by violence as well, but their suffering is rendered legitimate as an inner drama of the heightened soul. In contrast, is there a legitimate principle of identity that the heroes of global ballads could claim? Can these songs, in their nontragic yet harshly dramatic state, help us imagine an "ultimate" human condition—a condition in which depravity and loss become manifest as the potentially unruly base of today's world? If violence and monstrosities show a face that seems to erode the certainties of a Kantian universal order, where should critical ethics begin? Should it start by looking into the regions of imagination in which humans come closest to violence, without having the right to shape the destruction of their bodies and the abandonment of their souls into a legitimate form?

The distance of a fragmentary, sober drama from a sublime tragic posture could hardly be plainer than in the corrido *El contrabando del muerto* (The Contraband of the Dead) composed by Rafael Buendía.

> Life is so worthless
> Compared to money.

They killed a migrant
Who passed himself off as a farmworker.
Pretending that he was a soldier
Who ran away from battle.
They carried out an autopsy
To send him back home.
They took him across the line
To bury him.
They invented a wake for him
With relatives and widows.
It's said that at midnight
They dug him up
Because his belly
Was full of contraband.
The gang of drug traffickers
Had a terrible surprise.
They couldn't find the dead man
When they dug up the casket.
The devil stole him away.
There are those who say it's true
They are still searching
For the dead man's contraband.[73]

Thinking of World War I, Benjamin once observed that "never has experience been contradicted more thoroughly" than through the exposure of the "tiny, fragile human body" to the destructive forces of war, economic pressure, hunger, and moral degradation by the ruling powers.[74] To be equally compelling, a statement would have to account for the exposure of the migrant's "fragile human body" to the machinations of violence that proliferate along the hemispheric border. If tragedy is cathartic and "alchemizes" the catastrophe of an individual into sublime sensation, what, then, is the aesthetic experience emanating from the corrido *El contrabando del muerto* like? Doesn't the conversion of the migrant's body into a container for smuggling goods contradict the possibility of experience as such? However, the corrido does not share in the collapse of meaning that critics like to call upon when dealing with trauma and atrocious events, nor does the song borrow from tragedy's "sweet violence." In that it does not share the suggestive depiction of hazardous performances observed in the aggressive part of Hollywood genres, *El contrabando* relates something that does not have to be invented. When the dreadful matter is brought to the fore, it is done so on the grounds of an inherent reality, connected to the sort of "economic vampirism" that flourishes in the twilight zones of globalization.[75] *El contrabando*, by "keeping the story free of explanation"[76] as well as of aggressive dramatism, achieves a specific intensity that both media news and tragedy lack: it is breathtakingly paratactical. This makes the corrido different from literary works that have thematized a similar topic, such as Alberto Ríos' short story "The Child."[77] As Auerbach would have it, "the poet explains nothing," but who is really the poet of the corrido? Whose storytelling voice is, in the end, resonating? Ballads like *El contrabando* have emerged as somewhat cryptic "voices," opposed to the general trend in which entire segments of the communications industry have downsized social memory. The song provides the outline of an unnamed destiny that has been absorbed in the desert of transnational space. It makes explanation obsolete by turning memento mori into a repetitive, prosodic, and thus reterritorializing tale. We might recall one of the "non-sequiturs" of novelist Alejo Carpentier, when he spoke, in 1979, about the pressures of drama emanating from state violence and social conflicts in Latin America and referred to an ever more pervasive environment of disappearing and destroyed human beings. Asking, "fear of excesses, of bloodiness, of dreadfulness?" he called upon younger novelists to explore "a notarial style" (a kind of ballad style) that would consist of "not swallowing your voice, of not raising your tones, of not indicating admiration, of not flinching from anything you see."[78] Carpentier insisted, toward the end of his life, that an alternative stylistic attitude was needed. This was a vision that called for narrative projects audacious enough to help liberate writers from the legacies of sublime tragedy and psychological novels. A "notarial style" would thus resemble what Auerbach called the "paratactical style," yet it would require, today, that we engage in the "non-humanist" posture of the corrido's becoming a paratactical drama of globalization.

Our reflections have outlined tensions that can help to address the intricacies of imagination in present times. We suggested the concept of *paratactical drama* to be applied to understand global corridos. If these dramas surprise us with their narrative effectiveness, and by constituting mimetic linguistic constructions at the moment at which language turns into a resonance of violence and death, the markers for conscious reflection are rarely found in the texts themselves. The song *El contrabando* deals in atrocious experiences, rather than in knowing subjects. Parataxis helps to rework the effect of "knowing the truth" into a defiant perception. In the final peripety of the song, a spirit is called upon to liberate the body from its instrumentalized state: "The devil stole him away... they are still searching for the dead man's contraband." The gesture of reaching for an elementary ethical act, grounded in religious belief and delivered in an impersonal voice, must be distinguished from mythical discourse. Myth enchants and tends to perpetuate the present as eternal. In this case, the enactment of faith takes the form of a "small" messianic act that is released out of collective despair.

When Eagleton suggests that we "democratize" the notion of tragedy relating to selected forms of writing and drama,[79] his purpose might seem to be similar to Carpentier's, mentioned earlier. However, the British critic is hesitant to venture into an imagination that is heavily infected with global problems. When, in *The Idea of Culture*, he touches more directly on the thematics of globalization, he states:

> The primary problems which we confront in the new millennium—war, famine, poverty, disease, debt, drugs, environmental pollution, the displacement of peoples—are not especially "cultural" at all. They are not primarily

questions of value, symbolism, language, tradition, belonging or identity, least of all the arts....Like any other material issues, these matters are culturally inflected...But they are cultural problems only in a sense which risks expanding the term to the point of meaninglessness.[80]

Expressed in a slightly different manner, the most dramatic "material issues," including war, poverty, drug traffic, and the displacement of peoples would not be worthy of scrutinizing analysis, even though they have a strong bearing on narration and identity. They become meaningless for the cultural critic because they are too "morbid and obsessional" to be "set in an enlightened political context, one which can temper these immediacies with more abstract, but also with more generous, affiliations."[81] We could not disagree more.

Can tragedy's promise still be seen as it helps to preserve an ultimate "abstract affiliation," set against the morbid immediacies of the globalized world? What does a formulation that asks us to stick to an "enlightened political context" strive for? Does not the discussed song point critical thought in a different direction? Why would *El contrabando del muerto* be embarrassingly untragic? Is it the anonymous hero's status of "not knowing" that means, if we remember Vico, not commanding an individual tragic consciousness that can be shared by an enlightened reader? Has not the accumulation of violence in the global orbit been posing new irritations, as far as the modern aesthetic canon and its relationships to suffering and death are concerned? If suffering implies affective heightening such as tragic catharsis, melancholic sentiment, or other postures often tied to reflexive elements, whose experience would escape these strategies of select sympathetic compassion? How should critics rephrase the relationship between "sub-human" suffering and aesthetic experience, where the tragic distinction of individual annihilation does not exist? Rescuing an individual subject's experience from the masses of anonymous "sad" heroes would be just that—an individualizing enterprise. A narrative like *El contrabando* remains disturbing by avoiding this gesture. Its starting line resumes what Mexicans have assumed as a fact of life: "life is so worthless, compared to money." "Death has taken its seat at our table, becoming so familiar that even our fear has been vanquished," was the public answer of Subcomandante Marcos from Chiapas when reprimanded by former Mexican President Salinas de Gortari for challenging the exclusion of Mexico's poor from the national political system.[82] The denial is, of course, a double one, culminating in the exclusion of the poor from the order of the sensible that commands knowledge and common perception, so that society can determine, with Hegelian certainty, the site for the deaths that are tragic, those that are just "sad," and all the other ones that do not exist at all.

Our interest has focused on the narrative articulation of experience in relationship to "non-enlightened" border crossing. The conditions of poverty and the different forms of violence in which border ballads engage are part of an antidialectic that has become devastating: it generates precarious life for the sake of uneven modernization and excessive progress in the northern parts of the world. And yet, the two main legendary persons who contemporary corridos have brought to the fore are not extensions of barbarism but of a resourceful, life-affirming affectivity. The unrelenting migrant as well as the stoic low-level drug trafficker are both multiply degraded and therefore keen figures, unheeded *mojados* (wetbacks) both literally and metonymically. Border ballads are paradoxical agencies, bound to irritate the avalanche of images and symbolic artifacts unleashed by the surplus power of global capitalism. Therefore, the migrant and the trafficker, both dispossessed by instrumental forces and transcendental reason, are what we have come to call *ethical persons* of an alternative imagination.

Both figures appear, at the same time, as conceptual persons who call attention to the rhetorical-symbolic struggles over border space. In "*Lazarillo* and Primitive Accumulation," John Beverley takes up Claudio Guillén's notion of the "pícaro" as a "half-outsider." He argues that the sociohistorical condition of the hero of the picaresque novel in early modern Spain makes him more than someone "who through crime, madness or rebellion has passed beyond the immediate space of social determination," and that he inhabits the space of those belonging to a "relative surplus population [...], expelled from its traditional forms of life," yet who are awaiting being absorbed into the context of a "developing labor market."[83] However, "surplus populations" are becoming less "relative" under contemporary circumstances, and global capitalism has made evident that the assimilation of dispossessed humans into scenarios of advanced accumulation and economic liberalism may no longer be the "natural' trend."[84] Rather, closing the gap by including disposable populations into a more democratically operating market may belong to the lore of "pretty lies" that border crossers are supposed to consume as their daily bread—"su pan de cada día." In the event that myth and the illusion of an eventual integration into the rich world prevail, this might turn out to be the most abject scenario that a state of "not knowing" can give way to: the migrants' not being able to read their own stories from the viewpoint of horrorific openness, devoid of legitimate closure, or of coming to terms with an ounce of promise, of hope. When migrants and small traffickers are turned into ballad heroes, their conceptual contours become visible through the figures of embodied and mnemonic engagement of space. In their "blind mobility" guided by *tropological behavior*, they help us read what they cannot spell out themselves. Stuttering legends, paired with a musical rhythm that boldly holds together the scarce, fragmentary, elliptical tales circling around being uprooted, deportation, and drug smuggling are part of a phatic language. It afflicts imagination, just as the actions of corrido heroes afflict the earth with their relentlessly striving bodies moving northward—parataxes unbound.

CHAPTER 4

Where Affection Meets Figuration: Corrido Language and the Intermedial Presence of Death

To read what was never written. Such reading is the most ancient: Reading before all languages, from the entrails, the stars, or dances.

—W. Benjamin

MONSTROUS SPEECH: THE REEMERGENCE OF ANAMORPHOTIC TROPES

The goal of the previous chapter was to discuss a narrative-rhythmic mode that is inherent in both migration corridos and narcocorridos, indicating a spatial "syntax," one that enables a particular sensuous perception of massive uprooting and transnational border crossing. This mode is called *parataxis*, and we have suggested a shift that helped to decenter the classical philological semantics of the term in favor of a spatial and sociocultural one. Paratactical drama, viewed in this new sense, signals a rhetorical construction of border space by virtue of "atavistic" storytelling. At the same time, this concept can imply unforeseen complexity. Philologists have resisted examining paratactical style from a viewpoint of radical heterogeneity, and they have generally despised it as unreflective and impure, contrasting parataxis with hypotaxis. Not only has the term been absent from the great majority of works that constitute the classical and postclassical rhetorical canon, but it is almost unrecognizable within the ramifications of literary studies today. Our approach, in turn, considers this notion to be crucial for understanding segments of social imagination in relationship to uneven hemispheric modernity. In particular, the historicality of paratactical narratives has been barely examined in those contexts in which no appropriation by legitimate forms of text production took place. More specifically, this chapter will introduce the problem of reflexivity into the analysis of paratactical drama by focusing on the intermedial connections between narrative and music.

When recovering Auerbach's notion of parataxis and reframing it as a mode of border imagination, rather than just a style that signals being "beside arrangement,"[1] we have been concerned with the phenomenon of a mimetic dispositif. What if Vico's assumption regarding "monstrous tropes" does not pertain to "first human nature"[2] alone but aporetically holds for those relations between body and space, whose density and plasticity cannot be linguistically restrained by discourse, expressions whose "form is content" and "content is form"?[3] Parataxes, in the shape of corridos, present themselves as contemporary "monsters," "animated" by the figurative power to metamorphose into spacing narration. The notion of an inherent metamorphosis, which Vico linked to the inability of "first human nature" to "abstract forms or properties from subjects,"[4] pertains to nonsophisticated language. Such language can be envisioned as a coupling of body and space through parataxis. Thus, corrido language appears contorted into "pure affect." It has become inseparable from embodied imagination throughout hemispheric border space, by articulating its historical predicament—the existential perseverance of "northward bound."

Global corridos are *acting narratives*, which sets limits on their representing the actions performed. Asking how corridos "represent" social depravation and physical danger is a legitimate academic concern.[5] This, however, is not their reason for being, and their dynamic status cannot be accessed in this way. Let us start by recalling several critical markers from the previous chapter. We have suggested a perspective wide enough to place corridos within the confines of an "other modernity," one whose vivid connections with early modern and medieval culture have allowed for a nonhistoricist approach. As we remember, Auerbach paid attention to the relationship between parataxes and hypotaxes in his search for the rising spirits of individualism, temperance, and rationality to trace a "figural history" of realism.[6] Culture, in its march toward civilization, would successfully overcome being contaminated by the impure forces of imagination. "Figural progress" was understood as increasing momentum away from "sadism, frenetic bloodlust, and the triumph of magic and sense,"[7] forces that were perceived to mark strong undercurrents of medieval realism. Auerbach stands out as one of the protagonists of what Patricia Parker calls the neoclassical rhetorical tradition.[8] Other critics have pursued the influential "progress narrative" that reaches back to Cicero and Quintilian, drawing on the idea of eventual displacement of "catachreses"— signaling the "abuse" of language—by "proper metaphors."[9] When Auerbach sets hypotaxis against parataxis, he declares the first a central stylistic device of the reasoning mind when serving an enlightening purpose, and the second an expression of brutal sensuousness where "everything must happen as it does happen."[10] The hypotactical desire is as much a symptom of the construction of the Western literary canon as it has remained a contested principle: hypotaxis has never quite ceased to be haunted by the ghosts of parataxis. We could say that the way corridos have emerged as epithet of a transnational dramatic style during late twentieth century helps to lead parataxis out of its subordination to hypotaxis. We have been moving the concept from the philological to the spatial-rhetorical realm and will pursue, from there, its peculiar potential for ethical critique.

Hans Ulrich Gumbrecht comes close to Auerbach's readings when he situates Spanish Golden Age literature in a historical framework of tension between "a Subject-centered world view and the superimposition of a Christian cosmology that eliminated the spaces of subjective choice, action, and interpretation." He describes "paratactical narratives" as corresponding to a "time construction of continuity" that expresses the helpless exposedness of a "non subject," in certain early modern texts to the theologically defined world. He points out that a totalizing Christian doctrine had infiltrated parts of Golden Age culture and literature to such a degree that "lived experience" appeared as paratactically abandoned to the doom of unescapable sequentiality. "The position of an auctorial voice, of a narrator, or of an author remains void.... paratactical narratives come to an end, but as they are never actively brought to an end, they are always open for continuation." In turn, hypotactical narrative is viewed as "historically structured" and complex, warranting the emergence of reflexivity in subjective, philosophically ordering terms.

> "Hypotactical narratives"...are based on the assumption of an asymmetry between past and future, and therefore alternate between a level of lived experience and a level on which lived experience is interpreted and structured. With their concern for distinguishing "stages" as parts of a "development," the discourses of the bildungsroman or of philosophy of history...are perhaps the most obvious examples of this relationship....The structuring interventions of the auctorial voice (or of the narrator) take place from a position of Protention [Husserl; HH] because they presuppose an awareness of the outcome to which the narrative will lead.[11]

These remarks apply in a controversial way to corridos where the "auctorial" agency is absent or, at best, works in the interest of a weak subjectivity that resists closure or fulfillment. The absence of a sovereign narrator's voice is not necessarily predicated on the loss of a knowing, however. It can also be associated with an immanent collective imagination "to which even the deepest shock of every individual experience, death, constitutes no impediment or barrier."[12] That is to say, global ballads deal with specific heroes yet their affective wisdom is deindividuating.[13]

Neither Auerbach nor Gumbrecht seems to have been inclined to extending his rhetorical-structural analysis to these narratives. However, it is here that we can find different answers to well-known questions. Would it come as much of a surprise if ancient corridos and folk ballads were affected by the same spell of "non-historical" time experience that Gumbrecht attributes to certain more established forms of the Spanish Golden Age? Traditional corridos may indeed have little stake in tropes that lend themselves to historical development and temporal reflexivity. Yet this was not the question that, in early times, allowed them a forceful existence by keeping them active within the dark zones of culture. It was a kind of immanent performative consciousness that enabled ballads to act in public, to be seen and heard and renarrated by others, partaking in the spontaneous power to gather people together. While in early Christian culture the "abstention from wordly things" was lived as the phenomenon of "worldlessness,"[14] an impoverishment of public space, popular performance has often projected its sensuous inscriptions into the public realm as a diverging and community-building set of practices. As soon as we pay attention to the narratives' informal, body-driven relationship to spaces, the phenomenon becomes accessible in its own right: it does not need a hypotactical corrective to be approached as an alternate force of imagination and public action. The use of parataxes thus signals a frame of relevance that is different from that of "abuse of speech."[15] If there is a poetological dimension to parataxes, then these could be considered—to borrow an expression from Anselm Haverkamp—as quintessential "figures of latency."[16]

Quoting Gumbrecht's assessment of parataxis and hypotaxis allows us to recall that which constitutes one of modern discourse's central principles: the longing for narrative closure in the name of a speculative (qua "auctorial") consciousness. In contrast, an examination of contemporary corridos can lead toward a shift in the notion of reflexivity itself. The well-known assumption that with "postmodernism" or "poststructuralism" closure becomes highly problematic[17] is not of much help either. If the paratactical style of corridos were placed in a framework of speculative time experience, these narratives would appear to be pressed into the closedness of their sense of fatality. At the same time, since ballads are not "actively brought to an end" by a structuring consciousness that "knows of" history's moving forces, no hypotactical device serves a subjective, that is to say autonomous agency. However, we have to overcome the constraints posited by the paraphrased insights of literary criticism by defamiliarizing the way questions are asked: *how* do corridos know? Is their's a particular "knowing" that can shape affective imagination in a reflective way? Under which conceptual premises can paratactical drama reveal a reflective bearing? These questions ought to replace the usual one: what do corridos represent? A modernist conclusion would have it that corridos do not possess a reflective dimension, at least not from the angle of narrative focalization and configuration. A poststructuralist take would seek to demystify the idea of closure itself, while certainly denying ballads this metareflexive capacity. We will try to move beyond both attempts.

There is one figure that has somehow mitigated poststructuralist skepticism toward rhetorical constructions of sense, praised by Paul de Man when referring to Locke's attack against figurative speech: catachresis. Catachresis means "abuse of language," a dismembering of the "texture of reality" and a reassembling of it "in the most capricious of ways": "something monstrous lurks in the most innocent of catachreses."[18] But is it really a dismembering of the "texture of reality" or rather of the texture of any kind of realism, which strives to represent the world by hypotactical means? "Monstrous" would perfectly describe the terminology used by Auerbach when dealing with parataxes. Speaking from distinct mindsets, a modernist one and a poststructuralist one, Auerbach and de Man may have shared a similar perception of liberating impurity when exploring the aesthetic potentials of parataxis and catachresis. Both terms are etymologically different, however, they share a marginal position within contemporary literary and linguistic theory, perhaps because they cannot convey a clear sense of "human ingenuity."[19] Parataxes and catachreses are fundamentally anamorphotic, since they are employed where no proper term is available. The way these anamorphotic tropes could be appropriated and justified in their violent "abuse" of language is a concern that was raised by Auerbach and de Man in different contexts. Not surprisingly, both critics can barely hide their fascination with a disguised other. A distrust of the aberrations of figural language has almost naturally been attracted, at the same time, by their transgressive powers. A strange potential lurks in catachresis, and perhaps more strongly in parataxis: its faculty for positively staging the impure and the monstrous customarily associated with nonmeaning. But what is "nonmeaning" if not an investment in the potentiality of acting sense, inherent in the affective and narrative structures of culture? In other words, are we not dealing with the rhetorical conditioning of cultural praxis beneath "uncritically preconceived text models such as transcendental teleologies or, at the other end of the spectrum, mere codes"[20]? When the ordering mind fails to conceive the identity of language in terms of symbolic "advancement," it runs the risk of becoming itself affected by the spirits it has sought to control. Otherwise Samuel Beckett, celebrating a "primitive economic directness" of language, would not have formulated in "Dante...Bruno. Vico.. Joyce," a sensation of "elemental vitality..., corruption of expression,...furious restlessness [of] the form": "We notice that there is little or no attempt at subjectivism or abstraction, no attempt at metaphysical generalisation. We are presented with a statement of the particular."[21]

An Intermedial Approach to Affectivity

Global ballads have led us to revisit the landscapes of contemporary culture, pushing the paradox inherent in the paratactical mode beyond the limits of modern literary history: how can we understand, in the case of posttraditional corridos, the relationship between a rhetoric of atavism and versatile figuration? As we will show, the notorious sidestepping of specialized discourse by the corridos is linked to their intermedial constitution. Intermedial relations are conceptual relations,[22] in that the "work" at question is not a definite realization but "one possibility" that unfolds between rhetorical and theatrical material, between literary and cultural patterns, and media formats without necessarily satisfying the criteria of artistic synthesis. In the case of numerous corridos of Los Tigres del Norte, it is here that the relationships between tropological "action" and reflexivity can be assessed in new ways. The concept of intermediality does not refer only to the fact that their tales are accompanied by music, supported by rhythm, and performed in public. Intermedial relationships can be approached, for example, when we start asking about music in narratological terms. We already made a move in this direction when we addressed the rhythmical and performative "logistics" of paratactical drama, a faculty that helped link narrative to the construction of spatial experience. Now we have to take another step forward, discussing affectivity from the vantage point of musical narration.

As a musician, Wald pays only slight attention to the interactions of the rhythmic, vocal, and acoustic features in his study on narcocorridos, since their specificities seem to lie in the logics of the genre itself. He speaks of an "old-fashioned and rurally rooted" style "based on accordion-driven polkas and waltzes."[23] Rather than being directed toward a generic musical expression, our interest, in turn, will focus on the paradoxes of *musical diegesis* (diegesis: narration). This allows us to ask for a potential narrative effect produced by music "without really telling a story at all."[24] Why would we ask for the music's diegetically producing meaning effects if storytelling is already so obsessively brought to the fore by the lyrics of the ballads? Doesn't the textual part render the legitimate (and some critics might hold, the exclusive) realm on which narratological analysis should be focused? And where else should we look for narrational devices, if not in lyrics displaying a universe of peripeties regarding contemporary border outlaws and their legendary yet down-to-earth adventures? Precisely at this point, a doubt arises about reducing the narration of corridos to a single semiotic level. If the musical components merely complement or enforce atavistic storytelling, then the interpretation of corridos might add up to a list of stereotypes attesting to popular culture's scandalous Manichaeism. But things are not that simple.

We will now take a closer look at the music of Los Tigres del Norte especially those songs whose lyrics we discussed earlier. This step is necessary, on the one hand, to avoid rash generalizations and, on the other, to advance a conceptually more thorough inquiry than those undertaken in the pioneering studies we have been mentioning. Taking an approach distinct from Valenzuela and Wald, as well as Edberg, we are looking for intermedial clues that can help frame the peculiar nature of the speech-songs called global ballads that have aroused so many contradictory spirits. Posttraditional or global corridos, the category under which we have subsumed migration corridos and narcocorridos, will remain a contradictory, extremely ample phenomenon that resists unifying interpretation. Within their range there exist different and even opposing tendencies. However, the work of Los Tigres is crucial for addressing characteristic links between narrative phenomenology and cultural rhetoric. The pervasiveness of their music, which originated in Sinaloa, accounts for the breakthrough, beginning in the early 1970s, that has made corridos on both sides of the hemispheric border a transnational style. Residing in San José, California since the 1970s, the musicians are the first regional Mexican group that has become internationalized while singing exclusively in Spanish. The creations of Los Tigres have condensed a double dimension of experience, expressed in the simultaneous presence and interaction of migration corridos and narcocorridos into a unique rhythm. Rather than merely producing a variety of stories about border crossing and drug trafficking that rely on commercially effective patterns, their ballads emerge out of and feed back into a wide repertoire of Mexican and border culture that has not lost a single bit of its dramatic intensity.

An additional distinction has to be made. We do not subscribe to an all too easy equation between the migrant and narcoballads of Los Tigres, on the one hand, and gangsta rap, on the other, as has been expressed by Wald. It was the adventure story of a self-promoted singer, Chalino Sánchez, that catapulted contemporary ballads into the center of "dangerous urban dance music."[25] In 1992, after one of Chalino's public performances ended in a shoot-out near Palm Springs followed by Chalino's violent murder in Culiacán shortly thereafter, the message to his young public, strongly fueled by the record companies, was straightforward: corridos have turned into the Mexican equivalent of gangsta rap. Chalino became, after his early death, the antistar of "ugly singing," "the real thing," and "the true voice of the drug traffic."[26] In this manner, Chalino's music contributed to the creation of a cutting edge style for the more recent corrido boom that started in the early 1990s, a style that was set in Los Angeles. It reassembled a pattern that had already proven effective in the case of gangsta rap. This model emanates from the Manichaean power of countercultural expressions whose repertoire relies on explicitly violent icons, gestures, and modes of performance. To be clear, we are not dismissing gangsta rap for the gestures of protest it has enabled in sociocultural terms. However, our purpose is to inquire into a reflective potential of contemporary corridos that has not yet been addressed, let alone explored, by existing studies. An undifferentiated equation of narcoballads to hard rap would likely do away with the problem of reflexivity all together. Yet again, our concern is not to single out a type of drug ballad that can be intellectually tamed or dignified. On the contrary, the lived spaces of violence in which meanings are affectively shaped is what we are interested in.

If, as Diana Taylor argues, the notion of "repertoire" stands for a sphere marked by a preponderance of embodied practices open to the "transmission of social knowledge, memory, and identity pre- and postwriting,"[27] then Los Tigres' repertoire is an exemplary case calling for analysis. Migrants and immigrants witness drug trafficking daily as they cross the border. However, and contrary to statements by political conservatives and the Catholic Church spokespeople on both sides of the border, the stories sung by Los Tigres have never presented an affirmation of drug trafficking or a celebration of violence. Speaking more specifically, although myriad new corrido *bandas* (groups) have emerged during the last decades to join in the rise of what has become a global mass communicative phenomenon, Los Tigres have maintained a special *sympathetic* posture seldom achieved by other groups. Perplexingly, since they kicked off a massive commercial craze, the group has continued to cultivate a mode both more distinct and diversified than that of the great majority of their imitators. This is not a stylistic question alone, but rather their way of working through immanent social knowledge.

Wald discusses one of the group's first records that came out in 1972, seeing in it a style unlike anything else on the radio.[28] The record was created around the song *Contrabando y Traición*. Was it its *lyrics* that were different? The extraordinary rise of a group whose songs seemed to be, at first glance, nothing more than the typically Mexican *norteño* (country) music sprinkled with timely adventure stories, continues to puzzle the critics. Ethnomusicologist Helena Simonett, who characterizes Los Tigres as one of the "most influential binational bands," writes, "although the group succeeded in capturing with its bitter-sweet immigration songs the imagination of hundreds of thousands of Mexicans living in 'el otro Mexico' [the North], it initiated its career with *Contrabando y Traición*, a corrido about drug smuggling." The author then resorts to a prejudice explaining, on the one hand, that the appeal of the band is owing to its "migration-related corridos and border-crossing themes," which are seen as expressions of "widely shared experiences." On the other hand, however, she maintains that "the production of its songs is based not on emotional and sentimental consideration but rather on unrelenting calculated commercial interests."[29] Narcocorridos, according to a conclusion in toto, would have to be taken as responsible for the commercial success. Her distinction between narcocorridos and migration corridos seeks to carve out secure terrain through which the critic can still walk without risk. But the times in which this could be done have passed, and the trajectory of Los Tigres tells a story that is revealingly anachronistic. Adornian formulations such as the above-mentioned ones create a blind spot, pretending that big media are located on one side of cultural conflicts, instead of seeing mass communication as a conflict-driven arena. Market distribution does not suspend the articulation of "widely shared experiences;" there is even a component to the history of the distribution of narcoballadry that relies on "rebel elements" in the way corrido composers and performers confronted, during the 1970s and 1980s, the stratifying power of the music and media industries.[30] The media, in one form or another, are unlikely to be avoided. They can, however, be used under certain historical conditions for different purposes.

Those "shared experiences" can be accessed at the point at which the question of their ethical stance is explored within uncommon aesthetic settings. Shared experiences start to build up at the point where *affect meets figuration* in particular ways. Asking how to make distinctions at the level of "sentiment" can help to reinforce our diegetic interest in the musical form of corridos. But can the affective side of music be approached in figural ways? We should state our hypothesis. Los Tigres del Norte have turned narcocorridos into a subtle yet startling apparition, a kind of ghostly presence, allowing an ethical consciousness to take shape. The group's music has permitted, among a diversified public, the possibility of an affective awareness of violent conflicts whose consequences are predominantly "tragic," but they are not allowed to bear a legitimate tragic code. This understanding of awareness enables a specific reflexive dimension. When *Contrabando y Traición* was first released in Mexico in 1972, a sensuous experience started to resonate forcefully. Beckett's words can be recalled, albeit out of context: "You complain that this stuff is not written in English...It is not written at all...It is to be...listened to."[31] There had been corridos about smuggling long before that time, but something was missing that could speak to a transnational public—a public that has a background related to an interculturally diversified prevalence of the Spanish language. Global corridos are linguistically conceived and actively performed in Spanish, as has been stated earlier. These corridos have introduced a need for contemporaneity into an old genre. Something that made the blatant contrast between the spirit of the old and the pressure of the new not only attractive but also part of a profound experience regarding violence and life; something that opened a passageway between atavism and a reflexively active stance.

In chapter 1, we commented on the epic sobriety of *Contrabando y Traición*, and we addressed the anachronism at the level of its narrative matrix: melodrama's being led into crisis by paratactical soberness. Instead of an emotionally heightened dramatization, a style of expressive overstatement and acting out, there seemed to be "pure deeds" carried out by Camelia, and a few words, voiced by Emilio. When Emilio announced that he was heading off to meet with his beloved, "seven gun shots rang out— Camelia killed Emilio."[32] That the woman rejects melodramatic gestures and kills Emilio with seven shots that can be heard in the song is so radical that in the years after its release, a corrective cultural unconscious has hailed a series of follow-up songs in which Camelia is called to account by a patriarchal moral taste. Significantly, in the Contrabando song, a melodramatic pattern is used so that it can be inverted in such a way that the aesthetic procedure turns *inter-rhetorical* (if we prefer to avoid the term intertextual). This inversion already signals an element of reflexivity, its semantic attribute being contextual rather than textual. For this reflexive gesture to be effective, it requires the preexistence of what White calls "narrational knowledge" on the part of both the composer and the listeners, "the kind of tacit knowledge"[33] necessary for the existence of diegetic common sense. That is to say, a narrational awareness of, or preference for, a melodramatic encoding can speak of gender-related, religious, or other social desires. In the referred song, melodrama is first alluded to at the level of the plot structure, but it is soon suspended as an aesthetic resolution by Camelia's laconic act—the shooting of her business partner Emilio. Because of the absence of any signs that could indicate more specific motives for her, the corrido makes an aleatory point. It foregrounds transgression: the woman sidesteps the melodramatic terrain and moves into a different plotting of gender role. This feature has notably influenced the entrance of the corridos into a new, postnational wave of imagination. As we will show, although most of Los Tigres' corridos do not present defiant female heroes, the affective posture of these songs—different from gangsta rap—cannot be termed to be properly masculine, either.

If *narrational knowledge* is to be understood as a force field that is immanent to cultural experience, the undermining of the melodramatic mode by paratactical drama is not a matter of opposition or homology. It signals rather the ability of the corrido to resonate in accordance with powerful fantasies. Melodrama, understood as a matrix through which affective meaning is drawn from social experience, can be discerned as intrinsic to subaltern borderland imagination. Gloria Anzaldúa, who focuses on immigration and transculturation, provides a paradigmatic case. In *Borderlands / La Frontera* (1987), the expression of suffering serves as an empowering strategy: "The U.S.-Mexican border *es una herida abierta* [is an open wound] where the Third World grates against the First and bleeds. And before a scab forms it hemorrhages again, the lifeblood of two worlds merging to form a third country—a border culture."[34] In Anzaldúa's poetic and essayistic account, Mexico is epitomized as female agency, invaded, occupied, and forced "to give up almost half of her nation" in the U.S.-Mexican War. Since then, border crossing has become the main issue of "her" ongoing suffering—a melodramatic odyssey. For Anzaldúa, border crossing bears an emotional scar that is historically inherent in a gendered way, and it is thus related to the body in a twofold sense. Dismembered Mexican territory has become a melodramatic scenario that is now projected outward from the female body: "The Homeland/ Aztlán" portrays the female narrator as an agency whose suffering body lends itself to serve as a bridge between conflicting worlds: *Yo soy un puente tendido / Del mundo gabacho al del mojado* (I am a bridge extending from the gringo's world to that of the wetback.) And the voice continues, in a disembodied way: "A borderland is a vague and undetermined place, created by the emotional residue of an unnatural boundary."[35]

In this case, melodrama is charged with an existential political meaning: suffering and endurance are the symbols through which border crossing is imagined as a momentous experience. Melodrama articulates protest as it expressively acts out grief and body metaphors. Ethically speaking, melodrama demands legitimacy for a nonsovereign yet collectively and sexually identified agency called "border culture." It is related to the subjects of massive immigration, and especially to the most desperate and victimized ones, "las mujeres indocumentadas"—the undocumented women.[36] A dramatic, "expressionist aesthetics of the body"[37] is directed against violence and exclusion in their totalizing, instrumental logics. Border culture has been imagined by a significant number of literary, essayistic and filmic artists during recent decades as one of the most intense melodramatic experiences, giving resonance to uneven global modernity.[38] This is a sign that the trope of border crossing affords a constant tension regarding the projections of multicultural citizenship.[39] Within the critical realms of Chicano and Latino culture, melodramatic depictions have been developing a consciousness that seeks identification with the precarious subjects of border existence instead of renewing a cosmopolitan epistemology of travel narratives. Now, corridos foreground a different affective strategy. One of the reasons that this difference pervades imagination may be the predominance of migration experiences in contrast to immigration and transculturation. Global corridos attack good taste, a world of universal rules, and the values of the neoliberal state in their own way. This leads us back to the sympathetic style of Los Tigres. The differences from, and the closeness to, Anzaldúa's narrative politics offer insights into the paradoxes of subaltern affectivity.

The pioneering role of Los Tigres in the end-of-the-century hemispheric imagination is due, in the first place, to their obsessive repetition of the trope of border crossing. But it also owes to the ways in which the group has changed the expression and performance of this trope. In the cases of *Contrabando, La Banda del Carro Rojo, Una Camioneta Gris* (A Grey Truck), and numerous other songs, the music is characterized by close harmony, a short-driving rhythm guided by the monotonous strumming of a "low-tuned twelve-string guitar known as bajo sexto," and "sprightly accordion breaks."[40] The minimalism of these features in dozens of songs is literally memorable—the sober and straightforwardly iterative ballad groove seems unchanging. The de-melodramatizing gesture becomes rigorous, something that bears a conscious artistic note since the plot structures of corridos refer to adventures and crime stories. Despite the overtly dramatic matter, the narrative outline is anticlimactic. Referring back to an exorbitant balance of harassment, violence and also death that accompanies contemporary border crossings, these ballads produce the impression of stoically taking stock of this reality. Remembering the first stanza of the *Contrabando* song:

1 *They left San Ysidro*
2 *Coming from Tijuana*
3 *The tires of the car*
4 *Were full of bad grass*
5 *They were Emilio Varela and Camelia the Texan.*[41]

The singer keeps his voice at low pitch. He seems to show no emotion, so that his inclination seems at best "notarial." The singing is as short-driving as the rhythm, while the rhyming has two basic elements: first, a *cuarteta*, (stanza of 4 lines) through which the action unfolds, and a subsequent fifth line, which provides a resuming statement. With the statement, a slight rhythmic change is conveyed. In vocal terms, the fifth line comprises two isolated extensions: the words "Varela" and "Tejana" are sung in a chant-like sort of extension, "Vareeelaa" and "Tejaaanaa," so that the broken yet monotonous mode of singing is traversed, after every four lines, by a counterpoint. The four *cuarteta* lines, together with the fifth line, conform a stanza. The vocalizing extension of each name, "...Varela" and "...Tejana," is followed by an accordion break, respectively. The accordion thus leads up to the counterpoint that is exercised in the fifth line, producing two measured acoustic upbeats in each stanza. The result is a sober, somewhat monotonous insistence in the resounding presence of a story, similar to the one aroused by shamanic songs, but intercalated by the described vocal isolation (the chant-like extension of the names), together with the cheerful accordion breaks every five lines. Even during the vocal counterpoint that is repeated twice in the fifth line, the singer does not raise his voice. This instantaneous reaching beyond "monotony"—an anamorphotic change—introduces a specific affective moment into the performance of the ballad.

It is this anamorphotic strain on the vocal flow that suspends the possibility of melodrama by creating a different affective mode: if melodramatic expression relies on excitement and overstatement, then hyperbole meets its other in the nonhyperbolic yet deeply sensuous—as we will see—musical counterpoint. This regular anamorphotic element in the flow of the music would obviously remain secluded at the level of the text. How can its affective charge be further understood? We have to continue examining the possibilities of "musical diegesis." On the one hand, parataxes in corridos, as should be remembered, reduce the extreme exposedness of the characters to precarious existence to the level of nontragic sensation. Tragedy, on the other hand, in one of its "dialectical" Hegelian assumptions, should deploy oppositions such as suffering and life, or particular destiny versus a universal subjectivity. Only in this manner can "suffering"—in tragedy—become transcendentally charged, typically expressed by the sublimation of mythic or aristocratic heroes. For the corrido heroes, dialectical opposition is nonexistent, as are the values of noble sacrifice and auratic suffering conventionally associated with distinctly masculine connotations of tragedy. *Corridos* rely, not on the opposition constitutive of the sublime spirit, but on an earthbound, discomforting insistence. But they also provide a space of desire different from that in which melodramatic heightening takes place. Both categories, the tragic sublime and the melodramatic, find a counterpart in the exorbitant stoicism of the corridos—extreme in the sense that they are located beyond the scope of dialectical assumptions as well as hyperbolic expression. In the following section, we develop a conversation with philosophical hermeneutics at the point at which it comes close to the ontological status of fear, and of death.

A Non-Heideggerian Prolepsis:
Affection beyond the Ontological Sublime

Ballads, in their memorizing immediacy, reveal a mode of *time expression* that inheres in their affective language. Here we have to think within the criteria of a nonmetaphysical inflection of time and will therefore revisit the Heideggerian concept of "care." The notion of *caring about time* that should be understood as a way of "reckoning with" time in life helps us imagine the relationship between past, present, and future as an interplay of "intentionalities." Ricoeur calls these intentionalities "memory, attention, and expectation."[42] If these are to be considered hermeneutic notions, philosophical hermeneutics itself has, to a certain extent, helped to weaken the boundaries between totalizing abstraction and affective understanding. Might not the concept of *care* even suggest an interplay of emphatic concerns whose abstract layout must give way, today, to conflicting ontological involvements? Behind this question stands our interest in rethinking the ontological realm of experience.

Heidegger refers "care" (*Sorge*) to the condition of "being-in-the-world"—a "slumbering fearfulness," a "susceptibility to fear"—whose affective basis derives specifically from an attitude toward death.[43] The finite and thus unified structure of time arises from the recognition of the "centrality of death, or, more exactly, of being-towards-death."[44] Regarding the status—the authenticity—of care in Heidegger's thinking, Ricoeur formulates, "The resoluteness with which we face our own being-towards-death, in the most intimate structure of Care, provides the criterion of authenticity for all of our temporal experience."[45] It is probably fair to say that for Heidegger, *care* as the central notion designating an "ecstatic temporality" saturates "time" with an existential *Gefühl* (feeling); yet the assumption of an authentic being-towards-death (caring as dwelling–protecting–preserving) produces the ontological abstraction that immobilizes affect in the unhistorical realm.[46] Now, can this concept of emphatic time experience that is ingrained in *Dasein* (being in the world), which once mobilized a new ontology against modernity's metaphysical spell, be imputed to ballads? The issue at stake in this unusual case of comparison is the ethical status of death, at the point at which death is "reckoned with" as an affective reality.

As observed earlier, corrido tales are enveloped by diegetic force fields, obtuse meanings, which partly lie outside their specific referential traits. Their inmersion in an embodied flow of knowledge–experiences–sentiments accounts for their basic mode of *Dasein*, in virtue of which these meanings are always already present before or beyond the textual universe. Ballad time is haunted by violence and a sensation of unnatural death. To paraphrase one of Heidegger's stilted formulations, life resonates in its thrownness (*Geworfenheit*) into violence. In the case of ballads, this is a kind of (historically inflected) violence that the German philosopher would have contemplated only from an ideational distance. Corridos *take care* of disturbing the "wholeness" of mortal being toward death—they irritate the ontological authenticity of the finite human life. What is suggested by this statement, if not a different, a terrifying dimension of *affective time* shaped by the immanence of perilous death? At this point one might perhaps wish to do away with Heidegger altogether. Yet the notion of care, as it can signal a nonindividualist as well as a nontranscendental *attitude*, calls for being dissociated from a static concept of *Dasein*.

Among the central notions of hermeneutics, *historicality*[47] is the one that defies explanation in favor of the more difficult concept of understanding. Ricoeur, in his reading of Heidegger, speaks of "historicity," derived from the German word "Historizität" (as opposed to "Historismus").

> We move in the direction of the inauthentic pole when we proceed from temporality to historicity. Historicity…refers first to our way of "becoming" between birth and death. The stretching-along of life is thus more emphasized than the wholeness provided to life by its mortal termination.[48]

"Stretching-along" and "becoming" acquire a sarcastic tone when the historical situation of the subaltern's being-in-the-world is at stake. Historicality can, under certain circumstances and for certain subjects, be as fragmentary and cataclysmic as it can result, under others, continuous and repetitive. This concept allows us to question an ontological notion of death, which freezes temporal experience into an "authentic" horizon of being.[49] After all, at issue is everything that renders human life-worlds, local belongings, and shifting sensibilities recognizable as they contrast (as well as complement) the big circles of instrumentality and abstraction. Repetition and interruption, contiguity and contingency, action and speech taken together are characteristic features of historicality. Paratactical drama, in the way violent impulses of historicality are absorbed by embodied figuration, extracts an "other" ontological experience from border fantasies. What concerns us, alongside the poetry of Los Tigres del Norte, is a different sense of "care."[50] The kind of sensation on which this other perception of care can draw has no system and no proofs, but there is something like a logic to it, more stable than purely subjective preferences, yet less effable than a coherent idea.

The *novum* that is brought forth by *Los Tigres* is related to the way in which their music "reckons with" the proximity—the prosodic, pulsory, ugly pervasiveness—of death. These ballads stand out as *paratactical memento* that have absorbed a common sentiment of border crossing, to the extent that *being-towards-death* appears thrown into *being-with-death*. Differently put, ballad time is invested with the energies of a destructive, ontologically inauthentic global modernity. There is, above all, the balance of unnatural death pervading the reality of border crossing, caused by the spiral in which several dimensions of violence intersect. The affective resources of the corrido mode excel because of its particular capacity to "reckon with" death. What accounted for the ethical thinking of the later Heidegger, in close relationship with his reading of Rilke and Hölderlin, was an attempt at overcoming "the terror of death" and achieving "ontological security" by proposing an "ecstatic," somewhat pantheist concept of dwelling. "To dwell is to experience oneself as safe in, cared-for by, the dwelling-place in a way one is not safe in or cared-for by the foreign..."[51] Affectively speaking, the philosopher distinguishes between *fear* (intrawordly involvement) and *Angst* (the nakedness of pure *Dasein*).[52] Heidegger's "pure Dasein" is not Benjamin's "bare life." For Heidegger, the notion of *dwelling* signals an ethical realm beyond "involvement," that is to say an overcoming of "Angst" as the innermost feeling of being-in-the-world, together with an acquired "equanimity (Gelassenheit) in the face of death."[53]

In contrast, the sensation of immanence of death that resounds in Los Tigres' speech-songs associates a different ontology. This sentiment is located beyond us, yet it is nurtured and sustained by the intraworldly, material and social junctures of violence and everyday life. Notorious dangers surrounding the lives and emotions of the population on either side of the border come from two directions. There is, on the one hand, the pressure of capitalist instrumentality on ontologically authentic existence, especially in the peripheries—the unveiled face of neoliberalism; and, on the other, the reorganization of global-local spatialities by the pervasive spread of the narcotics economy. Thus, the popularity of the group Los Tigres poses tricky questions. If the most pervasive corridos tell the adventures of unhappy drug traffickers in a way similar to that in which they exalt the stories of poor migrants, and if musical storytelling can produce affective empowerment on a massive scale, who are the protagonists of global corridos? In addition to the bold peripeties of contraband, betrayal, atavistic survival, and loss of life, how can the real powers of these depraved antiheroes and antiheroines be accessed, at the point at which they enter public imagination? The majority of corridos' listeners, not sharing the heroes' immediate adventures themselves, seem to look over the protagonist's shoulders from a close, yet aesthetically mediated, distance.[54] When they do this, what is it that they perceive and "care" for?

Musical-rhetorical analysis helps to identify a notion of *care* that emerges from the edges of collective existence. We have commented on the pathbreaking song *Contrabando y Traición*, and its intermedial matrix. Ballads such as *La Banda del Carro Rojo, Una Camioneta Gris,* and numerous others can be placed within similar registers. Given that their narratives are imbued with straightforward, laconic features (a diegetic downsizing of the dramatic content), it is necessary to ask for the affective interaction of music and text and to pay special attention to the "surface" of the sound. Let me recall our previous analysis of the musical counterpoint that is exercised during the fifth line of each stanza. This counterpoint, as set out earlier, reaches beyond monotony by introducing difference into the performance—an anamorphotic change. Hence, parataxes cannot be reduced to the sensation of one seamless rhythm—there is room for it to be affected and modified. Owing to the counterpoint, a new figurative element comes into play, one which invigorates a non-Heideggerian mode of caring about time. We will call this element of difference, embedded in the paratactical construction, prolepsis. By prolepsis (anticipation) we mean an effect by which a sense of narrative attention is aroused. This attention is directed toward the phantasmic presence of death.[55]

If music is capable of narrating through prolepsis and other figures, and not only by making verbal sense, says White, then music "utilizing the figure of prolepsis can be said to project a possible story."[56] Interpreting the ballads of Los Tigres, we are applying the term prolepsis in a somewhat different manner. Stories are told through the lyrics of the songs, and the music's inducing a proleptic moment would not necessarily require it to "project" a story of its own. The proleptic effect is, rather, an intermedial effect, sustained by the counterpoint. Prolepsis emerges, at the end of each stanza, from the anamorphotic strain on the otherwise unchanging relationship between rhythm and voice. In fact, the way the singer's voice indulges, from the very beginning, in a vocal anachronism anticipates the counterpoint created in every fifth line. The lamentful voice already carries a double emphasis that is placed, on the one hand, on monotonous and laconic performance, and on the other, on a sensation of foreboding (which, in certain songs, can even acquire an ironic overtone). This tension between what we could call an archetypical ballad groove and a diegetically active counter-point is what marks the intermedial character of the song. It is that which makes narcoballads so ominously timely. What is anticipated by prolepsis is not the outcome of the story, which is overtly known to corrido listeners; it is a feeling that guides the group's sympathetic style, shaped into paratacti-cal drama, which accounts for the paradox of popularity: Los Tigres can be considered the real forerunners of the attraction caused by narcoballadry, yet they have at the same time been able to maintain an emphatic posture over several decades and into the twenty-first century. Their music neither focus on the instrumental act nor on the stunning power of violence, but on a knowing sentiment, one which seems to claim a critical and yet therapeutic awareness toward death. Prolepsis translates into a form of vocal attention that allows for "reckoning with" death in a way similar to that in which it disturbs a Heideggerian ontological stance. Future, past, and present appear fused into a single painful yet caring sentiment. It is here that a phantasmic relapse of "expectation" into narrative-performative "attention" takes place, drawing on a terrible state of immanence—the proximity of a destructive existence. This way of paratactically actualizing the memory of death effaces the authenticity of care. Listening to narcocorridos is like catching the glance of "the daimon" who watches the daring actions and mortal deeds of drug traffickers from a close yet constitutive distance.

Let us briefly use Jonathan Sterne's metaphor of "a resonant tomb,"[57] to describe this peculiar form of attention to a sentiment of existential "thrownness." From here, *immanence* can help by alluding to two things at once—to the narcotraficante, being on steady and familiar terms with death, and to the listener, indulging in the potentiality of death from the viewpoint of a mimetic insight. Mimetic recognition means that the expe-rience of death is not just a fact that shatters the *Dasein* of those who could not—as citizens—obtain the rewards promised by neoliberal society and recurred to illicit adventures and crime as expressions of despair or corrective action. It rather "reckons with" death in the way in which death is latent in the knowledge that accompanies border culture as a whole. "Implicit social knowledge" has been understood as that which "moves people without their knowing quite why or quite how, [...] and above all [...] what makes eth-ical distinctions politically powerful."[58] There is the repertoire of affliction, resistance, and stoicism expressed by the ongoing diaspora of the poor and the movements back and forth of migrants, as well as of immigrants. Its his-torical and geographical implicitness gives it a spectral presence. Not only does the spell of death, as caused by violent border afflictions, break through the Heideggerian passivity of "care." An experience of *being-with-death* has entered the wider collective unconscious to the point that violence is as real as it is normal. We may tentatively describe Los Tigres' early corridos as "resonant tombs." However, the expression is applied differently from the way in which Sterne, who studies the consequences that sound reproduc-tion has generated for the preservation of living voices beyond peoples' lives, uses it. The voice of the corrido singer engages in affective figuration in a paradoxical way. Vocal prolepsis anticipates a sensation that makes death a resonating experience, an immanent reality. It gives a reiterative, laconically rhythmicizing presence to those anonymous deaths that society is unable to efface. It renders the uncontainability of those deaths present. By doing so, the group furnishes an affective awareness of death as a form of resistance from a viewpoint of multiple affectedness.

POSTSCRIPTUM: AN ETHICAL PARADOX REGARDING VIOLENCE

Let us recall a specific example—*La Banda del Carro Rojo.* The early success of this corrido in the 1970s, and its long-lasting presence thereafter, appears somewhat enigmatic in comparison with *Contrabando y Traición.* As will be remembered, *La Banda*, first performed in 1975 by Los Tigres and still sung today, tells the experience of a small Sinaloan gang on its way to Chicago, carrying a load of cocaine. After crossing the border, they are trapped in San Antonio by the Texan police and killed in a gun battle in which three policemen lose their lives, as well. Here it becomes still more evident that the textual dimension is insufficient for understanding the aesthetic particulars. *La Banda* shares the antimelodramatic posture of Los Tigres' performance, despite its lack of the trope of female empowerment. The song plainly serves the paradox: while the ballad tells the story of an ordinary gang of *traficantes* (traffickers), the issue at stake is not their roving criminality. Instead, it is the roaming presence of the deaths of people who have no place in society. We would be dealing with one of innumerable coarse gangster stories, were it not for the inherent clues that Mexicans on both sides of the border immediately recognize. *La Banda*, the collective protagonist, displays an aura of stoicism reduced to a condition of bare life—the "thrownness" into a desperate state within the global flows of cross-border exchange. Yet, it is not the absence of agency that manifests the exposure of their existence to latent destruction. There is an affective link between deviant action and complete vulnerability: the kind of balance that has been so rarely and distinctly condensed by paratactical drama. The paradox is this: whereas it has been widely assumed that judgment without generalization (and moral hierarchies) is impossible, or otherwise there is "art" that supposedly transcends judgment as such, the ethical charge inscribed in corridos moves discernment to the level of immanence.

The intermedial clue of the song *La Banda* is already conveyed by its first three lines where we find a proleptic construction *in nuce.* Prolepsis speaks, first, out of the text itself: "It is said that they came from the south in a red car/ . . . / That's what the snitch said who had squealed on them." At that point, when the direction the story will take has become clear, diegetic attention wanders to the auditive level where music and voice take the lead. It makes prolepsis nuanced, since what is anticipated in the first lines is at the same time contrasted by a voice that knows more than the text can convey. The singing is utterly sad, but its grief is restrained by the "notarial" laconism that is so characteristic of ballads. Sadness is not the only component of the affective momentum. It vibrates, thanks to the timbre of Jorge Hernández, the main singer of the band, with a dose of irony that introduces tension between literal and nonliteral meaning. Thus the first lines provide us with an explicit narrative prolepsis, but the overall effect of *anticipation* is charged with an ironic knowledge that belongs to the voice. Can there be such a thing as "affective irony"?

The tentative answer is to be found, as well, in the proleptic promise of intermedial corridos. In paratactical drama, there is no autonomous place left for irony. Ballads' knowledge is inseparable from their embodied narration. Therefore, the ironic tone can hardly be more than an anamorphotic digression of the sad intonation. However, it is here that subtle changes give way to active momentum. As described earlier, in Los Tigres' early songs, anamorphosis is based on a musical counterpoint that agitates the monotonous rhythm.[59] The ironic undertone comes ingrained in the way these corridos "duplicate" death by way of its proleptic recounting: what is anticipated is not death but the ontological inauthenticity of its "normalized" stance. The voice of the singer does not become sarcastic; it enacts suffering but points to the absurdity of this experience: a drastic exposedness to bare life, rather than the death of the criminal, lies at the heart of the suffering. This is critical knowledge condensed into affect. The ironic tone makes its point by recalling the anonymous deaths whose presence in the life of border regions is felt as an ongoing interpellation of the living. Affectively speaking, narcocorridos perform a sort of ghost-song ritual[60] in which the slight irony is directed against mythifying violence, that is to say, reducing it to the stereotypes of a unifying discourse. This may well be the substantial point at which Los Tigres' corridos are different from those sung by other groups.

Narcocorridos interact with modes of common feeling that cannot be termed aggressive and illegal, even though they endlessly indulge in outlaw tales.[61] At the same time, they do not draw on commentaries and opinions whose norm is backed by official institutions and media. Their residence in liminal zones allows for a genuine critique. On a larger scale, at stake are issues that concern the places and possibilities of ethical awareness, especially those that are on the alert in view of an overbearing nihilism.[62] Paraphrasing Badiou, ethics today should pursue that which is not yet domesticated by conservative desire or by the murderous (Western) mastery of life and death, but which a particular yet nonindividualist consciousness is able to conceive.[63]

The present conceptual journey has developed several vantage points from which the notions of fear and guilt now seem to appear in a different light. As we argued when engaging Heidegger, an indefinite notion of *Angst* versus an innerworldly entity called "fear" collapses in the face of a different, a violent ontology. The succinct laconism of the corridos—pointing toward an extreme attitude of endurance—blurs the distinction between anxiety and fear. The diegetic consciousness that maintains the impact of corrido music among segments of the public on both sides of the border knows of no condition of dwelling that offers a peaceful, preserving "equanimity." However, such affective knowledge has no fear of involvement in the "existential spatiality" either. *Dasein* has been deprived of its primordial existential identity—*Angst*. For Heidegger, this identity resides in an "individualized, pure" *Dasein* (being): "*Angst* individualizes and thus discloses Da-sein as 'solus ipse.' "[64] What lends ballads a strong posture of their own—expressed in paratactical endurance and proleptic awareness—can neither be associated with an existential anxiety of the individual nor with more immediate figures of fear. *Being-with-death*, sensed and transmitted by narcocorridos and migration corridos alike, is not even proportionate to the sentiment of fear that one might expect to result from the amount of instrumental violence that is carried out daily along the hemispheric border.

Several intriguing questions ensue from here. If there is one sphere of "machinations" that has capitalized on, and somehow expropriated (Heidegger's idea of) ontological anxiety, it is the metamorphosis of the most powerful branches of mass media into endless "production lines of fear." Brian Massumi traces the need for a "political ontology" of emotions back to the historical, social, and technological mechanisms of subject formation. In his understanding of the way fear has become immanent in the collective ground of contemporary experience, he expresses concerns that—in principal—are similar to those that have been raised by Brennan in her discussion of modernity as containment. Saturation of contemporary social space by fear, the complicity with "capitalized fear" that inheres in wide realms of social life itself, referring to *low-level fear*—"naturalized fear, ambient fear, ineradicable atmospheric fright,"—is related primarily yet not exclusively to the ontological status that mass media have acquired toward the end of the past century. The kind of media-induced fear Massumi discusses shifts attention to the materiality of the body as the ultimate mark of the machinations of fear—the onto-anthropological site at which immanence "dwells" as experience. Fear can take hold at the low level when it is carved "into the flesh habits, predispositions, and associated emotions [...] conducive to setting social boundaries, to erecting and preserving hierarchies, to the perpetuation of domination."[65] Once the saturation of existential space by fear is addressed, violence is made to reveal its Janus-like face. The question of how to discern actual violence if one is in collective complicity with fear, buying into fear on an everyday basis, reaches into the tacit realms where imagination and action intersect. It signals back to what we have already identified as the conceptual space where affection and figuration meet—where the imprint of imagination resonates in life by virtue of rhythm, flow, and embodied energies. The power of difference, inherent in the global corridos of Los Tigres, is one that makes experience vibrate as embodied figuration. It is here, as well, that ballads can be shown to oppose the very forces that are at work in the immanent conditioning of fear.

There is reason to suppose that the saturation of existential space in contemporary societies, by mechanisms of fear production, has acquired a cultic dimension in a Benjaminian sense: no special dogma guides its pervasiveness that unfolds *sans trêve et sans merci* (without truce and without mercy). As we have argued in chapter 1, a crucial yet underestimated notion for addressing the aura that advanced capitalism has been able to unfold is *guilt*—"a vast sense of guilt" has been turned immanent by capitalism's pseudo-religious forces. For Benjamin, *Angst*—similar to Massumi's perception—emerges from there; being closely related to guilt it indicates a neverending reproduction of "Sorgen" (worries). "Worries: a mental illness characteristic of the age of capitalism," are induced by the "Angst" of communal hopelessness.[66] What lends advanced capitalist societies a religious pervasion is a unique (a cultic) enactment of powers and images that work on the body, the flesh habits, the collective subconscious. Guilt and "Angst" can be said to be central notions for debate. In the context of our study, their problematization allows for an alternative critique of violence. It helps to extend analysis beyond the influential paradigm of means and ends, to make invisible mechanisms of the production of violence palpable. Intermedial analysis, the way it has been conceptualized, allows for analytic perceptions that defy a sense of intelligible representation. The particular boldness of corridos is to be understood not as affronting existing law but as directed against sentiments of fear and guilt that constitute an inner core of the current status quo. At stake is nothing other than the psychic-political grounds of subjectivity, those that have been characterized by Butler in terms of an "intact" relationship between subject formation and subtle subjection. Global corridos would have to be placed either outside of that balance or described as uncontainable by it. These ballads contend against a culture in which contemporary spaces of subjectivity are saturated with guilt and fear.

Let us, finally, suggest that a shift be introduced into the way discussions have been paying increasing attention to biopolitical analysis. When Agamben identified "the concentration camp and the structure of the great totalitarian states of the twentieth century" as exemplary sites of modern biopolitics, he did not consider a transnational scenario that has spread its networks throughout the Western hemisphere. The U.S.-Mexican border is one of the spaces in which sovereign power's penetration of "subjects' very bodies and forms of life" has acquired a dimension of its own. We may well allude to the figure of "homo sacer"—a man "who may be killed and yet not sacrificed."[67] This figure allows us to reemphasize the relationship between bare existence and its superior regulation regarding the populations of migrants and "desperados" who are pushed into crossing the border, if necessary, a hundred times a year as corridos report. The wording of the "Corrido of the Deported" laconically says "don't condemn me, it's poverty's fault." Today, the geopolitical and economic conditioning of the migration process from Mexico northward reads as one of the most extensive spatial recodifications of bare life in the entire world. Death caused by accident during illegal border crossings and by the "graduated" permissiveness of coercive state power while controlling the border and protecting peoples' lives work as simultaneous exclusion and inclusion. Remembering Benjamin's thoughts on the exception and rule,[68] we cannot but point to a catastrophic historical logic by which the lives of innumerable peoples have come to bodily substantiate the civilization process of the North, with the southern border turned into a *sacred* space on highly secular grounds.

Metonomyzing the life of the "bandit," Agamben wrote:

> [H]is entire existence is reduced to a bare life stripped of every right...; he can save himself only in perpetual flight or a foreign land. And yet he is in a continuous relationship with the power that banished him precisely insofar as he is at every instant exposed to an unconditional threat of death. He is...caught in the sovereign ban and must reckon with it at every moment, finding the best way to elude it or deceive it. In this sense, no life, as exiles and bandits know well, is more "political" than this.[69]

The transnational areas that are marked by human displacement and its biopolitical regulation indicate an "other" state of exception, not the one outlined by Schmitt, not declared but immanent, in which killing and sacrifice become, at a certain point, indistinguishable. It is the point where the trafficker and the migrant enter a common space that is eventually reduced to bare life but whose fatalism has been contested by the affective perseverance of corridos. The aesthetic strategies of border ballads help introduce a difference into the perception of the condition where *homo sacer* "can be killed and yet not sacrificed." This is precisely the condition paratactical drama can penetrate and unravel its double meaning. We have been dealing with ballads as secular speech-songs that nevertheless convoke the powers of ancient ghost-song rituals. Corridos interpellate the living by monotonously stretching out their memento mori, traversed by the anamorphotic digression of the sad voice. Thus, death is made an experience of ongoing resonance and ironic awareness. However small the space of *affective reflexivity* seems to be, there emerges genuine knowledge about those border crossers who, with their very bodies and lives, have made *homo sacer* a transnational yet, above all, ethical figure. Its ominous closeness has come to bear the mark of distance from a mainstream notion of citizenship, especially when its perception is guided by neoliberal promise. There may be a point at which the precarious knowledge performed by global ballads can teach us more about life, politics, and violence today than certain moral codes or instituted laws whose task is to hold violence at bay. At a related level, we have set forth a concept that provides new insights into how transnational imagination is being reshaped. Paratactical drama, contrasting with both tragedy and melodrama, has helped by bringing into focus uncomfortable questions to whose gravity further studies will hopefully do justice.

PART III

Colombian Marginalities and the Culture of Exception

CHAPTER 5

Young, Alien, and Totally Violent: Marginal "Kings of the World"

Approaching the Culture of Exception: The Testimonial Project of Alonso Salazar

Colombia—crossroad of global trafficking in drugs, armaments, and female sex workers, with the unresolved conflicts of its national formation. Colombia is not the most violent country on earth, but the country in which the violence and fears of the end of the second millennium most visibly cross with those of the first.

—*Jesús Martín-Barbero*

When we start looking into Colombian realities, the dearth of strategies for approaching violence conceptually as well as for discussing the problems involved ethically becomes striking. Historians and social critics speak of the peculiarity of the Colombian case in phrases such as: "Organized crime, guerrilla struggle, dirty war, and diffuse social violence [. . .] can be part of a single situation."[1] Mainstream depictions produced by the media during the past few decades have been delivering shocking images, oversimplifications saturated with the drug lord–violent perpetrators–corrupt society schema.[2] It looks as though Hollywood provided, during the 1980s and 1990s, efficient narrative and psychological strategies for making the "war on drugs" intelligible as the primary global crusade against the forces of evil, taking Colombia as its main example for illustrating sanitizing strategies as they are applied in the hemisphere.[3] Parts of the media industry, together with imperial policies that use fear, coercion, and force, have been patterning a language that demands a war of cleansing and of enforced geopolitical security to be imposed on the "country of violence." At the same time, writers, artists, and social scientists in Colombia have developed perspectives that shed a different light on the scenarios of conflict in which the local and the transnational, the formal and informal spheres of economy, the drug wars and prerogatives of sovereignty are intertwined in complicated ways.

Our inquiry will depart from one of the most dramatic conjunctures of the Colombian process, especially in terms of the political conflicts and cultural controversy that stretched from the mid-1980s to the mid-1990s. An area that has received special attention from writers, film directors, anthropologists, and communications specialists in Colombia but also in Mexico and Brazil, is the reconceptualization of the cultural identities of young people. Martín-Barbero observes that from the day in 1984 when, in the streets of Bogotá, two adolescents riding a small motor bike assassinated the Colombian minister of justice, Rodrigo Lara Bonilla, the entire country seemed to realize that a new social actor had taken the stage—the adolescent with a previously unseen determination to interfere in civic life by producing an avalanche of killings together with stunning images of self-sacrifice.[4] Marginalized young men—recruited and trained, in the above-mentioned case, by Pablo Escobar and the Medellín drug cartel[5]—moved to the center of public anxieties. These young people started to be the protagonists of news headlines and TV programs and became a new object of study. But this interest that society suddenly developed in the world of the young was heavily stigmatized. The attack on Lara Bonilla was part of a concerted operation that was being undertaken by the drug mafia against the government of Belisario Betancur. According to Martín-Barbero, general preconceptions were easily fed. Actions generated by the drug trade now seemed to feed into the old prejudice that associated youth, and especially the poorest young people, with a threat to social order and rule, allegedly owing to their lack of integration or strict control. But what if, for many youngsters, social integration has not worked at all or has so far relied on the wrong assumptions? What if the point in question were also to be understood as a global phenomenon weighing on multiple localities and entire regions throughout Latin America? At issue would be the intersection of two types of economy that cannot be reduced solely to their national scales: an economy of dispossession and unemployment and the so-called narcotics economy. Related discussions would have to address the destiny of huge segments of young people from the standpoint of abandonment in terms of social inequality and human regression, before scrutinizing their involvement in the drug wars.

What appears to be a barrier to understanding the status of an important yet forgotten part of Colombian youth has, at the same time, provoked critical interest in the status of *exception and rule*. This refers, in particular, to the city of Medellín, which has metamorphosed into an epicenter of different forms of violence machinated by drug cartels, paramilitaries, armed forces of the state, and sectors of civil society itself.[6] A new critical perspective on culture and violence has received decisive impulses from there, one which during the 1990s pursued questions different from those of the *violentólogos*.[7] According to Martín-Barbero, the "violentologists" have explained the political history of *La Violencia* that has traversed Colombian society for many decades,[8] but "they did not help us understand the anthropological dimensions, the density" and sudden cohesiveness of the contemporary spheres of violence.[9] One of the major studies that started to unravel these enigmas while breaking away from a range of epistemological shortcuts and moral anxieties was Alonso Salazar's and Ana María Jaramillo's *Medellín: Las subculturas del narcotráfico* (1992). Medellín, Colombia's second largest city, has been repeatedly termed the murder capital of the world, although the statistics that are usually distributed by Reuters and other major news agencies draw on infamous balances of daily killings without providing major clues for interpretation. Salazar writes more succinctly:

> Towards 1985, the drug trade had already taken over the city, and the peace process with the guerrillas of the FARC, M-19, and the EPL begun by president Betancur had failed. In addition, Justice Minister Rodrigo Lara Bonilla had been assassinated, and the so-called holocaust of the Palace of Justice had taken place in which, after being taken by a group of M-19 fighters and the reaction of the military forces, dozens of people died, among them a good part of the high court judges. These occurrences were something like the breaking of a dike, giving way to a period of institutional crisis in the country and the increase in violence that brought us to more than twenty years during which death reigns. In this context an unprecedented phenomenon was produced: the organization of young men into dozens of armed bands that terrorized first their neighborhoods and then the country.[10]

It was particularly the so-called sicariato that spawned a new and terrifying sensation among a wide public at a time when the country was at last trying to come to terms with modernity, only to become more deeply immersed in Colombian capitalism, characterized by a violently exclusionary political system whose center stage seems to have been successfully seized, under the post-2002 presidency of Uribe, by an exceptionally powerful "narco-paramilitary" right.[11] The expression "sicariato" refers to the organization of adolescent boys into armed gangs whose occupation is killing for money, and whose members are, in their majority, less than seventeen years of age. Salazar notes that the phenomenon began to develop in Medellín in the late-1970s without being recognized by the state authorities until the youth gangs emerging from, above all, poor marginal neighborhoods had become actors of incredible magnitude, under the guidance of paramilitary forces and drug cartels. Attacks against politicians and important representatives of civil society in broad daylight have become notorious. However, it is the quotidian normality of violence, proliferating mostly within the *barrios* (marginal neighborhoods), on which the society has tried to close its doors. There have emerged literary, cinematic, and research projects that helped bring this nameless reality to the fore—an existence that is completely devoid of future, a life, however, of rituals and forceful desires as seen in Víctor Gaviria's pioneering film *Rodrigo D* (1988). Focusing on the experiences of teen-age gang members in the *comunas* (marginal neighborhoods) of Medellín, Salazar has been one of the first to assemble their testimony in categories of what we will call a culture of exception. His book, *No nacimos pa' semilla: La cultura de las bandas juveniles en Medellín* (We Were Not Born to Life: The Culture of Youth Gangs in Medellín, 1990, poorly translated in the English version as *Born to Die in Medellin*, 1991), inaugurated a pathbreaking series of Colombian narratives and ethnographic projects whose protagonists are members of the gangs of "sicarios."

Gangs of sicarios have made themselves visible by their "absolute" commitment to death, stepping out of the darkness of marginal existence to take the nightmare of secretly plotted assassination to whatever public site in which the victim can be intercepted. These killings raise a series of questions, among which the perpetrators' own disposability—their coming close to being sacrificed themselves as they carry out their assignments— is ostensible. Salazar sees the sicarios as dissidents whose aspirations and modes of life, in which diffuse images of freedom and elementary justice flicker, are inaccurately represented by their criminal deeds, often reflecting the instrumentalization of poor children and adolescents by the narco-paramilitary complex. Salazar's book, therefore, explores the sicarios' sacred spaces and transgressive practices, and their dreams and peculiar commitments. The six testimonies gathered in *No nacimos pa' semilla* are linked to a background of socioethnographic activism during the period when Salazar was a student of communications at the University of Antioquia between 1984 and 1990. It was a time of profound political crisis in Colombia, during which the author was involved in communitarian educational projects that were carried out in the marginal neighborhoods of Medellín. This experience created the framework that allowed his inclinations to crystallize into a narrative project of exceptional force.

We Were Not Born to Life consists of seven stories in which a scorching reality is put forth without dramatic exaltation. At issue is cultural diagnostics of an uncommon type. These are stories born out of the testimonies of different subjects who have been directly involved in the actions and the life of the gangs. In the case of authorship which is, we might say, an artistically restrained one, the writer has set out from an elementary ethics of narration. His driving force has been neither a striving for adequacy of representation when he deals with marginal adolescents nor a search for literary distinction, but instead it is the possibility of making voices speak that already carry the burden of utmost stigmatization. It has therefore meant making an incursion into an "abject" mode of communication. The sicarios' personal accounts that Salazar records seem to emerge from a corporal and verbal sphere of both aberration and "incompleteness," producing a "gaping"[12] whose result is of the kind of singularity that is opposed to specific literary modes of individuation.[13] Salazar's aim is to uncover a "contamination" that is inherent in the language, not only of the "unstabilized" (Kristeva) but of the nonexistent subject. It is no surprise that the book's glossary of *parlache*—the slang spoken by youngsters who inhabit the extreme margins of the country's symbolic order—is missing in the English edition.[14]

Salazar's project was based in the fact that the words and deeds of the neophytes of violence could tell astounding stories, provided that they could be unearthed. When this author enters into the testimonial adventure, nothing initiatory can be claimed, if one takes "initiation" to be an "accession to...the unadulterated treasure of the 'pure signifier'"[15] or in a different vein, as granting the subaltern subject an essential portion of "autonomy." Nor does Salazar focus on the atrocities that sicarios have committed as gang members, the end results of their presence in society of which the public takes note—the notorious *what* they have done. What marks Salazar's attitude of "care" is the question of *who* the sicarios really are as agents of the life stories in which they have been actively engaged. The literary solution itself can only be understood as paradoxical, if we remember Arendt's locating a "narratable self" at a place where actions cannot coincide with being the narrator of his or her own life story. However, this is not an empirical insight, nor can it be reduced to an ontological constant like the one Arendt constructs in an (un) conscious act of subalternization.[16] We are dealing, in Salazar's case, with the nondiscursive (yet narrative) world that is immanent in the construction of life testimonies, as well as the rare, nontotalizing talent for objectification that certain storytellers call their own. In that sense, Salazar writes life stories for the sicarios, not in their place, but for them.[17] Making their existences tangible and sometimes strangely coherent, the author makes their life of exception neither sublime nor cynical, nor does he become fascinated by a world where exclusion and poverty, if taken as signs of fatalism, would lead to cruelty and perversion. He renarrates the stories contained in his subjects' signifying manners of acting, talking, and recorded remembering as he attempts to manifest, so to speak, an immanent linguisticality, and the ways in which it is bound to the space-time experiences of Medellin's teenage gangs. It is from here, where singularity contests the possibility of individuation, that Salazar's protagonists start to appear as peculiar ethical figures.

At the beginning of *No nacimos pa' semilla*, in the first story entitled "We Are the Kings of the World," there is a ritual taking place.

> Silhouetted on the face of the full moon, the shape of a headless cat strung up by its paws. On the floor, in a bowl, the blood has been collected. Now just drops are falling, slowly and intermittently. Each drop, as it lands, makes small waves that grow until they form a tormented sea. Waves that shake to the rhythm of the heavy rock that is playing at full blast. To the side is the head that still watches with its green, luminous eyes. Fifteen people participate in the ritual. In the background, the city is spread below them.[18]

A young man, Antonio, remembers his initiation ritual into one of the gangs in Medellin's "Comuna Nororiental." His memory is enacted through "immediately lived speech" (in German: *erlebte Rede*) in which the event seems to tell itself:

> Blood of the cat that climbs over walls, that leaps easily..., that walks on its silent padded paws across rooftops, vanishes effortlessly in the shadows of night. Feline blood, full of the urge to pounce unerringly on its prey. Blood that conjures up strange energies, that accelerates the soul.[19]

The mimetic sacrifice of a cat, with its blood being recharged by blasting rock music, as well as its phantasmagorical images of feline energies and a savage state of soul are ecstatic features. They may be associated, according to assumptions that have become common since the French school of sociology, with sacred space. Before entering into the analysis of the text I would like to dwell, for a moment, on the notion of "the sacred," to mark out the status of religious experience—a feature that is strongly intertwined with violence—for our considerations. Emile Durkheim, together with Marcel Mauss, Henry Hubert, and others the pioneer of an influential tradition, once asserted that "there are two kinds of sacred, one auspicious, the other inauspicious. And not only is there no continuity between the two forms, but the same object can pass from one to the other without changing its nature."[20] Agamben has taken a critical stance against the explanatory model that is based on the "ambiguity of the sacred"[21]: a theory that places generic religious practice and experience next to both terror and attraction, horror and reverence, and the pure and the impure. This has conceptual resonance for our study of Salazar's and later Vallejo's narrative, since it calls for a double critical awareness. The first is almost self-understood but needs to be remembered: religious imagination should not be reduced to doctrinaire thought and practice. The second is related to the need to deal with cultural ambiguity in a "non-ambivalent" way. Once we consider the emotional and psychological forces that lie at the heart of religiosity, it becomes crucial, however, to avoid a "psychologization" of the social world, one that might be the result of the researcher's own unease before the "brute" cultural matter. What relates Salazar's narrative to concerns articulated by recent political philosophy is a perception of the sacred as closely linked to profane conflicts over social agency and political power. What lends his approach an original character is his questioning of the determinism of religious practices, related to his study of the sicarios' modes of embodied imagination and their singular moral postures, as they have become manifest in territories such as the marginal *comunas* of Medellín.

Referring back to the ritual performed by the gang in "We Are the Kings of the World," it seems to belong to a repertoire of "life techniques" that is learned through initiation into that adolescent community. Doubtless its relationship to daily practices of violence, death, and survival is more pertinent than its rootedness in a particular religious ideology or universe. A sacrifice like the one described earlier seems to serve the purpose of creating a "non-autonomous" sacred sphere, a sphere in which preexistent forms of violence practiced by different powers and on different scales in Colombian society are either countered or reterritorialized ("substituted").[22] The cultic event—charged with the power of techno-rock—, can be perceived as pertaining to an aberrant sociocultural situation. However, it is far from conveying an archaic residue or belonging to remote spaces within today's world. In Colombia, given an unprecedented proliferation and interaction of several "executive powers" over extended periods of time, with civil-war-like conditions traversing almost the entire second half of the twentieth century,[23] René Girard's question of "substitutive" as self-generating form of violence appears in a new light. The referred ritual performed by a gang of sicarios in

Medellín can be seen as their response to and, at a low level, participation in a larger dynamic in which major sectors of Colombian society possessing extensive amounts of logistic and economic, as well as biopolitical power, have taken coercion beyond the legal norm, enacting "mimetic" networks of terror by way of an endless chain of killings—the physical extermination of opponents as a cleansing of the political spectrum. This is not a matter of functional disorder, that is to say chaos as the opposite of an orderly arranged state. It is rather linked to a historical situation in which the Schmittian approach to sovereignty as a borderline concept (*Grenzbegriff*)[24] encounters an unforeseeable resonance from one of the disaster zones of global modernity.[25] Salazar's narrative thus deals with a dynamic by which life is systematically sacrificed on a major scale by an abnormal political system in the heart of the Latin American continent, a system that served capitalism at the brink of its global reorganization during the 1970s and 1980s.

Why would approaching the experience that pervades the lives of marginal teenagers in Colombia's peripheral modernity have to draw on the problematics of the sacred to gain a closer understanding of the relationships and paradoxes involved? The question becomes more pointed when we start asking if it is not the relationship between life and death as a *political* nexus that lies at the root of the Western concept of "sacred life." Within this unusual framework, as we have already discussed in chapter 1, it is the reproblematization of the term "bare life" from which a largely underappreciated concept of "sacred life" has been set out anew. The current advocate of this hypothesis, Agamben, discusses the historical sources of this figure in archaic Roman law and its timeliness regarding the (re)constitution of sovereign politics during the twentieth century.[26] In other words, against a belief in the sacredness of bare life as a pacifistic, or a silently convening notion established by Christianity and eventually reshaped by liberal-humanist moral ideologies, there is a different—a terrible—notion of the sacred that is revealing its archaic as well as timely contours. Agamben's approach to the concept of life relating to sovereign power is, on the one hand, appealing, as it reworks violence conceptually and addresses its opaque status within democratic societies. It tends, at the same time, to leave an epistemological framework that is constitutively European unchallenged. Agamben shows, again, the way in which critical European thinking continues to foreground the exception within itself. The experiences of countries like Colombia and other peripheral territories, despite their immediate presence and conceptual urgency still lack an equal place within strategic philosophical thinking. Those who plead that renewed attention be given to the nexus between violence and the sacred must consider a map on which the role of peripheral modern spaces is not only included, but becomes paramount, for analyzing the contemporary.

Let us put a formulation on the "state of emergency," taken from Benjamin's *On the Concept of History*, into a singular frame by relating it to the problems illuminated by Salazar. While fleeing from Nazism, Benjamin wrote in 1940, shortly before his death, "The tradition of the oppressed teaches us that the 'state of emergency' in which we live is not the exception but the rule."[27] We may slightly alter the formulation: if a *state of emergency* becomes the rule, the very notion of exception can lose both its juridical and its epistemological meaning, a risk whose infiltration into historical knowledge Benjamin denounced. It is this intricate problem that concerns Salazar, as well, when he addresses the existential realities of young people from the poor, lower-class neighborhoods of his home town, Medellín. *We Were Not Born to Life* will reveal an immanent state of exception that is different from Agamben's view. Regarding the status of the figure of *homo sacer*, an indistinguishability between "his" exemption from explicit killing and "his" perpetuous exposure to death can be recognized not just as a juridical paradox,[28] but as a political-existential and thus cultural one. That is to say that Salazar's testimony allows for a no less compelling yet different image of "sacred man." The title, *We Were Not Born to Life*, draws on a particular meaning of exception, inverted in relation to both a ruling sovereign's decision, and to a dualistic scheme where it would signal the reverse side of normality and rule.

In his preface to the 2002 edition, Salazar reflects on the strong reaction that his title has been causing among young people and social workers in Medellin's *comunas*. The claim expressed by these people is that the title itself stigmatizes life in the marginal neighborhoods, as though the arduous and resourceful confrontation with the task of survival does not entitle people to proclaim the opposite: "Yes, we were born to live!"[29] Nevertheless, the author makes his case for his wording, and he does so with the intent of verbalizing the most shocking estrangement that human beings born into the world can ever face—not being born for life. The title implies an effort of understanding that is conceptually intrepid. If "action has the closest connection with the human condition of natality" ("the capacity of beginning something anew"[30]), and if the adolescent subjects of Salazar's narrative have "not been born for life," how can their actions then become meaningful within their state of existence? The brutal paradox is this: these actions can become eloquent when, due to a state of emergency that is permanent rather than conditional, a cultural fabric is generated in which life is defined and organized as something with no essential, let alone normative value. The difference between a "culture of fear,"[31] as it incrementally strikes the Latin American middle classes due to the threats that afflict their perceptions of social order and security, and a "culture of exception" becomes evident. The first designates an imagination that legitimately longs for a civilian existence that is fundamentally incompatible with violence, whereas the second foregrounds a notion of life whose conditioning power is likely to be a deadly one. It may well be the (un)conscious resistance to distinguishing a "culture of exception" from a "culture of fear" that makes it immensely difficult to address the exception at the point, or within those spaces, where it tends to become an all-pervasive state. In this manner, the meaning of *No nacimos pa' semilla* is informed by an underlying concept of culture of exception.[32]

Sacred Labor: Death and the Gendered Space of Survival

In the end...many more lives would be stolen by "planned misery" than by bullets.

—*Naomi Klein*

Let us return to the event of initiation from which the first story in *We Were Not Born to Life* sets out: *Somos los Reyes del Mundo*—We're the Kings of the World. The sacrifice of the cat calls forth the framework within which the memories of Antonio, leader of a gang of sicarios, are embedded. When "immediately lived speech" enacting the recollection of the ritual is suspended, we find out that Antonio, twenty years old, is remembering his baptism as a sicario from a hospital bed. This is the moment when he is "dancing between life and death" at the Saint Vincent de Paul Hospital, after having been shot by a *pelado*—a young kid from a rival gang. Antonio has not been blessed with a sudden death. After spending four days in a coma he "returned" to endure, for several months, the slow disintegration of his body and his spirits. So the inaugural ritual scene is followed by what critics tend to consider as the focal frame that gives access to the deeper layers of the mind: a first-person narration. The traumatic state opens up a space for Antonio to think back and reflect. The sicario's first person singular now displays, with retrospective calm, a picture of his undertakings within the social metier of a murderous gang, an environment whose codes and mannerisms are recounted in detail. Toward the end, the reader returns to Antonio's deathbed in the hospital to listen to the adolescent gunman summing up his philosophy of existence: "The thing is, dying doesn't matter. Truth is we're not born to live. But we should go quickly, not feel ourselves so miserable and so alone."[33] It is not the brute fact of death that resides at the core of Antonio's lament, but the accident of not being killed the right way, of being lonely for a long time within the space of death. To become a first person narrator reflects the contingency of utter solitude.

> Everyone has his day, and this one was mine. What hurts is that I didn't go quickly, without having time to take another breath, to feel any pain, without even being able to say that they've killed me. It would have been better than feeling how my body is falling apart, and my spirit....Better to die at once, and not be abandoned by those who say they're your friends.[34]

In the world of Medellin's sicarios, death is perpetually counted on, and it is even praised when it happens all at once. But there is a *conditio sine qua non*: death should not be "the deepest shock in...individual experience..."[35]; it should occur in a straightforward way. The individualization of death—its painful extension into reasoning invoked by Salazar's recording the memories of the hospitalized sicario—is what brings about literarization. This means that Salazar's narrative is built on an ethical limit. Sicarios, in real life, do not possess a place for solitary mourning. In the final paragraph of the story, a vision in which Antonio is enticed back into the world of his fierce gang is called up, paralleled by a return to lived speech. In his last dream, he returns to the nocturnal site of his initiation, "flying, hallucinating to the beat of the drums and the electric guitars, with all his buddies."[36] The spot, in the hilltops where Medellín's shanty towns have spread out, offers a blatantly panoptic outlook. The dream creates an apocalyptic image of Medellín, especially of its monstrous center that is burning and collapsing, and still looming up as a phantom—seen from the distance of the hilltops where the sicarios have established their stand. "... [W]e're as high and as far away as a cloud. We're on the heights where we look down on everything, where nothing can touch us. We're the kings of the world."[37] This dream taking Antonio "home" is actually happening at the moment in his extinguishing life when he is at the furthest point from home.

The framing of "We're the Kings" around Antonio's core experience places the role of death in a disturbingly constitutive place. More specifically, it is Antonio's mourning the inadequateness of his death that brings us closer to the ways in which violence and *sacred* life interact. It leads us to ask how the (decision about the) deaths of all those who have been killed by Antonio, together with the attitude toward his own death, can be understood as—do we dare to say—enabling factors in the life of the sicario. What is the place that human life occupies at a threshold where it has indeed fallen under an exception? If, according to carl schmitt's expression, "sovereign is he who decides on the [state of] exception" (*Ausnahmezustand*),[38] for decades the Colombian government was neither able to act as "properly sovereign," on behalf of its country,[39] nor has at last—under the Uribe government—a democratic framework been consolidated as a confluence of the "fundamental horizons of all communal life."[40] Since the historical period of the so-called *Violencia* (1946–1957), the state has been immersed in and has itself been the instrument of, an ongoing struggle for sovereignty culminating, from the late-1980s to 1993, in what has been epitomized as *la guerra del narcotráfico* (the drug trade war).[41] It was during this time that gang youths were mobilized in the war by which Pablo Escobar and his cartel indeed succeeded, temporarily, in shaking state power. However, sicarios represented, throughout this period, the disposable agents of a struggle for political and economic power from whose ends they were essentially excluded. Following Escobar's defeat and, especially after 2000, the "pacification" of Medellín in an extreme neoliberal makeover, most of the members of this informal adolescent reserve army have fallen prey to the concerted terror by which these impoverished youths were either exterminated in mass or put back in their place as creatures with equal rights to both exclusion and bare life in poverty. In this process of biopolitical tabula rasa, in which concerted action between a consolidated (and later "demobilized") paramilitary wing, the army, and security agencies achieved spectacular levels of "state- and elite-orchestrated" gangsterism terror was the main weapon of pacification.[42]

Let us move back into Medellín's marginal barrios, post-1985, one of the epicenters of violence where impoverished youths were coopted by powerful narco-gangster terrorism and exposed, at the same time, to state repression. In the accounts of sicarios like Antonio from which Salazar's testimony arises, there is a characteristic motive that organizes the lives of the young criminals: killing for hire.[43] Terminating a person's life is conceived of as regular "work," and the mode of action that allows for this type of activity appears as an exorbitant form of nomadism: micro hit squads based in the *comunas* are launched to carry out their deadly actions in different parts of the city as well as throughout the entire country. An image that started to haunt Colombian society during the eighties was that of two adolescent boys riding a small motor bike, *una moto envenenada* (a poisonous bike), making a sudden appearance in all kinds of urban settings, executing someone on a sidewalk or in the middle of a crowd with terrible versatility, and disappearing as quickly as they arrived, or, in other cases, being shot by the police. Antonio tells how he went about completing his duties.

> We don't care who we have to kill. Whoever it is, I'm no devotee of any kind. I turn on the bike and, if I have to, I get them myself. Sometimes you find out who the guy was in the news.[44]

In detailed fashion, Antonio relates a sinister action—the assassination of the leader of an opposition political party, for which he and his gang were paid approximately three million pesos (nearly US $1,500). The grotesque tone of the narrative, not pointedly aesthetic but instead implicit, is caused by the casual way in which Antonio relates his tale as if it were an ordinary event, and by his detachment from any concern regarding the victim as an individual human being and a public figure. The hit was followed by a triumphant communal fiesta in the hillside neighborhoods that might have resembled an archaic custom of warfare. What was celebrated was not the action itself and its implications, which remained circumstantial to the sicarios (presumably the killing of a politician opposed to the connections between narcotraffickers and state officials), but rather the fact that they had made a huge amount of money. An action that in any case would appear as the execution of a political enemy turns out, in fact, to be a ritualistic deed. The victim has been sacrificed for the sake of obtaining *el billete* (big bucks). After the act, the money is immediately "wasted" in celebration, and the place where the sicarios launch a gregarious fiesta is their own poverty-stricken *comuna*.

> That night, once we got paid, we put on a big neighbourhood party. As they say, "dead guy to the hole, live guy to the dance." It was like a preview of Christmas Eve—we bought a roast pig, cases of beer and booze, we set up a sound system in the street, and we went at it till the next morning.[45]

Since the sicarios speak of their *trabajo* (work), a closer look at this concept is necessary. "Work" is literally a modern term, referring to the sum of activities related to production, fabrication, and exchange, surplus value, and abstraction. However, there is a second semantics to the term that has not received due attention from materialist theory. It refers to the realm of "labor" that weighs heavily on the human condition, although its looming presence was once supposed to be reduced and finally overcome by "work" associated with progress and development. Arendt's distinction between "work" and "labor" suggests a shifting of perspective.[46] Distinct from productivity and the abstract notion of work in the modern sense, labor provides for sheer subsistence. It leaves no products behind, yet, "despite its futility, [it] is born of great urgency and motivated by a more powerful drive than anything else, because life itself depends upon it." Labor has disclosed—since Arendt, whose blindness regarding modernity's peripheral constituents is an astounding fact—its massive global expansion, so much so that it finds itself ingrained in the ground of biopolitical and geopolitical control of the world. Perhaps it has been the "cunning reason" of neoliberalism, magnifying and corrupting labor in the name of consumption, which has outwitted the Marxist conviction of productivity-based social, cultural, and intellectual identities over time. Since in capitalism "labor and consumption are but two stages of the same process,"[47] in which the fetishism of the commodity has epidemically infected everyday life, the differences between wealth and poverty have been progressively obscured. At issue, when we revisit Arendt's thinking at this point, is a shift of attention from productivity (productive forces and means of production) toward embodied life, in that labor calls for readdressing those human activities and fantasies today, which are directed at sheer subsistence.

We Were Not Born to Life becomes radically involved in the problematics of labor. Its first story, We Are the Kings of the World, devotes an entire section to the testimony of Antonio's mother, Doña Azucena, who refers to her son as "Toño":

> What I can tell you is that Toño has been a good son. All these years, I've had to work in bars to earn enough to take care of my family. But for a single mother it's hard. He's the one who has helped me the most. He hasn't been lavish, and when he works, he shows up with something for the house.[48]

The seemingly trivial statement confides discomforting insights. Antonio's mother refers to her son's "work," that is to say "labor" as a habitual undertaking in regard to which no special distinction is made. What really matters is that Toño has helped keep the family alive. Under different circumstances, a situation in which a child resorts to organized killing and is then injured and hospitalized himself might have caused a cathartic reaction, or some sort of repentance about the person's occupation. But nothing like that occurs, and the mother instead praises her son's supporting her under all kinds of circumstances. The fact that he landed in prison several times during his short life is part of the same normality. The mother asserts, "When he's been in jail, I've never missed visiting him. Many times I've had clashes with the police, and as a woman I've made them respect me."[49] Within a culture of exception, being in prison, or being fatally wounded, or carrying out brutal revenge are fundamental labor practices that Doña Azucena vigorously defends.

Who is this woman who has been a waitress most of her life, stoically accustomed to being abandoned by one man after the other? She remembers that in one of the shabby bars where she tried to make a living, there was a mural painting showing

> a man hanging from the branch of a tree, about to fall into a pond in which crocodiles were baring their teeth. He couldn't try to climb back into the tree because there was a rattlesnake in it, and on the ground, a tiger was trying to climb the tree. What can the man do? At times I looked at that picture and thought that my life is like that: no way out. Everywhere I've gone, I've been lost.[50]

There is an unacknowledged caricature in the image: its victimized subject is a man, and we could probably not easily imagine a woman hanging from the branch of a tree in an analogous fashion. This may be seen as pointing toward an allegorical dispositif that emerged out of the Christian tradition, according to which the sacredness of life, as it is crystallized at the moment when death is imminent, is still attributed to the male subject. In Doña Azucena's case, the irony inheres in her entire experience: the fathers of her four or more children have abandoned her with the burden of survival. Thus she has been enslaved by the inescapable task of *pure necessity* that has been so strong that the departures of the "heads" of the family were not even perceived as dramatic events, owing to the regular failure of males to arrive at the same degree of abnegated endurance that women have inherited under the global conditions of poverty.[51] Given these circumstances, one might have suspected that Antonio's mother would have literally led a *bare life*—a condition of sheer endurance. Yet the ancient postulate of the exposed creature, its vulnerability, was imbued with an Aristotelian moral assumption. There should "possibly [be] some noble element" in the mere fact of living itself: "And we all see that men cling to life at the cost of enduring great misfortune, seeming to find in life a natural sweetness and happiness."[52] The episteme behind these ancient words belongs to an aristocratic ethics: "simple natural life was excluded from the *polis*" and remained confined to the sphere of the *oikos* ("home").[53] For Doña Azucena, the mother of the sicario from Medellín, there is no home in the classical political sense. There is only survival as fierce resistance.

Remembering the painting that makes her own suffering meaningful when projected onto the figure of a man evokes Azucena's hidden personal drama. On the one hand, hers is at very least a claim of active suffering; she confronted the police and other threatening forces, or, as Antonio recalls, she was "una guerrera"—a female warrior.[54] On the other hand, as the invisible side of the allegorical picture suggests, the character of the labor that weighs on her is distanced from the conditions of a man's—a husband's—life. Her laboring is, in fact, invisible. Women like Azucena exist at a threshold where they are excluded from a common ethical pathos of suffering by virtue of their position at the most precarious end of the laboring process. Azucena's way of dealing with this contradiction is due to what can be described as a *sacred pact* between violent sons and supportive mothers. At its core lies a peculiar affective exchange. According to *We Were Not Born to Life*, this pact precedes symbolic language, yet it pervades the signifying behavior of the persons involved. If we used the aspect of "taboo" that has often been referred to as sacred,[55] then taboo, in a more arbitrary sense, would indicate this intimate relationship: a kind of untouchable zone in which the moral order of society finds itself suspended or even reversed. The son's taking responsibility for his mother's bodily life (as well as those of his younger siblings) is matched, in turn, by the devotion that the mother gives to her son. This is not what it looks like according to prevailing images of maternal abnegation—the woman's silent acceptance of the criminal deeds of the adolescent. Mothers like Azucena actively function at the threshold where death is always pending, and they do so by consecrating their sons to the successful occupation of the space of death. It is from this inherently violent, strongly gendered constellation that we will derive the term of "sacred labor."

Azucena, not at all a devote Catholic, speaks as if Antonio's critical condition were merely an imposture:

> I promised Our Fallen Lord of Girardota that if this boy gets better fast, I'll pray ten novenas. That's what I want, that he gets out and finds that guy who shot him, because things can't stay like this. My family will not be at peace while that guy is still out there.[56]

Why is vengeance so excessively present in these environments? If Antonio's enemy is to be sacrificed (in the event of Toño's recovery that does not, in fact, occur), the driving force is a primordial desire for justice,—justice not as a universal or normative good, but as a manifestation of the efficacy of living at the edge of the human condition. We are thus dealing with a fairly untheorized experience of the sacred: sacredness—in the perception of more than one of Salazar's protagonists—reemerges outside of the notion of the ignoble endurance of bare life. It commands, rather, power over death for the benefit of those who live at the threshold.

We have implicitly addressed a vanished figure—the father as head of the family. Fathers are strangely absent (or fiercely contested) in the hit-boys' narrations, and so is the residual social tie that binds an adolescent son to the authority of his father. This far-reaching phenomenon will give rise, in Vallejo's *Our Lady of the Assassins*, to a very different literary construction: that of a homosexual paternal authority figure who takes sicarios under his care, not to protect and educate them, but to eventually "sacrifice" them for a higher goal (see the following chapter). The fact of the matter is that the majority of the sicarios depicted in Salazar's book have assumed, while still adolescents, the role of protectors of their families. This is a position that is characteristic, above all, of the most hardened gang members—those who have become protagonists of the utmost violence and, at the same time, rendered almost unconditional support and devotion to their mothers. When the hitboys take on this sort of father function and head-of-family role themselves, it should be viewed in the light of a particular abandonment.[57] The case is not simply that paternal authority is missing, but, rather, that these adolescents have no access to public society at all. The missing possibility would be that of becoming engaged in worldly life through labor and social integration. However, this involvement would require a moratorium ("la moratoria social"),[58] like that during which the young of the middle class and higher social sectors usually are prepared for the normative public world by an extended period of education and—to extend Freud's expressions beyond the childhood phase—internalization of aggressive instincts by virtue of the intellect. The moratorium thus bears a double relevance for adolescents in that it contributes to both formation and repression. The second aspect epitomizes an adaptation process to society's gendered symbolic order—the formation of the subject by more or less subtle subjection.[59] However, humans who have no access to the moratorium state are not only socially excluded, they are abandoned to an overall condition of affective marginalization and thus to a brutal contradiction. On the one hand, they lack the learning process and other means that can make them civilian subjects. On the other, their function within the public moral economy is that of being the "natural" bearers of guilt, paradoxically exposed to expiation— bare life's traditional symbolic function—but not to justice. At this point, the sacred pact between Doña Azucena and her son Antonio excels as a complex *affective* empowerment. Such mothers counter the abandonment of their fierce sons by consecrating them to survival. Becoming criminals—the official term—does not quite hold in this kind of case since it would mean the transgression of order and rule. Most sicarios have never come close to, nor have they learned to interiorize, civil norms that they could transgress. Their condition entails being turned into neophytes of violence as an ultimate empowering state that sets them apart from their abandonment by society, yet at the price of turning their bodily life into the exception. As a result, and different from the common, Christian-based perception of the life of poor communities, the hitboys' most precarious and yet most forceful position is not docile mere life or, in the same logic, rampant crime, but a particular form of "sacred life." There are, in *We Were Not Born to Life*, several narrative clues that emphasize the pivotal role of mothers in this respect, attesting to their consecrating authority.

Salazar himself provides a hint, in a scholarly text, regarding the phenomenon that we have termed the sacred pact. In the sicario's discourse, the image of the mother takes on special power. She appears as the unquestioning companion, the one who would give her life, and is, in many cases, the justification for the delinquency.[60]

We have emphasized an *exception* under which a culture emerges that does not regard life as a superior good. However, it validates life in that it is lived as a sacred condition: elementary and often stunningly archaic forms of communal interaction rank higher than individual existence. Salazar's narrative is not intended to be a statement in favor of any kind of marginal practice of violence. It points to the nerve centers of an *exception* that escapes both normative judgment and the model of a sovereign's conscious (instrumental) decision. So, how has the exception become the sinister rule? Here we are taking Arendt's formulation—that labor provides the means of subsistence on which life itself depends—beyond her own premises. The experiences related in Salazar's testimony cannot belong to "*zoē*," as the Greeks understood the mere condition that all living beings have in common. We are dealing, rather, with existence on a social and ethical edge that is both threatened and reaffirmed. Hence the paradoxical meaning of what we have termed *sacred labor* in the case of the sicarios and their single mothers. Life comes to be consecrated in the limbo where social subsistence is threatened with collapse. Here life exists at a threshold where its conditioning power is not only a most violent one, nor will it necessarily produce irrational violence in turn; however, to labor under these circumstances implies complex relationships with violence daily. This insight sheds light on the drama of gendered ritualistic identity that emerges from the hitboys' struggle.

If we are dealing with creatures born into an existence where their only real protection is their mothers' consecrating presence, we may think of an analogy to the axiom of "inclusive exclusion" that is foregrounded in *Homo Sacer*. In the ancient figure of the sacred located "before or beyond the religious," life is sacred only insofar as it is taken into an exception where it may be killed beyond or before the rules that are prescribed by both law and religious sacrifice. That is a figure according to which the relationship between life and violence has fallen outside the officially sanctioned practices of killing. It applies to cases where, according to Agamben, sovereignty generates a state of exception and can be seen during the twentieth century, most strikingly, in the concentration camp as the "exemplary place" produced by "modern biopolitical totalitarianism."[61] But what occurs within certain territories of global modernity, where human labor finds itself incrementally exposed to the extremes of exhaustion or fierce transgression, if not a latent virtual killing of uncountable lives at any moment, that is beyond or before the rules?

A peculiar figure—sacred labor—has been brought forward as a feature of the culture of exception in Medellin's *comunas populares*. Regarding the phenomenon of matriarchs, we must repeat that the mothers of sicarios do not primarily consecrate their sons to killing but to vigorously and aggressively defending life at its limit. These women can be considered the secret administrators of the threshold. Above all, and regarding the roving criminality, they relieve their sons of the burden of guilt. Who other than mothers could perform such a gigantic deed? Who other than mothers could provide the unconditional affective support that can turn labor into (power over) life itself? And who other than mothers could generate the immanent forces of "legitimacy" in favor of those living on the abandoned side of the social edifice and hence the legal apparatus? Herein lies one explanation for the fact that the word crime does not exist in the language of Medellin's hitboys. They think of themselves not as evildoers, but as outcasts in a universe in which the distribution of money, order, and rule are wrong anyway. Their sacred laboring results from establishing and following their own rules regarding violent killing, rules that range beyond the law in the same way that they themselves become the victims of them. Readers of *We Were Not Born to Life* may perceive, of course, these practices and aberrances as part of the Colombian predicament. However, an uncomfortable question arises from this. Is the heterogeneity of the world system today susceptible to new drastic situations, in which flight into different scales of *sacred labor* might not be limited to Colombia's "city of terror" alone? From the perspective of the South, the invisible hand of deregulating capitalism destroys human life without accountability.[62] Are not vast disposable or lateral parts of labor power included just by exclusion—being included in the neoliberal fabric by being exposed, to an increasing degree, to the potentiality of either abrupt or decelerated death? The "less than totalitarian" state of affairs through which this type of exception is normalized is called massive poverty. The human subject becomes intensely exposed to the realities of hunger, disease, and death but still cannot be put to death in sanctioned form under conditions where it is "destitute, excluded, repressed, exploited—and yet living." Seeking to reinvent a "materialist teleology" in Spinozian terms, Negri writes, "Today there is not even the illusion of a transcendent God. The poor have dissolved that image and recuperated its power."[63] Salazar's work helps to contrast the abstractness of these words. The project of the Colombian writer should read as follows: No sensationalist pose and no transcendental ideology shall be allowed to mythify the immanent relationships between existence and violence in the marginal zones of modernity into which many young people "have not been born for life." The question of whether there is, in Salazar's testimony, a place outside the exception will continue to inform our discussion. Yet the real alternative, the one where the neophytes of violence could claim an existence at an equitable place of Colombian society, seems to have been closed down.

Collapsing Consumption: Religiosity and Ethics beyond Guilt

The sicarios' unusual relationship with religiosity calls for further reflection. Our observations have thus far proceeded with caution as far as the term religion is concerned, perhaps remembering Derrida's remark: "How dare we speak of it in the singular [...], this very day?" How can we address "the clearest and most obscure: religion"[64]? We have been moving the problematic toward a specific notion of *sacredness* that allows us to emphasize relationships between extreme teenaged violence and informal laboring practices. Let us now pay more explicit attention to that which several Colombian analysts have framed as the neoreligious demeanors within the "subculture" of the sicarios.[65] Here religiosity will reappear as a phenomenon that is charged with grim impurities. On the one hand, the religious question traverses the life of the hitboys in an intense manner. On the other, at issue is not a proposal that the church was making to them. Father Jorge Galeano, vicar of one of the *barrios* in northeast Medellín and testimonial voice of *Una palabra en medio de la muerte*, (A Word While Dying), the fourth story of *No nacimos pa' semilla*, recounts his experiences with "the powerful gangs":

> They, as the saying goes, sin and make up. They come to mass, take communion, they make vows, wear religious medallions everywhere they go, and once in a while go to confession...

> These lads...with deep feelings talk to their dead, they touch them, play them their favorite music....Even though this disturbs the traditional service, I know they are not doing it as sabotage.[66]

Galeano, who works daily in the environment where most of the hitboys grew up, admits his astonishment at the peculiar rites he has observed among them. His intention of not accusing them of blasphemy reflects his admiration for the way in which the practice of veneration has been reinvented among these young people. Characteristically, popular culture in Latin America is held accountable, once more, for the most unorthodox phenomena: "This is part of the popular tradition, our people have always been very faithful, and these teenagers are, too, in their own way."[67] Yet this view of the extraordinary, in terms of tradition, tends more toward esoteric description than subtle illumination. One would have to assume that the neophytes' violent but nonetheless religious practices have led to a point where preconceptions crumble.

Salazar experiments with different forms of inquiry to avoid cutting his project off from the incongruent aspects of testimonial insights. His focalizing practice relies, in the first place, on the efficacy of lived speech—a narration that is governed by the sensuous immediacy of experience and memory, one that displays both tenacious and fragmented exposures without sublimation. To take one of Paul de Man's expressions, the kind of "screen of language that controls its own representational mastery"[68] is kept free of "narrative narcissism."[69] This puts Salazar at a certain risk when he uses, especially in one particular case, a focalizing situation that is entirely invented. In the story *La vida no es una película* (Life Is Not a Movie), the young protagonist, Níver, "speaks back" from the world of the dead.[70] Níver has been killed in an act of vengeance. His memorizing perspective is placed in a no-man's-land that does not evoke, however, a Christian imagery of the afterlife. This situation, where there is no return from the space of death, may be characterized, on the one hand, as an aesthetic estrangement from the sober testimonial style. On the other, the peculiar focus helps question a facile image of religion "without a church." One of Níver's remarks seems guided by a tone of contemplation where moral insight reigns: "Only on this side have I had time to think about many of the things of life." Toward the end of the story, the young man expresses repentance. His remorse gives way to the desire for a less aggressive way of living and enjoying happiness, not to a Catholic purging of worldliness as such: "What I'm sorriest about is that I didn't take advantage of my time on earth to shoot less and live more."[71] The expressions of Salazar's heroes are mixed up with certain common Catholic words, but this should not prevent us from perceiving what their antitranscendent focus is. The guideposts for recognizing an immanent religiosity, one which is not predicated on a coherent notion of faith but on an ethics of action, are scarce. However, it is one of the unacknowledged merits of *We Were Not Born to Life* that it can point readers in that direction.

When Níver speaks from the "other side," he has literally become the subject of a sacrificed life. At the outset of the story, his voice blends implicit sarcasm with a desire to renarrate what otherwise might have looked like—in his own imagination—a movie. But "Life is not a Movie," as he realizes from his death. "I live in the neighborhood of those who have been put to bed." "We are going to put him to bed" (¡vamos a acostarlo!) is the metaphorical *parlache* expression of the sicarios who phrase their intention to kill someone with those words. Similar to Antonio's retrospective speech in "We're the Kings of the World," Níver's voice is (re)constructed with the aim of piercing through the morass of horror. Perhaps it is Salazar's particular achievement that he has found a way to allow the *renarration* of experiences that are impossible to be told in a proper way. So he uses either an antirealist focalization or else keeps to the neophytes' *parlache* style of speaking. The subtitle of the story says: "Níver, soldier of the militias of the people and for the people." Níver belonged to the generation of marginalized Colombian youth that reached adolescence in the mid-1980s. He was the son of black parents from Medellín's Santo Domingo barrio who, as a child, experienced the dual repression of racism and poverty. Recalling, now "from life below," how he became a street kid after trying to protect his mother from his father's aggression, he tells a story that takes him from a rehabilitation center for adolescents, to army service where he became involved, in 1989 and 1990, in disarming guerrilla forces of the Ejército Popular de Liberación (EPL). When he returned to his barrio afterward, the presence of violent gangs that looted and killed had created disastrous scenarios. So he joined one of the armed defense groups—"popular militias"—, whose purpose was to clean the area of thugs and gangs.[72] According to Forrest Hylton, "militias were dedicated, at least in theory, to community empowerment and uplift." They were successful, after 1987, in fighting gangs of sicarios, "only to give rise to more violent, professional gangs with closer ties to narcotrafficking, and, ipso facto, elements within state security agencies."[73] As in the majority of the cases presented in Salazar's book, even defense groups were unable to avoid uncontrolled killing, so Níver, by circumstances of vengeance, is led into the "barrio de los acostados" as well—the neighborhood of those who were put to bed. Throughout his book, Salazar presents an astonishing series of protagonists, most of whom belonged to the "reserve army" of neophytes of violence during the 1980s: young people from the disinherited sectors, trained in the use of weapons and coercive intelligence by drug cartels and paramilitary groups or alternatively schooled by the guerrilla forces, who were soon expelled back into zones in which informal survival practices, together with rapidly generalizing violence reigned. This is the realm where bare life has not just been located at an extreme end of the "biopolitical fracture of the West."[74] It has instead been converted into a form of daily sacred labor that has degenerated into practices of ritual killing for hire. Among this reserve army of impoverished youths, a terrible "subjectification" has taken place, to the point that sacred labor has come to imply the active self-sacrifice of persons who are perpetrators and victims. If this can happen, there must be something more terrible than death,[75] yet more desirable than the "next world," which propelled the lives of the Colombian hitboys.

Let us continue exploring the traces of religious practices without a church. Owing to the existence of powerful players of violence, among which the guerrilla forces (especially the FARC) and their specific dynamics have a high stake,[76] people like Antonio and Níver fall prey to instrumentalizing interests reaching beyond their own influence, being abandoned by both public society and the law. However, they don't perceive themselves as victims. In their fantasies there seems to exist nothing that demands consolation, at least not in a way that would give religion its traditional affective role. Religion as a spiritual basis of tranquilization—the anodyne for the poor—does not work in the case of these antiheroes. For the "sacred" young people of the *barrios populares*, religious practice has no aura that could release the "sigh of the oppressed creature,"[77] alleviating the burden of labor at the limit. The fantasies that accompany the atrocities committed by the muchachos are thoroughly pagan. Their rituals create a domain in which the "vale of tears" (Marx) is contested and "remedied" in an active manner, at a distance from the enchanting devices that are provided by the church, either in the realm of Protestant or Catholic morality. In "A Word While Dying," Father Galeano recalls what he describes as the strangest funeral he has ever seen. The person killed, that is, sacrificed in the process of war-like gang rivalry, was "el Flaco, a dark-skinned young man, tall, about twenty-two years old, head of one of the powerful gangs in this sector."[78]

> The wake and the burial were a complete carnival. The gang members kept the body at the house for three days. They were listening to salsa, sniffing and smoking, drinking. Finally the family, in spite of the gang's opposition, decided to bury him. That Wednesday they came out with the coffin on their shoulders...At every corner where Flaco used to operate, they put down the coffin, they played wild music, salsa and rock...They put the coffin on a table and continued their ceremony until, again, the mother made them go into the church. When mass was half over, they put a battery-powered tape recorder on top of the coffin and played several salsa tunes for him...they went by hitting him and saying things: "It's neat that you're ok," "Neat that you're still with us." "You always came through for us"...as if they were paying homage to a god.

> At the cemetery they took him out of the coffin, they carried him on their shoulders, and shot their guns in the air...[79]

What kind of fetishism is on display in this exuberant funeral? He who is treated as an idol is not a saint but the former chief of a gang, "el Flaco." Two ways of approaching this phenomenon come to mind. One is invoked by a strange pagan ritual that Padre Galeano uncovers in his account.

> These leaders, like Flaco, put themselves forward with bullets, with power, with heroic acts. The guy who drives the bike best, who shoots best and kills the most people ends up being the boss. They amass such power that their orders, no matter how ridiculous they seem, are not questioned, they're just obeyed. The boss, with his contacts in the world of money and his role as war chief, is venerated.[80]

Father Galeano is careful about not acknowledging the issue of transgression directly, especially at the point at which it cannot be codified by mainstream Catholicism. In the above-mentioned scene, an intense power is induced that converts the inanimate body into the staging ground of the ritual, thus supporting a state of worship that lasts four days. An interpretation relying on the mimetic force of similar practices might understand the funeral rite as performance in which a "use-value relationship" is transferred from one domain to another: strength and charisma of the leader are fiercely remembered, and thus acclaimed by his fellow men. But is the creation of power that works by animating the dead sicario really driven by the desire to draw "on the character and power of the original, to the point whereby the representation may even assume that character and that power?"[81] We may have to again ask who or what is being hailed by the surviving gang members? The sicario Antonio, in "We're the Kings of the World," who was abandoned by his *parceros* (buddies) as he lay in the San Vicente Hospital was just as well-known for his spectacular actions as was "el Flaco." But Antonio proves to be of no use as a fetish, for he had become vulnerable, incapable of embodying the substance of the empowering drive.

The relationship of the worshipful sicarios with "El Flaco's" body is not moral, nor is it driven by bad conscience. It is rather a profane relationship with a mystic smack, in which religious fetishism is taken to its limits in a strange way. The dead body is kept for three days in a move to sanction what appears as a rough party. What stands out is the thumping of the body, its removal from the casket, culminating (in the case of another funeral reported in the same story) in a situation in which the muchachos of the gang have their picture taken together with the corpse. This is why the padre's observation that hailing a dead sicario is like paying homage to a god is not quite correct. Last but not least in the ceremony, a boom box blared out an antisolemn sound, with salsa and rock music setting the tone for the boys' ecstatic mood. In other words—what is at issue is the phenomenon of radical profanation of a Catholic ritual. In Agamben's study "In Praise of Profanation," the religious concept of profanation is reformulated as a strategy of returning sacred phenomena and objects that have been kept separated from the public domain to general, nonhierarchic use.[82] In "El Flaco's" case, one should speak of the digressive practice of rituals by those who have been entirely displaced from the public sphere. The notion of profanation becomes telling at the moment at which it must be distinguished from "secularization."[83] The culture of the sicarios is traversed by practices of informal veneration: elements of Catholic ceremonies are not only integrated into quotidian use but forcefully transgressed. As we will show, the dominance of exchange-value relationships over use-value orientations, established by the economy of capital, is intercepted the moment that violent sacrifices and actions function as profane rituals signaling, for example, the appropriation of market benefits by noneconomic actions.

One of the standing tropes in the language that sicarios use among themselves is *conseguir billete*[84]—getting money. *El billete* translates literally as "the banknote" or "the bill" that is often referred to as if it were a religious fetish. The impact of what Marx called commodity fetishism on the hitboys is not difficult to observe. At the level of linguistic expression, it is manifest in the verb *sicariar* that means something like "laboring for money."[85] With the verbalization of sicario, the gang members reappropriate the designation that a terrified society has given them and convert it into a job description that sounds more neutral than killing—at least to them and their clients. The word *sicariar* permits the hitboys to elevate their actions to the status of a craft, comparable to other crafts that are capable of generating "el billete." They have thus ended up posing as though they were carrying out a sort of reifying labor. On a related level, *sicariar* stands for the self-conscious pose of those who have challenged the moral concept of bare life's superior value.

It would be a mistake to conclude that what started out as a desperate attempt to survive eventually turned into a profit-driven activity transmuting into an endeavor of informal enrichment such as the one that characterizes mafia power. One of the points made by Salazar and Gaviria, as we will discuss later, is that most neophytes, despite their sometimes sizable incomes, remain at the lowest end of the economic ladder. Sicarios serve as the disposable agents of complex structures of organized crime whose scope is local, national, and transnational. The young warriors do not, however, perceive themselves as functional gadgets being used by more powerful agents. They view themselves as undaunted protagonists in their own territories and undertakings. Nevertheless, as extreme outlaws, the neophytes have no access to the major systemic and global alliances that make a political and social crisis like the Colombian one a profitable enterprise for others. In acting as perpetrators and victims of sacrificial practices, sicarios pursue dreams that are different from those usually associated with the aspirations of high crime—gaining access to, or piercing, the ruling economic and political system. Nor do the hitboys pursue, in a strict sense, the illusions created by market capitalism. In several sociological commentaries, Colombia's hitboys have been pictured as particularly ruthless protagonists of a culture of consumption. The flaw of these studies is that they apply an ideological critique of consumerism to cultural life practices that function in contradictory ways. The possibility of the neophytes' joining in a "true" consumers' society is not applicable to the manner in which these warriors approach consumption. Instead, the ways they waste the money they earn offers us a glance into a peculiar dystopian space.

The amount of money that can be earned by the gangs (the equivalent of between US $ 300 and $ 4,000) should be considered exorbitant only in relationship to the extremely low living levels in the northeastern *comunas*. This money is neither saved nor submitted to productive criteria with the aim of leading the adolescents and their families, over a period of time, out of poverty. *El billete* serves to purchase weapons and some lower-value market items such as Nike shoes, and money is given regularly to the mothers who are the administrators in the destitute families. Most compellingly, and despite the severity of necessity, considerable sums are spent for exhaustive celebration in communal environments. A typical feature of "expenditure" (Bataille) is expressed in statements like the following:

> We could spend a hundred thousand pesos or more in one night.

> We'd go wild until all the money was gone and we were broke again. Then we'd wait for the next assignment.

> …I spent whatever I got. If I had two million pesos, I'd put together a group and we'd go off to the coast, two weeks or a month living like Arab sheiks. Until we'd spent every last cent. When I came back I was as poor as before I'd started.[86]

It seems odd that sicarios would probably not try to settle down in society for good even if they could get away with a big enough "take." Their economic behavior would be qualified as a total waste by any norm that relies on rational acquisition and consumption. Academic studies of popular culture have provided certain generic explanations for similar phenomena, for example, Mikhail Bakhtin's work on carnival as the temporal suspension and inversion of established structures of domination. Yet Bakhtin's view is detached from the violent materiality of these practices.[87] What comes to mind, from another angle, is Georges Bataille's reflection on expenditure, arguing that the rational control to which "unproductive expenditure" is submitted by a developed Western market economy occurs at a high cost, among which we find the exclusion of the poor from all circles of rationalized social activity.[88] Reading his thoughts on "utility" and "conservation," one might feel tempted to say that, from a contemporary angle, an excessively exchange-value- oriented culture of consumption associates a type of expenditure that destroys the bases of "conservation"—sustainability of the planet, its human and material resources.

Searching for the nerve centers of the sicarios' spending habits, we have to understand their controversial nature. Arendt once formulated: "No man-exerted violence, except the violence used in torture, can match the natural force with which necessity itself compels."[89] As a "libertarian existentialist,"[90] she had no concern whatsoever for the laboring classes at the lower ends of mankind, let alone the informal economies as they affect primarily modernity's peripheries. Her thoughts were guided by the intention to discuss an assumption of Marx from the advanced territories of *homo faber*, the fabricator of things. Arendt historicized a logic of modernity as follows: "It is as though the growing elimination of violence throughout the modern age almost automatically opened the doors for the re-entry of necessity on its most elementary level." Differently put, in the age of industrial capitalism, a turn from noneconomic violence to the dominance of economic forms of oppression occurred: necessity starts compelling without visible coercion. Marx proposed the utopian idea of surmounting the separation of labor-power from the means of production—the political emancipation of laborers. Thus, living labor as the "subjective factor," once emancipated, was supposed to diminish (and finally overcome) necessity by submitting the objective factors of nature and technology to its collective interests. Arendt, in contrast, perceived the emergence of a consumers' society as an extreme form of emancipation of the laboring activity itself (as distinct from that of the laborers). For her, consumption after mid-twentieth century epitomized the degradation of humans toward "making a living"—away from the political concerns of public life—and an abundance of the resources that provide for limitless consumption. But what does it really mean that modern age is supposed to result in "forcing all mankind for the first time under the yoke of necessity"? Is there reason to wonder "whether the utopia of yesterday"— the eventual liberation from necessity—"will not turn into the reality of tomorrow," to the point that "nearly all human labor power is spent in consuming, with the concomitant serious social problem of leisure," etcetera? Or does the neoliberal revamping of the organization of labor suggest a reading from a more timely vantage point? In other words, the "paradise of consumption" is not, as Arendt believed, the "age-old dream of the poor and destitute," that threatens to become "a fool's paradise"[91] as soon as capitalism makes it a reality. Consumption and its annihilatory forces have been built into an increasing biopolitical control of the human condition on the grounds of its "modern" vulnerability. As the Colombian phenomenon of the culture of exception makes perceptible, the "paradise of consumption," besides eroding the public realm as the center of a politically qualified life (*vita activa*), risks sudden collapse or, literally, the destruction of life in its most valuable state—childhood and adolescence.

It is important to problematize the puzzling relationship between consumption and sacred labor. If, according to Salazar's testimony, Colombian sicarios are the deterritorialized and debased, yet all the more desiring victims of commodity fetishism, why does the fetishistic aspect of their behavior look so complex? Given the amounts of money that the hitboys, now and again, make in some excess, and viewed from the point of view of exchange value, the products they purchase, except for the weapons, are entirely banal. Above all, their "economic" behavior does not respect market ideology as it serves the accumulation of capital. For them, the main fetish is not the tangible and representative commodity that successful gang leaders could eventually afford but *el billete* as such. The muchachos do not regard money as capital—as an exchange value that can beget ever growing values—but as a potential for radical use. Money is a fetish that allows audacious and excessive spending, its only rational aspect being the support that is lent to the mothers. As the customs of gang life demonstrate, money is distributed illogically.[92] The earned *billetes* are usually divided between financial help for mothers and families (including the eventual upgrading of their households with refrigerators, TVs, and sound equipment) and, in the first place, outrageous celebration, that a calculating mind would consider to be an abusive, nonproductive luxury. Such an incursion into the universe of exchange values can in no way be subsumed under the concept of striving for a better life. Neither can we explain those fetishistic desires by recurring to the common sensical phrase that the Anglo-American mind invented for labor: "making a living." To make a living implies the immersion of the *animal laborans*, who is occupied with the "devouring processes" of life (Arendt), in the routine of a day-to-day striving whereby the promise of happiness exists in a state of constant deferral. The sicarios reject this state by all the means at their disposal. Society itself has placed them outside the circle where the "universal demand for happiness and the widespread unhappiness"[93] in modern society are mediated by obsessive consumption, so that they can strike an efficient balance. The practices of the neophytes show how this balance is in fact attacked by those whose exclusion from the normative conditions of *animal laborans*—mutated into *animal consumens*—has not succeeded in turning them, to paraphrase Aristotle, into serene suffering beings. Their marginalization has contributed to their entering into a peculiar state of transgression. The astounding feature of this state is this: Salazar's hitboys break the exchange-value chain that Benjamin had identified as part of the guilt-generating spiral of pseudoreligious capitalism. Sicarios do so by submitting earned money to a praxis of excessive profanation. We are dealing with a dystopian practice of utopian scope—consumption as utter expenditure, yet still as a communitarian act among the disenfranchised. In other words, the myth of the "consumer's paradise" collapses when the sicarios turn it against itself.

As we analyze the exorbitant spending and obsessive celebration among Medellin's hitboys, as they present themselves in Salazar's book, we also have to go beyond one of the concepts that has marked the rethinking of popular culture during recent decades: "consumption" understood as *tactics*. "Tactical consumption" would mean, according to de Certeau, the counterpart of a "rationalized, expansionist, centralized, spectacular, and noisy production,"[94] conceiving of "use" as a hybrid activity that allows for an endless decodification and sometimes subversive renarration of established hierarchies. In turn, the practices of consumption that are under discussion are anarchically "strategic," not "tactical." Are we confronting a reemerging form of archaism that lacks any competence for the nonviolent rationales of exchange? Or has the contemporary downsizing of use-value oriented cultures directed at sustainability and restrained growth, together with global conditions under which new social agents arise, generated scenarios where violent noneconomic appropriation erupts precisely in the realm of economic behavior? Let us remember that the unacknowledged aspect of Western commodity culture lies in the administration of "unhappiness" by making the guilt-debt spiral universal (Benjamin): a logic that functions by constant libidinal deferral that ties the *animal consumens* to the permanence of the commodity cult.[95] The following question is essential for understanding the affective stakes of our discussion: what are the deeper effects of the neoliberal promise that are holding "happiness" in today's peripheries at bay, to keep fueling a "wide-spread unhappiness" in the richer countries?[96] The conceptual implications of Salazar's narrative are severe: what if, at the point at which the "human animal" reaches its most destitute condition, the market-regulated balance between labor and consumption enters into an unforeseen dilemma, together with the emergence of forms of sacrificial violence that threaten society as a whole? The sicarios' practices provide a space for imagination that unveils that the nightmare of the culture of exception is not just an accident. It stands, rather, for a symptom showing how market- and profit-driven globalization, intersecting with a national crisis of state sovereignty, and the rise of the narcotics economy, have together disturbed any human consistency between the individual, the social, and a publicly organized civilian space that might still lend the subject of modernity its ethical name.

Let us remember the first and the last scenes in Antonio's dream in "We're the Kings of the World." The fatally wounded sicario, dreaming his last dream, envisions a return home within the space of his death, leaving us with a difficult question. How can the destructive order of things, where the transcendental God is absent, be intercepted in such a way that being at home in the midst of catastrophe can still be imagined? Is there an ethical place left, able to contradict—from within—"the passage of the planet 'Human' through the house of despair?"[97] How troubled has the relationship between religion and ethics become, after all? Salazar holds that, under the modernization of the region of Antioquia and especially Medellín during the second half of the twentieth century, religion and ethics have drastically fallen apart. His intention is not to restate an abstract claim of secularization—to wrest ethics away from religion—, but to elucidate how parts of regional Catholic traditions have metamorphosed into an economic ideology that values monetary success by all means and at all costs ("a religious-empresarial formulation").[98] As revealing as this observation may be regarding the structures of local economic politics, and especially the incorporation of patriarchal elites into the expanding narcotraffic of the 1970s and 1980s, it is equally incomplete for explaining the dystopian economic behavior of the forgotten youth. Catholic-based values and affiliations have contributed to the game of powerful players of violence in various contexts of Colombian history. However, nothing is more deceptive than the appearance of religiosity in the behavior of the violent gangs. We will now consider, at last, how *We Were Not Born to Life* contributes to destabilizing an ominous notion of guilt, one that has come to characterize capitalist culture at the point where the crisis of secularization turns out to be linked to the pseudo-ritualistic dimension on which commodity fetishism relies.

Recalling Benjamin's seminal remark from his fragment "Capitalism as Religion," we can address the concept of guilt at a particular conjuncture at which, in the culture of exception, religious behavior and the imagination of righteousness intersect. Sicarios commit murder while observing certain Catholic practices (obsessively wearing "escapularios" and visiting church), yet they do not strive for atonement. The worship of local versions of the Holy Virgin (and of their own mothers), as well as prayer, is used by them to be successful in their adventures, and importantly—to stay alive while others are "put to bed," which lends the question of guilt an even stronger tone. When Antonio, only twenty years old, is "about to take off from this world,"[99] he declares that he does not feel guilty, except for regretting the fact that his elderly mother will be without his support in her struggle to survive. Only mothers could, under these circumstances, generate feelings of guilt, for their secret mission has always been to provide relief to their adolescent sons. On the one hand, what is missing in muchachos like Antonio is any feeling of guilt similar to the standing moral habitus inherent in Christian belief. Guilt is also absent, as we have observed, relating to the law pertaining to the order and the myth of the state. Nevertheless, sicarios follow a codex of mandates that defines the relationships between duty and guilt in unconditional terms. A guiding rule of behavior for those living on the edge is defined by the verb *cumplir*. To "comply" refers to the task at hand, an order to kill someone and to the mutual relationships among the participating hitboys.

"To have complied" means to be free in a mystical sense. This kind of freedom is first circumscribed as a relationship between the muchachos and their *trabajo*. It means to leave virtually no duty or commitment behind, a connotation that is closely related to living on the edge of existence. If we think genealogically of the imaginary figures of *the bandit* or the outlaw, this state of freedom does not quite resemble the image of the *Friedlos* (the "man without peace"), which permeates popular legends and romantic literatures.[100] It rather resonates with Marx's description of the person who becomes "vogelfrei" ("bird-free") in the process of capitalist accumulation, especially under the proviso of primitive accumulation. However, a singular aspect of the culture of the sicarios relates to their peculiar moralizing stance. For them, the opposite of freedom is the state of duty or debt when it persists unpunished over time, spelled out by the slangy neologisms *falsear*, or *faltonear*. *Faltonear* signals a behavior that continually owes something to someone, a condition that the debtor is supposed to pay off with his life. This kind of "debt-fetishism,"[101] practiced among the neophytes by "leaving nothing behind" is strangely discordant with the worker's freedom to sell his labor, as well as with the outlaw's indebtedness to sovereign power. It would have to be labeled an aberrant form of egalitarianism relying on a moral superlative, as it has functioned, to keep intact the structure of the teenaged gangs of northeast Medellín during the late 1980s.

To appreciate the practical meaning of this state we have to consider the notion of the gift. One approved relationship between gang members is referred to as generosity, and it equals respecting—even celebrating—an unwritten law. Antonio remembers his vigorous times by affirming, "we helped each other a lot"; "...if you don't have any of this and I do, then I give it to you. Understand? Not a loan but a gift. And if somebody's bad off, you give to him, too. But you can never keep owing something." The gift appears as a crucial regulatory element of exchange between sicarios but also between "serious" gang leaders and the inhabitants of the barrios where they have established their dominance. The standing term for supporting the neigborhood is *colaborar*, collaborate with needy people.[102] Collaboration is what has been described as wasteful spending—radical expenditure.

A double tendency speaks out of the fetishism of the hitboys, one that we now recognize as their radical attitude regarding guilt. Theirs could even be termed a merciless *war on guilt*. The muchachos reject, via *sacred labor* (as they are unable to gain "normal" access to labor, in their marginality), the enslaving mechanism of making a living. What they disdain is a reality where the "yoke of necessity" would besiege the laborers with torturous routine. The sicarios are obsessed by ostentatiously spending their money with nothing left over. During their communal fiestas, abundance is celebrated, comparable to a simulacrum of plenitude that can afford spending wealth in one single act. At first glance, the triumph of consumerism as it is instituted by the global market seems unrefutable. However, this interpretation would be misleading. For many sicarios, the rejection of guilt implies a distancing from the formal practices linked to the debt economy as an instrument to increase capital and thus augment wealth among a select few. Leading an existence at the edge of life, and free of guilt, the neophytes "save" their violently obtained income from reinvestment by anarchic spending. Wanting all or nothing, and "not born for life," sicarios perform a terrifying simulacrum of the Marxian dream—the overcoming of alienating labor. Immanent in their behavior, their language, and unwritten rules is an ethics that propels them to fight guilt from an extreme end of exposure. Their triumph over the hypocritically deferred happiness on which a hegemonic market culture relies appears to be directed against labor as such. For them, labor has never been an instrument for a "man-made" world. Their violent perversion of necessity through rituals of sacrifice and by their ecstasy of spending has undermined the religious-capitalist spiral of guilt. If the Western universal dream of happiness persists, today, by reproducing widespread unhappiness, sicarios have created their own dream of fulfillment. In their impending mortality they cannot demand to be happy. Instead, they are driven by a desire to be free, free of the curse of docile bare life as it is prescribed by poverty or subjugation—that means free of guilt. Their actions and dreams, within the culture of exception, betray an ethical craving at the expense of Christian religion—and of an equitable human life itself.

POSTSCRIPTUM

Finally, Salazar's project requires that one make a distinction between an aberrant ethics of action and an ethics of narration. We have explored how Salazar lends his marginal protagonists an *ipse*—a singular narrative identity. The author does so by establishing a relationship that rests on his faculty of conferring a gift—the gesture of writing life stories for the sicarios, not in their name. There is no justification for Salazar other than telling stories that are not his own, which means that his is not a project of authorship structured around his own substantial self. One might argue that his narration does not appeal to the protagonists of *We Were Not Born to Life* as it does to the reading public, or that he has given a subjective signature to material he encountered in Medellín's hotbed of violence. However, it is the reciprocal activity expressed by his role as the storytaker before he turns into the storyteller that constitutes the basis for his public statement in the form of the text. There is no doubt, the writer has committed himself to life as opposed to violence. This engagement rests on an ethical complicity that has enabled him to prevent his project from turning into a moralizing gesture vis-à-vis criminal behavior, as much as it resists the desire to produce an artistically outstanding text. Could we still assume—in an Arendtian fashion—that the value of the "narratable self"[103] is to be accessed in terms of unique life-stories, so that each of the violent sicarios would excel in his distinctive being? In contrast, if we'd referred to them as a collective plural, where would the uniqueness of their identity lie, the way it is related in *We Were Not Born to Life*? How do we recognize in the words of Antonio, Níver, and Mario an experience that only they can provide in unrepeatable form? Salazar avoids the figure of a collective protagonist, so to speak. The narrative is compelling because of the peculiar singularization of the collective phenomenon.

It is the imminence of death within the culture of exception from which Salazar has wrested the epic force sustaining his book. It grounds its strength in the discovery that sicarios, exempt from the possibility of advanced age, possess an astonishing authority—the authority of youngsters alive but soon to be dead, from which "the unforgettable emerges."[104] *We Were Not Born to Life* calls for us to uncover the feelings, images, and peripeties among which these muchachos have made their terrible choices without even being aware of having done so. Adopting Orwell's assertion that conditions abound under which "human life cannot be lived at all,"[105] and having been introduced into contemporary spaces where life is placed within a permanent state of sacrifice, we are struck by the sensation that each of Salazar's protagonists possesses an unrepeatable posture. More to the point, the more the narrative withholds specific psychological and physical traits that could make them tangible as individuals, the more it omits descriptions of the dreadful violence that accompanies sicarios in real life, together with the flagrant face of murder. It is not terror but experience that plays its strong part in this extraordinary book, and narrative experience is something that is to be shared. But is it at all legitimate to ask *who* the sicarios are (to search for the narratable self), given *what* they have done? We cannot decide on the ethical dimension of the book on the basis of this question alone, because there is the fact of the gift preceding (or following) this kind of question, crystallized in a singular, nonviolent narrative pact between Salazar and the testimonial actors. If radical otherness, or more precisely, the singularity of a culture of exception, can tell stories that are taken on by others—connected to precarious lives whose stories only the others can and will recognize and recount—, then violence may have succeeded in cancelling the possibility of truthful representation. But it has not been able to suspend wisdom—the wisdom that lies in shared experience, as incomplete as it may be. We can say that Salazar's attitude is expressed in an inversion of the sentence that concludes one of Benjamin's essays: "The storyteller is the figure in which the righteous man encounters himself."[106] Muchachos like Antonio and Níver, and so many others, who have labored by killing people and have been killed themselves, could never—while alive—opt for a legitimate morality. The discovery of their *narratable selves*, however, can place their memories vis-à-vis the exception, although their identity remains bound to the intolerable state: not having been born to life.

CHAPTER 6

Autobiography as Eschatological Project: An Intellectual Struggle Regarding Freedom and Guilt

Approaching Ritualistic Masculinity: Our Lady of the Assassins (Fernando Vallejo)

If there is a book that has invented a strategy of abjection by incorporating the figure of the sicario into a raging tale of transgression, it is Fernando Vallejo's novel, *La Virgen de los Sicarios* (1994; *Our Lady of the Assassins*, 2001). Different from *We Were Not Born to Life* and its artistic asceticism, this text has the power to excite a literary community of global scope, and it has provided the storyline for a successful film directed by Barbet Schroeder (1999). Differently from existing assessments, we contend that *Our Lady of the Assassins* is not a narrative essentially dedicated to adolescent sicarios but rather to the problematic of the intellectual Self that, as we read at the beginning, can "make[s] you want to give humanity a kick on the ass, send it headlong over the cliff of eternity so that it vacates the earth and never comes back."[1] The first-person narrator of the same name of Fernando, is an allegedly famous Colombian writer, who excels by an extraordinary fundamentalist rhetoric, driven by an obsession to attract by appalling. The novel has the capacity to injure, to injure by language and by argument.[2] We may eventually perceive Vallejo's project to aim at a verbal assault directed at the text's readers, generating effects that make Charles Lawrence's characterization of racist speech that it produces the perception of "receiving a slap in the face,"[3] a somewhat milder innuendo.

There have been several attempts to place Vallejo's novel within established literary frameworks. Assertions that *Our Lady of the Assassins* "constitutes some of the most challenging writing of the Colombian post-Boom period,"[4] rely on presupposed evidence. Terms such as "boom" and "post-boom" continue to haunt the unconscious of parts of Latin Americanist literary studies, as though a controversial aesthetic and political imagination could be conceptualized by historicist axioms and molds of fiction. In a more sarcastic vein, the Colombian writer Héctor Abad Faciolince coined the term "sicaresca"[5] to typify a tendency within Colombian literature that deals with the destinies of young hitmen from the marginal barrios of Medellín and Bogotá,—"sicaresca" a play on the Spanish genre denomination, "picaresca." Critics are eager to adopt labels of this sort, yet one should be skeptical about the stylish alliteration. It operates on the basis of a metaphoric and phonetic deduction. de Man's dictate applies to this case: "Metaphor is error because it believes or feigns to believe in its own referential meaning."[6] Symbolically speaking, the picaresque novel has earned a respectable place since it was appropriated in the service of a literature of manners offering, in Harry Sieber's reading of Stephen Greenblatt, "an integrated rhetoric of the self, a model for the formation of an artificial identity." Morally speaking, the "pícaro," the masculine marginal in the "growing urban population that contributed to Madrid's demographic explosion at the end of the sixteenth century,"[7] overcomes his precarious position by obtaining, at last, a place within the ruling social pact. Neither premise holds for the figure of the "sicario" the way it is portrayed and imagined, in entirely different ways, by Salazar and Vallejo. In *Our Lady of the Assassins*, the sicario will appear as a figure that is taken into service, and later dispensed by the intellectual hero—the narrator Fernando.

For better or worse, Vallejo's novel confronts the literary scholar with more disturbing issues. One of the questions that it makes resonate with deep irony could read as follows: Is there a vantage point of the literary and the political, from which both postmodern as well as properly modern writing strategies are susceptible to being led into collapse? Few critics have ventured into such perilous terrain, a region where unwelcome rencontres set the tone for interpretation of, for example, a *ménage a trois* of religiosity, violence, and perturbing imagination, fused into a literary event of considerable power. A problem pertaining to the incongruences between rhetorics and poetry or, differently put, to the status of the work of fine art since Kant is placed at center stage: what would it mean when the assumption of the freedom of "artistic" writing is confronted with virtual aggression whose agency is . . . fictional discourse? In *Our Lady of the Assassins*, aggressive acts can be perceived in the narrator's diatribes directed toward the assumed reader. These reproaches are set in the registers of literary "free speech," but they are also being reproduced on a different level—that of Vallejo's rampant public discourse from the moment he becomes a well-known author.[8] The relationship between the "secondary levels" of aesthetic experience (linked to modes of reflexivity) and "primary aesthetic identification" (on the basis of explicit judgments and strong emotions) is not simply a stylistic question that postmodern writing has succeeded in dehierarchizing and ironizing, as Hans-Robert Jauß, among others, has contended.[9] It is a relationship that may have its actual matter in affective as intellectual commitment, to the extent that literary writing is susceptible to turning into polemical ethical discourse.

Le Figaro Littéraire has produced a marketing label that gives the novel an esoteric rank between refinement and exaggeration: the book is said to present the most beautiful tale of deliriousness that "literature has bestowed on us in a long time."[10] Vallejo's maneuver is in any case skillful, and it might be interesting to recall Barthes' treatise on Ignacio Loyola in which the French author makes evident the timeliness of the Jesuits' contribution to the artifices of Western literature.[11] With a perception of the aporias of Western culture that is as ample as Auerbach's, Barthes shows that interpretive reason should be alert to the manifold connections between sophisticated composition and doctrinary discourse. Regarding *Our Lady of the Assassins*, it is astounding that critics have overlooked a stratagem that our study will analyze, one that consists of surrendering aesthetic reflexivity to religious metaphorization. Both a modernist and a Weberian concept of culture have helped dismiss certain moral issues as irrelevant for the literary specialist vis-à-vis a distant academic neighbor, the theologian. Vallejo, when he calls his narrator a "letrado," an educated man, does away with such modern differentiation of labor. What if the author desired, suddenly, to reinvent himself as a Platonist literary subject searching for Christian values to be built on the ruins of a shipwrecked profane world? Benevolent readers appear to believe that the novelist carries an ontological mission of dissent, even when humming the demagogic melody. Is not the Jesuitical lesson referred to by Barthes the one that makes rhetorical goals especially succinct when they are placed in multilayered fiction? To put it differently, might we not overlook the sublime vibrations of power, its "sweet coloniality," if we requested that violence reveal its authentic, unmediated expression to be taken at face value? Even in that case, Vallejo's novel stands as a bold statement in which the obvious is nevertheless difficult to assess, making us wonder, what makes violence so perplexing when it comes disguised as eloquent discourse?

Franco reads the narrator's project in *Our Lady of the Assassins* as one that advocates the loss of all criteria of both meaning and value.[12] It may be that the scholar, for ethical reasons, eschews the grimace of a "letrado" who will not refrain from making terror axiomatic and meaning controversial, yet who is far from lacking criteria of value as well as historical judgment. For there is a difference between the narrator's attacking the "corruption and collapse of civil society" and a moralizing project that offers absolution from responsibility when the narrator himself is driven to violence. To anticipate one of our hypotheses, absolution from guilt,[13] however, may not be the central question raised by the novel. It is rather the creation of a new circle of guilt and punishment in which violence becomes a foundational intellectual act. The following dictum of the autobiographical narrator is not a balance but a point of departure: "I am the memory of Colombia and its conscience...."[14] There has been a strange hesitance to submit the novel to scrutiny. The traps and artifices Vallejo has set out are real, and critics even tend to approve of the narrator's exorbitant ego by softening its discursive constituents.[15] Does the literary self, disguised as a renowned writer, really have to be "'our' ally"? Franco leans toward an interpretation in which the strategic affinity between "lettered hero" and "lettered readers" should prevail, or where an ironic reading should provide a last proof of doubt: "The question is whether he [the narrator] is deliberately forcing us to face the 'fascist within' or whether he expects our complicity."[16] A map of debatable issues is taking shape. Yet, interpretation seems to become powerless at the very moment when the novel pushes readers into its vortex. Assessing this situation implies questioning the unity of the literary work. Cultural battlefields are marked by transgression. As coherent as it may seem to place Vallejo's novel within a compulsive realm of new novelistic texts on violence, it is necessary to show how the novel is traversed by and has itself become an agent within a wider *querelle* (dispute).

Let us look at the actual narrative features of *Our Lady of the Assassins*. The protagonist, named Fernando like the author, speaks in first person singular and calls himself a famed philologist. Throughout the book a perspective prevails that fuses narrator and protagonist into one agency—the voice of the "grammarian." It is a voice—allegedly autobiographical—that, by moving ahead in first-person narration, directly comments on Fernando's actions and expresses his convictions, in addition to calling upon the reader. The reader is often addressed pejoratively, "because I know you won't know the word," "something you've never even heard of, I bet," or "my idiot friend."[17] The entire construction is somewhat unusual if we look for specific genre characteristics. Whereas autobiography tends to evoke the past, as it indulges in the hidden, complex dimensions of a narrating self, what surfaces in the novel is a torrent of inexorable statements, together with the momentous actions of the "grammarian" for which he himself becomes chronicler and guide.

Having spent the active part of his life abroad, Fernando returns to his place of birth, Medellín. The return to Colombia, "the world's most notorious cradle of violence," serves a double strategy. It helps to aggravate the tensions between his self and the world. Second, it provides the center stage for living out his desire of coming home, be it physically or transcendentally. It is not the sublime longing of a lonely individual for a place to die that structures the novel. Vallejo has elected an element of insubordination that equals, in the words of his protagonist, the true residue of love in a miserable, mendacious world: young sicarios who are gay. The aged "grammarian" falls in love with the hitboy Alexis, and later with Wilmar, whom he calls *mis niños*, my children. One must learn about the spectacle of initiation accompanying Fernando's return to Colombia. The real coming home sets out, apart from the hero's visit to his birth village Sabaneta and the church that hosts the Virgin Maria Auxiliadora, from an apartment owned by "José Antonio Vasquez"—Fernando's old gay friend and a survivor of the "antediluvian Medellín."[18]

> 'Here, I'm making you a present of this beauty', José Antonio said when he presented me to Alexis. 'He's already got ten or more victims to his name.'[19]

The setting for initiating a homosexual romance gives Medellín a mythic flair. As Fernando enters, together with Alexis, the butterfly room, he is surrounded by innumerable old dead clocks, all stopped at different moments. How does this reliquary relate to the hitboys? Young homosexual sicarios like Alexis come and go without the host "laying a finger on them." A threshold situation through which Fernando's search is put into perspective becomes manifest. This point of departure has a ritualistic bearing, and throughout the book it will guide the flame of imagination that nurtures the protagonist's fate.

> ...through the apartment of José Antonio's, in amongst its clocks stopped like dates on the tombstones in a cemetery, there passed an infinite number of very alive boys. Or rather, I mean to say, alive today and dead tomorrow....[20]

The second detail characterizing the spot, in addition to the mute clocks, is a "furious television" from which one soap opera after the other spews forth, insinuating a peculiar duality in the lives of the sicarios: "emptiness" and death on the one hand, a pervasive flood of images and noises on the other. Yet one keeps asking, what is this strange, shadowy apartment all about?

> Just what did José Antonio gain from that coming and going of young men, of criminals, through his house? That they might rob him? Might kill him? Or is it that his apartment was maybe a brothel? God forbid. José Antonio is the most generous character I've ever known. And I say character and not person or human being because that's what he is, a character, like something from a novel, something not encountered in real life.[21]

Asked from a different perspective, what can people like our hero the grammarian gain from a meeting place like this? Fernando's statement shows that he acts as the observer-participant of his own initiation.

> ...who but he [José Antonio, the antedeluvian character] would take it into his head to make presents of young boys, the best present there is? "These boys belong to nobody," says he, "they belong to whoever needs them." Put like that, this is Communism; but the way he put it into practice was a work of charity, the fifteenth good work missing from the catechism, the greatest and noblest of all, more noble than giving drink to the thirsty man or helping the dying man die in peace.[22]

As we read about "making presents of young boys,..." we can recall the caprices inherent in aristocratic practice, present in different historical scenarios. One might even think of Plato's allusion to adolescent homosexual eros as an inspiration for the search for sublime ideas, together with the philosophical and moral debate leading from Plato, Xenophon, Isokrates, and Aristotle to Foucault and continuing still further.[23] More obviously, what comes to mind is the figure of giving privileges to selected adolescent boys of poor descent in exchange for homoerotic devotion. In Vallejo's novel, an initial constellation is set up that spans homelessness and adoption, and which anticipates the reversal of common rules of the game. There must be something ceremonial that suspends the more immediate possibilities of José Antonio's place—like, for example, the host's active involvement with violence and crime, the sicarios' serving his practical interests, or the consumption of drugs and the indulgence in worldly pleasures, among others. But none of the profane sorts of business deals, criminal conspiracies, and addictive entertainment occurs, as Fernando, the newcomer, asserts. The "temple" emerges as a place of superior, nonutilitarian exchange. Subject to this exchange are boys who "belong to nobody."

When Fernando starts acknowledging his concern with the neophytes of violence, he evokes his defunct grandfather, who was a farm owner, a Catholic, and patriarchal figure. "Dear Grandfather, if by chance you can hear me from the other end of eternity, I'm going to tell you what a hitman is: it's a young guy, sometimes a kid, who kills to order." When the narrator continues his explanation, alluding to the absence of the father in the lives of the sicarios, he knows that his autobiographical tale will not touch upon his own father either. In the region of Antioquia, homosexuality was not an option in Catholic families of oligarchic descent. But this is an aspect about which he will keep silent, as much as his accumulated wrath may bear the signs of repression. "And the men? In general, they're not men; here, the hitmen are kids or young guys, twelve, fifteen, seventeen years old..." When Fernando keeps talking about the mythic apartment, we encounter José Antonio as the friend whose advanced age has "cured" him of any active homosexual joy, thereby allowing him to reach "perfection" by hosting "los muchachos" without touching them. At this point, for Fernando, any personal genealogical traces are erased by the new adventure, in which José Antonio acts as a kind of ideal father figure for the grammarian. Fernando, who has no children and prefers not to remember his own mother, needs to rebuild his autobiographical base. He will henceforth refer to his lovers, the hitboys Alexis and Wilmar, as *mis niños*, my children, for whom he develops a most complex affection. Here, the role of the "temple" erected by the surreal José Antonio becomes pertinent: it is a place for adoption created through intimate rules of exception. The exception is defined as "communism," and "the greatest and noblest work of charity." Available for adoption are the neophytes of violence, "alive today and dead tomorrow," "murdered young murderers, freed of the ignominies of old age by flagrant dagger or compassionate bullet," with the only prerequisite being that they be gay. There is no doubt for Fernando, who does not cease to complain about Colombia's fall, that the real exception from where the sicarios originate lies in the country's political and economic situation.[24] This way, the mythic place from which his actual coming home begins can be viewed as an "exception within the exception." This second exception will inspire the hero to work on his own sovereign ambitions as Colombia's "last" intellectual.

A place like the one described can be thought of as a sacred territory, within which select encounters are performed, if there is an authority that sicarios are neither competing with nor working for. A power to whose rules the young criminals would happily obey: a suspense of the other exception—the real one—that they are fiercefully confronting daily. If the visiting sicarios "belong to nobody," they might remind us of the bare life of poverty-stricken adolescents who take refuge in violence to survive, and who are now meeting at José Antonio's in an act of self-exoneration in exchange for certain privileges. Is there, in the scenario of initiation, a force of subjection at work, one that has the power to lead the muchachos away from being subjects and victims of violence, to becoming objects of charity? Or, on a different note, is there perhaps a secret force being exerted by the sicarios over their benefactors? How can we understand that Alexis, Fernando's first lover and a crude hitguy, not only delicately respects the hero's belongings and well-being, but treats the grammarian with utmost devotion? At the point at which certain things are "not done," and the intention of doing them hardly arises, who would not think of the refined standards sometimes associated with homosexual behavior? Yet, we are dealing with an initiation that leads the protagonist to an empowerment that will turn out to be violent in itself.

Fernando's relationship with Alexis, the muchacho who is given to him and takes him to the butterfly room, starts with the mutual experience of falling in love, followed by a story of adoption. Adopting the sicario is not an act whose consequences will include the older man's taking care of the future of the teenager. It is rather a gesture of empowerment, driven by the desire for a pact that helps the man transcend ordinary life: "Alexis began undressing me and me undressing him; he with an innocent spontaneity, as if he'd known me forever, as if he were my guardian angel." The romantic affiliation produces and from now on will give rise, on Fernando's part, to an apotheotic vision. "I realised that Alexis didn't correspond to the laws of this world; and I, who hadn't believed in God for a long time, stopped believing in the law of gravity."[25] It appears as though the homosexual hitboy represented, for the protagonist, a radically masculine path to God. But since God is out of place in this world, especially in Colombia, a ritual of incorporation is needed, an experience through which a holy substance is incorporated into the intellectual self. What prefigures this incorporation is the encounter with an image the grammarian had been longing for a long time: the Guardian Angel.

Scholars have overlooked the theological matrix that traverses *Our Lady of the Assassins*, taken in by a title that seems to foreground the religiosity of the sicarios. It is Fernando, however, who seizes on the pathos of revelation and self-apotheosis as devices for organizing his "autobiographical" course.

For him, calling on the closeness of death and decline is a rhetorical means that helps to prepare his transcendental path. Death, the idea that looms large from the beginning of the novel shall give the longed-for unity to his life. Surprisingly, it does not function as a vantage point of remembrance and reflection but is eventually turned into the instrument of manic intellectual sublimation. The autobiographical edifice is thus only the lose frame that accommodates the nexus between the described ritual of initiation and what will turn out as an active incursion in the reign of terror.

"Vir Clarisimus—Unum et Idem—Summum Jus": The Reinvention of the Master and the Battle of Language

Fernando, who in a clumsy allusion to Nietzsche,[26] claims that "a person doesn't know what he is thinking himself" and opts not to rationalize the sicarios' crimes either, knows from the beginning the words that should be engraved about him in eternity. It should say, next to his name and in capital letters, in Latin, to one side of the door of the house where he was born, at the moment when death "rounds off the epitaph": "*Vir clarisimus, grammaticus conspicuus, philologus illustrisimus, quoque pius, placatus, politus, plagosus, fraternus, placidus, unum et idem e pluribus unum, summum jus, hic natus atque mortuus est...*" The lettered man is striving for a self that can be solidified—via distinguished language—into a lasting, publicly elevated quality. A temporal indication frames the image: "And there they would put the year the plaque was installed, not the years of my birth and death, because I'm a believer in not constraining eternity between two dates, as if in a straitjacket."[27] Obsessed with the idea of eternity, Fernando aspires to supersede the frailty of human affairs with the power of his illocutionary speech,[28] trying to lay bare, and then, to purge, a degenerated world that finds its apocalyptic scenario in the city of his birth, Medellín.

Among the surprising traits of Vallejo's novel is the fact that the author, who constructs a narrator bearing his name, discards any arbitrary aspect that could be implied by the search for an exclusive identity. He is even less concerned about the possibility that the notion of the lettered subject might in itself result problematic. The enunciation chosen for when Fernando enters abstract time, a time carved in Latin words, is articulated as a foundational act of naming: *unum et idem e pluribus unum, summum jus*. Let us recall an aporetic concept of the name. A name is the most immediate and, at the same time, the most elusive way of addressing an individual's self. There is, for example, Ricoeur's doubt when pointing to the strange permanence of a "proper name." "What justifies our taking the subject of an action, so designated by his, her, or its proper name, as the same throughout a life that stretches from birth to death?" Ricoeur is offering an Arendtian formulation—the answer to the question of "who" the subject of a *bios* (a life that merits a biography) is "is to tell the story of a life,"[29] that is to say, to confer a diversity of meanings to one single name. Vallejo's *grammaticus* heightens his celebrity carved in Latin, yet refrains from telling the story that could emerge from his past. This man, who has returned to Medellín "in order to die," withholds the clues that could tell us *how* he became the outstanding grammarian he claims that he is. He also refrains from disclosing the roots of "the same tired rancour that forgets all grievances, being too lazy to remember them."[30] When Vallejo withholds the life story of the autobiographical subject, except for acknowledging the childhood local-ity of Sabaneta, he instead provides the demand for an essence, fused into the Latin epitaph. From here, Fernando can act as a missionary, discarding any collateral experience and making his task abundantly clear: "I am the memory of Colombia and its conscience and after me comes nothing,"[31] equalling perhaps the delirious claim of a lettered outsider for hegemony at the point of the nation's catastrophe. What allows the novel to make a bold strike against aesthetic expectations is the way the self-empowerment of its protagonist is sculpted, as well as the virtual absence of distancing devices in that regard. The rhetorical stance of the narrating subject is overbearing, and the entire novel excels owing to its peremptory tone.

The replacement for Fernando's missing life story is a fleeting childhood nostalgia contrasting with an abominable present that is marked by the agony of the home country. Let us follow Ricoeur's unraveling of the paradoxes that span the concepts of identity and narrative.

> To answer the question "Who?" as Hannah Arendt has so forcefully put it, is to tell the story of a life...Without the recourse to narration, the problem of personal identity would in fact be condemned to an antinomy with no solu-tion. Either we must posit a subject identical with itself through the diver-sity of its different stages, or, following Hume and Nietzsche, we must hold that this identical subject is nothing more than a substantialist illusion, whose elimination merely brings to light a pure manifold of cognitions, emotions, and volitions.[32]

The described dilemma disappears at the point at which identity can be perceived as a practical category, when "we substitute for identity under-stood in the sense of being the same (*idem*) identity understood in the sense of oneself as self-same [soi-même] (*ipse*). The difference between idem and ipse is nothing more than the difference between a substantial or formal identity and a narrative identity."[33] In the event that no reified narrative exists, then the *ipse* finds its script in the actions and experiences that, taken together, conform the potential life story (Arendt). The distinction between *idem* and *ipse* has an implication that neither Arendt nor Ricoeur addresses. How do we perceive and describe the narrative identity of creatures, such as the sicarios, who even a non-Platonic discourse is likely to ignore? On the other hand, how can we be mindful about that flaw that is now and again ingrained in the work of literary criticism: to conflate *idem* and *ipse*, due to the claim that fiction essentially embody narration. If, indeed, nar-rative should be understood in the sense of a practical category, then at least the possibility should be conceded that stories "resulting from action" can be "misconstructed as fictional stories" when they rely on authors who "pull the strings and direct the play."[34] Or inversely, fictional stories can be understood as ruling over "stories of action," qualifying an identity for representation. This holds, of course, for Salazar's narrative project as well. However, it is here that the differences between both writers could hardly be more emblematic.

Our reflections on Vallejo's novel can thus be carried further by recalling an ethical crux that we addressed when discussing *We Were Not Born to Life*. What is the literary status of the adolescent criminals from the *comunas* of Medellín—those subjects who could not be the authors of their own stories, but who carry a unique potential for narratable selves? Would not the autobiographical question of *who* Fernando, the grammarian, really is become more pertinent when we simultaneously ask *who* the young sicarios are? Can a narrative self-constancy be attributed to the figures of the hitboy Alexis, and later to Wilmar? Once we ask this question through the lens of Fernando's desire, the accent shifts: what is the identity of the sicarios supposed to be? What does it need to be for the *grammaticus* to slip into a universal self? It is here that the question of *purity*, together with that of "absolute truth," emerges within the novelistic realm. A look into Fernando's and Alexis's views about women becomes pertinent, and we notice how Alexis' voice—speaking in focalizing terms—is "taken by the hand" by the Master. Throughout the novel, Alexis' perspective is embedded in the enunciation of the protagonist who either directly addresses his lover ("See here, Alexis . . ."; *Our Lady of the Assassins*, 10), or refers to him through indirect personal speech: "he asked me if I liked women."

> . . . for me it was as if women didn't have souls. Empty upstairs. And for that reason love was impossible with them. "It's 'cause I studied with the Salesian Fathers at the Colegio de Sufragio. Through them I learnt that a carnal relationship with women is tantamount to the sin of bestiality, which is when one member of one species is crossed with a member of another species, like for instance a donkey with a cow. You get me?" Then, knowing that he was going to answer yes, and so as not to let him, I threw the question back at him and asked if he liked women. "No," he replied, with a "no" so emphatic, so unexpected, that it left me speechless. It was a "no" for all time: for the present, for the past, for the future and for all God's eternity: he'd not slept with one nor did he ever intend to. Alexis was unpredictable and was turning out to be more extremist than even me. So that was what was behind those green eyes, then, a purity unsullied by women. And the absolute truth, without extenuating circumstances or it mattering a damn what you think, is what I stick to. That was what I'd fallen in love with. His truthfulness.[35]

By this skillfully hegemonic focalization, the sicario is converted into an "absolute being"—the discursive invention of the sacred creature. A delicate moment has arrived, in that it initiates the novel's evolution into a treatise of truth statements, as they are formulated in response to Colombian contemporaneity. Fernando perceives the development of his country as a degeneration qua feminization, which is said to be due to a procreative mentality that punishes the country with poverty, and to the weakness and corruption of state authority[36] together with the catastrophe of the nation. An idiom is set forth whose determination is stunning. In Colombia, what "all poor people know how to do, along with having kids" is "to beg, beg, beg." In an eschatological image that introduces the core issue of guilt, we find assembled together procreative femininity, poverty as a massive body of perversion, and uncontrolled violence.

> Neither in Sodom nor in Gomorra nor in Medellín nor in Colombia are there innocents; here, everything that exists is guilty and if it goes on reproducing itself, even more so. The poor produce more poor and misery produces more misery, and the more misery there is, the more killings there are, and the more killing there is, the more dead bodies there are. Such is the law of Medellín, which will henceforth rule throughout the globe. Mark my words. (ibid., 89)

Whereas many people and, according to the testimony of Salazar, especially notorious sicarios in Colombia believe that motherhood is sacred; the *grammaticus* views it as a "genuine lack of Christian charity." He even judges it to be an extreme form of delinquency and guilt, expressed in a picture of wretchedness that "any pregnant human bitch" presents to the rest of the world. In turn, it is from the figure of the sicario who lives at the most radical end of violence that a counter image of purity and truth arises. Hitboys who are gay embody, once and for all, a fundamental renunciation of women. Only in this way can they be turned, like Alexis, into an image of sanctity representing such eternal values as truth, heavenly beauty, and death. When reading, at the beginning, that Colombia is consecrated to Jesus in whose "open breast nestles his bleeding heart,"[37] and, a bit later, that selected young sicarios are destined to complete the work that is still missing from the catechism, one can recognize the role that a sublimized masculine sexuality is bound to play. Between Fernando and Alexis, pleasure reigns without the spark of desire. Love, Fernando holds, is a fireplace without wood that keeps burning, like a miracle, while the fire is out. This attitude may sound oddly old-fashioned, yet it points toward the current state of affairs. For Fernando, what is at stake is the nexus of power, sexuality, and eternal truth. His is a drive toward power that necessitates making the discourse about Colombia universal.

Let me draw an imaginary link between Fernando's "extremist" take on the status of women, and the viewpoint of the German political psychologist Hans Blüher, whose major text is *The Role of Erotics in Male Society* (1921). Blüher's words, written in 1914, are associative, especially regarding the link between homosexuality and state sovereignty.

> What would be the result if we would exclude the whole branch of [homosexual] inversion from the fonds of humanity's libidinal forces? There would be no compulsive sexual drive between man and man. Humanity would be relegated to the family principle, and the family—as is well known—never constitutes the basis of the State.[38]

The concept of "inverted" charismatic men in favor of illuminating male adolescents was directly informed, in Blüher's vision, by the desire to engage in the "essential sociological event of the socio-human formation of the state."[39] There are reasons for pursuing this connection. What is the strategic function of religious speech in Vallejo's text? Are we concerned with just an individual search for eternity? Fernando's claim that he represents the memory of his country is not an allegory but a categorical metaphor. Colombia is consecrated to eternal suffering and may, therefore, need an elect voice that can act prophetically, someone who foresees what will happen as a consequence of the fall, acting as *advocatus diabolis* (the devil's advocate), but who cannot alter the course of events. But is it true that Fernando cannot interfere in the course of events? Or does Fernando's project reach beyond prophecy? One would have to speak, perhaps, of a theological world view that reaches beyond contemplation. The way that rigorism is set forth by the narrator Fernando will turn the issues of guilt and freedom into the most debatable battleground that a contemporary novel can push for.

At the beginning of the book there is a journey—the trip Fernando takes to Sabaneta, together with Alexis. It serves to redefine the relationship between the protagonist and "his country" in a way that leads from the pronoun "we" to the word "they." During Fernando's absence from the country, after his childhood, "Colombia...went all over the place as far as we were concerned, or rather, just like it went all over the place as far as 'they' were concerned, but not me, because I wasn't here, I came back later, years, decades later..." If there is an agency that informs this formulation, it is the transformation of an allegedly shared responsibility into an imperative of guilt that is imputed to the other party. When traveling in a taxi to Sabaneta, Fernando exclaims, "Aren't those pigs in the government capable of asphalting such an essential road, one that runs through the middle of my life? *Gonorreas*! (*Gonorrea* is the strongest insult in the slums of the *comunas*...)". This is a situation in which Fernando sets up his fundamental authority as lettered outsider. The journey marks his passage from his natural authority to interfere in public affairs, which belongs to any male child from the country's upper class as he is growing up, to the legitimacy of a *philologus illustrisimus* who, on his return home, aspires to become the main voice for moralizing about Colombia and even resorting to punishment. The reader learns that none of Colombia's recent presidents—as the "idiot faggot, arms manufacturer and distiller of liquor, the forger of constitutions that cannot be challenged...the cocaine profiteer"[40]—could have been entrusted with resolving the crisis, nor could they be absolved from guilt in view of the crying evil surrounding them. From here, the image of a lettered messiah starts to grow out of the link between homosexuality and a sublime masculine force of action.

The street that leads to the place of his childhood, still not paved, leaves Sabaneta an underdeveloped place in the middle of faceless, desolate urbanization, and enrages the hero about those who should have "taken care" of it during his absence. The kind of resentment he demonstrates is worthy of an uncrowned, forgotten magistrate. On his arrival in Sabaneta, while watching the Tuesday pilgrimage that overcrowds the church of the Virgin, Fernando decides for himself, "I am not from around here. (I am ashamed of this beggarly race.)" Distancing himself is, of course, necessary for him to become the "conscience" of Colombia. At the same time, he launches a request for immediate action by the state on his behalf, addressing the entity that he most mistrusts. To act as the country's "memory," the *grammaticus* demands that he be protected by the law: "Mister Public Prosecutor or District Attorney or whatever you're called, observe how I walk the streets risking my life: with the powers invested in you by the new constitution, protect me."[41] The demand is made in the form of a negative illocutionary speech act. The other party is asked to take action to show the inappropriateness of doing it at all. Addressing Colombia's legal authorities in that manner is calculated lunacy, or irony used as a rhetorical weapon, since the statement itself enacts the negative outcome.

The unbelievable is indeed going to happen. Fernando will launch a wave of killings on his own, and he inaugurates this with a coup de théâtre that seals his judgment over the state as the country's "first lawbreaker." With the television in his apartment on, Fernando asks Alexis to lend him his revolver ("I can't take it any more").[42] The hitboy, suddenly concerned about the suicidal gesture of his lover and benefactor, grabs the weapon and empties it into the TV set, just at the moment when "the president" is on the screen. The negative illocutionary speech that we mentioned earlier has prefigured the act by which the personalized image of the law has to be "wasted" ("quebrado," in the argot of the sicarios). The outcome produced by the symbolic killing of the president is the unleashing of the bond between masculine homoerotic love and the quest for supreme power. If the state has sunk into total disrepute relating to its duties, especially the protection of law and order, then the grammarian is entitled to act as *summum jus*. Could there be a solution other than seizing on the spirits of an undeclared (state of) exception? An eschatological vision is not far away, one that can promise a unique kind of freedom for those who have to walk through the valley of debasement, cutting the Gordion knot to make their conversion into higher beings complete.

While roaming through Medellín, and suddenly walking through the middle of a shoot-out, Fernando laconically reports, "bullets were flying this way and that, windscreens exploding and passersby going down like ninepins in the fiendish uproar." When people scream "Get down," he counters with indignation, "Get down, who? Me? Never! My dignity prevents me. I carried on through bullets that were whistling around my ears like cut-throat razors. And me thinking of the old verse, who's it by? 'Oh death, come silent in the arrow.'" Back in the apartment, when telling the TV-watching Alexis about the incident, he realizes that the boy "...'d have beat it." So Fernando gets emphatic, "Me, run for it? Beat it? Never in a month of Sundays. Never. Death is my errand-boy, kid." The scene is not as trivial as it sounds, and pretense can be a method. Fernando has started to build his authority at the threshold between life and death. The general state of evil is due to the absence of sovereignty in a country where "nobody is innocent." The only way to regain innocence (purity) and to overpower the general guilt, as the *grammaticus* puts it, consists in imagining a state that relies on punishment and repression. "Does this little problem have a solution?" he asks regarding Colombia's national history of violence as it became a malignant hotbed in the marginal *comunas*. "My reply is a yes as emphatic as a bullet: up against the wall, say I. Anything else would be like squaring the circle." And to be more specific, "Don't human rights me! Summary justice and then up against the wall and from the wall to the rubbish dump. The state is there to repress and do the shooting. All the rest is demagogy, democracy."[43] According to this assessment, the difference between popular sovereignty (the political body), and the excluded class of *populus*[44] has collapsed in Colombia, so that the existence of the "people" as political reality, as well as concept, has become impossible. Fernando sustains that only a debased sphere can be associated with this name—the multitude of the poor and greedy that threatens to overthrow society all together. Therefore, a new normative pact is necessary, an aristocratic masculine bond capable of breaking all taboos and bringing disorder to a halt.

There is a particular ambiguity inherent in the view that the protagonist defends, and it does not consist of doubt as to whether or not utmost violence "from above" is (proclaimed to be) necessary to put society in order. The question calling for resolution is, rather, who can claim the authority to pose or to act as the all-knowing corrective force—the state, God, or the *grammaticus conspicuus* himself? It is from the viewpoint of this implicit dispute that the transformation marking the autobiographical core of the novel is set on course. If evil is recognized as an all-pervasive force, where can power capable of coping with it come from? A distinct stance in front of national sovereignty's catastrophe is implied, and there is not one moment of doubt regarding Fernando's transcendent range of insight. Speaking of his perception of the refined subject in a world that appears mortally wounded by evil, his melancholic attitude would fall short in view of a more ambitious project. Applying a Sartrean wording, could not the perception of extreme evil allow for an imaginary annihilation of the abominable in such a way that freedom can then emerge? At issue is an attitude at the point where the subject's consciousness is pushed toward experiencing its utmost state of torment. The disgust in view of the catastrophe of the nation state is simultaneously presented as personal crisis and as metaphysical problem. The solution Fernando imagines could perhaps be viewed as a hysterical escape into authoritarian desire, if it were not for a ritualistic strategy bearing still different implications. What becomes more and more palpable is that, since that early moment when Alexis was adopted, an imperfect solution to the problem of evil has started to become obsolete.

We can now approach the epistemic root of the master's relationship with the sicario, a homosexual romance in the midst of darkness. The pact with the adolescent killer, Alexis, is staged as a joint experience of transgression. The hitboy has already been abandoned to the confines of a deadly destiny; the protagonist, for his part, affirms that he is close to death, always contending that his return to Colombia serves the purpose of leading his life to its end. So the illustrious man works on realizing his ultimate desire: after coming back from Europe, or from the North, where he led a "normal" and professionally successful life, his goal is to become an outlaw as intellectual, and to fuse his self-determined proscription with his search for transcendence. The *grammaticus* wants to share the intensity that marks the short life of his beloved child, Alexis, yet in a sublimized way staging—as we will see—an unprecedented vendetta of punishment.

When Fernando adopts Alexis as his lover, he becomes his benefactor, but this relationship of "unbridled love," as opposed to the lives of those who live as prisoners of "fat wive[s] and five kids"[45] has its price. Fernando "abandons" the hitboy to a type of violent action of which he—the *grammaticus*—will become the *spiritus rector*. The lettered man is capable of ultimate cunning. He establishes his own power over life and death by virtue of discursive action. For instance, when Fernando reproaches a taxi driver, Alexis kills the driver so as to complete the verbal outbreak. In Alexis' eyes, Fernando appears as an adored alien, a higher being, even a sorcerer—he has sufficient money to start a business but has no personal belongings; he can afford to throw boom boxes and TV sets out of the sixth-floor window of his apartment; and his verdicts come down on presidents and God alike. What Alexis cannot recognize is that representation, as it sustains the symbolic order of Western culture, is situated at the opposite end of action, so that an idea can be taken as an intervention without generating practical consequences. In the short lives of the sicarios, in turn, where law as an abstract rule is absent, and where community relations are guided by ritualistic codes, the spoken word vibrates with immediate political power.

When the lettered man drops his words into the delicate ears of the young sicario, he cannot suppose that the adolescent is aware of the double sense of language. Yet his "discursive action" is well calculated, so it excludes the possibility that meanings get "lost in translation." Only in this way can the master achieve Alexis's total submission. At least, this is the dream on which the novel bases its fictional structure. To be seen as superior by his neophyte lover, Fernando does not need any warrior-like qualities. Once the older man is accepted as the one who "knows," he is, in Alexis's eyes, the person invested with the most thorough power to act. That is to say, he is not what he might represent for most people—a person whose relationship to social language is defined by the language games that he can afford to perform as individual citizen. He is, in Alexis's eyes, the master who rules and acts *by* his word. This is the way he actually becomes Alexis' father, via an adoption that creates the image that Fernando belongs to a mysterious aristocracy.[46] His power does not have to be exerted, it is there, and the young killer subordinates his life to it. Thus, the adoption reveals the contours of an abandonment that is not the "untying to" a sovereign's power per se, the way it is described by Agamben. It is, more specifically, the abandonment to a calculated misunderstanding, a language gap, a *trompe-l'œil* that makes language appear as action, a disavowal, ipso facto, of its representational function.

For Fernando to become his country's violent Messiah, Alexis has to misunderstand him. Let us look into the linguistic politics through which the master seizes power over the act of killing. Paradoxically, the suspension of language's representational complexity is due to a collapse of cognitive into performative language or of "trope" into persuasion.[47] Alexis does not understand the double sense of Fernando's words that, in turn, generates a chain of killings. How could he know that he was not supposed to take his master at his word? Or was he perhaps supposed to do just that? One day, Fernando complains about the apartment's neighbor, a "fucking heavy-metal freak" who "is fucking up our night. [...] I'd like to kill the bastard." (22) On the following day, Alexis spots the neighbor on the street and acts with uncontrollable speed. He "went on ahead of him, half turned, pulled out the revolver and from a few inches away planted a bullet in his forehead, dead centre, right where they mark the holy cross on Ash Wednesday. Blam!" (24) The shock into which the reader is led is not relieved by the realization that Fernando "didn't mean it" that way. But the grammarian's surprise does not last for long; his horror of the unexpected is soon replaced by sublime admiration.

In an essay called "Pure Violence," Žižek has addressed what he calls the "racist prejudice of the theories of 'rationality.'"[48] This bias is supposed to consist of an assumption: the actions of those who commit the most brutal and incomprehensible acts are driven by condensed intentions and ideological goals. This premise, according to the Slovenian critic, is bound to a need to construct an evil-other, while making it "similar to us" (Western rationality) by inverting the ideological purpose. Žižek holds that, for example in the case of Islamic terror, the explanation does not lie in a counter-ideological or counter-cultural project of the fundamentalists (striving for superiority through difference), but rather in their own perspective of inferiority (unconsciously admitting their likeness to the West). When applied to the Colombian scenario, Žižek's argument about reversal (the slip from superiority to an inferiority complex in the perpetrators) falls short, yet it helps unravel Vallejo's strategy. On the one hand, the sicarios' actions can certainly not be judged to be purposeful acts of rebellion. On the other, their use of violence, to turn things to their own benefit, does not respond to an inverted scheme either. The drives that are immanent to the culture of the hitboys are less tangible, and it is revealing that the master Fernando takes care to suppress any paradox that could speak of the narrative identity of "his children," that is of their bare lives as personalized experiences. To give Žižek's thesis a twist, why not dare to look into identities that cannot in any way be subsumed under the Western principle of idem (and its aberrations)? Then it would be obsolete to search for an inferiority complex in the Colombian neophytes, or for any other scheme that reduces their identity to likeness or difference from a prevailing matrix. By introducing the notions of "culture of exception" and "sacred laboring," we have already led the discussion beyond the scheme of violence as pure difference versus likeness. Vallejo's novelistic enterprise in turn provides a magisterial, that is, plainly Western, construct of otherness: homosexual sicarios as mythically empowering creatures. What surfaces through *Our Lady of the Assassins* is a literary coup that returns the perception of violence to the need of a mythical Other, from which universal meaning can be obtained, with autobiography engaging in the ultimate battle.

The moment at which Vallejo's grammarian realizes how Alexis can be led into killing by a single word of his, he discovers the power of his desire, its reality in Lacanian terms. If, at an advanced point of catastrophe, violence equals truth, as the *philologus* asserts when admiring the beauty of the hitboy, there is a sinister sphere left where the most improbable intellectual act can be fulfilled. Since an idea will not collapse into its consummation if its authorship is "authentic," someone else is required to carry out the business. So the adoption of sicarios encounters, in the grammarian's project, a Schmittian variant of its own: sovereign is he who has the "right to decide life and death."[49] Vallejo's fiction does away, with a single stroke, with the concerns that the relationships between sovereignty and reason have generated over time. How can an educated fundamentalism be treated today when it emerges by surprise, taking marginal subjects into service to redeem the contemporary world from catastrophe?

Now, how does Fernando Vallejo's "Fernando," the "memory of Colombia," and the judge of its destiny, become involved in murder? We have described a praxis by virtue of which "his child," the sicario, is abandoned to a calculated linguistic misunderstanding. Fernando exposes Alexis to the actions that taking the elder's words literally generates ("I'd like to kill the bastard…"). If it is the authority of discourse over action that is at stake, here it appears at an extremely efficient point. Alexis becomes an instrument in the service of social sadism, stirred up by hatred and sexual repulsion that the self-appointed "magistrate" directs against the "human hordes," the "riffraff invading everything, destroying everything, smearing everything with its crapulous misery." As Alexis indeed starts reading the grammarian's thoughts on the matter of punitive action, he is converted into a sublime assassin. While actually killing passersby in the middle of Medellín's streets, preferably children and pregnant women, the hitboy is characterized by his benefactor to be "su servidor." This means, on the one hand, that he serves Fernando's interests but, on the other, that he acts on behalf of divine matters. The true informant [of this designation] is Thanatos, eventually called the *Santo Rey*—King Herod.[50]

Angels of Terror versus Marginal Subjects

It is difficult to find a level of comparison for the rash of assassinations into which the hitboy is released from now on. A few pages after indulging in how "the condemned hippie" was sent to the "depths of hell," Fernando informs us that Alexis's "next victims were three soldiers" (36), trying to intercept them when they were walking through the Parque de Bolívar. "Dead men do no searches. A bullet in anyone's forehead and their computers wiped." (37) The account continues alongside the couple's roaming along Medellín's suffocating streets. "Alexis's next little victim turned out to be a loutish passerby...But this time, just for a change...he didn't give it to him in the forehead, no, in the mouth, in the foul mouth he cursed us out of." (41) If we do not count the battles between rival sicarios, the next person who is terminated is an "arrogant taxi-driver" (48) who, when asked to turn down the radio, turns the volume up to ghetto-blaster levels. So Alexis, after leaving the taxi, "releases" him from work. "Death released him: Lady Death, the lover of justice...retired him." (49) Before the car hits a post and explodes, it still "takes out...a pregnant women with two little kids...thus cutting short what was promising to be a long maternal career." (ibid.) We then read about the encounter with Eve, a bar employee: "When the sweet thing threw coffee at us because we asked her for a whole serviette and not those tiny little triangles of paper not even an ant could wipe its mouth with, the first thing that occurred to Alexis was her mouth, and through the mouth is how the wretch bought it." (50) By the time that Fernando the narrator and Alexis have walked past the Cathedral, they run into a scene where "a dirty, foulmouthed kid with tears running down his face" is insulting a policeman: "Gonorrea...why'd you hit me, gonorrea!" (56) Three people in the street crowd sympathize with the kid, and the narrator explains, "They were the kind of champions of 'human rights,' or delinquents' rights who spring up spontaneously round here and lay claim to that 'defender of the people' role instituted by the new Constitution convoked by that idiot queer" of a president. (56) The narrator admits that he does not know why the cop would have hit the boy, but this is not the question; what, rather, strikes him is that "the kid's tone was the most rancorous and hate-filled I've ever heard in my life." (ibid.) Fernando settles his own obsession in reverse: "If this little bastard...behaves as wild as this with authority at the age of seven, what'll he be like when he grows up? He could turn out to be the one who does for me." (56, 57) As in previous cases, the narrator lends the executions that are now successively carried out by Alexis, a sanctifying voice that is loaded with religious metaphors: "...the Exterminating Angel [i.e., Alexis] unsheathed his sword of fire, his 'rod,' his 'piece,' his plaything, and like lightning did for each one in the forehead. The three of them? No, my idiot friend, all four" (referring to the boy and the three sympathizing people). It is the reader who is addressed as "idiot friend" ("bobito"), so as to be sardonically reminded of the a priori that guides the crusade. Fernando affirms that "Lady Death" has chosen him and Alexis to cut the Gordion knot of Colombia's vicious circle. "Lady Death" makes them act while acting upon them.[51]

Fernando keeps performing as the envisaging, commenting, all-knowing mind, but "Alexis was the Exterminating Angel who had descended on Medellín to finish off its perverse race." By virtue of a single stroke of the devining rod, the sicario has become the Angel of terror. The victims that now follow are "another señora, heavy with child," a "mime," a "defender of the downtrodden," and six men who are out drinking late at night in a cantina close to the grammarian's apartment: Alexis "dispatches" all six "with a bullet in the forehead...he punished them for their drunkenness, their 'bender.'" The chain of killings follows its course, reported in the same voice of controlled passion, which knows what it is talking about: the country's purification from guilt. During these scenes, the personal plural of the narrator is the guiding voice. The "dead is what we came for." "Ha! Death belongs to me, you jerks, she's my paramour and goes wherever I go." Before Alexis, the Guardian Angel, himself dies at the hand of another hitman, the list of people who are wiped out in public goes on to include a caretaker of a tomb, two "recently born innocents," four adults, a horse carter, and another taxidriver. As Fernando sums up, "After Alexis reached a hundred stiffs, I lost count altogether."[52]

An interpretation of these acts has to return to the matter of poverty and procreation. If this entirely abject sphere, in the eyes of the grammarian, is addressed as the root of all evil, it is the poor and the women who are punished. At the same time, poverty constitutes an ambiguous trope: the gay hitboys adopted by the protagonist are themselves the product of poverty. Elevating Alexis (and later Wilmar) to saintliness (the Guardian Angel/the Exterminating Angel) turns them into "unsocial" beings. This transformation draws, it seems, on an intertextual prop. Vallejo, who likes to invoke Latin and Roman classics, has chosen a name for his beloved child that calls up Vergil's *Eclogues* (or *Bucolics*) completed in 37 B.C. "Alexis" is the name of the beautiful slave whose favor the homosexual lover Corydon, in the Second Eclogue, desires in vain. Paul Julian Smith confirms the "traditional assertion that in the figure of Corydon, the jealous lover, Vergil chose to represent himself; and that Alexis... was a slave whom Vergil had met at dinner and had received from his host as a gift."[53] In *Our Lady of the Assassins*, the initial scene in the mythic apartment in which Alexis is given to Fernando by his old homosexual friend resembles the ancient source. What matters are the differences Vallejo introduces. A figure of subalternity is latent at the point at which the slave/the marginal outlaw is taken out of his proscribed condition. In Vergil's case, Alexis is transferred from mere life (*zoē*) to "qualified life" (*bios*), as Aristotle would have it.[54] In the novel in turn, "Alexis" is removed from his social background yet is not absolved from bare life. (He will even be sacrificed toward the end of the novel.) In both cases the exchange deals in strictly biopolitical values. Bits of legitimacy and a more decent life are conferred to the previously excluded subject in an exchange of youth, beauty, and homosexuality. Now, Vergil did not leave the youths he loved "unlearned [*non ineruditos*]. For Alexander became a grammarian and Cebes a poet."[55] Fernando on the other hand, takes Alexis and later Wilmar into service by turning "pedagogy" into a dark weapon that we have examined in relation to the language the master uses when he directs the hitboys into action.

Fernando's assertions seem to compete with each other in terms of exhortation and vindication, tearing to pieces that which is called hope—that which could still maintain positive images of Latin American historical and cultural identity.[56] His statements about poverty are so stunningly sexist and uniform that their literalism can lead sophisticated reading astray.[57] The narrator's abhorrence of sociologists has not kept himself from entering into sociological simplicities.[58] The general solution he would suggest for his country's catastrophe is twofold. On the one hand, he would have saluted a state authority capable of not housing the "ones who suffer...and who insist on not being rich," but, rather, willing "to poison their water once and for all and bingo!" On the other, and since the first solution has vanished in Colombia's "rotten modernity," what remains is the drastic biopolitical imperative: "For genetic reasons, the poor have no right to reproduce themselves. Rich people of the world, unite!"[59] Imagination decides the status of "the fact" and, interestingly, the paragraph that follows these words is the one already cited, which elevates Fernando to the heights of *vir clarisimus...unum et idem e pluribus unum, summum jus*—the select subject speaking with the voice of "extreme justice." In the process of recurrent self-definition versus an external world, as well as versus the reader who, by rhetorical attestation, does not "know enough," that which results is the construct of a fundamental consciousness. After all, the antipsychological gesture that traverses the novel is not surprising, although it is situated at the opposite end of Salazar's artistic asceticism.

The fact that Vallejo has chosen hate as a formula of self-legitimation allows to draw on a specific relationship between religion and cognition. The mediating link is *affect*. Even if one would like to be cautious about addressing the fictional text in these terms, the narrator's own indulgence in imperative tone, moralizing discourse, and scholastic rhetoric is too overbearing to be judged incidental. What the modernist critic would be inclined to view as mere phantoms of literary language—extraliterary elements, so to speak—becomes aesthetically crucial in that they defy plurality. As has been noted, personal memories are for the most part missing. From the perspective of the construction of hatred and guilt, a compulsive disorder is likely to lie at the center of the missing biography. An attempt to uncover it would require facing the known Freudian dilemma as phrased by Santner: the unconscious is supposed to work in a "machine-like" manner. Unconscious formations "are ultimately insensitive to the question, Why are you doing that?"[60] Fernando the grammaticus has found an efficient way to ward off these levels of life experience. The metaphysics of the novel functions as a towering authority to block its possible traumatic substratum from expression. What serves as a monolithic circle is the connection between the extreme subjectivity of rhetoric and an objectifying discourse. This tie is supported by the unity of author-agency and narrator voice—an irritating aspect for any reader whose expectations are molded by a worldly reflexivity. The novelistic discourse is thus difficult to handle. For the narrator, the Colombian situation is essentially due to the hatred that reigns in the population. Hating back becomes his strongest passion, to the degree that it sustains his autobiographical identity. How irrational is this passion? If it is a predisposition to hatred that nurtures the discourse on poverty, one might decide to take it as "inadequate idea."[61] However, one cannot cope with Fernando using enlightened criteria. The man of letters is not a lunatic but a master of cunning reason. His extended treatise on poverty serves as the calculated method by which degradation is assumed to be inverted, so that it can serve as an act of sublimation or spiritual freedom. The dilemma Fernando cannot overcome otherwise is a series of secular restraints of his own life—a personal history that prevented him from either becoming a sovereign magistrate or an "essential criminal."[62] His desire might have been to learn from Jean-Paul Sartre's *Saint Genet* to convert life into the "lucid free act," on the basis of the metamorphosis of "the criminal, the aesthete, the writer."[63] This is, as Susan Sontag shows, an enterprise that is inherently Hegelian: the world is established "as a closed system consciousness regards from without, in the manner of the divine understanding."[64] And we may perceive, in Vallejo's imagination, a dark caricature of—or a bold return to—Hegel's view of the relations between self and other. Hence the *methodical* deployment of poverty that is defined as a mythical condition that only the intervention of sacred power can remedy. Sanctity, to be established, needs degradation from where it can depart. This matrix relies on one of the oldest principles of religion: that of establishing a distinctly sacred sphere vis-à-vis the profane world. According to an etymology of the term *religio* as pointed out by Agamben, things are considered *sacred* or religious when they belong, in one way or another, to the gods. Therefore, "*Religio* is not what unites men and gods but what ensures they remain distinct."[65] By spelling a similar pattern, Vallejo's grammarian has started to engage in the consecration of "his children" (their passage from the profane to the sacred)—a transcendental project whose inner mechanism remains to be revealed.

Both literary works, *We Were Not Born to Life* and *Our Lady of the Assassins*, are "global localizations" of a conflict in which imaginaries regarding the relationships between violence, ethics, religion, and modern life are fought out. In both texts, the concept of the sacred is a cornerstone for addressing cultural and survival practices looming over Western contemporaneity. Salazar and Vallejo, both Colombian intellectuals who share a critical sensibility toward globalization, confront their readers with projects, each of which displays its own extraordinary oeuvre. According to our reading of Salazar, *sacred laboring*, an extreme state of violence generated within territories that are traversed by local and neoliberal dynamics alike, weighs heavily on social fantasies. *We Were Not Born to Life* conveys the images of marginal adolescent outlaws pertaining to a multitude of violent outsiders who have no entry into official society. The stories that make up Salazar's book can be read as experiential layers, each of which relates to a somehow different sociopolitical framework into which young people from the *comunas* have been absorbed (drug traffic, paramilitary self-defense groups, and—to a lesser extent—guerrilla activities). Through testimony, Salazar has captured intricate personal, logistical, and social threads that connect the destiny of Medellín's harshest shantytowns to Colombia's history of political violence. Vallejo's narrative, conversely, is designed in a way that enables an antisocial argument. Similar to the construction of certain colonial metaphors in Colombian history, Vallejo's narrator introduces Medellín's hitboys as creatures essentially lacking consciences. Consonant with what Taussig calls the colonizers' mimicking of the savagery they previously imputed to indigenous populations,[66] Fernando's craving is to take the young assassins out of their context (make them alien to themselves), and thus draw on their actual powers. At the core of this mimetic appropriation of the other lies the expropriation of its materialized narratives—the sicarios' own rituals, modes of life, and manners of speech and silence.

INVERTED CHRISTIANISM: A SACRIFICIAL ROMANCE

Vallejo's novel has become more notorious than Salazar's text, due to the book market's fascination with the acrimony and mystification that the central voice applies with great versatility. There is, for example, the title itself—*Our Lady of the Assassins*. The image of hitboys in Medellín venerating the Virgin Maria Auxiliadora appears several times, always maintaining its mystical flair. If one were to follow traces of inquiry that the lettered hero dismisses as the caprices of sociologists, one would probably ascribe the "inner emptiness" of adolescents like Alexis to their pagan use of Christian artifacts and symbols. The neophytes do not participate in the Christian tradition that works by injecting feelings of "debt" into the souls of believers, especially when guilt is eternalized through atonement.[67] Sicarios cultivate different religious practices—pertaining to the culture of exception—which Fernando is unwilling to accept. Religious sacrilege is not his cup of tea, unless it is supervised by an elected agent who holds claim to the *summum jus*. Yet more than that, the pagan facet of the hitboys' identity could provide them with a narrative of their own. For example, a minor evil self that would not attune itself to the idea of an abstract God but would venerate the deities of rock music and salsa. The recognition of a pagan narrative matrix would, ipso facto, be concerned with a subversive figure of the ipse toward which society has remained blind. Hitboys from the margins have been the inarticulate targets of moral and legal discourses whose foremost concern has been to determine *what* they have done, not *who* they really are. This youth has thus been utterly given over to others to be instrumentalized: they cannot demand a space of self reference. What excels in an adolescent killer like Alexis is the absence of guilt, yet what is compelling about Fernando is a fundamental recreation of guilt. Therefore Fernando must attest Alexis an "emptiness" of mind and an "absolute truth" as noncontaminated being. Otherwise, it might become obvious that the absence of guilt, in the case of the hitboy, is not a transcendental phenomenon; it is more than anything else a cultural fact and a survival praxis.

The linguistic misunderstanding that prefigured the vendetta carried out by Fernando, together with his "baby boy," served as the maneuver that undermined Alexis's potential narratable self. The sicario is deprived of the motives for action that would respond, in a different imaginary setting, to sacred labor as laid out in relation to the testimony of Salazar. Instead, Alexis is converted into a creature in the service of the satanic mastermind and will become an *object* of sacrifice. As the grammarian wants us to believe,

Alexis's eventual death is due to external circumstances: he dies from the bullet of another sicario in an act of revenge. But Alexis's death is, above all, a necessary element in the plan of the master. The young homosexual killer has to be sacrificed, not because he committed violent acts against the civilian population or is a victim of gang warefare, but due to the purifying strategy for which he has become the vessel. The meaning of the homosexual romance lies in the transgressive pact in which redemption can be achieved only by one. Without Alexis's death, given, for example, an earthly happy ending, Fernando's evolution into "the Invisible"—his absolute freedom of guilt—would be impossible. Toward the end of the novel, the narrator feigns his own transfiguration into a disembodied essence, mimicking the figure of a revenant from the reign of death, one of Herod's angels. Fernando claims that he is finally restored "to what I am, the invisible man."[68] Crucial things have to occur before he can pretend to leave "this world"—the embodied, guilt-loaded earth of ordinary man. Alexis dies from the bullet of another hitboy, Wilmar. Wilmar becomes Fernando's next lover, also called "my child." The grammarian even confuses the names of the two.

The death of the adolescent can be associated to the Eucharistic ritual in an aberrant way. A sacred strategy makes the body of the other available for incorporation: Alexis pays with his body and life so that Fernando can achieve transubstantiation. The ritual is supposed to help the protagonist to fulfill his will to arrive at eternity by joining the dark, violent divinity. The ritual mechanism that serves this goal occurs twice. Alexis dies first, at the hand of Wilmar, and afterward, Wilmar has to die. It is as though the practice of transubstantiation passed through different stages, first embracing the actual body of Alexis and then, as a second step, the mystical body of Alexis that has taken shape in the person of Wilmar.[69] Both killers, Alexis and Wilmar, are catalysts and victims within the same ritualistic circle of purification. Fernando thus becomes an authentic hero, entering the reign where violence finds its real, its transcendental, place. Only from the standpoint of a ritualistic incorporation of the adolescent lovers, together with violence made transcendental, can one understand the unexpected movement of the romance—Fernando's adopting the killer of his first lover without bad feelings. The grammarian has repeatedly claimed that he returned to Colombia to die, however he is far from dying. To contend that at the moment at which "his child" (Alexis) dies, "he," the father, dies as well is just another *trompe-l'œil*. It implies, linguistically, the fulfillment of the categorial "we"—definitely obliterating otherness: "We think we exist, but no, we're a figment of nothingness, a *basuco* dream."[70] The adolescent sicario, who was never allowed to speak on his own behalf, is authorized to practice a direct, third-person speech act, one single time—at the moment of his death.

As the great seer, Fernando is not only the one who commands higher consciousness; he is also the agent of extreme justice. In fact, he holds that *vir clarisimus* and *summum jus* are one. The whole rhetoric sounds like blasphemy—not accidentally, it resembles Jesus's speech as it is portrayed in the Gospel of John. Jesus tells the crowd that "I and *my* Father are one," a pronouncement that causes the Pharisees to stone him.[71] The astounding gesture consists in erasing ambiguity on the grounds of an ambivalent statement. The zealous homily that comprises the better part of Vallejo's novel is not focused on a positive ideal, nor even on a positive vision of the God of the Old Testament. Murder was carried out by Alexis under the guidance of the master, so that we are supposed to ask: what is more blameworthy than cold-blooded murder? More terrible than murder, according to Fernando, is the absence of innocence and purity in the light of poverty and unruly procreation, which is viewed as equaling the absence of truth. According to this rhetoric catalogue, the qualities that matter are manifest not in actions and deeds but in something else. There are victims of Fernando's crusade who are killed for the same conducts that others are absolved of. Being susceptible to hatred by sharing the stigmata of evil, by being female or being poor, on the one hand, or by unlawful behavior (such as the corruption of state authority) is essential for judgment, followed by punishment. The motion that approximates Fernando's discourse closer to that of a vindictive Christ in the Gospels of John and Matthew is found in the extirpation of righteousness in its relationship to human action and behavior. Let us repeat this criterium: people are punished not for their deeds but for their beliefs, which means the lack of authentic belief. Here we may remember Saint Paul's statement, as cited by Badiou: "Faith is what saves us, not works."[72] Only in this manner can one uncover the "method" that underlies the killing of so numerous a group of passers-by in the streets of Medellín. Fernando was offended by the sheer physical presence of his fellow countrymen rather than by any active immoral behavior. These victims are guilty because they live in a country and in a world where, *per dictum*, their existence cannot serve a good end. Participating in a superior mission does not admit ifs and buts. It requires an elect chastity, manifest in the veneration of homosexual masculine love, as the way that can lead to (violent) salvation. If one keeps thinking about Saint Paul, one would have to add a second side to the "perilous metonymy." The first aspect was "faith is what saves us, not works"; the second says, "We are no longer under the rule of law, but of grace."[73] Has Fernando turned into the apostle of grace since law has vanished from today's rotten earth?

A further clue is found in the polemical interpretation of the figure of Christ. "Christ is the great introducer of impunity and disorder in this world. When you turn the other cheek in Colombia, with another blow they end up depriving you of your retina. And once you can't see, they do for you with a knife in the heart." The grammarian's preference becomes chillingly clear when he asks, "And Christ? Where's he? The rage-filled puritan who whipped the moneylenders out of the temple? Did the cross cure him of his tantrums, and does he no longer see nor hear nor smell anything?" With an ironic blow against the principle of the Trinity, Fernando exclaims, "Here you have my new theology of Duality…: the twosome needed for love; three's already an orgy." Despite the irony, the duality referring to Alexis and the master is not entirely remote from biblical semantics. It allows us to imagine a constellation in which the Father in heaven and Jesus unite efforts to mount a reign of punishment against a wicked humanity, a human race that has been corrupted by the fall. In the light of Jesus's declaration "I and my Father are one," the theology of duality appears as an old dictum. But the grammaticus inverts God's sacrifice of Jesus by sacrificing his lovers instead of himself, his "children," his "baby boys."[74] Detesting the forgiving and loving side of Jesus, as it also shines through the Gospels, Fernando reinstates an image of the fanatic Christ. This Christ[75] has the power—of the word—to balance the erosion of the law with grace. But owing to the state of affairs epitomized by Colombia's fall, he also needs to draw on the power of the "event." *Grammaticus*, after having bestowed purifying terror on the city of Medellín, shedding much innocent blood, has emptied himself of the attributes of the profane, and he becomes omniscient and transparent. As the "Invisible man" of Medellín, he quotes from the Gospel of Matthew:

Let the dead bury their dead.[76]

And between the living dead, walking without going anywhere in particular, thinking without really thinking, I strolled along the motorway. The living dead were passing me mumbling to themselves, talking gibberish.[77]

The thread that connects biblical words and a guiding principle in *Our Lady of the Assassins* is marked by an erosion of human agency in its bearing on moral values. To use Shadia B. Drury's words, the religion of the New Testament "ranks the right thoughts and beliefs so highly that they overshadow good conduct and eclipse right action."[78] Similar to the autocratic Jesus portrayed by the Gospels, Vallejo's grammaticus punishes his fellow countrymen, having more than one hundred of them killed, not for their behavior but for pertaining to a contaminated race. Hence, guilt does not arise—as properly modern morality would have it—from criminal actions but from a condition of evil that people have no chance to chose or reject. Guilty people are singled out by the *summum jus*. It is part of this antilogic that the agency of the narrator can indulge in murder and crime, and still claim to be free of guilt.

Fernando's feelings about the Roman Catholic Church are ambivalent. On the one hand, by imagining—and perhaps mimicking—a fanatic Christ, he seems inclined toward a Calvinist or Lutheran radicalism rather than to the "more palatable doctrine" of Catholic provenance,[79] which balances out sinfulness by righteous actions to make salvation achievable. On the other hand, Fernando and Alexis regularly visit churches where they meet with the all-forgiving Virgin. Fernando is reluctant to give up his adoration of Maria Auxiliadora, and he rejects any secularist ("sociological") explanation of the devotion of the sicarios to the Virgin. Is not the Roman Catholic religion pragmatically wise, incorporating the worldly into the sacred? Is not Vallejo's narrator unforgivingly inscrutable? If a sinful population, including the sicarios, had the right to practice expiation and to atone for their sins in the houses of God, how could he resort to violent punishment? Ironically,

Medellín's churches acquire, now and again, the role of highly useful places; Fernando visits these sacred sites regularly to find relief from the aggression of the streets. When Vallejo's narrator, acting as an amazing ventriloquist for the writer,[80] unleashes his wrath against a wicked humanity, it is not accidental that he wages his mission by engaging metaphysical issues. He draws on an ambiguous hermeneutic space where the relationships between the Old and the New Testaments regarding the role of the God, His competence over the status of sin and salvation, violence and the law, belief and understanding are still apt to puzzle ethical thinking.[81] Fernando is aware of both ambivalence and belligerence when he digs the face of the God out of the New Testament—especially the face that favors terrors, traps, and ambushes to sustain the image of sinfulness.

A mystery remains to be addressed at last, one that might appear as the most irritating aspect of the novel. By regularly incriminating religion and God, Vallejo's narrator has set an interesting trap. Is not a sense of what readers could discern as atheistic skepticism present in the novel? Is not the grammarian's autocratic discourse obstructed by his own disbelief in God? And should one not attribute to his mindset, therefore, an agnostic rather than doctrinaire leaning? Our reading suggests otherwise. Having been raised in a family of Colombia's landowning oligarchy, Fernando was by the conservative character of his class naturally exposed to Catholicism from early childhood. The persistence of such legacies can be detected in his use of religious allegories, and of metaphors referring to the biblical concept of creation. At the same time, a desire for salvation pervades the conscience of the narrating voice; it has been the hidden yet pressing stamina that shapes the attitude of calling upon death, preaching purity, and actively engaging in violence. The references to creation, in turn, bring out the grammaticus as the great apostate. When he and Alexis encounter a wounded street dog that has no chance to survive, Fernando declares, ostensibly blaming the God of the Old Testament:

> Only God will know, he who is guilty of such infamies: He, with a capital "H", with the capital letter that's reserved for the most monstrous and cowardly being there is, who kills and maims by using the hand of another, the hand of man, his plaything, his hitman.[82]

It is astounding that the Master and his child, after terminating the lives of dozens of passers-by, care intensely about the wounded dog, so much so that Alexis is unable to give it the *coup de grâce*, which Fernando then carries out. This scene and other references to animals (like the singing birds that humans are not supposed to imitate by whistling), help us realize that existence is looked at from the standpoint of creation (or termination), not through a lens of social or historical conflict. This holds for poverty and female impurity, as well: they stand for the abject outcome of *Genesis*. Different from a politics supported by the Roman Catholic canon, as it balances teachings about creation and the doctrine of salvation,[83] *Philologus ilustrisimus* challenges this balance. He confronts readers from a strange position of religious syncretism. Roman Catholic doctrine is not despised as such, but it can barely hold on to its authority. The defilement of humanity that is pervading the earth is too disastrous. "God doesn't exist, if he does, he's the big gonorrea," continues Fernando, while an apocalyptic rain pours down on him.[84]

The missing link that completes the theological syncretism of the novel is Gnosticism, especially those ideas that bear an interpretive memory of the Old Testament. Several of Fernando's pronouncements would fit into the decalogue of heresies as they were formulated during the second century AD, described, for example, by Hippolytus in *Refutatio omnium haeresium*: "The God of this world at the blood rejoices. This is the one, who in the last days of the time of Herod appeared in human shape..."[85] Jacob Taubes has assigned Gnosticism a "move out of history,"[86] consciously carried out, based on experience that reworks mythical thinking under the impact of early Jewish and Christian eschatology. According to this hypothesis, *parousia*, understood as real expectation, conflicted with the timeframe inherent in the Gospel. Gnostics, while being educated about the narrative of salvation—"the eschatological salvation God holds in store for them in Jesus"[87]—were confronted with the waning of any historical ground on which the coming of the Apocalypse could rely. In Taube's view, this experience was molded by Gnostics into a fantasy in which a reprehension of the God of the Old Testament cohered with the heightening of notions of inwardness, with *Gnosis* designing secret and elitist knowledge—a subversive stream of Neoplatonism—which would generate its own revelations. Such knowledge becomes capable of enlightening the soul by assuming that negative forces had always been at work. Evil became personalized in a variety of versions, "absolute Genesis" emerging out of the contentions and rivalries between the celestial powers. Second-century Gnosticism, which the church soon sought to suppress, is ironically recalled by Borges: its intention "is to resolve the problem of evil without scandal." What makes Gnostic narratives appealing, according to Borges, is "our imprudent or guilty improvization by a deficient divinity, of ungrateful material."[88]

If we look for imaginary patterns, an insinuation regarding the relationship between the grammarian and the killer Alexis is provided by the figure of the "Light-Jesus": the divine person who enters the lower world of human depravity and ignorance to bring the life-giving Gnosis. This refers, above all, to the enlightening of souls, and Alexis' inner emptiness becomes the right destination. Taubes refers to a Manichaean cosmogony in which a new narrative is superimposed on the story of Genesis.[89] The Gnostic tale reports how Light-Jesus wakes Adam from a deadly sleep, liberates him from the demon, makes him taste from the tree of life, and thus enables Adam to open his inner eye and raise his voice against God the Creator. The analogy still holds: it is not so much that Alexis be awakened to his own self (his soul) that is important, but rather that he be led into transcendental action against evil under the tutelage of Fernando the master.

Gnosticism entered into the appalling, unbearable enigmas of God and, according to Gershom Scholem, later Messianic mysticism has sought to "summon up and to release all the forces capable of hastening the End."[90] In terms of historical imagination, if there is a parallel between the novel's take on the crisis of Colombia and the Gnostic imaginary edifice, it can be found in the enabling link that connects a prehistorical vision (the fable of creation) and a posthistorical construction (a story of punishment and redemption). Fernando's posthistorical obsession is not driven by naive assumptions. He sees himself as a dinosaur who is sent off to die in a rotten Western world, but who—as the "only" remaining grammarian of his country—has decided that his last craving will be a singularly radical one. The subtitle of our study speaks of an intellectual struggle regarding freedom and guilt. Freedom and guilt are understood as categories that have accompanied diverse experiences of intellectual self-conception throughout Western culture. Could it be possible that both notions bear a common root that goes back to late Antiquity, namely to the emergence of monotheism? What is the specific relationship of "freedom" to the historical world, according to Fernando's Christian syncretism? Freedom is linked to his condition as the enlightened yet autocratic subject, member of a universal, spiritual elite who, by seeing clearly, can take hold of the abyss. His embodiment of supreme justice follows from here—it becomes manifest in the gesture of "grace" extended to a lawless, degenerated world.

But what does the *grammaticus* see, and what does he know? Taubes wrote, while affirming the Divine presence in history: "Chosing or rejecting evil must be a real possibility."[91] In this vein, to uncover the secret of evil's origin or—conversely—to cover up its truth belongs to a prospect of essential freedom. On the potentials of Gnosticim, Taubes also writes, "Man does not become insane, but always and only acts within insanity... To perceive the madness that pervades the world as madness is the only path to not becoming insane. Recognizing insanity as insanity is the way out of madness [and] toward the revelation of truth." The Gnostic transcendental bias supposes that "every construct of history must remain susceptible to being perceived as insanity, if truth is to be brought to light."[92] Thus, freedom allows for driving guilt out of the inner circle of sin and atonement by means of those mystic insights that Gnosis is capable of providing to an elect few. The Gnostic excursus could probably explain, as well, how Fernando has come to terms with the presence of "evil" in his own class. In that sense, his Gnostic wrath would appear as a means for repressing the trauma accounting for his missing autobiography.

Fernando's origins in a Catholic oligarchic background of Medellín must have left him, rather sooner than later, at odds with the ways of how the traditional lettered elite has handled the issues of gender identity, as well as "public politics." The initial image of his antediluvian friend José Antonio Vásquez, who makes presents of young boys, could either be read as mythic compensation for a traumatic past or as an example of how exclusivity is celebrated by a few. Erna von der Walde, commenting on the nation-founding protagonism of the conservative lettered elite in Colombia—*los gramáti-cos*—in the late nineteenth century,[93] argues that Vallejo's heresy is the balance of the definitive collapse of a hierarchic notion of national identity. The thesis that contemporary, and especially postmodern literature has helped to deconstruct the normativity of a modern lettered city qua nation in Latin America has been around for a while, but its either nostalgic or euphoric overtones have sometimes obscured the vibrant stance taken by writers and artists within the alleged no-man's-land of global culture. The protagonist, Fernando, the "last" of his country's grammarians who omits the story of his personal—should we say national-political?—fiasco, is heading toward a singularly ambitious goal. To mourn, for example, the historical infeasibility of a homosexual conservatism in Latin America is not his cup of tea. We may want to phrase it in a more Deleuzian way: within a posttraumatic state of affairs, the explanatory power of the hidden trauma might turn out to be a limited clue. Fernando's project is an all-out assault, not just on a traditional hegemonic culture unable to coming to terms with the crisis of Colombia, but on the perversions of modernity as a whole.

Here, modernity is seen in its relationship to the kind of worldly Catholicism that Fernando has learned to despise. Both have become plural, "feminine," and moderate; both have proven unable to secure the authority of the law, thus betraying the Christian dualistic principle. When *grammaticus* declares there are no innocent people, it becomes difficult—despite his masterminding the killings among the civil population—to regard him as a terrorist. When all choices are polarized in advance, alternatives are eclipsed. One might disqualify the novel as a sophisticated example of biblical neo-fanaticism. However, this would fall short of its timely horizon. The discourse of *Our Lady of the Assassins* intensely associates the discussion of what Foucault has called the "Right of Death and Power over Life." If one recalls the political frames of reference regarding Colombia's situation in the 1980s and the 1990s, what excels is the existence of different territorial and logistic fractions, forces that commanded—each in its own right—tremendous amounts of biopolitical power.[94] Now, would not a perception of the disastrous coexistence of these forces call for a model according to which the "power of the sovereign over his subjects could be exercised in an absolute and unconditional way"?[95] Is this what Vallejo imagines to be the superior truth of violence brought to the fore by his belligerent narrator?

This is possibly the point where the debate over the biopolitical dimension of modernity would have to open up to global heterogeneity. Foucault observed how the ancient Roman, that is, absolute, model of power has been turned relative and limited in its modern forms; however, as he pointed out regarding developments that resurface during the twentieth century, there is suddenly a rejoinder of absolute practices of political power, for example in the case of wars in which wholesale slaughters have been carried out in the name of "basic necessities." As for Foucault, his much cited insights must be considered incomplete: they leave the incorporation of peripheral regions into the global sovereign design unexplored. Let us recall a few words of his:

> If genocide is indeed the dream of modern powers, this is not because of a recent return of the ancient right to kill; it is because power is situated and exercised at the level of life, the species, the race, and the large-scale phenomena of population.[96]

Distinct from this rather general evaluation of sovereignty's passing from a juridical to a complex biopolitical issue, Vallejo's novel unfolds a sweeping biopolitical vision whose very center is the globalized periphery.

The logic of the hero of *Our Lady of the Assassins* is dazzling. It may look like a perverse stroke against concepts such as that which holds on to the fundamental distinction between power and violence: "power is…of the essence of all government, but violence is not…Power needs no justification,…what it does need is legitimacy." According to Arendt's liberal existentialism, the notion of legitimacy stands above "justification" because it is based on an appeal to the past. Justification, in turn, "relates to an end that lies in the future."[97] In the case of the *grammaticus*, legitimacy is an issue that merits no trust. Creation and genesis have ended in corruption and insanity, putting the world out of order. Justification, in turn, rather than being necessary for enabling violence, is produced by its very action, anticipated by a type of reason that appears to be either fundamentalist or cynical, perhaps both. The Colombian case seems, at first glance, to foster this logic. Doesn't it suggest that the notion of sheer violence has been able to gain so much influence because sovereign power was lost? However, this would be the moment at which Colombia's social and political history, together with its conversion into a strategic arena of local and global conflict would have to be put on the table again. If this is too bothersome, the call for a biopolitical tabula rasa may indeed be the order of the day. Since Colombia is not in a position of unfettered national sovereignty, it would either be destined to drag out its miserable condition or have to be geopolitically sanitized under foreign guidance. The second solution has actually been taking shape since 1998. In any case, if Vallejo's novel could be viewed as premonitory, shockingly bold and self-consciously dogmatic, the point could be made that it is so by virtue of imagination. In the end, its protagonist is just a traveler who—against his original plans to die in his home country—decides that he will be leaving Colombia again. The answer to the question to what extent Fernando's eschatological violence has fueled his "worldly" ambitions as intellectual missionary is, as well, just a matter of imagination.

A postscript comes to mind, and it brings us back to the hidden affective drives inherent in the intellectual condition. On the one hand, Vallejo's narrator calls for attention and admiration, mimicking a new universal apostle, an authoritarian heretic but still a heretic who works toward Colombia's point zero. On the other, his curious mixture of preaching, ritual transgression, and self-purification, more than gaining control over

the predicament of guilt, seems to be trapped within it. What kind of protagonist is Fernando, a question that might invoke, again, the issue of abjection. Michael Bernstein, in his genealogy of a modern yet ominous type of
hero, and following Kristeva's characterization believes that "abjection" has
received little scholarly attention because of its lack of grandeur, its fusing
together a deep coarseness and a reflexive attitude in the very person of the
modern subject:[98] a proto-Nietzschean figure driven by strong energies of
"ressentiment." As we argued earlier, when evoking Sartre's Saint Genet,
there are experiences of "absolute prestige" in the matter of violence that
are denied to Vallejo's lettered hero. His striving to fuse constituencies such
as that of the writer and that of the great criminal remains prone to passion, wickedness, and demagogy. According to Bernstein when approaching
the work of Dostoevsky, Céline, and others, the "abject hero" is lacking
the monstrous single-mindedness and self-absorption of the essential criminal. We leave it open here whether the ontological identity attributed to
the "monster" or the "great criminal" is not an invention of the modern
writer's mind. But it is worth noticing that "the Abject Hero often longs
to be exactly such a creature; his rare words of praise are reserved for the
transcendent villains, and his whole being is a helpless dialogue between
the urge to curse and attack without restraint and the anxiety immediately
aroused by even the slightest danger."[99] Is Vallejo's narrator not the one
who turns a deep "bad conscience," together with a passion for intellectual
freedom and sovereignty, into an empowering condition? Nietzsche speaks,
not by chance, of "that terrible inner artist's egoism," even of an "artist's
violence": "This *instinct of freedom*, forcibly made latent...this instinct of
freedom forced back, repressed, incarcerated within itself and finally able to
discharge and unleash itself only against itself: that, and that alone, is bad
conscience in its beginnings."[100] Bernstein believes that, by being denied
the pride of an authentic rebel (or magistrate), "by occupying the logically
impossible space created by the intersection of the satanic and the servile,
the Abject Hero is both a more complex and ultimately a more subversive
figure than the monster..."[101] Subversiveness is not the suiting term in the
case of *Our Lady's* ultimate grammarian. However, one might want to give
the *philologus* Fernando some of the admiration that he seeks. Fernando
Vallejo could claim to have afforded the literary world with a stunning tale
of masculine sacred erotics. These purifying erotics could succeed in burying
the late capitalist "Whore of Babylon"[102] under its obsessive scorn, because
this passion engages in magic at the same time that it enters into violence.
Its work of intellectual abjection is so radical that the Colombian imaginary
scenario surfaces at center stage of today's troubled world. With a fierce spark
of sarcasm, the narrator bids the reader farewell:

> And so my very best to you
> May you be flattened by a truck
> Or have a train cut you in two.[103]

PART IV

Affective Politics and the Image

CHAPTER 7

Beyond Bare Life: Affection-Images of Violence in Latin American Film

QUESTIONING THE "DOGMA" OF BARE LIFE

Audiovisual imagination in Latin America can be perceived to have generated affective territories in its own right. Many films that were produced during the 1990s and afterward, in Mexico and Colombia, Argentina and Brazil, as well as in other countries, have started to intervene in peculiar ways into cinematic spaces that are saturated by hegemonic networks of "fear production."[1] To the extent that filmic works originating in the globalized South occupy significant realms of either artistic recognition or commercial distribution, some of them can be perceived to be strong indicators of an epistemic change. These works have generated aesthetic-affective assemblages that introduce new features into mainstream perceptions and images of violence.

The present study focuses on ethical-philosophical questions rather than on advancing media-specific arguments. If the medium of film has a specific propensity to bring out the affective side of bodies, environments, and thus "the stuff itself of human life,"[2] is it not fair to say that innumerable movies in the past century gave the presence of violence a natural, that is libidinal form? Didn't they intensify the visibility of terror to the extent that it has become atmospherically ineluctable from modern life? Wasn't one of the major efforts that has guided Hollywood's most ingenious strategies of fear-production aimed at putting Third World realities at a salutary length? Were these efforts of sanitizing our life worlds not promoted by screen and media images capable of keeping the ignoble zones of the planet at a fantasmatic range, not to speak of their Manichean representations? To paraphrase Paul Gilroy, knowledge of geopolitical conflicts arrives, more than ever before, on very long loops, usually via expensively manufactured surrogate images.[3] Of course, the cultural coordinates that determine that which is experienced as reality are at issue. A denial that these symbolic networks account for becomes especially compelling. There is no doubt that the largest amount of screen violence has been propelled into the world by the United States. Yet as much terror as there has been on the screen, there was a common perception before September 11, 2001, presuming that "we," the sophisticated centers of the world, have removed from ourselves the atavistic side of violence. "Our" violence, to paraphrase Auerbach's sharp remark on Christianity, is supposed to be cleaner, "more ordered," and even "more human."[4] To follow the tracks of this massively interiorized logic a step further, there has even been a strange revival of the "dogma of bare life" (which Benjamin called into question): that life as such in the highly developed West is still worth more than "just life," to the extent that the criteria and categories by which just life can be assessed today have become virtually invisible. It is on this perception that an important number of contemporary Latin American films cast doubt.

Benjamin's formulation continues to resonate: "The proposition that existence stands higher than a just existence is false and ignominious, if existence is to mean nothing other than bare life..." It is necessary to be aware that bare life and just life are not sociological concepts nor should they be viewed as abstract ontological notions. Benjamin's argument against the dogma of bare life—the assumption of its sanctity under any circumstances—can be read in two ways. On the one hand, as I have argued in chapter 1, it refers to the pronouncement that *bare life* has been regarded sacred, in an "attempt of the weakened Western tradition" to recover its "lost saint" within the "impenetrability" of the existential cosmos.[5] On the other, the narratives that we have examined in this study convey urgent insights into the paradox that life itself, even at its lowest level, can be turned into a critical concept at the point at which it starts to resist being the "marked bearer of guilt" and the uncontested, docile expression of fate. I must repeat here that to turn "life itself," at its supposedly most precarious level, into a potentially alternative concept is uncommon, especially from several vantage points in the Marxian cultural tradition. The purpose of this chapter is to extend our analysis further and look for the interfaces of filmic expression and affective experience that help us address the tensions between bare life and just life, not at the level of content but at that of the "content of the form," to take White's expression. We will therefore put in a new perspective an aesthetic concept that we have previously introduced in relation to narcocorridos— *paratactical drama*.

Film can be considered as symbolic formation(s) constituting a wide, that is, multilayered, realm within which experience is translated into features and figures of immanence. At the same time, film helps radicalize the discussion of immanence: an "anthropological materialism" becomes a kind of sine qua non, in that it is necessary to read life, action, and desire through the lenses of images. In our reading, the concept of immanence points toward experience without transcendence, faith without doxa, and action without discourse. For example, when embodied and enacted, ethical differences take the lead over absolute moral dispositions.[6] At this point, influential categories like, for example, those of tragedy and melodrama are to be reviewed from an angle that perceives their limits. The concept of paratactical drama can help further explore those border zones in whose light reflection suddenly appears to be pushed toward absurd or incredible phenomena, hidden within the material surfaces and the experiential rhythms of immanence. Benjamin's distinction between the concepts of mere existence and just existence acquires a strong bearing because it challenges us to read it as a question of *immanent* difference. The absence of "just existence" from the plane of conclusive historical or theoretical categories requires that we explore the surfaces of the visible and palpable world in search of hidden ethical clues. Benjamin's distinction will thus be taken into the dimensions of that which is dealt with in terms of embodiment, figuration, and recognition rather than cognition and "meaning."

My study enters into dialogue with, among others, Deleuze's reflections on cinema. However, it advances the hypothesis that distinctive cinematic projects of Latin American descent give prominence to paradox over abstractly ontological, or suggestively fashionable, or pseudoreligious visions of a violent world. A series of questions arises from this. What are the affective zones, regarding the production and dissemination of images, where the density of experience is not simply erased by anthropological simulacra that nurture what Massumi calls the pervasiveness of "low-level fear," as it joins in the reproduction of violence as commodity? On a different plane, what are the territories where the Western transcendental apparatus becomes shallow, even as it remains redundantly prone to a dominant concept of reason? Let me reaccentuate the question that has been leading our entire study. How can bare life be meaningfully approached in such a way as to go beyond nihilistic sentiments, neoliberal cynicism, or a refashioned Christian morality? What are the conceptually and morally compelling spaces in today's world, where bare life—despite an omnipresent domination—avoids representing the lowest level of existence, and where there is an investment in energies and concepts directed against the toleration of suffering and holding on to life as if it were an unconditional given? How can contemporary films from Mexico, Brazil, Colombia, and Argentina help us to map out, or understand, these timely yet drastically unworldly spaces, in which life itself, having become *immanently political*, is at stake? Placing Benjamin in this context makes his concept of "legibility"—"each 'now' is the now of a particular recognizability"—more suggestive than he himself could have foreseen. His words about the junctures between bare life and just life, both ambivalent and urgent, call for an awareness that, from unfamiliar, non-European territories, can grasp those images anew "wherein what has been comes together in a flash with the now to form a constellation."[7] How can experience be wrested away from the powers of exhaustion or epistemological idealism? How can it be recuperated from its saturation by the deceitful forces of either cynicism or "post-humanist" comfort—the simulacrum of good life in today's privileged spaces of the globe?

Viewed in relation to Latin America, the periphery that has been incorporated into strategic neoliberal assets and at the same time converted into wastelands, while being besieged by the gifts of the "almighty's" empire (Harvey),[8] life acquires new urgency. Recalling current discussions, our point is not that "there is no place in Agamben for the democratic project of renegotiating the limits that separate full citizens from *Homo sacer*."[9] At issue, in fact, are global changes taking place in that very regard: in particular, the geopolitical placement or invention of democratic capitalist systems to make the periphery "contemporaneous." These systems can then function as masks concealing the fact that, "ultimately, we are all *Homo sacer*."[10] In other words, what some critics would perhaps view as being too immoderate a statement by Agamben when used to refer to the representative countries of the West, we perceive as being susceptible to critical spatialization that must, in the first place, consider the status of the global periphery. Globalization is about the uneven distribution of bare life. This chapter explores relationships between the uncanny territories of contemporary imagination and life by concerning itself with that order of immanence that is related to the aesthetic and existential presence of the image through film. Filmic creation has been addressing the history of neoliberal adjustment and the pacification of Latin American countries during recent decades in a particularly intense, sometimes existentialist, strongly paratactical yet not unreflective way. New tendencies in the cinema of Mexico and Colombia, Brazil, the Southern Cone, and other countries have rearticulated the problematics of violence by questioning geopolitical inequality, together with the mechanisms of distancing by which the ruling capitalist societies continue to protect their symbolic order from recognizing that guilt and deformation are their own invention. We will now discuss a selected group of movies stemming from different scenarios throughout Latin America.

After Tragedy, If Not Melodrama, What?

The Argentine film *Un Oso Rojo* (2002), directed by Adrián Caetano, is made up of elements of montage that seem conventional, together with an argument that appears to be ordinary at first glance. Yet, common typological takes are of little use once we accept "sensuous elaboration"[11] as a quality in its own right. The narration starts on the day on which *el Oso* ("the Bear"), a taciturn man in his late-thirties, is released from a Buenos Aires jail into which armed robbery had propelled him seven years earlier. The robbery had occurred on the first birthday of his daughter, Alicia, a coincidence that discredited the man in the eyes of his pretty wife, Natalia, who struggles to make a living in a suburban, lower middle-class neighborhood. On the day of *el Oso's* return, Natalia is living with another man, and eight-year-old Alicia is being raised with the knowledge that her father is a criminal. However, *el Oso* does not accept being treated as an unwelcome intruder; he instead strives to regain his authority as father and to provide the family (including Natalia's new partner) with the financial support he thinks he owes them. His economic condition is as precarious as it was before, so his project cannot be carried out without violent means that lead him, once again, into the arena of delinquency. *El Oso*, who now works as a driver, becomes involved in retaliation and murder ("el Turco," who owes him big money from the time before prison, is killed for betraying him again), but he manages to get away with it and to provide the family with an impressive sum. Natalia and Alicia's stepfather can thus pay their debts. After that, *el Oso* walks away and into the dark, following the principle: "At times, in order to do right by the people you love, you have to be far away."[12]

Caetano is one of the main directors of the so-called *nuevo cine argentino*, a movement that has been evolving since the second half of the 1990s, originating in independent film and short film productions, and carried forward by a generation of well-schooled filmmakers who came from television or advertising. David Oubiña, in his essay on new Argentine film, speaks of the recovery of a

> submerged universe of marginalized people (at times, a *lumpen* pose, at times an exotic perspective, and only occasionally an authentic search), a youthful look (that can lead to understanding a sphere that has been very badly mistreated by earlier films [...]), and a discursive tone dominated by populism (in which costumbrist and anti-intellectual tendencies combine to construct new common cinematographic spaces.[13]

In Argentina, a controversial recovery of marginality and violence by contemporary filmmakers came to bear later than in other countries like, for example, Mexico and Colombia. Caetano's film should be judged against the grain of an interpretive tradition in Argentina that favors the adherence to Adornian values of high aestheticism. Hence, one criterion for evaluating the status of violence lies in the possibility of tragedy. Oubiña, in his analysis of the film, asserts that the construction of the hero misses the point: "the figure lacks transcendence" and does not display the traits of a "modern," properly tragic, hero. From the balance between lacking "grandeza (greatness)" and "densidad (density)," it is only a small step to dismissing the legitimacy of Caetano's protagonist: *el Oso* is disqualified as a creature that is "simply violent"—"He's *lumpen*."[14] This approach becomes still more problematic when *el Oso* is denied the status of a "popular hero." At this point the critic discloses his wish to speak in representation of a tragic subject: popular agency would be recognized only if it offered a matrix that fits the "educated" sentiment—it would have to become sublime by striving for absolute values of good or evil; otherwise it remains inauthentic.

To mourn the lack of transcendence in the marginal subject has become a most inadequate, although not uncommon argument in ethical discussions. "Tragedy" still marks a powerful watershed that has, for a long time, been in the service of either an aesthetic purification of violence or a sublimation of political and social conflicts. As believed by the above-cited critic, *el Oso* fails to be authentically tragic because his crisis is not a catastrophe translatable into an individual's inner drama that could claim for genuine truth. *El Oso's* condition is not tragically significant in that he does not deserve "true pity." To say it with Hegelian criteria, his actions (and failures) cannot be measured by the "eternal and inviolable" values that a tragic subject would summon up against itself. Hegel wanted to be overtly clear: "Beggars and rascals cannot inspire us with pity of this kind."[15] In that vein, *el Os'os* is, rather, a "sad story," "a misfortune as such. Such miseries may befall a man [...] merely as a result of the conjuncture of external accidents," not of deeper *necessities*. Hence, "sad" collisions and "tragic" conflicts are separated by the famous essentializing partition.

Contemporary Latin American films have generated a narrative and visual repertoire with which a "normative concept" of tragedy[16] has been widely challenged, although it was sometimes affirmed. Melodramatic affective strategies, in particular, question a sublime pathos that refers back to God, the law, or other transcendental insignias. Melodrama has subverted good taste and established rules by staging incredible and absurd stories whose only promise consists of limitless love, heartbreak, and quotidian negotiations between these two. It has engaged obsessive narrations nurturing the day-to-day desires of those whose lives have been emptied of the hopes for superior justice. Film melodrama in Latin America also became increasingly self-reflexive during the 1990s, recharging and contrasting its affective investments with ingredients of irony, mockery, and even horror.[17] However, to approach cinematic imagination in these present times may require still different conceptual frameworks. Films such as *Un Oso Rojo*, together with others such as *Pizza, Birra, Faso* (Argentina 1997), *Amores Perros* (Mexico 2000), *De la Calle* (Mexico 2001), *Cidade de Deus* (Brazil 2003), *Días de Santiago* (Peru 2004), *El Colombian Dream* (2007), and *La Vendedora de Rosas* (Colombia 1998), to name only a few, introduce modes of experience at the edges of life that also seem to suspend, aesthetically speaking, the possibility of melodramatic empowerment. This tendency was pioneered by the Colombian film *Rodrigo D. No futuro* (1988), which we will discuss in the final section of this chapter. We are dealing with contemporary forms of paratactical drama whose appraisal can enable a specific involvement in the current discussions on ethics and violence.

We now return to *A Read Bear*, for it provides a significant case of this change. Its hero is disconcerting, if one does not share the prejudice that the figure is just another criminal. Let us look at two scenes in which the status of exception regarding the meaning of life is at issue. Shortly after his release from prison, *el Oso* overhears in a street conversation that a young, elegant, business type has received a salary advance. *El Oso* approaches him to ask for ten pesos, to which the haughty character answers: "Andá a trabajar (Get a job!)." *El Oso* violently drags the fellow into his luxurious car and steals all his money. Intensity arises from the emotional abyss between the two men. Whereas *el Oso's* posture, behind his aggressive act, is entirely passionless, the rich man bursts into inconsolable tears. This leads ad absurdum any possibility of individual tragic distinction in the Hegelian sense. The emotional contrast is grounded on common knowledge shared by both men. For the social outsider and the businessman, sheer life is at stake, although from opposite angles. That is to say, they share a strange sense of a contemporary "state of exception," which is pervasive, yet not directly dependent on the positive power of the law nor on a sovereign decision known as the Schmittian paradigm. This scene extends historical insight beyond the assumptions of the juridical theory of the state. In Argentina's post-dictatorship, the political state of emergency has passed, since democracy implies the perception of a stable society. However, this normalized existence in market society has become anachronistic, in that it is now contaminated by situations of exception in the spaces of daily life.

Another still more significant scene constructs an encounter between *el Oso* and his daughter Alicia, leading to a traumatic revelation. The father has taken the eight-year-old girl to a suburban fairground where she climbs on a merry-go-round. The camera is mounted on it, so that every time it goes around, when Alicia travels past the man, she sees him up close, then moving out of angle until he disappears from sight, before circling back, and so forth. *El Oso* watches his daughter on the carousel from behind a fence. Alicia notices two policemen approaching her father. The girl grows anxious while she is stuck on the moving platform. The father looks toward her in a state of emotional attachment until he "awakens" at the moment when the policemen, from behind, push him against the fence to search him for weapons or drugs. The girl's stupor is heightened—the carousel keeps spinning so she can only turn her head as far to the left or right as possible to keep her father in sight. It is there—in the silent relationship between the girl's face and that of her father marked by successive reencounter and separation—that the film produces its argument by virtue of the "affection-image."

According to Deleuze, film has reshaped the problematics of affection, especially with visual figurations related to the use of the close-up. The molding and the tectonics of the face have made affect apprehensible through visual ecstasies that surpass the immediate coordinates of space and time. Deleuze addresses particular powers of "abstraction" and intensification in their relationship to the image. To say it again, we are concerned with the complexity of experience and even reflection when they are related, not to transcendence but to immanence. It comes as a necessary surprise that, through filmic expression, affect can be made specifically independent of the coordinates of a concrete place. Montage is able to create entirely new relationships between visual isolations and contextual environments: affect becomes an "entity" by means of image construction. The relationship between *el Oso* and Alicia can thus be addressed in terms of intensity and empathy, or of "proposition." Proposition discloses a virtuality that is "not a sensation, a feeling or idea, but the quality of a possible sensation, feeling or idea." Deleuze describes the "affection-image" as distinct from the "action-image": "it is quality or power, it is potentiality considered for itself as expressed."[18] Regarding the scene described earlier, the traumatic encounter of father and daughter is, on the one hand, owing to the specific circumstances of the situation. At the same time, the particular *affect* created by the silent communication between the two faces, both depicted as alternating close-ups, is "distinct from every individuated state of things"—it is like a new experience, powerful and transgressive in itself.

The mutual mirroring of the two faces as intimate close-ups expresses the "compound affect"[19] of longing for proximity and of a sudden bewilderment working against the longing. The affection-image gives shape to a double abandonment as proposition: Alicia is abandoned by her father, who is taken away from her by the unlimited power that the police force can exert on the man even in a moment of togetherness with his daughter. Second, *el Oso* is abandoned by the existing law. This abandonment rests on the assumption that interventions of the police can go beyond "law-preserving" violence with practices of "law-making" violence. The fact that the policemen finally walk away after searching the man does not diminish the affective state that, on the contrary, is pushed toward a perception of the virtual omnipresence of the police. An abandonment of the daughter is caused by the exposedness of the father—his being susceptible to discipline by superior coercive violence at any time. To use Agamben's expression, the father in *Un Oso Rojo* has become a "sacred" person. This is the moment in which the immanent guiltiness of *el Oso* is crystallized by an image of singular intensity. The man had not been doing anything wrong—his mere existence, together with his suspicious appearance in the eyes of some people of the neighborhood, sufficed to expose him to reprehension. At last, the affection-image gives shape to a double exposedness: in his abandonment to the ghostly presence of the police, the father is exposed to the eyes of his daughter, which is worse than his being in prison. While *el Oso* watches his daughter watching him, he is forced to recognize himself as a criminal-in-advance—a kind of wandering delinquent. In that sense, both father and daughter are taken away from each other, since the father cannot overcome the immanent *sacredness* that characterizes his condition after having left the prison.

Viewed from the standpoint of multiple abandonments, the next step toward *el Oso's* relapse into criminal action does not make an essential difference: if he is only a "revenant" to life—not being able to assume a normal existence after jail—his transgressing the rules constitutes his only freedom. Oubiña, the critic referred to earlier, is not interested in the affective situation created by the film when he asserts: "In a country where taking justice into one's own hands has so frequently been the clearest indication of fascism, at very least a heroic character like *el Oso* should be in doubt."[20] The atavism of Caetano's movie points in a different direction, in that it is a historical phenomenon—as is fascism—yet it is subjectified by those who have been biopolitically dispensed by authoritarianism and by neoliberalism alike. In the film, the loss of the melodramatic option still enables a strategy of empowerment. Once *el Oso* realizes that his longing for love and harmony has broken down owing to his immanent criminality, he decides that he can still help Alicia, Natalia, and her new partner get out of indebtedness. He does so by participating in a robbery and settling scores with old companions, finally being able to contribute big money to Alicia's new family. The final scene shows the compact body of *el Oso*, seen from behind, framed in a medium-shot, as he walks away from the camera into the darkness of urban nocturnal space. Now it is no longer the face that constitutes the site of the affection-image. Instead, it is the body of the protagonist that has become "pure affect." The nocturnal, empty streets are depicted in such a way that they lose their specificity and become "any space whatever."[21] The affection-image reveals its magic to abstract from spatiotemporal coordinates; moreover, it can even move beyond a face or a body. In that sense, the man's body expresses a deindividualized experience, a posture of life at its limit revealing a strange and powerful consistency.

Realistically, *el Oso* would be dead after the shoot-outs that he, alone, had with many other men. To attribute his endurance to the marketable ideal of heightened masculine power would overlook the affective argument. The film places the man in a virtual space "beyond death," since society has abandoned creatures like him. In conventional terms, two possible solutions would have sufficed. On the one hand, death could have occurred in a way that enabled the tragic distinction of the person, a situation arising, for example, from Alicia's losing her beloved father so dramatically. On the other hand, violent death could have sealed the destiny of a person who did not deserve otherwise. Caetano's film avoids these schemata, both of which are inherent in a long-traditioned, morally affirmative middle-class imagination. Within this tradition, violence and death represent the abject side of modern life. In other words: violence has occupied its legitimate place within a means-ends dialectics that has always seemed to be ultimately secured by enlightened law, normative universalism, or regulative Christian morality. When cinematic ethics, however, engage bare life as a quotidian condition, the problem is not violence as an ultimate, remote possibility, or as a means that under certain conditions serves either the attainment or the preservation of the higher end, nor as a sad occurrence suddenly irrupting into someone's destiny. At issue is existence qua experience under the conditions of life's having been sacrificed to an omnipresent, virtual nonexistence of the human condition. Seen from this perspective, an atavistic philosophy resonates in the affective makeup of the film. This posture has corrosive implications for the ways in which modern life has been conceived and dreamt of. Violence is suddenly made visible outside the means-ends dialectics: it has become the central feature of immanence in the life of figures such as Caetano's hero, *el Oso*.

The affective arguments set forth by a series of recent films from different Latin American countries can be placed within a similar framework, an observation that allows us to historicize the perception of ethical survival in times of advanced global capitalism and imperial rule. Speaking in narratological terms, at issue is the conscious decision of the outsider-protagonist to move beyond the docile endurance of a destitute life, even at the coast of death, not for a higher end but for the sake of sheer existence. This is neither a simple question of counter-violence, nor of terrorism, although it could be viewed as a form of "active nihilism."[22] Distinct from Nietzschean postures, this attitude is not a matter of intellectual vehemence. It has to do with the heroes' seizure of the space of abandonment created by society at the point where no other alternatives can be seen, yet where the creation of violent events serves as an act of solidarity—the support of loved ones or family members who still have a chance to outlive the exception. In the case of these antiheroes, violence does not serve personal enrichment or the creation of corrupt networks of power. For example, at the end of the Mexican film *Amores Perros* (2000), the protagonist *el Chivo*—a former guerrillero who eventually worked as a contract killer—walks out of the picture and into an affective, visual space "beyond death"—a semi-dark, desolate country-side, his stature becoming one with the mass of dry, broken earth extending toward the horizon. Is it accidental that *el Chivo's* adoring love and supportive attitude, as was *el Oso's*, is focused on his only daughter who—living on the side of "full citizenry"—has become inaccessible to him? If, from a father's perspective, the sentiments toward the daughter become more essential than his own being, then existence appears as an active stance that contests the supposed impotence of bare life.

Before paying attention to *Amores Perros*, a second Argentine movie has to be mentioned: *El Bonaerense* (2002) directed by Pablo Trapero. *El Bonaerense* narrates the story of *el Zapa*, a man of thirty-two who works as a locksmith in a village in the province of Buenos Aires. His boss, el Polaco, advises him to help two men open a safe, after which *el Zapa* is arrested by the police. His uncle, a retired police officer, succeeds in getting him out of jail and sends him, with a recommendation, to the big metropolis of Buenos Aires where he is expected to become a police agent. This turnabout indicates an ambiguous mechanism in the social production of discipline. Society recruits male members of the lower classes to serve its "law-preserving" needs. Behind the integration of *el Zapa* into a strict system of rules and codes, the film allows the viewer to discern the machinations through which the local urban police interacts with street crime and drug traffic. One of *el Zapa's* teachers is Gallo, an experienced agent in his forties, who holds that "we have to resolve the problems of the community, because we are part of the commu-nity." The real lesson taught by Gallo, who lives in a better-off middle-class neighborhood, is that police violence must skillfully emancipate itself from its limitations as merely a force for the preservation of law. Without any pre-tension of a legal purpose, Gallo kills the elder criminal el Polaco who had already been arrested by *el Zapa*; and before *el Zapa* can start protesting, Gallo shoots him in the left thigh, making him a cripple for the rest of his life. *El Zapa*, who has never been a man of words, silently understands the lesson that binds him even more strongly to the side of the police, since he has now experienced with his own fragile body how the law is made.

In this film a remarkable, slowly increasing intensity is evoked by the depiction of *el Zapa's* face. *El Zapa* is played by Jorge Román, a nonpro-fessional actor whose face is mostly framed through medium shots. By the repetitious, speechless expression of a countenance that resembles the child-like features of a hedgehog, the story of the man's entering the police and thus becoming part of society, is contrasted on the level of affection. It is as though the face were unable to completely understand what its own body is doing almost automatically. *El Zapa's* face appears frozen in a kind of childish astonishment, or naive cynicism, which remains dominant even in situations of unbridled sensuality—when he has sex with the police officer Mabel, or when he is severely injured. According to a dark, yet not fortuitous logic, *el Zapa* (similar to *el Oso*) is denied the possibility of melodramatic conflict. The film avoids devices of "overstatement, [...], hyperbole, excess, excitement, and acting out."[23] In terms of melodramatic empowerment, an "expressionistic aesthetics of the body" would have allowed for a force field helping to affirm life in the ordinary and even abject spheres of daily normality. However, this strategy seems to lose its meaning under the spell of an exception that becomes real life's norm. *El Zapa* has a wife and a small child whom he had left when he became a police rookie, and with whom he meets again after recovering from his injury, when he pays them a platonic visit. In the meantime he has begun a relationship with Mabel, the police officer, but she wards off his attempts to continue the sexual romance, knowing that he has been co-opted by the dark forces of the institution. His previous encounters with Mabel were driven by hunger for sex in a world without meaningful words and deeds, that is to say—without love. Hence, *el Zapa* is entirely lost to bare life, not being prone to the deviant stoicism and the ethical energies that distinguish a figure like the *Bear*.

The concluding scene shows how the man enters into the abyss of a "no-life," devoid of alternatives as well as of tragic posture. When *el Zapa* visits his home village after receiving a promotion, the situation of reencounter with his mother, his wife, and child shows a lamentable tableau. His mother appears to be resigned to whatever life presents to her, not even paying attention to her son's limp. The family and some members of the local police force have set up a table outside a barn—an image of rural fatalism based on poverty and monotony. Robot-like, *el Zapa* joins people drinking to his promotion, while his inscrutable, immobilized face absorbs everything instead of reflecting it. The final camera movement draws on the chasm that lingers behind a motionless face covered by a barely perceptible veil of sadness. His farewell to his family is set in a series of images that seem to blur concrete space and time. With his police cap on, *el Zapa* is seen from a distance, walking away alongside a fence and back toward where he belongs—the police force. He walks slowly, favoring his left leg. The camera moves from long shot to medium shot, slowly catching up with the man until his face is caught in profile by the close-up, at which point the face turns away from the onlooker. Thus he walks out of perspective, his countenance being effaced while making the spectator rebound to the close-up image of his head now shown from behind. *El Zapa* and the *Bear* can be viewed as embodying two sides of extreme biopolitical conditioning of the human being. The one is based on the machinations of law-making violence at the lower end of state domination, where legal police power mutates into an arbitrary, all-pervasive, and formless presence. The other is linked to practices of existentialist violence—in the case of *el Oso*—arising as vigorous reaction to the negation of the modern social contract and its worldly as well as communal spirit.

Among Latin American films of the beginning of the twenty-first century, the Mexican production *Amores Perros*, directed by Alejandro González Iñarritu, has probably earned the most spectacular attention, along with an impressive array of festival awards. Sharply condensing a world of urban squalor that envelopes Mexico City, the film deals with a variety of topics that are all linked to contemporary cinematic conventions. Its characters are grouped around the idea of a vertical slice through society where meanness and poverty contrast and suddenly collide with wealth and frivolity. There are marginal youths engaged in underground dog-fighting, robbery, and a violent search for romance; there is a top model, together with her wealthy lover, who is crippled in an accident that destroys her precious body; furthermore, there is a mythic street character—an old vagrant—who was once a guerrilla rebel, spent many years in prison, and then became destitute, surviving by occasionally hiring himself out as a hitman. In addition, there are car races, dog fights, scenes of street violence and obsessive passion, jealousy, hate, and revenge—offensive gestures and belligerent acts looming everywhere. The onlooker can recognize features of the telenovela supergenre that are synthesized in a well-made action drama. At the same time, dramaturgical ingredients come as a matter of "generational' schooling—González Iñarritu has not hesitated to borrow stylistic elements from Tarantino's *Pulp Fiction* and *Reservoir Dogs*.

But there is something that compels beyond these parameters of success. The title "Amores perros" reveals a twofold meaning. The persons involved in the three love-and-repugnance relationships that together constitute the narrative grid of the film are all attached to dogs. Second, the obsessive presence of dogs within all three constellations marks the centrality of (dog-)life—and death—as the catalyst of a visceral force. It is a compulsion that accompanies and even enables human life the way it is shown to pervade an end-of-the-twentieth-century Mexico City. The film starts with brutal, smash-cut images of a fleeing car driven by two young fellows, and a bleeding, mortally wounded dog in the backseat of the car. Later, dogs are present in different settings of human interaction, either behaving aggressively or being vulnerable and victimized by other dogs. González Iñarritu thus creates a stunning allegory of bare life. These dogs do not symbolize the affection that humans often devote to animals in situations of personal loneliness. They lend bare life an ongoing physical presence. Their role is attached to both aggressiveness and the extreme vulnerability of the body, constituting a parallel that unites humans and animals under the circumstances of what appears as a shared abysmal state.

Humans and animals sharing a common state of exception is one of the aspects that lends the film particular strength and a great deal of the dismay that it has generated among viewers. However, it is necessary to perceive this archaic component as a conceptual factor. At issue is politicization of urban life as it unfolds in a realm spanning the operative capitalist dynamics of power, palpable as an omnipresent drive toward commodification, and an exhaustion of the spaces of daily existence in Mexico's capital. Historicization by filmic images does not need to be explicit; it requires reading the traces of affection through which the audiovisual project makes its argument. When discussing *Un Oso Rojo*, I alluded to democratic society's susceptibility to daily situations of exception. *Amores Perros* shows, in an even more accentuated way, disaster zones irrupting from beneath the surfaces of democratically normativized life. Within these peripheral territories, democracy, which is supposed to define the space that separates "full citizens" from "homo sacer," is neither self-understood nor is it guaranteed to the people through the unity of law-preserving structures and the role of the state itself. This is one of the substantial subjects addressed by all the works discussed here. Scenarios like those created by González Iñarritu can be viewed as "global localizations" suggesting that, for example, countries like Mexico and Argentina have come close to each other, not in terms of homogeneous development, but from the standpoint of perturbing experiences inscribed in the postmodern zones of destitution that characterize the "cities of the future."[24]

Illustrious metaphors circumscribing Mexico's stake in modernity seem to display a genealogy of decline. There is Octavio Paz' *Labyrinth of Solitude*, Roger Bartra's *The Cave of Melancholy*, or Monsiváis' *Rituals of Chaos*. The director of *Amores Perros* abandons them all and creates another one: rituals of violence. Has modernity, beyond all premonitions, generated public territories in which a huge number of people survive by ritualistic incursions into violence? This question is not a deterministic one, and it should not be seen as merely dependent on the specific conditions that threaten Latin American civil societies. At issue in these films is not a violent Latin America, but violence in global, and yet modern terms. To put it differently—what distinguishes González Iñarritu's perspective from the playfully unhistorical, cynical, yet entertaining blood-spilling violence in several of Tarantino's films? Are the protagonists of *Amores Perros* like Octavio and Ramiro, and El Chivo, "natural born killers," to paraphrase Oliver Stone?[25] It would be difficult to imagine that a film like *Amores Perros* could incite teenagers to follow the examples of these protagonists in real life. There is an ethical difference that prevents affective montage from being absorbed into those terror scenarios whose function is to hijack the attention of an exhausted international public mainly consisting of parts of the middle classes. Latin American cinema's new outcasts from the urban poor are physically vulnerable, yet in their atavistic deftness impressive machos, or gang youths, or children without childhood who—together with a scorching class of underground heroines—have come to challenge the mythifying images of the Hollywood-style post-human warrior.

Let us look into how the three juxtaposed narratives in *Amores Perros* form a conceptual grid. First, there is the story of "Octavio and Susana," set in a poor, working-class neighborhood where numerous youngsters live together within a small housing space, facing all kinds of trouble. Cofi is the name of a stout Rottweiler that Octavio uses to raise money from dogfights, as he dreams of running off with his young sister-in-law, Susana.

Ramiro, Susana's aggressive husband, works in a grocery store and applies his respective know-how to robbing other stores at night. Things go wrong and Octavio, threatened by the chief of the local dog-fighting scene, has to resort to a wild car flight, producing the accident that entwines the three different story-spaces of the film. All these are ingredients of common action plots. Yet the film's dramatic gift lies in the surprises it creates. The handsome, almost sweet Octavio, who pursues Susana against all odds, turns the Rottweiler into a sacred animal: to assume Agamben's definition somewhat drastically, Cofi can naturally be sacrificed in the dogfights, but Octavio is inconsolably shocked when the owner of some pit-bulls shoots his dog. That same Octavio hires three men and sacrifices his brother Ramiro to a terrible beating, with the condition that he not be killed. Octavio is then severely injured himself in the car crash.

The implications for the structuring of affective space are telling. Octavio is presented by "action-images" that relate to physically and socially defined environments. Close-ups of his face are notably missing, except for the frantic initial scene of Octavio's driving the pursued car, in which his grimace appears as part of hyperkinetic cross-cuts showing his terror, the bleeding dog on the back seat, and glimpses of the passing streets. According to a phenomenology of the "action-image," character and milieu are organically tied together: "The milieu and its forces...act on the character, throw him a challenge, and constitute a situation in which he is caught. The character reacts in his turn (action properly speaking) so as to respond to the situation...."[26] Now, the purpose of the protagonist's "realistic" construction through action and reaction lies in situating the "affection-image" elsewhere. What acquire intensity in their own right are the depictions of Cofi the Rottweiler, as well as of the other fighting dogs. Canines crashing into each other cause a sensation of pure combustive energy, of bodies in their immediate crossing of the threshold between life and death. The director's editing logic is explicit in forcing abject sensations: repeatedly, a cut interrupts the scene of fighting dogs at the moment at which they attack each other, so that the deadly spectacle is deferred, that is to say transferred into the realm of human relationships. Affection-images, in this context, are not centered on the body or on the appearance of a particular dog; they are the result of a deindividuating motion that makes affect "pure" and all-embracing. The viewer is thus haunted with the sheer potentiality of blood-soaked, ripped-apart bodies to surface everywhere and at any turn of the film. The movie induces experiences of fear as aesthetic sensations. However, shock-like effects are not produced wholesale but require thinking.

In the second story, "Daniel and Valeria," the ritual constellation is different. Although the director is said to have borrowed several shots from Kieslowski's film *Red*,[27] a sacrificial constellation lends his subplot an atmosphere of its own. The relationship between Valeria and her boyfriend Daniel, a married businessman, becomes problematic at the point at which the supermodel is injured in the car crash caused by Octavio. Put in the terms of the intimidated citizen, Octavio has been ruthlessly endangering, and potentially sacrificing the lives of innocent people around him. Innocent people? Indeed, the laceration of Valeria's right leg equals the end of her career. This is one of the few experiences prone to generating tragic sentiment, since it is the future of a young and sophisticated woman that is at stake. Visual contours of tragic sensation are framed in a match-cut, a sort of establishing shot in terms of intensity, moving from a gigantic street poster that shows a supermodel towering over the heads of passersby, to Valeria's stupefied face depicted in close-up. It is the model who now sits in a wheelchair, staring out of the window of her new apartment at her commodified, timeless image displayed on the street, and unable to make sense of her situation. At this point, the director invents a doubling of sacrifice that will turn out to be devastating to the tragic momentum. While Valeria is paralyzed physically and mentally, her puppy Richi falls into a parallel drama: the little dog disappears beneath the floorboards of the apartment, and the vision that takes hold of the woman is her pet's being devoured by rats. Daniel, the lover, is drowned in stupidity, unable to understand how Valeria relives, through the disappearance of Richi, her own laceration, only to end up in melancholic hysteria revealing that the center of her love was the perfect icon of her female body. The body of the model loses its select sacredness—its existence as a superior fetish object—when it is physically shattered: sacrifice as collateral damage among the rich.

The film contributes a remarkable hero to contemporary imagination, and he belongs to the third story: "El Chivo and Maru." It is Martín who bears the nickname of *el Chivo*, referring to the popular metaphor given to a trimmed gun or, more satirically, to the man's being a strange apostate. *El Chivo's* attire is that of a long-haired and bearded Methuselah in tunic-like rags and tatters. As a phantom figure, he inhabits an abandoned storage-shack, frequently roaming through the streets with a horde of dogs surrounding the wheelbarrow in which he collects trash and recyclables. People tell each other that this urban nomad started out, decades ago, as a professor at a private university, but he left his job and family—his daughter *Maru* was then two years old—to join a guerrilla movement. On his return he was convicted to twenty years in prison for kidnapping a wealthy businessman and committing other crimes. After his release he occasionally carries out contract killings to survive; at the same time, he arrives at a point where his only desire is to reintroduce himself as a human to his daughter who doesn't know that he is alive.

El Chivo has already been lurking throughout the previous stories, establishing an uncanny authority. In a scene of the first story, the man is seen in front of a garbage pile, standing with a raised machete in his right hand like a threatening statue, to symbolically shelter his dogs from a pit-bull that is about to attack them. On seeing this saintly admonition by the man whose eyes emit dangerous-looking sparks of obsession, the goons to whom the pit-bull belongs call their dog away. In the central scene of the car crash, Martín, who was strolling along the sidewalk, takes action immediately. Helping the injured Octavio out of the shattered car, he makes sure to rescue the money that was earned by the youngster in the dogfight for him. He then rescues the wounded Cofi, Octavio's brutish Rottweiler to heal it. These acts function as skillfully edited counterpoints to Martín's pursuit of a young rich fellow he's been hired to kill by the man's business partner. Everything has been prepared for the assignment to be carried out, but when the moment arrives, Martín cannot use his gun because a group of children gets in the way. On another day, returning to his shelter, Martín has to face a terrible picture: his stray dogs have all been mauled to death by Cofi, who has recovered from his wounds. Inconsolable and with tears streaming down his face, *el Chivo* gets ready to punish the Rottweiler with a shot in the head, but in the final moment decides to let the animal live. All these scenes suggest a peculiar stake that Martín has in the issue of power over life and death—a disturbing image of the nonsovereign reterritorialization of "sacred power" enacted by the marginal subject. The disconcerting aspect is Martín's role as a marginal person who is equal to someone who self-consciously decides about the killing, or not killing, of other beings. Both humans and animals are exposed to bare life; the rich business people are destined for a good and protected life, but Martín shows a strong sense for the exception. This sense is displayed in one of the final scenes in which *el Chivo*, instead of carrying out an execution, kidnaps the client along with his victim, and then faces both businessmen toward each other as they are lying, tied up, on the floor. *El Chivo* places a revolver at an equal distance between them and leaves them to a destiny in which each will try to get the advantage that will allow him to kill his partner. In other words, to view *el Chivo* as a brutalized individual or as an ideological fanatic would miss the point that the film is offering to critical readings.

It has been observed that *el Chivo* is constructed as a conservative parody of the image of Karl Marx. Sánchez-Prado suggests an interpretation according to which the director fell prey to a prejudice that conceives of the urban criminal terrorist as a natural outcome of the political rebel. In that vein, the film could be read as a tribute to the fears of a conservative Mexican middle class during a time of the decay of the symbolically and legally protective nation state.[28] However, the film is more complex. What if *el Chivo* functioned, in a diffuse yet compelling realm of "post-national" imagination, as a revenant, embodying deep-rooted religious-political myths and masculine moral fantasies? Martín unites in his personal history representative figures of identity: the educator, the family father, and the political rebel. What we see is his having become a phantom figure roaming through present-day urban life. Like Freud's *Moses*, Martín has been repressed by the community; his contours are those of a martyr or of a prophet presenting an image of cursed and sometimes violent saintliness. When he shuffles down the city's sidewalks at a steady pace, pushing his wheelbarrow in a majestic manner, exhibiting an immutable, charismatic appearance, surrounded by his dogs and avoided by the passersby, he inhabits a world beyond. However, the penetrating look behind his apparent detachment shows that he is more from "this world" than many others. His is the posture of the forgotten prophet, an excluded and impoverished prophet, a post-traumatic hero, still an over-bearing presence in his ghostliness. He is disavowed by his own daughter and banned from the space inhabited by a citizenry that has become corrupt, amnesic, and mindless. His only community is the pack of dogs and, in a sense, youngsters like Octavio and Ramiro who have become violent in their own struggles against aborted hope.

Somewhat theatrically construed as a prophet without doctrine, *el Chivo* confers an image of authority—an archaic father who is relegated to the side-lines, but claims an occasional right to violence that is ambiguous in that it belongs both to the pater and to the marginal at the same time. This father, unlike Freud's *Moses*, takes action to be restored in the consciousness of his former family, secretly introducing his picture into the array of photos in the house of his daughter and his former wife. If that which resonates in *el Chivo* is the fantasy of a fallen original father, a sacred figure prone to the hopeless search of a community, then this character stands out as a postscript to the difficult dialectics of secularization in Latin America. Several associations regarding the relationship between politics, religion, and national trauma could be drawn from here. What makes the hero special is his opposition to a Freudian psychopathology. The repressed figure is neither restored to a pub-lic (or family) consciousness by virtue of collective guilt nor can he sustain a symbolic order as a metaphor of (lost) morals and law. Yet nor is the impossi-bility for the prophet to rise again by virtue of a collective neurosis converted into tragedy. On the other hand, a melodramatic turning point might have conferred a proper aesthetic place for an unrecognized father. *Amores Perros* shows how far a director can go, using a conventional dramaturgy and still undermining influential aesthetic styles. He succeeds in heightening strong passions without bending his knee to either tragedy or melodrama. It is, of course, a question of "values" that goes with these dispositifs, since modern incursions into the possibility of either melodrama or tragedy are "exercises in cultural diagnostics."[29]

After the adopted fighting dog has slaughtered *el Chivo's* animal com-munity, the man experiences sensations of torment that lead him to a point of conversion. He decides to abandon his legendary appearance and to take on an external facade that seems, at first glance, absurd. A closer look reveals the parodist touch of what appears to be the formal outfit of a weary profes-sor, his fierce eyes veiled behind a pair of very old, broken glasses. It is this image of his that he now takes a picture of, and which he secretly mounts among the photo collection of his former family by breaking into their house in their absence. He also leaves a bundle of banknotes under his daugh-ter's pillow, a fetish that middle-class families tend to equate with a father's traditional responsibility. Martín then chooses to go away, based on his expe-rience that there is no choice to make. One might paraphrase Deleuze at this point—his thoughts on the immanent links between knowledge of "missing choice" and "pure potential"[30]—but it is necessary to surpass the abstract ontological frame. In *el Chivo's* case, the "pure potentiality" of assuming a space beyond despair is negatively defined. He departs from the role of the urban nomad whose reterritorializing habitus could rely on occasional acts of violence. He moves from his previous sphere of abandonment into an open space, a "plain" space where such distinctions as the ones between "nomad" and "migrant," vagrant and prophet are becoming blurred.

El Chivo is the only figure in the film whose appearance is framed by "action-images" and "affection-images" alike; yet at the end, his presence mutates entirely into an "affection-image," erasing any tie between character and milieu. The man's final walking away from the camera, depicting both his and the dog's bodies from behind as they move into an inscrutable void, evokes the affective metaphor of "any-space-whatever."[31] His stature is gradually absorbed by the somber grey, broken earth that potentializes the void as an expressionist darkness. There is nothing left except bare life. Yet it is important to note the shift that takes place at the end of *Amores Perros*. The subject of "bare life" is no longer the vagrant. It is the conscious intellectual who is excluded from all meanings, that is to say from the constituent possibilities of society's public space. The fact that *el Chivo* "chooses" to (re) enter this affective space, not as a prophet, nor as a marginal figure, but as a ghostly intellectual, makes González Iñarritu's film an extraordinary statement on the situation of today's world.

A Brazilian film acquires significance as an adjacent yet strongly contrasting case: *Carandiru* (2003), directed by Héctor Babenco. "Carandiru," once located in São Paulo, was Brazil's largest penitentiary and existed until October, 1992, when police squads stormed the complex, putting an end to a prisoners' uprising by carrying out an atrocious massacre. The slaughter by the state forces caused a wave of nationwide indignation, which led to the closure of the facility and the relocation of remaining detainees. On the basis of *Estação Carandiru* (Carandiru Station, 2000), an eyewitness account written by Drauzio Varella who had worked for several years in the penitentiary as a physician, Babenco, together with Fernando Bonassi and Victor Navas produced the script for the film.

Babenco has been well known since *Pixote* (Brazil, 1980) and his adaptation of Manuel Puig's novel *El beso de la mujer araña* (*The Kiss of the Spider Woman*, 1985). His recent work is not a prison movie of Foucaultian style. How does he address the "exception" that comes related either to prison reality or to a possibly wider context of state intervention? Babenco decided to mold his central hero based on the original prison doctor, Varella, the author of the testimony. The book, *Carandiru Station*,[32] evokes the trope of the *medicus* as benevolent ethnographer: Varella appears as an attentive and thus committed chronicler, that is to say, as the author gathering the tales of prisoners who desired to tell their stories "back to the world." The design of the film corresponds to this model, in that it is constructed around the actions and the perspective of the "Doctor." This physician, about forty years old, is a model caregiver, calm and attentive, professional, with infinitely gentle eyes—a man of goodness and confidence. He offers basic treatment to all inmates, irrespective of their chances of being cured. His infirmary becomes a meeting place where patients tell their stories, and from where—through retrospective montage—a panorama of human histories unfolds: some anecdotes, others parables, and still others dramas with epic and tragic peripeties. There are the gorgeous transvestite "Lady Di" and her dwarfish lover; the mulato Ebony ("Nego Preto"), the highest authority of the prison population; "Majestade," an ebullient black man who is courted and cursed—during visiting hours—by his two "wives" who are also the mothers of his several children; there is "Deusdete," an adolescent who was detained for killing his sister's rapist, and his pal "Zico," who will soon kill his young friend in the throes of a drug delirium.

The epidemic reality of AIDS and venereal diseases is addressed as the doctor regularly performs blood tests. However, these are rather symbolic examinations: the tests give the doctor access to the men's stories, a reality that can still be appropriated anecdotally or epically, and thus escapes an abyss that is life-destroying. AIDS is a medical issue or a narratological device, but it is not an immanent experience that involves patients as much as it could affect the doctor. Probably for that reason, prisoners are depicted mainly through action-images, even when they convey the narrative memory of their past. The doctor is the only person who is occasionally absorbed into affection-images like his astonished or melancholic face. There is another, very different transcending image at the end of the film. It shows the remnants after the massacre that has put down the prisoners' revolt, in which more than a hundred inmates were brutally slaughtered. When the camera slowly moves through ghostly corridors filled with bodies that are spattered with blood, one might have the sensation that the images belong to a different film. The doctor had finished his humanitarian assignment a while ago. He will return to the place once more, weeks after the massacre, only to see cleaned-up, dark, and empty spaces. A salomonic subtext, looking strangely out of place, expresses his inner voice: "The only ones who know what really happened are God, the police, and the inmates."[33]

A peculiar evolution from melodrama to tragedy has taken place. During extensive parts of the film, one could be reminded of Brooks' thesis: in a world deprived of traditional religious beliefs in higher justice, melodramatic imagination can generate a "moral occult," illuminating and sustaining life under the most profane circumstances. Romantic personal memories and entanglement kept the prisoners alive—their marginality was emotionally defined, and their heightened expressive behavior often transgressed sane language but always held tight to the meaning of existence as happiness, thus resisting bare life. The film's ethical argument was defined by the presence of the doctor-narrator, combining charity and human understanding. At the end, the massacre indicates the moment in which law-preserving force suddenly turns into a frenzy of "law-positing" invasion. When the images of special police units performing the massacre replace the perspective of the eyewitness, the moral purpose as it has been unfolded earlier crumbles into an apocalyptic, tragic void. Affective involvement is remade into a distancing aesthetic strategy, seconded by the above-cited subtext: only "God, the police, and the inmates" could know what really happened. If there is "involvement," it either works "in representation" or from the distance of the ethnographer-citizen that is kept intact. A glimmer of a Hegelian transcendental fear emerges, according to which "true tragic sympathy" is inspired by our "fear of the power of the...order" that has been violated.[34] There is a deep, perhaps unintended irony in Babenco's film: the appearance of the doctor as self-determined, compassionate individual, together with his empty words at the end are the markers of a fantasmatic abyss—the real sign of the prisoners' abandonment. A normative separation turns into a chilling perception—that between the secure place of the qualified citizen and the power of the body politic to practice the exception. *Amores Perros*, in turn, confers a strategy that draws the viewer, and the critic, into a space of immanence where no salvation exists. In other words, the *Doctor* in *Carandiru*, and *el Chivo* in *Amores Perros* can be viewed as opposing figures regarding the subject-oriented experiences of violence, ethical agency, and life. They both represent affective postures whose strange synchronicity forms part of contemporary critical imagination.

Resurgence of the Forgotten: Víctor Gaviria's Project of Immanent Critique

The ways in which contemporary films from the global South explore bare life in relation to figures of *violence without guilt* intersect with larger cinematic trajectories. Historical understanding is a question of discontinuity, including the repetition as well as change of status of features and modules that are already known. On the one hand, there have been marked shifts in the work of ethically committed filmmakers during past decades. However, more acute attention is needed to decipher similarities that appear in the guise of difference. Let me mention, before touching on the work of Colombian director Víctor Gaviria, an episode from the documentary *Tire Dié*, created by Fernando Birri in 1958. The film was dedicated to the children of Santa Fé (Argentina) and other places for whom, due to their life in poverty, the word childhood does not exist. The sequence by which Birri's movie keeps impacting memory captures images of barefooted children, as they run along the narrow struts of the steel frame that takes the train rails across the Santa Fé River lying far below. The low grounds along the river, regularly flooded, devoid of trees and any scenic attraction, show the huts of countless families of Santa Fé's marginal population. "Tire dié!"—"throw ten (cents)!"—is the daily cry of the children who, while balancing on steel planks alongside the trains during those few moments when they cross the bridge, ask the passengers behind the windows for ten centavos.

Among the impressive number of references to Italian postwar neorealism that have come to traverse Latin American cinema, Birri's film offers a vibrant example. The scene in question starts with a locomotive's whistle, accompanied by a cut from a long take of the river lowlands to the structure of the bridge on which boys between the ages of six and twelve are quickly climbing upward. Suddenly there is a view of the upper scaffolding with groups of barefooted bodies lurking on the struts like little acrobats on the look-out for the starting signal. A train enters the steel skeleton, with the driver of the locomotive shaking his head: "It's always the same with those children!" The camera now looks out of the train. From above, the viewer sees the boys' eyes, hands, and arms raised toward the windows while their bare feet are rushing, with amazing versatility, over the planks to keep pace with the train. Their yelling "Tire dié!" is vigorous and sometimes breathless; for some it might even sound like a battle-cry. The spectator, while looking down toward the faces and arms of the "tire dié!," sees the narrow struts on which the children balance, and the deep void below. Fragile bodies on the verge of the abyss, yet their features are marked by an energy that makes them excel in the act of staying alive—which means providing their families with the wherewithal for survival. General concepts like "docu-drama," "poetics of poverty," and "subaltern representation" have often served as foci of explanation, yet they have sometimes obstructed an approach to embodiment as a conceptual issue of equal validity. For the duration of the bridge scene, Birri has suspended his narrating voice, the voice of the interviewing and commenting documentarist. In contrast to a politics of criticism that has judged Latin American social realism mainly by its content, a sudden commitment to aesthetics of immanence shines forth. We can reconsider *Tire dié* decades after its creation and realize that the described shots accomplish an astonishing passage between action image and affection image. *Who* are these children? They were what in Spanish are called "actores naturales" (nonprofessional, real-life actors) from the destitute neighborhoods of Santa Fé. But aren't these people susceptible, as well, to turning "natural acting" into a violently defamiliarizing gesture? We will return to this question when we discuss the films of Víctor Gaviria.

There is a segment in which the action of *Tire dié* produces "pure intensity" condensed in the rhythm of the children's bodies, their vivacious movement close to the abyss, manifest during the moments when velocity is shared by the passengers of the train and the running bodies—a synchronicity that is expressed in the momentary contact of two distant worlds. The viewers' sudden fear for the children's safety is not shared by the little acrobats. Affective contact means conflict in the space of experience. At the point at which the children adapt to the pace of the train while it slows down on the bridge, the "*passenger*-camera" looks into the boys' agitated faces and suddenly seems to capture their entire situation. This is a Benjaminian dialectical image insofar as it evinces the way in which violence reverberates as an immanent and one might say, *paratactical* mark of an action that, in its logic of means and ends, is not violent at all. There is an energy that—in a flash—emerges from poverty's hidden trajectories. What would lend this scene a glimpse of singular momentum if not a small yet potent difference between bare life and vigorous motivation in the case of the children of *Tire dié*? The mode through which Birri highlights an agency as subaltern works through sensuous imaging in the first place not by virtue of a social critique that is made into poetry. If the concept of affect has replaced that of judgment, the critical issue here is judgment sensed through affect: the lens of the subject is replaced by an immanent force of acting subjectivity. Birri's scene helps contrast a certain mode of abstractness, as it characterizes Deleuze's and Guattari's assumptions on immanence,[35] in that it is precisely that kind of subalternity that can be recognized as neither a transcendent value nor a merely empirical matter. It appears to be existing in a state of presence.[36] Aesthetic investment in the experience of the disenfranchized, as I have argued throughout the book, needs to be meaningfully discussed in search of an aesthetics of immanence—one which is capable of apprehending the modes of existence[37] by which subalterns make their active presence in the world. Similar conceptual concerns can be raised regarding various films that have started to explore marginality and childhood in globalized Latin America, yet whose intensity comes not simply condensed in their referential traits, such as *Pixote* (Brazil, 1980), the films *Gregorio* (1984) and *Juliana* (1989) produced by "Grupo Chaski" in Peru, and *Sicario* (José Novoa, Venezuela 1994), among others.

It would therefore be a misperception to relate the stakes that cinema has in historical and conceptual debate to thematic continuities and discontinuities, as though subaltern experiences like poverty, violent death, and harsh inequalities could be subsumed under the same abstract notion of time[38] that corresponds to the ontological unity of the *one* subject. This has been a main difficulty that has affected the interpretations of one of today's most startling directors: Víctor Gaviria who has in a singular manner addressed the question of violence in those globalized margins in which a Colombian culture of exception could emerge. His major works, *Rodrigo D. No futuro* (R. D. No Future, 1990) and *La Vendedora de Rosas* (The Rose Seller, 1998) have yet to be read in relationship to an experience in which the canon of abstract Western ontology is suspended from the beginning. What happened since Buñuel disturbed, with *Los Olvidados* (The Forgotten; Mexico 1950), a prevailing sense regarding the margins of social existence and its paternalistic depictions, as had been expressed in Ismael Rodríguez' famous film *Nosotros los Pobres* (We, the Poor; Mexico 1947)? As we will show, the Colombian poet and director Gaviria has taken up several of Buñuel's stimuli. Gaviria, similar to Salazar, has focused his major works on the marginal *comunas* of Medellín during the second half of the 1980s and beginning of the 1990s, a time when these spaces had been turned into one of the most violent informal war zones that a peripheral global modernity would generate. If one situates Gaviria in relationship to postwar Italian neorealism, the fact that the criterium of social content says nothing about his strategy to elevate untimely experience over representation can easily be overlooked. For it is necessary to mark those nonplaces—hidden territories of the state of emergency in the contemporary world—which have been written off from normative space and time by societies. It is here that the particular lessons of affective aesthetics become all the more telling. Deleuze, reminding us of Bazin's work, has characterized neorealism as a movement by which European cinema introduced fundamental aesthetic distinctions vis-à-vis an action-image dominated American tradition. A somewhat comparable shift is carried out by a series of contemporary Latin American films that challenge the sophisticated mechanisms of violence-production of the North. The case of Gaviria is crucial, not only because of his emphasis on the global slums and their young people not destined to life. The director has converted the territories that surround his character *Rodrigo D* into "any spaces whatever," whose "visual and sound nakedness, crudeness and brutality" nevertheless oppose moral paternalism and aggressively market-oriented contours of filmic violence. Let me repeat that, for Deleuze, it was not the French New Wave nor German cinema that, from the 1950s onward, broke with the prevailing "sensory-motor situations of the action-image in the old realism."[39] The breakthrough was instead achieved by Italian neorealism—its critical and intuitive consciousness of a new aesthetics of the image in the course of its emergence. The paradox whose political implications Deleuze names only indirectly, consisted of a specific perception of violence (social, sexual, moral, and spatial): its figurations were notably freed from the convention of means and ends (action-images giving coherence to the real), yet they were also distanced from utopian postures. This new perception of social experience as optically immanent was directed against an ego-centered civilizatory pessimism, turning extreme sensations of everydayness into "thinking images." It is here that we find incentives in neorealism to which Gaviria has accorded a new appeal.

In *Rodrigo D. No futuro*, a title that is evocative of Vittorio De Sicas *Umberto D* (1952), there is no avantgardist pursuit of the unfathomable. However, in terms of composition and time structure and, above all, language, there is an appearance of inconsistency and rudeness, not to say of permanent estrangement from any common criteria of filmic expression. According to Gaviria, this is due to the obsessive part that real-life actors from Medellín's marginal neighborhoods played during the production process of the film: young people whose actual desire is to burn down the whole world and give movie director headaches. Similar to the protagonists of Salazar's *No nacimos pa' semilla*, these adolescents have "not been born for life." Like Carlos Mario Restrepo, one of the main actors in *Rodrigo D. No futuro*, several of the young collaborators were killed after their participation in the film. Many of them "still live in the streets where they are trapped by misery and drugs."[40]

Critics have viewed the work of the Colombian director as a substantial statement within a shift from the depiction of marginality by Latin American film in relation to "contestatory projects of decolonization" (the sixties and seventies), to existential conflicts and survival strategies in the case of lonely protagonists (the eighties and nineties).[41] Explanations such as these are part of the historiographical desire of interpreters. A more elementary way of looking into Gaviria's work is to take seriously the questions that materialist ontological critique is posing to cultural analysis. Today, at a much more powerful end than deconstruction, "disaster capitalism" (Klein) is waging its large-scale attacks on the modern ontological subject. By "ontological subject" I mean—alluding to ideas developed in chapters 4 and 5—a category that has, from Hegel to Husserl and Heidegger, conformed the basis of what Derrida calls "onto-theology": the idea of "finitude [viewed] as origin of mortality" and at the same time, as "origin of ideality" attesting to the incorporation of the topos of "mortality" into transcendental phenomenology.[42] The sublimation of mortality into an enabling condition of the human subject might at first glance be considered an outdated issue, had market culture not finally appropriated the obsession for an ever more sophisticated both heightening and "deposition" of death.[43] Not by chance, current theorizations of film and media have refashioned the topic of the "defensive subject," an example of which is provided by Philip Rosen's recovery of Bazin's "ontological objectivity" of the image together with the concept figure of "change mummified."[44] It is from such a background that Gaviria's concept of realism will be understood as an interdiction of the unified ontological subject as the blueprint for aesthetic critique. Young people like Rodrigo and his contemporaries, inhabiting the zones of differential ghettoization of the world, lack any stasis from which they could be shown to be handling death from a Heideggerian distance or sharing a fearfulness that is marked by the disciplined citizen's deferred motion of "being-towards-death." If one thinks of Arendt as perhaps the most lucid advocate of the distinct "human condition," her totalizing assumptions must be perceived as mistaken in a world where inequality triumphs over plurality. A "second birth,"[45] that is socialization through learned action and speech and dwelling is not an option for those obnoxious youngsters who have not been born to life. Can the work of Gaviria be understood as an attempt to *struggle for affect* on the side of children like Rodrigo and Mónica? What does it mean to lead such a project into filmmaking, leaving poststructuralist dicta aside, yet assuming resistance to capitalism from a battlefront of immanent critique?

Recalling Deleuze's concept of the *affection-image*, which we unlike the French philosopher do not subsume under either "action-image" or "time-image," we have been concerned about the paradox of indistinguishability, that is to say heterogeneity relating to image and reflection. When Deleuze touched on the "two poles of the filmic face," "power" and "quality," it seemed as if intensity and reflexivity could be approached as nondistinct aspects.[46] We will now relate the questions that refer to the reflective powers of expressive immediacy to Gaviria's films. Describing *Rodrigo D. No futuro* for those who have not seen it benefits from first referring to what the film does not. The film does not offer a dramatic plot, although it dwells in constant action at the brink of any possibility of meaningful life. It erodes the convention of an intelligible verbal core, be it dialogic, introspective, or even aleatory. The film undermines a generally assumed distinction between actors, participants, and spectators. It also shuns accepted clichés of aesthetic effect as to the depiction of insanity and violence, be they seen in the leading action genres of the Hollywood tradition, or more intellectually refined. The impression of the film's elliptical and unorganized structure also accounts for its underrepresentation within the fora of cinematic review. All this makes the point of reflexivity qua embodiment an intricate issue.

The protagonist excels because of his incessant movement through space. Seventeen-year-old Rodrigo is a kind of walking nomad within the environment of the poor *comunas* on the hillside from which the center of Medellín can be seen. At the beginning of the film, Rodrigo is kicked off a construction site, his former place of work that he sporadically used to skip. From there he drifts into the maze of unasphalted roads, half-finished houses, steep banks, and waste grounds that stretch across Medellín's northeastern slopes. His restless, somnolent striding is eventually perceived as a search for a set of drums to set up a punk rock group. This distinguishes his role from that of his *parceros* (buddies), who inhabit the labyrinth of the *comunas* where they hide from the police after robberies or drug dealing. Rodrigo, who does not participate in criminal activities, will not succeed in getting the money he needs for his instruments. His attempt to set up the band fails after long vagrancies; and there are recurrent takes that show the roaming teenager from behind fences—he is moving on the far side of love, friendship, education, sports, religion, and even the concerns of his buddies. Toward the end of the film, Rodrigo commits suicide by throwing himself off the top floor of an apartment. The suicide appears as depersonalized. What the camera shows, while framing a sight out of the window on one of the lower floors is the downward flight of a shadow.

Throughout the film there is a sensation that is as pervasive as it is discomforting. It emanates from a mechanism of "sound-over," a displacement and thus a reoccupation of the visual and verbal sphere by a soundtrack of anarco-punk and hard-rock.[47] What the spectator is forced to perceive—because it breaks the barrier of an ability to listen to—is made up of belligerent sound volleys by real-life groups such as that of Ramiro Meneses, the actor who portrays Rodrigo. In a crucial scene Rodrigo is shown drumming in excess, to the extent that the imposture of the shrill sound causes pain to the ear while we hear battering voices roar: "Dinero—Angustia, Dinero—Problema, Dinero—Sistema..." Words and loud screams become indistinguishable. Disturbing the independent, self-determined stance of the audience is the director's conceptual purpose.[48] The language spoken by Rodrigo and his buddies from the *comunas*, an atavically sounding form of *parlache* (the slang spoken by youngsters who inhabit the extreme margins of the country's symbolic order) is virtually unintelligible. One scene shows Rodrigo's almost naked body standing on a ragged roof terrace like a warrior holding on to a spear-like metal bar, pictured against the panorama of the valley of Medellín that stretches out down below. Rodrigo is thus seen overlooking, for a moment, the entire city as a person who has no place other than the moving spaces of his unquietness. What drives his existence is a sonorous energy that fuses his unhomely steps into the battering punk rhythm. Rodrigo's silhouette on the rooftop is quickly interrupted by the following scene in which his enraged sister calls him a "punk ass," a useless creature, someone who exists as an "entity." Rodrigo's presence is so powerful because his unpresence in the social and symbolic order lends his body, together with his displacement through space, an eschatological energy.

However, no sign of transcendence of human grief could come his way. What does all this imply as to a particular mode of existence? In other words, does *Rodrigo D. No futuro* provide a blueprint for "ethics without morality"?[49]

If one opposes the concept of an immanent "mode of existence" (Spinoza) to that of transcendent values, this might quickly instigate, according to Daniel Smith, the doubt of the normative thinker: without universal rules, the "chaos of subjectivism and relativism"[50] is supposed to loom large. However, once we deal with subjectivities that lack both a proper position in the order of discourse and the right to claim for transcendentals, their "conatus," embodied action as we would call it today, can only be addressed via an ethics of immanence. This means that we must go beyond the attributions of subalternity to the noncode realm, expressed by metaphors such as lack, rupture, or a delusive notion of the real. Where there is no distinction between bodily existence and political condition, social deprivation and symbolic exclusion have to be addressed in more proactive terms. The paradox of judgment that is conveyed by an "ethics without morality" becomes imminently political when it is applied to *Rodrigo D. No futuro* and *The Rose Seller*. In the first, the affection-images woven around, and emanating from, Rodrigo's pugnacious, morose unquietness become the tools of immanent critique. These images convey a sense of the peculiar agency of an adolescent like him, not just his condition of loss. Gaviria's project is to make an ethical point about immanence: Rodrigo goes to the outer limits of what his mode of existence compels him to do—to bodily assume. Deprived of both instrumental and universal means of integration, the adolescent still presents a singular vehemence. He renounces all the forms of violence with which his buddies from the slums are trying to survive. He moves himself to the edge where neither the members of his family nor his *parceros* can maintain a capacity to affect him, nor does he expect them to be affected by him. At that point, Rodrigo sort of metamorphoses into a plainly *paratactical subject*, driven by the punk rhythm that obsesses his vagrant body. His body becomes one with sonorous wrath—an eschatological force without transcendence. To commit suicide is his consequent choice—Rodrigo breaks away from the extreme banality of bare life. His sister can call him an "entity" because he leaves behind any practice of mediation that could help alleviate his life at the edge. What would have happened if Rodrigo had succeeded in setting up a punk band? The question becomes moot at the moment where he assumes the most radical act that this violent music could aim for—to perform the destruction and death of those not been born to life.

It is likely that nothing could distance Gaviria's film from nihilism if his project were not informed, from the beginning, by an unusual striving for the "thinking image"—the affection-image as embodiment of a reflexive power. How can resistance be imagined as the negation of the limits that exclusion imposes on the excluded? Can the misery that vibrates in the film help to anything other than attack the learned indifference of an audience comforted by a relative ontological "safety"? Can Rodrigo's vigorous mode of resisting adaptation contribute to intercepting the repressive agency of a culture that rests on the life-denying disavowal of death that the unpolitical subject reserves for itself? Is *Rodrigo D. No futuro* a statement about collective eschatological energies from where a resurgence of the forgotten is perceived? The affection-images that shape the perception of poverty and violence in this film are far from Vallejo's vision of catastrophe. Can Gaviria's movie utter amazement at a state of affairs that is social and global at the same time? Let me refer to a hypothesis that Hylton foregrounds:

> *Rodrigo D* gives the North Atlantic spectators the opportunity to favorably contrast metropolitan capitalism with the apocalyptic decline of the Third World, incorporating the latter into an imaginary that fetishizes violence when it smashes historical profundities and concrete policies.[51]

This contention is informed by the supposed lack, in Gaviria's film, of information that could illuminate the neocolonial complexity of the Colombian situation. It seems to imply that the film replicates one or the other mainstream style that is based on the dominance of action-images, together with the fetishized bodies of action-heroes. This might apply, to an extent, to Fernando Meirelles' movie *Cidade de Deus* (City of God, Brazil 2003). In Gaviria's case, we must argue differently, that the director intercepts the fetichization of violence with a strategy that is headed toward global and local spectators alike. It conveys a statement aimed at full citizens and their most desired possession—the ontological "safety" to be born for a "good life." Therefore, a specific scenario is constructed—the deployment of rhythmic movement through space, together with the accompanying sonorous siege by anarcopunk—that does not differentiate between Latin American audiences and metropolitan viewers from the North. Critical reflection does not precede the exposedness of the viewer to the affective violence that the film deploys. Gaviria's offensive aesthetic thus creates a counterforce to an all-pervasive, media-generated low-level fear. *Rodrigo D. No futuro* can be called paratactical aggression. It turns its disturbing soundscapes and language fragments against the spectators to harm and torment them without making distinctions. It also incites reflection, but it offends in the first place, not giving in to the attractions that can be drawn from commodified super-warriors and the vicarious pleasures they can incite. If there were, perhaps, a nonindividual climate that the film gives way to, it might be informed by a bodily, or physiological uneasiness, a sense of perturbation without salvation for a select few. This is what we alluded to when anticipating that Gaviria is committed to a struggle for affect on the side of adolescents like Rodrigo and children like Mónica, the protagonist of *La vendedora de rosas*.

The characteristic paradox that shapes *Rodrigo D. No futuro* (1989) reappears in *The Rose Seller* (1998) in a different manner. The ambiguity in this film comes from Gaviria's addressing the destruction of adolescent existence, working with real-life actors several of whom were killed before the completion of the films and, at the same time, his setting forth a strong, nonconforming affectivity at an opposite end of sentimental compassion, melancholy, or transcendental hope. *The Rose Seller*, drawn from the same sociospatial repertoire as *Rodrigo D. No futuro*, is the second and most complex of Gaviria's trilogy of feature films that was completed in 2004 by the movie *Sumas y restas*.[52] It tells a story whose dramatic minimalism goes hand in hand with the normality of distortion to which destitute girls between the ages of ten and fourteen are exposed and of which, to an extent, they are themselves actors. Mónica is a thirteen-year-old orphan[53] who is seen living on the sidewalks of *Carretera 70* and *La Bolera* district in Medellín on a 23rd of December evening, trying to sell roses in night clubs to buy Christmas decorations and celebrate with her drug-dealing boyfriend. The film provides a collation of two disjunctive visual rhythms: the street world with a sort of spasmodic presence, and a dream space across which Mónica remembers her dead grandmother who is evoked either as a fairy-like woman or in the image of the Virgin Mary. Petite Mónica whose eyes and demeanors already reflect the air of an elderly person, offers protection to Andrea, a ten-year-old girl who has escaped from her brutish mother. Both girls, enveloped in nocturnal space that is intermittently sprinkled with Christmas lights, roam through the dangerous urban district, with its drug hustling, street-stabbings, sexual harassment, and the glue-sniffing habit among poor youths. Gaviria uses a contrastive matrix: Hans Christian Andersen's story *The Little Match Girl*, a minute yet pioneer tale of nineteenth-century urban poverty in which a little girl dies of hunger and cold on Christmas Eve while lighting all together the matches she was trying to sell.[54] Andersen's two-page story becomes a blueprint for the creation of an expressionist imaginary of the closeness of death, as it is still lived by marginal children in late-twentieth-century Medellín.

Dealing with the issue of gender, *The Rose Seller* takes a surprising approach to the culture of exception, one that appears to be different from that offered by Salazar's *We Were Not Born to Life*. The film, although lacking the persistent sonorous bombardment of volleys of anarcopunk that appeals the viewer of *Rodrigo D. No futuro* presents its own vocal offensiveness. It seems as if the deep, crass voices of Mónica, Andrea, and the others who dwell in the *parlache* slang, could not belong to the fragile bodies from which they emanate.[55] It would appear that Mónica's crude voice is a matter of self-defense in the hostile street environs. However, there is a particular spirit of revolt among the teenaged girls who inhabit Gaviria's film, and it is directed against being confined to the lowest end of families that suffer the curse of poverty. Girls like Mónica and Andrea are exposed to harassment by their mothers and stepmothers in the first place, women who are strongly susceptible to matriarchal behavior, combined with permissiveness regarding offensive behavior by male family members. "The mothers are gonorreas,"[56] says one of the girls. Andrea endures and fights her mother's oppression, and Mónica, toward the end of the film, even leaves her sister's house to escape rape by her sister's boyfriend. She is thus sent back into the implacable space of street law where the thirteen-year-old orphan will be killed by *el Zarco*, an adolescent criminal.

It is necessary to return to our concept of *sacred labor* that has implied drastic transformations of gender roles under the conditions of survival and historically enforced conflicts in the northeastern shantytowns of Medellín. As outlined in chapter 5, and related especially to the cases of sicarios as gang members and leaders, the concept of "sacred labor" describes a specific form of consecration: this informal practice is carried out by mothers who endow their sons with the moral energy to actively inhabit the space of death. Throughout the territories of Medellín's *comunas*, in times of heightened narcoconflict, a culture of exception has been constituted at the opposite end of society's legal and moral order. Salazar's *We Were Not Born to Life* shows compelling cases of mother-son relationships, in which an extreme form of maternalism results in practices of emotional empowerment by virtue of which mothers relieve their sons of the burden of guilt. Mothers like Doña Azucena in "We Are the Kings of the World," living under the rigors of mere subsistence, and the role of the father having become vacant, tend to become a principal justification for delinquency in the imagination of the adolescent, male-bonding sicarios. Thus, mothers shield the informal economic behaviors of sicarios in affective terms. As for Gaviria, he focuses on a still ignored subject—the daughters who live under the pressure of the same phenomenon. *The Rose Seller* is programmatic for the director's incursion in gender drama, where he proposes an antidote to the ultimate mother–son relationships that we highlighted with the term sacred labor. If male adolescents are consecrated to aggressively inhabiting the space of death to secure the survival of the poor matriarchal family, then adolescent females carry the double burden of oppression by males and by the moral and physical inflictions that are imposed on them by their mothers. Set into an affective mood that is different from the aesthetics of *The Rose Seller,* the Colombian film *Rosario Tijeras* presents a female outcast from the slums whose destiny started out from a rebellion against the same conditions of repression.

Gaviria's is a bitter attack on the homophobia that dominates the habitus of Medellín's violent gangs. A scene that can be read as one of several allusions to Buñuel's *Los Olvidados* introduces the image of the wheel-chaired sicario. A long shot depicts a semidark space from which a group of strangers emerges, approaching the camera, accompanied by coarse laughter and the penetrating bleating of a goat. The scene shows an esperpentic procession of sicarios in whose center, pushed forward by fellow gang members, "Don Héctor" advances in his wheel-chair. "El Zarco," a figure that resembles blunt cruelty, performs a pirouette in front of the pack, so as to clear a path. A goat is walking on the right side of the entourage, and the youngest gang member, still a child, explains: "I found this goat at the University. It was just asking to be stolen." "No problem, man!" responds the crippled Don Héctor, the senior member who is not more than twenty-five-years old. As the group nears a frightened street junky, "El Zarco" runs after him as if he were chasing prey, throws him to the ground, and shoots him to death, then frisks the body for drugs and a watch. The entire gang of sicarios embodies complete aberrance, a mixture of deformation and savagery, the disabled body of Don Héctor echoed by the coarse babbling of his drugged friends. The periodic bleat of the stolen goat heightens the sensation of atmospheric dreadfulness, and while Christmas noises can be heard from a distance, the camera captures the moon that lurks in the nocturnal sky for a moment before it is covered by black clouds. The entire scene presents itself as a complex "affection-image," an esperpentic fusion of the territory occupied by the pack of sicarios and its abstraction into a form of "any-space-whatever," evinced by jumpy cutting that acts as a brake on narrative cohesion and by the archaic element of the goat, as well as the cosmic, ghostly appearance of the moon.

Reality, and not only dreams as Goya had it, engenders monsters. What connects Gaviria to Buñuel are neither stylistic elements nor an abstract notion of social realism. The affinity lies in a crude and, to an extent, transgressive way in which marginality and poverty are visualized. For both directors, surrealism has played its part. Millán speaks of aesthetics of cruelty,[57] as well as monstruosity, arguing that the figure of Don Carmelo, the blind beggar in *Los Olvidados*, is a victim and a fierce and astute tramp at the same time. Indeed, the irruption of *Los Olvidados* into the Mexican public sphere of the early 1950s drastically challenged both the compassionate, benevolent approach to the poor (as shown in Rodríguez' *Nosotros Los Pobres*, 1947 and other movies) and their exclusion from the sphere of representation. Gaviria, for his part, extracts an imagery of adolescent destruction from the junctures of Colombia's political history of violence, the rise to power and warfare of the narcotics trade, and the devastating effects that a global neoliberal economy has imposed on large numbers of Latin American youths. "Don Héctor," the sicario who commands his gang from a wheel-chair, wears an outfit that includes icons of the intricate conflict: cargo pants, an army shirt, and a ragged sweater showing the U.S. flag, all of which are displayed as symbols of power in decay. As Juana Suárez puts it: "His now broken body and his clothes are the results of drug trafficking, as well as the fight between the legal apparatus of the state and the sicarios, and the simultaneous influence of and opposition to the United States."[58]

Deleuze, in his reading of Italian postwar-neorealism, has identified the crisis of the classical "action-image," linked to framing and narrative figuration that foreground coherent relationships between modes of behavior and "determinate, geographical, historical and social space-times."[59] However, the risk of a narrow historicist view would hover over analysis if we did not acknowledge that there is no such thing, in film history, as a general overcoming of the "action-image" by what Deleuze terms the more complex and contradictory "time-image." On the one hand, an assumed logic of governing image models is fissured by filmic experience as it emerges from the globalized peripheries. On the other, during recent decades there has been a saturation of audiovisual space with trivial action-images, accompanying the hegemonic media forms with which the "war on drugs" has been visually constructed. When Gaviria undermines an action-image-oriented dramaturgy, the issue is not that children like Mónica find themselves thrown into a hostile milieu that overpowers them. Rather, the erosion of the action-image appears as an aesthetic procedure in that neither *Rodrigo D. No futuro* nor *The Rose Seller* allows for a formative or, even less, a normative relationship between the protagonists and their marginal world. Their modes of being are marked by a discomforting brokenness. It is this sense of disjointedness by which violence is distanced from a cause-effect relationship (realist depiction in conventional terms) to be sensed as immanent force. However, immanence is not extreme exposure to evil. It is, in the cases we are discussing, bound to the insight that beyond the world of sheer existence—Medellin's harsh streets, its poor neighborhoods, and especially the bodies of children, adolescents, their families—there is nothing else from which alternate visions could be drawn. This means that we must pay attention to the aspects of intoxication and use value that, together with the issue of gender deformation, play a crucial part in the film.

It is critical, in the first place, not to reduce the hallucinatory experiences of Mónica, which are centered on visions depicting her deceased grandmother, to a nostalgic trope. A more acute aspect comes to the fore: the reimagination of *consumption* in a frame of both survival and the envisioning of alternative values. Mónica's singular dream experience is shown to function as a negation of the aberrant effects that drugs and glue sniffing cause in teenaged boys. It is set apart from the stigma of generating violent behavior. Mónica's active dreaming, under her conditions of orphanhood, breaks with the assumption that relates adolescent deviance among the poor essentially to drug trafficking and abuse. It is not farfetched to recall Benjamin's almost unknown tale "Myslowice—Braunschweig—Marseille," especially its spirit of revising intoxication as a controversially modern concept.[60] The girl's hallucinatory journey becomes pivotal when she asks her adult sister Bibiana to give her the trunk that Mónica has inherited from her grandmother. The camera approaches the wooden box, placed on a semidark loft, like a treasure chest, which is then opened by Mónica's hands, shown in close-up, taking out a pair of old-fashioned white shoes that she happily puts on. Her sister's voice is heard: "They are too big for you." Mónica replies, "It doesn't matter, I'll put in some paper." Shortly afterward, a similar movement of the camera introduces a dream sequence—a door opens into a room where the grandmother is seen from behind, clothed in linen and wearing a headscarf, sitting at a table and sewing, with spheric music accompanying the scene. The woman, a fairy-like presence, slowly turns her head toward the door, smiling but with her face remaining slightly blurred. Mónica has prepared a cup of chocolate that, while approaching the sewing table, she offers to the old woman as if she were making a gift. Her smile has taken on its warmest expression in the entire film, when a sudden cut interrupts the heightened, slow-motion atmosphere. Back to real life, Mónica has woken up from her nap in Bibiana's house, at the moment at which her sister's boyfriend is grabbing her thighs. She is thus compelled to escape once again, on the morning of Christmas day, and to seek refuge in the streets where we see her walking in her new used shoes before she encounters death.

The gesture of giving that the girl, in her dream, directs toward her grandmother, together with the old woman's immersion in a sacred pose of embroidering, generates a tie between generations in which parents are absent. In view of the abyss that separates the orphan from the physical time of social integration (the nuclear family, the school, normative public space), life itself, for Mónica, takes on a transmissible, and emotionally formative value from the image of the dreamed grandmother. The enigma that often binds children to the voices and bodies of grandparents is not only related to the desire for protection and love; what is compelling is a sort of magic authority whose strength is parallel to the grandparents' embodying a different rhythm of economic behavior that is related to the *use value* of things, and of time itself. A sense of nonutilitarian exchange, mystically emphasized, emanates from the vision of the embroidering woman that comes to meet hallucinating Mónica. The image of the grandmother generates a sacred experience, whose meaning derives from the slow rhythm in which the hand, the body, and the soul make generations join in nonviolent accord.

This is why wearing grandmother's used white shoes lends Mónica a company that resonates with her dream hallucination. It is Christmas time. While male adolescents and other girls on the street are enticed to think in terms of some eagerly desired commodities, Mónica's intention is to give and to use in simplest terms: her appearance acquires a remotely Franciscan touch. She lends the scarf from her grandmother's trunk to Bibiana because it suits her nicely. Mónica also destines the cute watch that a drunk has given to her to be a present for her boyfriend Anderson, who is blind to the meaning of the gift while taking, from other revering girls, as many presents as they offer. Mónica's desire for love by giving what she has to others is finally destroyed by the myth of consumption to which most of the fellow adolescents fall prey. *El Zarco*, who forces Mónica to hand over the watch to him, is only interested in its attractive colors, and when the pictures on its dial vanish he will kill the girl, taking absurd revenge for the missing authenticity of the fetish object. As I have discussed earlier in relation to sacred labor, narratives such as these rearticulate the issue of consumption at the point of life's being obstructed in the dark night of social and economic exclusion. That is to say, the question of "expenditure" arises anew from territories where the economy of aggressive accumulation[61] regulated or adjusted by the formal world economy, functions at the expense of life. It is at this point, when it comes to the exclusion of the teenaged cohort of humanity from civil rights and the supply of formal jobs, that the issue of consumption acquires an unfamiliar meaning. Now, the way in which Gaviria maps naked adolescent life in Colombia is not only linked to the noneconomic value that objects like grandmother's shoes can acquire to counter both gender violence and a deceitful market society. At the same time, we are dealing with a vision that allows relating the question of self-intoxication of marginal actors to provocative practices of profanation. Profanation, in a more elementary fashion than in Agamben's recent discussion of the term,[62] means to oppose the segregation as hopeless creatures to which these children are exposed with their use of street psychoactives.

Irrespective of the devastation that opiates and other habits, especially glue-sniffing, cause under harsh conditions, they also allow their users to counterbalance the complete vulnerability of the body with excitement and a different fatigue. There are still vast territories of modernity, as Benjamin wrote in "Myslowice—Braunschweig—Marseille" where life vibrates in a permanent state of emergency,[63] spaces where intoxication provides a daily "diet" to existences that cannot count on the schooling that instrumental reason affords to the more privileged citizens, nor on the slightest amount of hope. And so it is that neither criminality nor accidental circumstances can account for the fact that *basuco*, marijuana, and other psychoactives are an ingredient of the refuges of destitute and forgotten youth. Neither esoteric projects nor biohygienic control could tranquilize the ambiguous forces that precarious drugs stimulate, as long as poverty exists. Gaviria views the territories from which *Rodrigo D. No futuro* and *The Rose Seller* originate as destructive of adolescence, the most valuable human and social potential. At the same time, his films present the *comunas* as spaces where terrible battles are being fought out. Is not the glue-sniffing that is practiced by the protagonist of *The Rose Seller* a way, as well, of wresting her own body and soul away from its confinement to total loss?

Gaviria's works, together with Salazar's *We Were Not Born to Life*, are new approximations to the problematic of use value today. There is the ancient, almost forgotten debate about poverty that reached a dramatic moment when Pope John XXII denied and proscribed the Franciscan concept of "simplex usus facti" (simple factual use) as heresy. At stake was a concept of life—of life's perfection in Franciscan terms—at an end where it could supposedly acquire its purest value by virtue of a strict separation from the domains of property and by the renunciation of commercial exchange directed at any form of surplus.[64] The Pope countered the idealizing Franciscan vision of property by dictating that, outside the sphere of law and thus of property of goods through dominion and exchange, there could be no autonomous use of things.[65] A similar assumption, adjusted to the needs of global capital in present times, sustains the excesses of ever more deceitful consumption for the sake of consumption. There is a heretic purpose inherent in Gaviria's shaping of Mónica, the rose seller, a post-secular figure that introduces a Franciscan moment into the depiction of the borderline scenarios he describes. Must not the use of things, of the environment, and of the human body be relearned from a vantage point of singular modesty and rigor at the same time? Paraphrasing Bataille, this question allows imagining a wider conceptual situation according to which Western societies are about to exhaust all the major reserves that have been at the disposal of the human species, to the extent that utility can only be assigned a *relative* value— serving subsistence and the reduction of suffering.[66]

Precarious territories have come into focus in which the body, use value, and life are not separated by the disciplining forces of guilt, property, and pervasive spirals of indebtedness. For example: *sacred labor* means the utter paradox of defending survival by putting the body in the service of violent death—the sicarios in Salazar's narrative. Glue-sniffing among poor youths allows for effects of transgression that, like in Buñuel's esperpentic surrealism, break with the circle of muteness and pity to which bodies are exposed—Gaviria's dreadful street boys. But intoxication is also shown to help the enchanted body reassess the use value of life itself—Mónica and the way she turns exchange practices into an ordinary ethics of the gift. Are we dealing, while writing of the struggle for affect that is liberated by Gaviria, Salazar, and other artists, with a positive notion of barbarism the way it was explored by Benjamin in "Experience and Poverty"? Can the youngsters Rodrigo and Mónica be imagined to be the "new barbarians" in today's global climacteric? Are their ways of confronting and challenging their informal exposure to latent death compatible with states of experience whose chance is to "start from scratch," and thus to begin anew?[67] And could this antiheroic, that is non-Nietzschean, yet barbarian *ethos* be turned into a learning experience, in which other creatures whose "qualified life" is, according to Heiner Müller,[68] only a more severe form of impoverishment could join?

I would like to provisionally conclude my study by returning the image of *Mónica, the Rose Seller*, to where it actually belongs—to a realm that extends beyond the domains of instrumental reason, neoliberal violence, and affective marginalization. This is an image-space that can make us recall, in connection with Benjamin's early text, "Capitalism as Religion," his unfinished writings about hashish, which he once layed out after crossing the poorer neighborhoods of Marseilles. It is from these territories, as they have extended to engulf peripheral humanity, that "intoxication" could serve a yet untheorized purpose of "profane illumination": "And when I recall this state, I would like to believe that hashish persuades Nature to permit us—for less egoistic purposes—that squandering of our own existence that we know in love. For if, when we love, our existence runs through Nature's fingers like golden coins that she cannot hold and lets fall so that they can thus purchase new birth, she now throws us, without hoping or expecting anything, in ample handfuls toward existence."[69]

CODA

The notion of "bare life," in its imaginary, social, and existential relationships to violence, has been emerging as a force field that concerns the very status of aesthetic experience today. Along the lines that our study has been developing, a larger number of Latin American films, literary texts, and other intermedial narratives could be discussed—being, as they are, genuine contributions to the historicality of present-time ethics. Our initial references to Benjamin were intended to serve a committed yet uncomfortable goal. In Benjamin's view, pointing toward the difference between "bare life" and "just life" did not only imply a bet on critical alertness toward justice. It also expressed a need to take bare life into the considerations of thinking anew. As became eminent, and against prevailing assumptions, this was not a category that modernity had rendered obsolete, pointing rather toward the intricate closeness of terror and guilt, as well as normative reason, violence, and sovereignty. In other words, bare life was neither an unrecoverable, archaic Other, or just the uncanny remains of the globally uneven dynamics of progress, nor was it an ahistorical, religiously conditioned state. The concept of bare life could reveal, first and foremost, the relationships between violence and life in the shadow spaces of the Western means-ends-dialectics. It could shed light at the underside of, and the energies directed against the famous venture of subject formation—the project of "affective civilization."

At stake, for Benjamin, was radical reflexivity. But where it seemed to call for articulation was probably at its most aporetical point. This challenge looked like the opposite of reflexive qua autonomous thinking, setting forth the possibility of criticism in its contamination by the immanence of life itself. As we have been arguing when we addressed the reflective side of affectivity, contemporary narratives from the global South have given this problematic amazing weight. And one might end up asking if literary understanding and epistemological analysis, together with cultural philosophy, have arrived at a point where ethical critique outside and above this condition may no longer exist.

NOTES

1 FROM WALTER BENJAMIN'S EARLY WRITINGS TO THE PERILS OF GLOBAL MODERNITY

1. Derrida, "Force of Law," 228–298. Haverkamp, "Kritik der Gewalt," 7–9.
2. Agamben, *Homo Sacer*, 28.
3. Significantly, "the historical index of the images not only says that they belong to a particular time; it says, above all, that they attain to legibility only at a particular time" (Benjamin, *Arcades Project*, 462, 463). See "Convolute N" regarding what has become eminent as Benjamin's concept of the "dialectical image" (ibid., 456–488). See also Weigel's reading of the thought figure of the "now of cognizability" ("Warum Walter Benjamin Now?" 4–6).
4. See Benjamin, "Critique of Violence," 251.
5. See Avelar on the role of ethics in literary studies ("Ethics of Interpretation"), and Lindemann-Nelson's outline of ethical positions that rely on the interpretation of literature (*Damaged Identities*, 37–64).
6. See Marramao, *Cielo e terra*.
7. Bové writes, "Literary critical state formations are essentially literary historical. They can, of course, be formalistic hermeneutic and semiotic structural. In the formation of nation-states, however, the historical canon-forming effect has priority over the others—at least politically." "Afterword: Memory and Thought," 376. At a related level, a term such as "emerging literatures" is intrinsically problematic, as discussed by Djelal Kadir in "Colonial Discourse and Emergent Cultures" (see "The Other Writing," 17–29). It is here that I take Benjamin's thoughts on "legibility" and "dialectical imaging" to destabilize a tendency of discursive judgment via "deliberative sublimation" by which Third-World literatures are sometimes welcomed into the canon.
8. See Reguillo, "Social Construction of Fear," 188–194. ; Valenzuela, "Recreación del melodrama en el narcocorrido," 166–168; Monsiváis, "Citizenship and Urban Violence," 240–246.
9. See Mitschein, Miranda, Paraense, *Urbanização*; Davis, *Planet of Slums*, 174–176.
10. See Monsiváis, "En los albores de la indústria heterodoxa."
11. See Debord, *Society of Spectacle*, 12–24.
12. Pérez Ramírez points to a distinction of narcoliteratures from those affiliations of modern prose that have in one way or another explored individual experiences of self-intoxication in terms of poetic strategy: "Narcoliterature is not about the personality of the addict, the 'yonqui' or the 'tecato' that has nourished the literary imaginary, starting with Samuel Coleridge, passing through Charles Baudelaire, Thomas de Quincey and William Burroughs, and up to Juan Antonio Ramos" ("La narcoliteratura," 6).

13. Davis, *Planet of Slums*, 176.
14. See Van Schendel and Abraham, *Illicit Flows*.
15. See Aristotle's ancient yet strongly evocative elaborations on citizenship and "mere life." In *Politics*, 69–70; Agamben, *Homo Sacer*, 1–2.
16. Franco, *Decline*, 14.
17. Benjamin, "Critique," 251.
18. See Hiller, "Linkspazifismus" [1920], 29, 30, 32, 41.
19. Arendt would later omit Benjamin's thoughts on that matter while attesting the critique of the Platonist matrix ("the degradation of politics into a means to obtain an allegedly 'higher' end") a central place in her reflection *Human Condition*. She would speak of her own generation as "perhaps the first generation which has become fully aware of the murderous consequences inherent in a line of thought that forces one to admit that all means, provided that they are efficient, are permissible and justified to pursue something defined as an end." (*Human Condition*, 229.)
20. See Hiller, "Linkspazifismus," 28.
21. Benjamin, "Critique," 243 (trans. modified).
22. See Hiller, "Linkspazifismus," 35.
23. Benjamin, "Critique," 251.
24. Butler, *Precarious Life*, XII.
25. Ibid.
26. Ong, *Neoliberalism as Exception*, 79.
27. Davis, *Planet of Slums*, 175.
28. See Hardt and Negri, *Empire*.
29. Boal et al., *Afflicted Powers*, 21.
30. See Butler, *Precarious Life*, 133.
31. See Brennan's reflections about modernity and exhaustion. In *Exhausting Modernity*. Also *Globalization and Its Terrors*.
32. See Foucault's "Introduction" to Canguilhelm's *Normal and the Pathological*, 17–19. According to Latour, if we were to follow the prevailing convention of strict divisions between "life" as either a matter of the social world or as an object of the natural sciences, "morality" (public space, normative orders, etc.) could easily be situated in a different register than "nature" (see *Politics of Nature*, 16–18; also *We Have Never Been Modern*, 1–12). The concept of "bare life" however, once it is deprived of the dogma of essential sacredness, helps cut across such epistemological ruptures that sustain modern reason in a quasi-religious way.
33. See Steiner, *Walter Benjamin*, 77.
34. See Agamben, *Homo Sacer*, 11–12, 49–51.
35. See Hallward on the theological undergrounds of an influential concept of otherness in "Translator's Introduction" to Badiou, *Ethics*, 35–36.
36. Benjamin reads the tensions between present and past through a "dynamic lens" that he calls "dialectical image." One of its metaphorical descriptions reads: "If one looks upon history as a text, then one can say of it what a recent author has said of literary texts—namely, that the past has left in them images comparable to those registered by a light-sensitive plate" ("Dialectical Image," 405). See also the letter "Benjamin an Gretel Adorno," 1148.
37. Kraniauskas, "Beware Mexican Ruins," 57. See the correspondence between Benjamin and Auerbach in which the latter suggests Benjamin an opportunity

to leave Europe for São Paulo, Brazil. In Barck, "5 Briefe Erich Auerbachs an Walter Benjamin in Paris," 689.

38. This is not a critique of Susana Rotkers' seminal volume *Citizens of Fear*. Today, a closer look at contradictory affective and ethical territories becomes necessary to understand narrative formations at whose center we find a renewed concern about bare life.

39. See Cornell, "Philosophy of the Limit," 68–71.

40. See Harvey, "Spaces of Insurgency," 81–88.

41. See Rasch, *Niklas Luhmann's Modernity*, 108–114.

42. Arendt, *Human Condition*, 129. Labor is used in this formulation, following Arendt's distinction of labor from work, in the sense that it secures for the laborer the necessities of life at the level of subsistence and continuance, while increasing the overall wealth of others.

43. See Pollock et al., "Cosmopolitanisms," 5.

44. Harvey, *New Imperialism*, 144.

45. According to Harvey, "some of the mechanisms of primitive accumulation that Marx emphasized have been fine-tuned" today to play an even stronger role for revamping and flexibilizing existing disproportions between centers and peripheries. See ibid., 144, 146, 147; also Perelman, *Invention of Capitalism*.

46. See Benjamin, "Critique," 243. As Rasch illustrates, "law-positing" (violence) is a more suiting translation of "rechtssetzend" than "lawmaking" (see *Sovereignty*, 93).

47. Rasch, *Sovereignty and Its Discontents*, 51.

48. Ranciére, *Politics of Aesthetics*, 85.

49. "Strictly speaking, 'distribution' therefore refers both to forms of inclusion and to forms of exclusion." Ibid.

50. See Damasio, *Looking for Spinoza*, 28.

51. Appadurai, *Fear of Small Numbers*, 29.

52. See on the concept of transatlantic modernity Quijano and Wallerstein, "Americanity as a Concept"; Quijano, "Coloniality of Power."

53. See Herlinghaus, "Walter Benjamin's Begriff des Rausches."

54. Ranciére, *Politics of Aesthetics*, 85.

55. Informal economy and war neither fit into an oppositional scheme, nor can the first be viewed as the simple cause of the second. As Brady holds, the so-called war on drugs is to be recognized as "an economy that includes both its formal manifestations (interdiction, education, treatment, imprisonment . . .) and informal manifestations (the business of growing, harvesting, processing, distributing and selling illegal narcotics and drugs)." This economy has to be placed within "broader changes from the end of [the] post-WWII economy to the transitional economy of the seventies, to the development of . . . flexible accumulation and economies of scale." (Brady, *Extinct Lands*, 240, Note 13).

56. DeGrandpre, *Cult of Pharmacology*, vii–x.

57. See Bertram, Blachman, sharpe, and Andreas, *Drug War Politics*, 9–10; Carpenter, *Bad Neighbor Policy*, 11–58.

58. Bertram et al. speak of a "drug war syndrome" that is based on a "politics of denial." [This policy] "would never reduce significantly the supply of drugs coming into the United States; it was wasting billions of dollars; and it was undermining democracy and human rights in the region by strengthening

the hands of repressive militaries and weakening already fragile civilian governments" (3). The authors continue: "Evidence of the drug war's failure and harm was widely available, not only in academic circles but also in government documents and media reports. Yet the reports of failure only reinforced the resolve of public officials to 'try harder', to apply a little more funding, a little more firepower—and the deeper flaws and harms of the policy were rarely part of the official debate" (IX, X).

59. See Arendt, *On Revolution*.
60. Agamben, *State of Exception*, 2; see also Rasch, *Sovereignty*, 90–93.
61. See Brennan, *Transmission of Affect*, 2–7; and *Exhausting Modernity*, 6, 47.
62. See Taussig, "Transgression," 362.
63. Žižek, *Fragile Absolute*, 147.
64. See Kuhn, Swartzwelder, and Wilson, *Buzzed*, 18–19.
65. Bertram et al., *Drug War Politics*, IX.
66. See Kristeva, *Powers of Horror*.
67. DeGrandpre, *Cult of Pharmacology*, vii.
68. See ibid., 239; Said, *Orientalism*.
69. "America became the world's most troubled drug culture not because the government conspired to allow access to drugs to some while denying access to others, but because more than any other nation, it was a full member of the cult— it truly believed" (DeGrandpre, *Cult of Pharmacology*, viii).
70. The decade of the 1970s marked a major turning point in the world economy. Regarding Latin America, in virtually all Andean countries, as well as in Central America and Mexico small peasant producers were massively driven out of basic traditional production, while their countries were forced to open borders to the strongly subsidized agribusiness of the North, resulting in a massive decrease of cultivation for local needs, and booming poverty. Owing to a lack of viable alternatives, the cultivation and processing of coca, poppy, and marijuana read as local responses to neoliberalism. See Bertram et al., *Drug War Politics*, 15–18. Harvey, *New Imperialism*, 145–152; and *Brief History of Neoliberalism*.
71. Benjamin, "Surrealism," 210.
72. Debord, *Society of Spectacle*. See a more recent elaboration on Debord's arguments in Boal et al., especially 20–23.
73. See DeGrandpre, *Cult of Pharmacology*, 103–137.
74. Arendt, *Human Condition*, 134.
75. At an extreme end of global narcotics trade, one finds the situation of Andean peasant communities who use drug plant cultivation as an essential, long-traditioned form of laboring to escape bare life. Here marginalization bears the triple mark of disgrace that has put them, from the vantage point of the war, and in accordance with neoliberalism's legitimate logic, in a social, legal, and moral no-mans-land. On the question of legitimacy and participatory projects regarding local Andean drug plant cultivation, especially in Bolivia, see Rivera Cusicanqui, *Las fronteras de la coca*, 161–166; Spedding and Colque (eds.), *Nosotros los Yungueños*; Medina, *El trueno sobre los cocales*.
76. See Marez, *Drug Wars*, 24–29.
77. On the concept of profanation see Agamben (*Profanations*, 73–76).
78. See Valenzuela, *Jefe de Jefes*, 40, 41, 103; Monsiváis, "En los albores," 30–33.
79. See Mignolo, *Local Histories/Global Designs*, 18–37, 278–280; *Idea of Latin America*, 51–94.

80. Brennan, *Transmission of Affect*, 13.

81. Brennan's approach is different from Deleuze's and Guattari's propositions in *Anti-Oedipus*. See also Deleuze, *Pure Immanence*, 25–32.

82. "Affects and impulses pre-exist the infant. We are born into them.... But people then, and this is our tragedy, take these impulses to be our own, filtering them through the 'I' or ego development in the first few months of life. The affect is held in common, but the ego makes up its own story." (*Exhausting Modernity*, 8).

83. See the distinction between emotions and feelings in Damasio, *Looking for Spinoza*, 44–49.

84. Brennan, *Transmission of Affect*, 12.

85. See Taussig, *Shamanism*; also *Mimesis and Alterity*.

86. See Latour, *We Have Never Been Modern*.

87. Brown, *Life against Death*, xix, also 13.

88. See Brennan, *Exhausting Modernity*, 41.

89. Brennan, *Transmission of Affect*, 6.

90. See Brown, *Life against Death*, 15; see Freud, *Civilization and Its Discontents*, 145.

91. I am using Badiou's citation (*Saint Paul*, 75). See St. Paul's "The Letter to the Romans," especially pages 73–75. Also Agamben's interpretation of the concept and performative use of "faith" (*Time That Remains*, 24–125, 130–132); and Taubes' historical comment in *Political Theology of Paul*, 13–16, 23–28.

92. See Butler, *Psychic Life of Power*, 3.

93. Brennan writes: "The question should be: To whom is the affect directed? Because whoever that object is will be prone to anxiety and depression (both the effects of aggression turned inward)" (*Transmission*, 15).

94. See ibid., 144.

95. I have been paraphrasing Arendt's formulation (see *Human Condition*, 224).

96. Courtwright, *Forces of Habit*, 1–2, 60–64.

97. See ibid., 152–167.

98. See Topik, Marichal, and Frank, *From Silver to Cocaine*.

99. See Ortiz, *Cuban Counterpoint*.

100. See Courtwright, *Forces of Habit*, 38, 167. Protagonized by the United States and Western Europe, an international system of treaties was put in place to eliminate production and distribution that was not "medically essential" (184).

101. Foucault, *History of Sexuality*, 115.

102. Ibid.

103. See Riley, *Snow Job?* 24–25.

104. Courtwright, *Forces of Habit*, 135.

105. See Barck, "Der Sürrealismus," 391.

106. Ibid., 386.

107. See Steiner, *Walter Benjamin*, 89–91.

108. See Buck-Morss, *Dialectics of Seeing*, 254.

109. Osborne, *Politics of Time*, 183.

110. See Horkheimer and Adorno, *Dialectic of Enlightenment*.

111. Benjamin, "Surrealism," 209.

112. Benjamin, "Main Features of My Second Impression," 89.

113. Benjamin to Scholem, July 26, 1932, 14, 15.
114. Auerbach's formulation about "ordered magic" as it pertains to the core of the Christian tradition comes close to Benjamin's concerns (*Mimesis*, 1957, 61; see Benjamin, "Surrealism," 209).
115. Benjamin, "Zum Aufsatz über Sürrealismus," 1023.
116. Benjamin to Scholem, 15.
117. See Wolin, "Experience and Materialism."
118. Ibid., 217.
119. See Benjamin, "Myslowice—Braunschweig—Marseilles," 107.
120. Ibid., 109.
121. Ibid., 115.
122. See Benjamin's sarcastic metaphor regarding "individuality" ("Surrealism," 208).
123. See Benjamin's early interest in "Mexican culture and language of the ancient time" (Letter "An Fritz Radt," 290); Kraniauskas, "Beware Mexican Ruins!" 355, 357; Witte, *Walter Benjamin*, 34, 35.
124. Benjamin, "Mexican Embassy," 448, 449.
125. See Benjamin, "An Gershom Sholem," Dec. 1, 1920, 109.
126. See Haverkamp, "Kritik der Gewalt," 7.
127. I have modified the translation (see *SW*, Vol. 1, 251). For the German original see *GS*, Vol. I–2, 202. *Ausgang* can also mean "consummation," which makes a modal semantic more appropriate than a strictly temporal one.
128. Derrida, *Acts of Religion*, 298.
129. See Agamben, *Homo Sacer*, 64, 65.
130. Ibid., 65.
131. See Agamben on the possible roots of the ambiguity of "divine violence" (ibid., 64, 65).
132. See Benjamin, "Critique," 251. See Taubes on Benjamin's messianism (Political Theology of Paul, 70–71).
133. Said, *Beginnings*, 347.
134. Ibid., 348.
135. My translation of "die Verschuldung des bloßen natürlichen Lebens" (*GS*, Vol. II–1, 200). For the English edition, see 250.
136. Said, *Beginnings*, 350.
137. See Benjamin, "Fate and Character," 203.
138. See Agamben's comments on Kafka, *Homo Sacer*, 49–50.
139. Translation modified (see *SW*, Vol. 1, 250; for the German original see *GS*(1977), Vol. II–1, 199–200).
140. See Hartwich, A. Assmann, and J. Assmann, "Afterword," 117.
141. Vico, *New Science*, 164.
142. See Benjamin, "Critique," 248; "Fate and Character," 203–204.
143. See Jewett, "Romans," 94, 97; St. Paul, "Letter to the Romans," 69–75.
144. Benjamin, "Critique," 249.
145. See Derrida on "differential contamination" ("Force of Law," 272).
146. Ibid., 239, 240.
147. See "Critique," 250. In German: "in ungeheuren Fällen" (*GS*, Vol. II–1, 2001). Benjamin refers to the commandment "Thou shalt not kill" and the way it was understood by Judaism.

148. See Baecker, *Kapitalismus als Religion*, 7.
149. Benjamin, "Capitalism as Religion," 288.
150. Translation modified, ibid., 290. For the German original, *GS*, Vol. VI, 103.
151. See Steiner, "Kapitalismus als Religion,"169.
152. "Capitalism has developed as a parasite of Christianity in the West…, until it reached the point where Christianity's history is essentially that of its parasite—that is to say, of capitalism. (Benjamin, "Capitalism" 289).
153. See Max Weber, *Protestant Ethic*.
154. Benjamin, "Capitalism," 288. See Bolz on capitalism as a "form of neopaganism." ("Der Kapitalismus," 196).
155. See the correction made by Steiner, "Kapitalismus als Religion," in Lindner (ed.), *Benjamin Handbuch*, 170.
156. Benjamin, "Capitalism," 288.
157. See Hamacher, "Schuldgeschichte," 93.
158. Agamben, *Profanations*, 82, 90.
159. See Benjamin on "phantasmagoria," Blanqui's cosmic speculation, and "mythical fear" of mankind (*Das Passagenwerk*, GS, V-2, 1256).
160. Benjamin, "Capitalism," 288.
161. Butler, in her study on "theories of subjection," pays no attention to Benjamin's reflections on the relationships between guilt, subjection, and bare life (see *Psychic Life of Power*).
162. Benjamin, "Capitalism," 289.
163. Ibid.
164. Negri, *Time for Revolution*, 197, 194–195; see also *Savage Anomaly*.
165. I am borrowing Rasch's expression (*Niklas Luhmann's Modernity*, 109).
166. See Hardt and Negri, *Empire*. Although Negri's ontology could be understood as open toward an alternate concept of bare life, the philosopher attests the notion (as it is used by Agamben) merely an "anthropological negativity." (see "Political Subject," 235).
167. Rasch, *Sovereignty*, 85; see also Weigel on the "demonic ambiguity" of the concept of guilt ("Literatur," 88).
168. On "public secrecy" see Taussig, *Defacement*.
169. Benjamin, "Zur Geschichtsphilosophie," 92.
170. See Deleuze, *Nietzsche and Philosophy*, 15.
171. This holds, for example, for his analysis of the "system of public credit" linked to the *Staatsschulden* (fiscal debts) from which, once established, a sacred aura accrues (see Hamacher, "Schuldgeschichte," 96, 97).
172. Marx, *Capital*. Vol. 1, 874.
173. Ibid., 873.
174. Benjamin, "Shaw: Frau Warrens Gewerbe," 613.
175. See Benjamin, "Capitalism," 290; Hamacher, "Schuldgeschichte," 98.
176. Harvey, *Limits to Capital*, 387.
177. Marx, *Capital*, 165.
178. Ibid.
179. See Agamben, *Profanations*, 81–83.
180. Sassen, "Globalization after September 11," B 11; on third-world debt after 1970 see Grandin, *Empire's Workshop*, 170–203. Benjamin's "Imperial Panorama" associates contemporary discussions on the global distribution of exhaustion and impoverishment (SW, Vol. 1, 451–453).

181. See the discussion of the term in Buck-Morss, *Thinking Past Terror*, 34–35.
182. Nietzsche, *On the Genealogy of Morality*, 39.
183. Ibid.
184. Ibid., 66–67.
185. Benjamin, "Capitalism," 289.
186. See Franco, *Decline*, 17, 18.

2   WHEN NARCOCORRIDOS WERE BORN

1. See Paredes, *Folklore and Culture on the Texas-Mexican Border*, 129.
2. Ibid., 132.
3. Wald, *Narcocorrido*, 2, 3.
4. See ibid., 1.
5. Edberg identifies a "narcocorrido community" as a listening audience: "according to interviews with recording industry respondents, there is a large and growing market for narcocorridos and norteño music in general among the Hispanic/Latino immigrant community in areas such as Los Angeles, Chicago, Florida, the San Joaquin and Central Valley areas of California, in cities in the midwest, some parts of the Pacific Northwest, and all along the U.S.-Mexico border (as well as in Mexico at large)," (*El Narcotraficante*, 67).
6. Mendoza, *El Romance Español y el Corrido Mexicano*, 115–119.
7. This problem has been addressed by Kittredge when dealing with English and Scottish Popular Ballads (see "Introduction," xv, xvi).
8. See Taylor's discussion of the concepts of "archive" and "repertoire" (*Archive and the Repertoire*).
9. Mendoza, *El Romance*, 118.
10. See Menendez-Pidal, *Romancero Hispanico*, 3.
11. Mendoza, *El Romance*, 118.
12. Ibid., 119, 120.
13. See Herlinghaus, "Zur neuen Krise der Kosmopolitischen Imagination"; Pollock, Bhabha, Breckenridge, and Chakrabarty, "Cosmopolitanisms," 5–6.
14. Saldívar, *Border Matters*, 61, see also 36, 40, 41.
15. See Saldívar, *Dialectics of Our America*, 49–56; Teresa McKenna, "On Chicano Poetry and the Political Age," in Calderón, Saldívar (eds.), *Criticism in the Borderlands*.
16. About intermediality see Herlinghaus, *Narraciones anacrónicas*, 39–42.
17. See Quiñones, *True Tales from Another Mexico*.
18. See Edberg, *El Narcotraficante*, 27, 28. Marez thinks that narcocorridos and gangsta rap have produced images and stories of the drug war from below: "These two musical forms imaginatively invert dominant state and capitalist relations that subordinate the poor. Which is not to say that *narcocorridos* or rap represent the unmediated voice of the subaltern as such, for both kinds of music are mediated in ways that partly embed them in dominant ideologies and structures. In their fantasies of subaltern power, both forms borrow ideas and images from dominant mass media, including newspapers, TV news, and mainstream action films...Nonetheless, the history of gangsta rap and *narcocorridos* suggests that subaltern audiences take vicarious pleasure in the narcotrafficker's opposition to state power. The tastes of such audiences contradict dominant representations of poor

people longing for patriarchal state protections" (Marez, *Drug Wars*, 23; on gangsta rap see Quinn, *Nuthin' but a "G" Thang*). Our study will focus on narcocorridos in their own right, since their close comparison with rap music carries assumptions in terms of "affective aesthetics" that may not be generalizable. The cases of Chalino Sánchez and Los Tigres del Norte are significantly different in that regard (on Chalino see Quiñones, *True Tales*; Wald, *Narcocorrido*.)

19. Astorga, *Mitologia del "narcotraficante" en México*, 37–38.
20. Ibid.
21. On the concept of "renarration" Herlinghaus, *Renarración y descentramiento*, 12–23, 220–249.
22. We are referring to a period previous to, as well as to a context that reaches beyond the vigorous urbanization of the narcocorrido that took place, since the early 1990s, within the Los Angeles Mexican cultural environments, including the huge immigrant suburbs. This development, in which the impact of rap culture among Los Angeles Mexican-American working-class youth was crucial, is given more specific attention by Quiñones, *True Tales* (11–29) and Wald, *Narcocorrido* (69–83).
23. Wald, *Narcocorrido*, 2.
24. See Quiñones, *True Tales*.
25. My translation. For the Span. original see Astorga, *Mitología*, 126, 127.
26. Kittredge, "Introduction," xi.
27. Wald, *Narcocorrido*, 40, 39, 33.
28. See ibid., 42.
29. See Toro, *Mexico's "War" on Drugs*; Bertram, et al., *Drug War Politics*.
30. My translation. For Span. original see Valenzuela, *Jefe de Jefes*, 176.
31. On "Operation Condor" see Toro, *Mexico's "War,"* 16, 17, 39–44, 57; see also Carpenter, *Bad Neighbor Policy*.
32. McDowell, *Poetry and Violence*, 206, also 205.
33. See the numerous examples provided by Valenzuela, *Jefe de Jefes*, 174–192.
34. Toro, *Mexico's "War,"* 1.
35. Ibid., 16–31.
36. Wald, *Narcocorrido*, 39.
37. Cited in ibid, 42.
38. Ibid., 43.
39. Kittredge, "Introduction," xxiv.
40. Wald, *Narcocorrido*, 11.
41. My translation. For Span. original see Astorga, *Mitología*, 127, 128.
42. Wald, *Narcocorrido*, 22.
43. Ibid., 19.
44. See Mondaca Cota, *Las mujeres también pueden*.
45. Mendoza, *Cada respiro que tomas*, 53–55.
46. See Uribe, "Presentación," 15.
47. See Pérez Reverte, *La Reina del Sur*.
48. See Brady, *Extinct Lands*, 172–175.
49. See Monsiváis, *Los mil y un velorios*, 54.
50. Wald, *Narcocorrido*, 19.
51. Valenzuela, *Jefe de Jefes*, 59, 60.
52. See Certeau, *Practice of Everyday Life*, 201.
53. See Kittredge, "Introduction," xxii.

54. See Taussig, *Shamanism*, 366, 393, 394.

55. See Hobsbawm's assessment of the "social bandit," in *Primitive Rebels*, 13.

56. My translation. Span. original in Astorga, *Mitología*, 128.

57. Ibid.

58. Ibid.

59. Ibid., 128, 129.

60. Ibid.

61. Valenzuela, "Recreación," 167.

62. Astorga, *El siglo de las drogas*, 89.

63. Ibid., 119.

64. Ibid., 89–92; on "Operation Condor" see 115–126; also Astorga, *Mitología*, 23–28.

65. Astorga, *El siglo*, 30.

66. Ibid., 31, 33–37.

67. This is how McDowell explains the timeliness of corridos. See *Poetry and Violence*.

68. Wald, *Narcocorrido*, 49.

69. Cited in Astorga, *Mitología*, 95.

70. See ibid., 96.

71. See Benjamin on storytelling and "experience" ("Storyteller").

72. Liera, in *El Jinete de la Divina Providencia*, "sums up" the social memory of Malverde which has circulated by virtue of legends into an ambitious theatre play. See Liera in Leñero, 431–435. Also the recreation of Malverde in Mendoza's *Cada respiro*, 57–58.

73. Lyotard, *Postmodern Condition*, 20.

74. See Wald, *Narcocorrido*, 62, 63.

75. Ibid., 66.

76. See Foucault, *Surveiller et punir*, 93.

77. See in Liera's play the critical dramatization of the Porfirista governor Cañedo.

78. I am taking the expression used by White (see *Figural Realism*, 151, 152). However, I do not share Ricoeur's and White's subsuming narration under the category of discourse, for it curtails the question of cultural and epistemological heterogeneity of narratives (see Ricoeur, "The Human Experience of Time and Narrative," 99).

79. White, *Figural Realism*, 152.

80. See also Vanderwood, *Juan Soldado*, 215.

81. See Wald, *Narcocorrido*, 64.

82. See Quiñones, *True Tales*, 230.

83. Wald, *Narcocorrido*, 64.

84. Quiñones, *True Tales*, 230.

85. Herrera-Sobek, *Northward Bound*, 305.

86. See Toro, *Mexico's "War*,*"* 1.

87. See Smith, "Place of Ethics," 251–252.

88. My translation. Span. original in Monsiváis, "Los mil y un velorios," 51, 52.

89. See the slideshow of the chapel: http://www.calecia.com/gallery/travel-malverde.

90. Wald, *Narcocorrido*, 61.

91. My translation. Span. original in Valenzuela, *Jefe de Jefes*, 42.

92. Monsiváis, "En los albores," 23, 24.

93. Valenzuela, *Jefe de Jefes*, 42.
94. Quiñones, *True Tales*, 228–229.
95. Wald reports a concert lasting six hours, which was sponsored by someone "behind the scenes." The sponsor who paid and sent the banda did not appear himself, since these days it has become "indiscrete to be seen spending too much money, too obviously, on El Narcosantón" (65).
96. See Žižek, *Lacan and Popular Culture*.
97. See Colebrook, *Deleuze*, 10.
98. White, *Content of the Form*, 24.

3 PARATAXES UNBOUND

1. Saldívar, *Border Matters*, 1, 14.
2. See Sassen, *Territory, Authority, Rights*, 1–4.
3. See Saldívar, *Border Matters*, 3.
4. Appadurai, "Grassroots Globalization," 6.
5. See Brady, *Extinct Lands*, 172–175.
6. Se the discussion of the notion of "surplus power" by Ronald Judy, "America and Powerless Potentialities," 130, 131.
7. See Harvey, *Spaces of Hope*, 15, 16.
8. See Ong, *Neoliberalism as Exception*, 79.
9. See Lorey, *U.S.-Mexican Border*, 162–169.
10. Huntington, *Who Are We?* 221.
11. See Judy, "America and Powerless Potentialities," 131.
12. See Hondagneu-Sotelo, "History of Mexican Undocumented Settlement."
13. Huntington, *Who Are We?* 225.
14. Ibid., 256.
15. See Brady, *Extinct Lands*, 172, 173.
16. See also Lorey, *U.S.-Mexican Border*, 163.
17. Ibid.
18. Ibid.
19. Herrera-Sobek, *Northward Bound*, 191, 192.
20. See ibid.
21. See Harvey, *Condition of Postmodernity*, 153, 154.
22. Monsivais, *Los mil y un velorios*, 52, 53.
23. See Quiñones, *True Tales*, 4; also Quiñones, "San José's Tigres del Norte," 3.
24. García Canclini's formulation is taken as indicative for both epistemological and cultural strategies that resist universalizing narratives (*Culturas híbridas*).
25. Anzaldúa holds that due to the geopolitical situation initiated by the Treaty of Guadalupe Hidalgo (1848), which confirmed the loss of Texas, New Mexico, and Upper California, Mexicans cannot refrain from migrating to the North (see *Borderlands/La Frontera*, 1987); see also Hamnett, *Concise History of Mexico*, 1999, 151–157; Villegas (ed.), *Historia General de México*, 763–768, 803–821.
26. See Geertz, *Interpretation of Cultures*, 10.
27. See Lorey, *U.S.-Mexican Border*, 164.
28. See Appadurai, *Modernity at Large*, 48, 49.
29. See for basic assumptions of linguistic speech act theory, Austin, *How to Do Things with Words*, 1–11.
30. See Herlinghaus, "Zur neuen Krise."

31. See Vico's intriguing elaborations on "poetic tropes, monsters, and meta-morphoses" (*New Science*, 87–91).
32. Certeau, *Practice of Everyday Life*, 97.
33. Ibid., 97, 98.
34. See Herrera-Sobek, *Northward Bound*, 196.
35. Ibid.
36. See ibid.
37. See ibid., 197, 198. See also Herrera-Sobek's study of feminine images in the Mexican corrido (*Mexican Corrido*).
38. My translation. Span. original in Valenzuela, *Jefe de Jefes*, 26.
39. My translation. Span. original in ibid., 42, 99.
40. See also two historical examples of immigration corridos provided by Herrera-Sobek: *Corrido de Inmigración* (Immigration Corrido) and *Corrido de la triste Situación* (Corrido of the Sad Situation). In *Northward Bound*, 138–144.
41. See Spinoza, *Ethics*, 171, 172. See Avelar's reference to Spinoza's concept of "affect" and its semantics of "to strive for," related to an "immanentist" notion of desire (*Untimely Present*, 237, note 1); also Goetschel on the concept of "affect" (*Spinoza's Modernity*, 49).
42. See Anzaldúa, *Borderlands*.
43. See the corridos *Los Alambrados* (The Wire Jumpers) and *El Bracero* (The Bracero), in Herrera-Sobek, *Northward Bound*, 198, 199.
44. White, *Figural Realism*, 88, see also 87, 97, 98; see Auerbach, "Figura." Karlheinz Barck and Martin Treml have recently published a remarkable volume of new studies on Auerbach (*Erich Auerbach*).
45. See Costa Lima's discussion of Auerbach's peculiar concept of "realism": "Zwischen Realismus und Figuration," 256–267; and Müller about "figure" and "realism," "Auerbachs Realismus," 274–277.
46. See Ginzburg, *Cheese and the Worms*; Chartier, *Cultural History*.
47. Auerbach, *Mimesis*, 88.
48. Auerbach, *Mimesis*, 86, 63, 84–87.
49. See Benjamin, "On the Mimetic Faculty."
50. Auerbach, *Mimesis*, 59.
51. Ibid., 61.
52. See Rozitchner, *La cosa y la cruz*, for a perspective that addresses the epistemic core of St.Augustine's work as a critique of global capitalism.
53. See my thoughts on the concept of "colonial rhetorical reason" in relationship to Bernardino de Sahagún's *Coloquios y Doctrina Cristiana* (*Renarración y descentramiento*, 91–96).
54. See Sloterdijk, *Critique of Cynical Reason*.
55. Auerbach, *Mimesis*, 59, 61.
56. See Plato, *Republic*, Chapter XXV.
57. Auerbach, *Mimesis*, 60.
58. See Negri, *Savage Anomaly*, 103.
59. Negri, *Time for Revolution*, 197.
60. White, *Content*, 24–25.
61. Vico, *New Science*, 88.
62. See Bachelard, *Poetics of Space*, 1964.
63. Certeau, *Practice of Everyday Life*, 193, 195.
64. See Augé, *Non-places*.

65. See for example Auerbach, "Figura," 47.
66. Santner, *On Creaturely Life*, 12, 13.
67. Menke, *Tragödie im Sittlichen*, 19. See Menke's differentiation between a poetic discourse of modernity and philosophical discourse. Ibid., 20–23.
68. See Hegel, "Aesthetics," 448.
69. See Eagleton, *Sweet Violence*, 93, 94.
70. Hegel, *Elements of the Philosophy of Right*, 279.
71. Hegel, "Aesthetics," 452.
72. See Benjamin, "On the Mimetic Faculty," 722.
73. My translation. Span. original in Valenzuela, *Jefe de Jefes*, 37, 38.
74. See Benjamin, "Experience and Poverty," 732.
75. See Schendel and Abraham, *Illicit Flows*, 7–9; Kraniauskas, "*Cronos.*"
76. See Benjamin, "Storyteller," 147.
77. See Ríos, *Iguana Killer*, 12–21. See also Saldívar, *Border Matters*, 69–70; Brady, *Extinct Lands*, 175–181.
78. Carpentier, *La novela latinoamericana*, 26.
79. See Eagleton, *Sweet Violence*, 96.
80. Eagleton, *Idea of Culture*, 131.
81. Ibid.
82. Subcomandante Marcos, cited in Montemayor, *Chiapas, la rebelión indígena*, 56.
83. See Beverley, "*Lazarillo* and Primitive Accumulation," 36, 37.
84. See Harvey, *New Imperialism*, 145, 151, 154.

4   WHERE AFFECTION MEETS FIGURATION: CORRIDO LANGUAGE AND THE INTERMEDIAL PRESENCE OF DEATH

1. See Cuddon, *Dictionary of Literary Terms*, 481.
2. Vico, *New Science*, 90.
3. See Beckett, "Dante...Bruno. Vico.. Joyce," 14.
4. See Vico, *New Science*, 90.
5. See Edberg's problematization in *El Narcotraficante*, 12–17.
6. See E. Müller, "Auerbachs Realismus."
7. See Auerbach, *Mimesis*, 59.
8. See Parker, "Metaphor and Catachresis," 67.
9. Ibid., 60–73.
10. Auerbach, *Mimesis*, 88.
11. Gumbrecht, "Cosmological Time," 305, 309, 310.
12. Benjamin, "Storyteller," 157.
13. Although it is difficult to make these distinctions, paratactical figures relate to borderline experiences that, since early medieval "realism," have existed within as well as outside literature. Their interpretation by literary historians, significantly obvious in the case of Auerbach, has been based on their being condensed into major literary forms rather than the "vulgar language," prevalent in minor narratives related to singing, acting, and oral communication.
14. See Arendt, *Human Condition*, 54.
15. See Parker, "Metaphor and Catachresis."
16. See Haverkamp, "Allegory," 51.

17. See Gumbrecht, "Cosmological Time," 319.
18. de Man, *Aesthetic Ideology*, 41, 42.
19. See Sander, "Tropes and Trojan Horses," 95, 96.
20. de Man, *Aesthetic Ideology*, 49.
21. Beckett, "Dante," 16, 17.
22. Higgins, a proponent of concept-art, has discussed a notion of "intermedia" to suggest a new take on the history and development of modern and postmodern art forms (see *Horizons*, 18–28; and *Modernism*, 93–94). Our study, in turn, applies a concept of "intermediality" to address the figural character of cultural heterogeneity (see *Narraciones anacrónicas*, 37–49).
23. See Wald, *Narcocorrido*, 2.
24. See White, *Figural Realism*, 153.
25. See the story told by Quiñones (*True Tales*, 24).
26. Wald, *Narcocorrido*, 71, 72.
27. Taylor, *Archive and the Repertoire*, 16.
28. See Wald, *Narcocorrido*, 12.
29. Simonett, *Banda*, 228–229.
30. See Edberg, *El Narcotraficante*, 95.
31. Beckett, "Dante," 14.
32. See for the lyrics chapter 2.
33. See White, *Figural Realism*, 152.
34. Anzaldúa, *Borderlands*, 25.
35. Ibid., 25, 29.
36. See ibid., 34.
37. Brooks, *Melodramatic Imagination*, x.
38. See for example Castillo's essays, *Massacre of the Dreamers*, 1994.
39. See Pollock, "Cosmopolitan," 44.
40. Wald, *Narcocorrido*, 14.
41. My translation. See chapter 2.
42. See Ricoeur, "Human Experience," 100, 101.
43. See Inwood, *Heidegger Dictionary*, 16. This "fearfulness" is closely related to Heidegger's notion of "care." "Care, rather than the persistence and self-awareness of an I or ego, or the continuity and coherence of experiences, makes Dasein a unified, autonomous self. In care Dasein pulls itself together: 'As care Dasein is the "Between" [birth and death].'" (Inwood, *Heidegger Dictionary*, 37).
44. See Ricoeur, "Human Experience," 101.
45. Ibid.
46. See Osborne, *Politics of Time*, 59.
47. Historicality, in Benjamin's sense of paradoxical recognition/image, cuts through historicism ("On the Concept of History," 390, 391).
48. Ricoeur, "Human Experience," 101, 102.
49. See Osborne, *Politics of Time*, 57.
50. I use the word "poetry" in contrast to Heidegger's text "What are Poets for?" (see Young, *Heidegger's Later Philosophy*, 66).
51. Young, *Heidegger's*, 64.
52. See Inwood, *Heidegger Dictionary*, 16, 17; Heidegger, *Being and Time*, 172.
53. See Young, *Heidegger's*, 71.
54. I am paraphrasing Arendt's formulation (*Human Condition*, 179, 180).
55. This can be seen in the way that our assumption of an affective potential, derived from the nonverbal repertoire that is activated by corridos, does connect

with an underlying narrative consciousness on the part of the public—a public whose main characteristic is not that it partakes in drug trafficking, but that it shares a sense of the conditions of drastically increased violence.

56. White, *Figural Realism*, 152.
57. See Sterne, *Audible Past*, 287.
58. Taussig, *Shamanism*, 366.
59. In several later songs, this counterpoint may even acquire a slight carnavalistic tone.
60. See Bierhorst, *Cantares Mexicanos*.
61. Critics have tried to address this phenomenon in different ways. Valenzuela leans toward a pedagogical interpretation: narcocorridos can serve as a warning that can prevent people from stepping into the abyss. Edberg argues in favor of a socially alert anthropology, drawing attention to the various implications that performative styles like that of narcoballads can acquire through "acting as if" under conditions of border liminality (*El Narcotraficante*, 30, 100). McDowell observes that Los Tigres have taken a moral position leaning toward social commentary and finds a "regulatory" potential for producing "lessons" out of despicable acts (*Poetry and Violence*, 206).
62. Badiou writes: "Considered as a figure of nihilism, reinforced by the fact that our societies are without a future that can be presented as universal, ethics oscillates between two complementary desires: a conservative desire, seeking global recognition for the legitimacy of the order peculiar to our 'Western' position—the interweaving of an unbridled and impassive economy [économie objective sauvage] with a discourse of law; and a murderous desire that promotes and shrouds, in one and the same gesture, an integral mastery of life—or again, that dooms *what is* to the 'Western' mastery of death" (*Ethics*, 38).
63. See ibid., 3.
64. See Heidegger, *Being and Time*, 132, 133, 176, 177.
65. Massumi, *Politics of Everyday Fear*, viii, ix.
66. See, Benjamin, "Capitalism as Religion." My translation (in the English version, the German "Angst" is changed into "despair," see 290.)
67. Agamben, *Homo Sacer*, 8, 73.
68. See Benjamin, "On the Concept of History," 392.
69. Agamben, *Homo Sacer*, 184.

5 YOUNG, ALIEN, AND TOTALLY VIOLENT: MARGINAL "KINGS OF THE WORLD"

1. Bergquist, *Violence in Colombia, 1990–2000*, 3.
2. See "Colombianos, mafia y muerte es lo mismo," in *El Mundo*, Medellín, July 15, 1979, 8 (cited in Salazar and Jaramillo, *Medellín*, 45, 46.)
3. See Marez, *Drug Wars*, 185, 150, 151.
4. Martín-Barbero, "Jóvenes," 22.
5. See Hylton, "Colombia," 15.
6. See Medellín's "neoliberal plastic surgery" in Hylton, "Extreme Makeover," 152–154.
7. See Jaramillo Morales, *Nación y melancolía*, 27.
8. About the historical phenomenon "La Violencia" see Hylton (*Evil Hour*, 39–50).
9. Martín-Barbero, "Jóvenes," 24.

10. Salazar, *No nacimos pa' semilla*, 15, 16 (translations are mine unless otherwise indicated). Condensed synthesis of the period in question is provided by Hylton in "Rodrigo D," 27–30.
11. See Hylton, "Colombia: An Evil Hour"; "War as Peace, 2005–6" (in *Evil Hour in Colombia*, 121–128).
12. See Kristeva, *Powers of Horror*, 27.
13. See Hallward, *Absolutely Postcolonial*, 6.
14. For a more extensive glossary see Castañeda Naranjo and Salazar, *Diccionario de Parlache*.
15. Kristeva, *Powers of Horror*, 27.
16. See Arendt, *Human Condition*, 184; Cavarero, *Relating Narratives*, 56.
17. See Cavarero, *Relating Narratives*, 56.
18. I have modified the translation. For the Engl. version see *Born to Die in Medellín*, 11; Span. original, *No nacimos*, 21.
19. Translation modified. Engl. see 11; Span. 21.
20. Durkheim, *Elementary Forms*, 306.
21. Agamben argues, in relationship to the ancient notion of *sacer*, that there is a conception of the sacred that, "before or beyond the religious, constitutes the first paradigm of the political realm of the West" (*Homo Sacer*, 9, 77).
22. See Girard, *Violence and the Sacred*.
23. See Bergquist, Peñaranda, and Sánchez, *Violence in Colombia: The Contemporary Crisis*, especially chapter 5.
24. See Schmitt, *Political Theology*, 5, 6.
25. See Klein, *Shock Doctrine*.
26. See Agamben, *Homo Sacer*.
27. Benjamin, "On the Concept of History," 392.
28. See Agamben, *Homo Sacer*, 28, 29.
29. See Salazar, *No nacimos*, 16, 17.
30. Arendt, *Human Condition*, 9.
31. See Rotker, *Citizens of Fear*, 7–21, 224; Kaminsky, Kosovsky, and Kessler, *El delito*, 77–87.
32. See, in addition, Salazar's testimony *Mujeres de fuego*, published in 1993.
33. See Salazar, *No nacimos*, 22, 40.
34. Ibid., 40.
35. Benjamin, "Storyteller," 157.
36. Salazar, *No nacimos*, 41.
37. Ibid.
38. Schmitt, *Political Theology*, 5.
39. See the example of "Plan Colombia." Stokes, *America's Other War*, 87–105.
40. See Agamben, *Homo Sacer*, 11.
41. See Salazar and Jaramillo, *Medellín*, 69–83.
42. Hylton, "Extreme makeover," 157–161, 163.
43. See, *No nacimos*, 25.
44. Ibid., 26, 27.
45. Ibid.
46. About Arendt's discussion of Marx' concept of labor see Ernst Müller who writes, "Arendt's polemic with Marx entails a sharp critique of bourgeois economy, yet her notions of politics and action are based on the relationships she criticizes" ("Hannah Arendts Marxkritik," 105).
47. Arendt, *Human Condition*, 86, 87, 126.

48. Salazar, *No nacimos*, 34.
49. Ibid.
50. Ibid. 28, 29.
51. See ibid., 28.
52. Aristotle, *Politics*, 70.
53. See Agamben, *Homo Sacer*, 2.
54. Salazar, *No nacimos*, 22.
55. See Taussig, "Transgression," 349.
56. Salazar, *No nacimos*, 34.
57. See the figure of abandonment in Agamben, *Homo Sacer*, 87–90.
58. See Margulis and Urresti, "La construcción social de la condición de juventud," 5.
59. See Butler, *Psychic Life of Power*, 2.
60. Salazar and Jaramillo, *Medellín*, 117.
61. See Agamben, *Homo Sacer*, 9, 85, 86, 119.
62. See Brennan, *Globalization*, 1, 20–23; Klein on the application of "States of Shock" to Latin American societies, beginning with Chile 1973, and what Pinochet called "a war" (*Shock Doctrine*, 75–97).
63. See the formulation in Negri, *On Revolution*, 156, 65.
64. Derrida and Vattimo, *Religion*, 1, 3.
65. See Salazar and Jaramillo, *Medellín*, 114–118, 123–124.
66. Salazar, *No nacimos*, 114.
67. Ibid., 114.
68. See de Man, *Allegories of Reading*, 22.
69. The term is taken from Hutcheon (*Narcissistic Narrative*, 17–21).
70. This story was not yet part of the first edition of the book of 1990.
71. Salazar, *No nacimos*, 126, 143.
72. Ibid., 126, 136.
73. Hylton, "Extreme Makeover," 157–158.
74. See Agamben, *Homo Sacer*, 180.
75. We are paraphrasing the title of Kirk's book.
76. Hylton provides a precise, that is demythifying analysis of the historical emergence, the political and territorial dynamics that have been characterizing the different guerrilla movements in Colombia ("Colombia: An Evil Hour").
77. See Bewes, *Reification*, 136–137.
78. Salazar, *No nacimos*, 113, 114.
79. Salazar, *Born to Die*, 99, 100.
80. Ibid.
81. Taussig, *Mimesis and Alterity*, 135.
82. See Agamben, *Profanations*, 73–92.
83. See Agamben about the difference between "profanation" and "secularization" ("Der Papst," 56).
84. See Salazar, *No nacimos*, 69, 70, 115.
85. See ibid., 70.
86. Translation modified. See Salazar, *Born to Die*, 60; 67–68.
87. See Taussig, "Transgression," 351.
88. See Bataille, "Notion of Expenditure," 120–123. On the concept of "utility" see 116–117.
89. Arendt, *Human Condition*. The citation continues: "It is for this reason that the Greeks derived their word for torture from necessity" (129).

90. See Flores d'Arcais, *Libertärer Existentialismus.*
91. Arendt, *Human Condition*, 130, 127, 131, 133.
92. A telling contrast is found in the perception of "innocent money," owing to moralizing public outcries in view of the burning of banknotes by criminal gang youths in Ricardo Piglia's novel '*Plata Quemada*' (Burned Money), 189–192.
93. Arendt, *Human Condition*, 134.
94. See Certeau, *Practice of Everyday Life*, 80, 81.
95. See Benjamin, "Capitalism," 288.
96. We have rephrased Arendt's formulation.
97. See Benjamin, "Capitalism," 289.
98. See Salazar and Jaramillo, *Medellín*, 114–116.
99. Salazar, *No nacimos*, 22.
100. See Agamben, *Homo Sacer*, 104–108.
101. Term taken from Taussig but given a different meaning (see *Shamanism*, 70).
102. Salazar, *No nacimos*, 24, 25, 75, 76.
103. See Cavarero, *Relating Narratives.*
104. Benjamin, "Storyteller," 151.
105. Orwell, *Collection of Essays*, 213.
106. Benjamin, "Storyteller," 162.

6 Autobiography as Eschatological Project: An Intellectual Struggle Regarding Freedom and Guilt

1. Vallejo, *Our Lady of the Assassins*, 9.
2. See Butler, *Excitable Speech*, 1.
3. See Butler citing Charles R. Lawrence III on "racist speech," ibid., 4.
4. O'Bryan, "Representations of the City," 195.
5. See Orrego, "Entrevista con Héctor Abad Faciolince," 3.
6. de Man, *Allegories*, 151.
7. Sieber, "Literary Continuity," 140, 155.
8. See Ospina's documentary *La desazón suprema* (Colombia, 2003), in which Vallejo replicates diatribes that have made his novel a provocation in terms of social racism: "People reproduce blindly and it's a disaster. Most are hypocrites...They've had the bad luck of being born. Don't be born! Don't have children!" The viewer can also perceive a speech habitus of the writer that has been recently called "apocalyptic electricity" (See Vallejo, "Electricidad apocalíptica," 1).
9. See Jauß, *Ästhetische Erfahrung.*
10. See the cover text of the 1998 Spanish edition.
11. See Barthes, *Sade / Fourier / Loyola*, 1997, 39.
12. See Franco, *Decline*, 225.
13. See ibid.
14. Vallejo, *Our Lady*, 18.
15. See Jaramillo Morales' reading of the novel as "caricatura de la realidad colombiana" in which melancholy is viewed to be the defining feature of the autobiographical self. In *Nación y melancolía*, 112–119.
16. Franco, *Decline*, 225.

17. Vallejo, *Our Lady*, 2, 3, 57.
18. Ibid., 5.
19. Ibid.
20. Ibid., 6.
21. Ibid., 7.
22. Ibid.
23. See Foucault, *History of Sexuality*, Vols. 2 and 3.
24. Vallejo, *Our Lady*, 5, 4, 6.
25. Ibid., 7, 13.
26. See ibid., 12. At the beginning of *On the Genealogy of Morality*, Nietzsche writes: "We are unknown to ourselves, we knowers; and with good reason...," 3.
27. Vallejo, *Our Lady*, 114.
28. See Butler, *Excitable Speech*, 3.
29. Ricoeur, *Time and Narrative*, Vol. 3, 246.
30. Vallejo, *Our Lady*, 8.
31. Ibid., 8, 18, 21.
32. Ricoeur, *Time and Narrative*, Vol. 3, 246.
33. Ibid. "The Notion of narrative identity also indicates its fruitfulness in that it can be applied to a community as well as to an individual....Individual and community are constituted in their identity by taking up narratives that become for them their actual history" (Ibid., 247).
34. Arendt, *Human Condition*, 186.
35. Vallejo, *Our Lady*, 14, 15.
36. "...the state in Colombia is the first lawbreaker" (ibid., 91).
37. Ibid., 109, 110, 2.
38. In German: *Die Rolle der Erotik in der männlichen Gesellschaft* (cited in Brunotte, *Zwischen Eros und Krieg*, 85).
39. Ibid.
40. Vallejo, *Our Lady*, 2, 8, 91. "Cocaine profiteer" refers to César Gaviria Trujillo, president from 1990 to 1994.
41. Ibid., 10, 18.
42. Ibid. 91, 35.
43. Ibid., 21, 108, 27, 109.
44. See Agamben, *Homo Sacer*, 176.
45. Vallejo, *Our Lady*, 22.
46. See Agamben's discussion of "Vitae Necisque Potestas," *Homo Sacer*, 88.
47. See de Man's formulation regarding rhetorical reading (*Allegories*, ix).
48. See Žižek, "Pure Gewalt," 36.
49. See Foucault's formulation in *History of Sexuality*, Vol. 1, 115.
50. Vallejo, *Our Lady*, 68, 64,110.
51. Ibid., 36, 37, 41, 48, 49, 50, 54, 56, 57. When Fernando advices the policeman, we feel reminded of the figure of "vitae necisque potestas": the policeman is addressed as if he, too, were one of Fernando's adopted sons, and he is adviced in matters of life and death, as well as of order and authority.
52. Vallejo, *Our Lady*, 57, 66, 69, 71, 72, 76, 75, 80, 81.
53. Smith, "Homographesis in Salicio's Song," 133.
54. See Aristotle, *Politics*.
55. See *P. Virgilii Maronis opera cum Servii, Donati, et Ascensii commentariis*, Venis 1542. Cited in Smith, "Homographesis in Salicio's Song," 133.

56. On the Colombian race we read in Vallejo's novel: "there is not a worse plague on the planet than rural Colombians" (Span. edition, 83, 84). Regarding Latin American ethnicities: "There is no worse mix than that of the Spaniard with the Indian and the black" (90).

57. See two examples: "The poor person is the asshole that never stops and the insaciable vagina" (68). "In Colombia debauched life is defeating death, and kids come from everywhere, from any hole or vagina like rats from sewers when they are overflowing" (71).

58. Vallejo's choice of subject is likely to be influenced by the publication, a few years before, of *No nacimos*, which he then implicitly ironizes by a dismissive rhetoric regarding "sociological" insights into the culture of sicarios (see Vallejo, Span. edition, 15, 16). Also note the narrator's comments on drug traffic, the role of the government, and the condition of Medellín's sicarios. His satanization of the *Comunas*.

59. Vallejo, *Our Lady*, 72, 73, 113. The expression reads more comprehensively as: "Ye poor of this world…sweep you away" (113).

60. See Santner, *On the Psychotheology of Everyday Life*, 28.

61. See Spinoza's formulation in *Ethics*, 169.

62. See Sartre, *Saint Genet*, 90. The title of Vallejo's novel seems to have been inspired by Genet's *Our Lady of the Flowers* (1943). See Russel, *Our Lady of the Assassins*, 1.

63. Sontag, *Against Interpretation*, 96.

64. Ibid.

65. Agamben, *Profanations*, 75.

66. See Taussig, *Shamanism*, 9.

67. See Deleuze, *Nietzsche and Philosophy*, 141.

68. Vallejo, *Our Lady*, 128.

69. I am drawing freely on Kantorowicz's *King's Two Bodies*, xi, 3–6.

70. Vallejo, *Our Lady*, 85.

71. *Holy Bible*, "John," 10:30, 1140.

72. See Badiou, *Saint Paul*, 75.

73. Ibid.

74. Vallejo, *Our Lady*, 78, 55, 56, 127, 156.

75. If Nietzsche believed that the Gospels did not provide a clear picture of the essence of Christ, so that the "real" Jesus had to be discovered by critical intuition, the *grammaticus*, in turn, overrides the ambiguity of these texts by calling for the autocratic posture of the figure. See also Jaspers on Nietzsche and Christianity.

76. *Holy Bible*, "Matthew," 8:21–22, 1005.

77. Vallejo, *Our Lady*, 131.

78. Drury, *Terror and Civilization*, 9.

79. See ibid., 15, 29.

80. See Faciolince, *Las formas de la pereza*, 117.

81. Drury writes, "In the Old Testament, sins are actions, not beliefs. In contrast, the New Testament makes abiding by the Law secondary to believing in Jesus. And when believing in him is itself a gift of grace, we get a picture of a very remote, arbitrary, and inscrutable God who is also beyond reproach" (*Terror and Civilization*, 32, 5–9).

82. Vallejo, *Our Lady*, 83. See Taubes on the symbolism of Gnosticism ("Der dogmatische Mythos der Gnosis," 583).

83. See the doctrine of "concordancy" of both Testaments (Taubes, "Der dogmatische Mythos," 584).
84. Vallejo, *Our Lady*, 83.
85. Cited in Taubes, "Der dogmatische Mythos," 152.
86. See ibid., 153.
87. Mitchell, "1 and 2 Thessalonians," 57.
88. Borges, "Una vindicación del falso Basílides," 215, 214.
89. See Taubes, "Der dogmatische Mythos," 153.
90. See Scholem, *Major Trends in Jewish Mysticism*, 247.
91. Cited in Goodman-Thau, "Auf der Kreuzung von Geschichte und Freiheit," x.
92. Taubes cited in Goodman-Thau, ibid.
93. See Walde, "La novela de sicarios," 35–37.
94. See Hylton, "Colombia," 10–15.
95. Foucault, *History of Sexuality*, Vol. 1, 135.
96. See ibid., 135, 137.
97. Arendt, *On Violence*, 51, 52.
98. See Bernstein, *Bitter Carnival*, 27.
99. Ibid.
100. Nietzsche, *On the Genealogy*, 59.
101. Bernstein, *Bitter Carnival*, 27.
102. Here we are using Drury's metaphor (*Terror and Civilization*, 153), not Vallejo's (see *La Puta de Babilonia*).
103. Vallejo, *Our Lady*, 132.

7 BEYOND BARE LIFE: AFFECTION-IMAGES OF VIOLENCE IN LATIN AMERICAN FILM

1. See Massumi, *Politics of Everyday Fear*, viii.
2. See Beckett, "Dante," 7.
3. See Gilroy, 'Postcolonial Melancholia,' 88.
4. See Auerbach, *Mimesis*, 61.
5. Benjamin, "Critique," 251.
6. See Smith, "Place of Ethics," 252.
7. Benjamin, *Arcades Project*, 463.
8. See Harvey, *New Imperialism*, 214.
9. See Žižek on the "(mis)appropriation" of European intellectual topoi by the American "radical" academia. In 'Welcome to the Desert,' 100–101.
10. Ibid., 100.
11. Sontag, *Against Interpretation*, 212.
12. Cited from the film.
13. Oubiña, "El espectáculo," 29.
14. See ibid., 32.
15. Hegel, "Aesthetics," 452.
16. See Eagleton, *Sweet Violence*, 8.
17. The list of examples would be an extensive one. To name some: "Estrategia del caracol," "Ilona llega con la lluvia," and "Rosario Tijeras" (Colombia); "Últimas imágenes de un naufragio," "El lado oscuro del corazón," and "La ciénaga" (Argentina); "Mi último hombre" and "El chacotero sentimental" (Chile); "Cronos" and "Y tu mamá también" (México).

18. See Deleuze, *Cinema 1*, 97, 98.
19. See ibid., 101.
20. Oubiña, "El espectáculo," 32.
21. See Deleuze, *Cinema 1*, 97.
22. See S. Žižek, *Welcome to the Desert*, 40.
23. See Brooks, *Melodramatic Imagination*, viii, ix, x.
24. See Davis, *Planet of Slums*, 19.
25. See Pisters, *Matrix of Visual Culture*, 79.
26. Deleuze, *Cinema 1*, 141.
27. See Kipp, "Amores Perros," 2.
28. See Sánchez-Prado, "Amores Perros," 41–43.
29. Sontag, *Against Interpretation*, 138.
30. See Deleuze, *Cinema 1*, 114, 115.
31. See ibid., 120, 122.
32. Varella, *Estação Carandiru*.
33. Cited from the film.
34. Hegel, "Aesthetics," 452.
35. See Deleuze and Guattari, "Plane of Immanence," 44–49.
36. See Gumbrecht on "effects of presence" (*Production of Presence*, 18).
37. See Smith's discussion of the notion "mode of existence" ("Place of Ethics").
38. See Rosen on "existential phenomenology" (*Change Mummified*, 11).
39. See Deleuze, *Cinema 2*, 1–4, xi.
40. See Jauregui, "Entrevista con Víctor Gaviria," 93, 94, 95, 96.
41. See Suárez, "Los estragos de la euforia," 34.
42. See Derrida, "Ends of Man," in *Margins of Philosophy*, 115, 116, 121.
43. See Heiner Müller about industrial society and death drive (*Jenseits der Nation*, 44).
44. See Rosen, *Change Mummified*, XXIII, 28, 41; Bazin, "Die Ontologie des fotografischen Bildes" ('*Was ist Kino?*' 21–25).
45. See Arendt, *Human Condition*, 176.
46. See Deleuze, *Cinema 1*, 87.
47. See Kantaris on the music of the film ("Allegorical Cities," 7, and note 20).
48. See Bruzual, especially on music and rhythm ("El espectador asesinado").
49. See Smith, "Place of Ethics," 251–252.
50. See ibid., 252.
51. Hylton, "Rodrigo D. No futuro," 31.
52. See Suárez, "Los estragos," 47–52.
53. See Domínguez on the real-life person of "Leidy Tabares," 19–37.
54. See Kantaris, "Peripheries of Globalization," 4, 5.
55. See the real-life actors of *The Rose Seller*, and their demeanors in the documentary "Como poner a actuar pájaros."
56. See Suárez, "Los estragos," 46; Castañeda Naranjo, *Diccionario de Parlache*, 106.
57. Millán, *Las huellas de Buñuel*, 19–31.
58. Suárez, "Los estragos," 44.
59. Deleuze, *Cinema 1*, 141–142.
60. See Herlinghaus, "Walter Benjamins Begriff des Rausches."
61. Bataille, "Notion of Expenditure," 118.
62. See Agamben, *Profanations*, 77–79.
63. See Benjamin, "Myslovice–Braunschweig–Marseilles," in *On Hashish*, 107.

64. See Lambert, *Franciscan Poverty*, 40–46.
65. See Pope John XXII, "Ad conditorem canonum," in Lambert, 247–253; Nold, *Pope John XXII*, 169–176.
66. See Bataille, "Notion of Expenditure," 129.
67. See Benjamin, "Experience and Poverty," 732.
68. See Müller, *"Jenseits der Nation,"* 27–28.
69. Benjamin, "Hashish in Marseilles," 126.

BIBLIOGRAPHY

FILMS

Aljure, Felipe. *El Colombian Dream*, Colombia, 2007.
Babenco, Héctor. *Carandiru*. Brazil, Argentina, 2003.
———. Pixote. Brazil, 1980.
Birri, Fernando. *Tire dié*. (Documentary) Argentina, 1958.
Buñuel, Luis. *Los olvidados*. Mexico, 1950.
Caetano, Adrián. *Un oso rojo*. Argentina, France, Spain, 2002.
Caetano, Adrián and Bruno Stagnaro. *Pizza, birra, faso*, Argentina, 1997.
Gaviria, Víctor. *Rodrigo D. No futuro*. Colombia, 1989.
———. *La vendedora de rosas* (The Rose Seller). Colombia, 1998.
———. *Sumas y restas*. Colombia, 2004.
Goggel, Erwin, Sergio Navarro, and Víctor Gaviria. *Como poner a actuar pájaros.*
    (Documentary). Colombia, 1999.
González Iñarritu, Alejandro. *Amores perros*. Mexico, 2000.
Grupo Chaski. *Gregorio*. Peru, 1984.
———. *Juliana*. Peru, 1989.
Maillé, Emilio. *Rosario Tijeras*. Colombia, 2005.
Marston, Joshua. *María llena eres de gracia* (Maria Full of Grace). Colombia, 2005.
Méndez, Josué. *Días de Santiago*. Peru, 2004.
Meirelles, Fernando. *Cidade de Deus* (City of God). Brazil, 2003.
Novaro, María. *Sin dejar huella* (Without a Trace). Mexico, 2001.
Novoa, José. *Sicario*. Venezuela, 1994.
Ospina, Luis. *Fernando Vallejo: La desazón suprema*. (Documentary) Colombia, 2003.
Schroeder, Barbet. *Our Lady of the Assassins*. Colombia, Spain, France, 1999.
Tort, Gerardo. *De la calle*. Mexico, 2001.
Trapero, Pablo. *El Bonaerense*. Argentina, Chile, France, 2002.

TEXTS

Agamben, Giorgio. "Der Papst ist ein weltlicher Priester." (Interview) *Literaturen,*
    Berlin, Feb. 6, 2005.
———. *Homo Sacer: Sovereign Power and Bare Life*. Trans. Daniel Heller-Roazen.
    Stanford: Stanford Univ. Press, 1998.
———. *Profanations*. Trans. Jeff Fort. New York: Zone Books, 2007.
———. *State of Exception*. Trans. Kevin Attell. Chicago–London: Univ. of Chicago
    Press, 2005.
———. *The Time That Remains: A Commentary on the Letter to the Romans*. Trans.
    Patricia Dailey. Stanford: Stanford Univ. Press, 2005.
Anzaldúa, Gloria. *Borderlands/La Frontera: The New Mestiza*. San Francisco: Aunt
    Lute Books, 1987.

Appadurai, Arjun. *Fear of Small Numbers: An Essay on the Geography of Anger.* Durham, NC; London: Duke Univ. Press, 2006.

———. "Grassroots Globalization and the Research Imagination." *Public Culture,* 12 (1), winter 2006.

———. *Modernity at Large: Cultural Dimensions of Globalization.* Minneapolis; London: Univ. of Minnesota Press, 1996.

Arendt, Hannah. *The Human Condition.* Chicago; London: Univ. of Chicago Press, 1958.

———. *The Life of the Mind.* New York; London: Harvest/HBJ, 1981.

———. *On Revolution.* New York: Viking Press, 1966.

———. *On Violence.* San Diego; New York: Harvest/HBJ, 1969.

Aristotle. *The Politics and The Constitution of Athens.* Ed. Stephen Everson. Cambridge; New York: Cambridge Univ. Press, 2005.

Astorga, Luis. *El siglo de las drogas: Usos, percepciones y personajes.* Mexico City: Espasa Calpe, 1996.

———. *Mitología del "narcotraficante" en México.* Mexico City: Plaza y Valdés, 1995.

Auerbach, Erich. "Figura." [Trans. Ralph Manheim] In *Scenes from the Drama of European Literature.* Minneapolis: Univ. of Minnesota Press, 1984.

———. *Mimesis: The Representation of Reality in Western Literature.* Trans. Willard Trask. Garden City, NY: Doubleday, 1957.

Augé, Marc. *Non-places: Introduction to an Anthropology of Supermodernity.* Trans. John Howe. London; New York: Verso, 1995.

Austin, J. L. *How to Do Things with Words.* Cambridge: Harvard Univ. Press, 1975.

Avelar, Idelber. "The Ethics of Interpretation and the International Division of Intellectual Labor." *SubStance,* 29 (1), 2000.

———. *The Untimely Present: Postdictatorial Latin American Fiction and the Task of Mourning.* Durham, NC; London: Duke Univ. Press, 1999.

Bachelard, Gaston. *The Poetics of Space.* Trans. Maria Jolas. Boston: Beacon Press, 1969.

Badiou, Alain. *Ethics: An Essay on the Understanding of Evil.* Trans. Peter Hallward. London; New York: Verso, 2001.

———. *Saint Paul: The Foundation of Universalism.* Trans. Ray Brassier. Stanford: Stanford Univ. Press, 2003.

Baecker, Dirk (ed.). *Kapitalismus als Religion.* Berlin: Kulturverlag Kadmos, 2003.

Barck, Karlheinz. "5 Briefe Erich Auerbachs an Walter Benjamin in Paris." *Zeitschrift für Germanistik.* Leipzig. Vol. 9, 1988/6.

———. "Der Sürrealismus: Die letzte Momentaufnahme der europäischen Intelligenz." In Burkhardt Lindner (ed.). *Benjamin Handbuch: Leben—Werk—Wirkung.* Stuttgart; Weimar: J. B. Metzler, 2006.

Barck, Karlheinz, Martin Fontius, Dieter Schlenstedt, Burkhardt Steinwachs, and Friedrich Wolfzettel (eds.). *Ästhetische Grundbegriffe.* Vol. I (2000) and IV (2002). Stuttgart Weimar: J. B. Metzler.

Barck, Karlheinz and Martin Treml (eds.). *Erich Auerbach: Geschichte und Aktualität eines europäischen Philologen.* Berlin: Kulturverlag Kadmos, 2006.

Barthes, Roland. *Sade / Fourier / Loyola.* Baltimore, MD; London: Johns Hopkins Univ. Press, 1997.

Bataille, Georges. "The Notion of Expenditure." In Allan Stoekl (ed.). *G. Bataille. Visions of Excess.* Selected Writings, 1927–1939. Trans. A. Stoekl with Carl R. Lovitt and Donald M. Leslie, Jr. Minneapolis; London: Univ. of Minnesota Press, 1994.

Baudelaire, Charles. *Artificial Paradises.* Trans. Stacy Diamond. New York: Carol Publishing Group, 1996.

Baum, Dan. *Smoke and Mirrors: The War on Drugs and the Politics of Failure.* Boston; New York: Little, Brown and Co., 1997.

Bazin, André. *Was ist Kino?* Köln: Verlag M. DuMont Schauberg, 1975.

Beckett, Samuel. "Dante...Bruno. Vico.. Joyce". In S. Beckett, Marcel Brion, Frank Budgen, and Stuart Gilbert. *Our Exagmination Round His Factification for Incamination of Work in Progress.* New York: New Directions, 1962.

Benjamin, Walter. *The Arcades Project.* Trans. Howard Eiland and Kevin McLaughlin. Cambridge; London: Belknap Press of Harvard Univ. Press, 2002.

———. "Benjamin an Gretel Adorno," Paris, Oct. 9, 1935. In *Das Passagenwerk. Gesammelte Schriften,* Vol. V–2, 1991.

———. "Capitalism as Religion." In *Selected Writings* [SW], Vol. 1, 1996/2004.

———. "Convolute N." In *The Arcades Project.*

———. "Critique of Violence." In *SW,* Vol. 1.

———. *Das Passagenwerk.* In *Gesammelte Schriften* [GS], Vols. V–1 and V–2, 1991.

———. "The Dialectical Image" (Paralipomena to "On the Concept of History"). In *SW,* Vol. 4, 2006.

———. "Experience and Poverty." In *SW,* Vol. 2–2, 731–736, 2005.

———. "Fate and Character." In *SW,* Vol. 1, 201–206.

———. "An Fritz Radt." München, Nov. 21. 1915 (letter). In *Gesammelte Briefe* [GB], Vol. 1, 289–292, 1910–1918.

———. "An Gershom Sholem." Berlin. Dec. 1. 1920. In *GB,* Vol. 2, 107–110.

———. *Gesammelte Briefe* [GB], Vols. 1–6. Eds. Christoph Goedde and Henri Lonitz. Frankfurt Main: Suhrkamp, 1996.

Gesammelte Schriften. Vols. I–VII. Eds. Rolf Tiedemann and Hermann Schweppenhäuser. Frankfurt Main: Suhrkamp, 1974–1978.

———. "Hashish in Marseilles." In *On Hashish.* Trans. Howard Eiland and Others. Cambridge; London: Harvard Univ. Press, 2006.

———. "Imperial Panorama" ("One-Way Street"). In *SW,* Vol. 1.

———. "Kapitalismus als Religion." In *GS,* Vol. VI.

———. "Main Features of My Second Impression of Hashish" [1928]. In *SW,* Vol. 2–1, 2005.

———. "Mexican Embassy" ("One-Way Street"). In *SW,* Vol. 1.

———. "Myslowice–Braunschweig–Marseilles." In *On Hashish.*

———. "On the Concept of History." In *SW,* Vol. 4.

———. "On the Mimetic Faculty." In *SW,* Vol. 2–2.

schtiften. Vols. 1 and 2. Eds. Theodor W. and Gretel Adorno, Frankfurt Main: Suhrkamp 1955.

Selected Writings. Vols. 1–4. Eds. Marcus Bullock, Howard Eiland, and Michael W. Jennings. Cambridge, MA; London: Belknap Press of Harvard univ. Press, 2004–2006.

———. "Shaw: Frau Warrens Gewerbe." In *GS,* Vol. II–2.

———. "The Storyteller." In *SW,* Vol. 3.

———. "Surrealism: The Last Snapshot of the European Intelligentsia." In *SW,* Vol. 2–1.

———. "Zum Aufsatz über Sürrealismus." In *GS,* Vol. II–3.

———. "Zur Geschichtsphilosophie, Historik und Politik." In *GS,* Vol. VI.

———. "Zur Kritik der Gewalt." In *GS,* Vol. II–1.

Benjamin to Scholem. Nice, July 26, 1932, 14, 15. In Gershom Scholem (ed.). *The Correspondence of Walter Benjamin and Gershom Scholem 1932–1940.* Cambridge, MA: Harvard Univ. Press, 1992.

Bergquist, Charles, Ricardo Peñaranda, and Gonzalo Sánchez (eds.). *Violence in Colombia: The Contemporary Crisis in Historical Perspective.* Wilmington, DE: SR Books, 1992.

———. *Violence in Colombia, 1990–2000: Waging War and Negotiating Peace.* Wilmington, DE: SR Books, 2001.

Bernstein, Michael André. *Bitter Carnival: Ressentiment and the Abject Hero.* Princeton, NJ: Princeton Univ. Press, 1992.

Bertram, Eva, Morris Blachman, Kenneth Sharpe, and Peter Andreas. *Drug War Politics: The Price of Denial.* Berkeley; Los Angeles; London: Univ. of California Press, 1996.

Beverley, John. *Against Literature.* Minneapolis; London: Univ. of Minnesota Press, 1993.

———. "*Lazarillo* and Primitive Accumulation: Spain, Capitalism and the Modern Novel." *Bulletin of the Midwest Modern Language Association,* 15 (1), spring 1982.

———. "Theses on Subalternity, Representation, and Politics." In John Beverley, Phil Cohen, and David Harvey. *Subculture and Homogenization.* Barcelona: Fundació Antoni Tàpis, 1998.

Bewes, Timothy. *Reification or the Anxiety of Late Capitalism.* London; New York: Verso, 2002.

Bierhorst, John (ed. and trans.). *Cantares Mexicanos: Songs of the Aztecs.* Stanford: Stanford Univ. Press, 1985.

Blumenberg, Hans. *The Legitimacy of the Modern Age.* Trans. Robert M. Wallace. Cambridge, MA: MIT Press, 1983.

Boal, Iain, T. J. Clark, Joseph Matthews, and Michael Watts. *Afflicted Powers: Capital and Spectacle in a New Age of War.* London; New York: Verso, 2005.

Bolz, Norbert. *Auszug aus der entzauberten Welt.* München: Wilhelm Fink Verlag, 1989.

———. "Der Kapitalismus—eine Erfindung von Theologen?" In Dirk Baecker. *Kapitalismus als Religion.* Berlin: Kulturverlag Kadmos, 2003.

Borges, Jorge Luis. "Una vindicación del falso Basílides." In *Obras Completas.* Vol. 1. *Edited by Carlos V. Frías.* Barcelona: Emecé, 1996.

Bové, Paul A. "Afterword: Memory and Thought." In Rob Wilson and Wimal Dissanayake (eds.). *Global/Local: Cultural Production and the Transnational Imaginary.* Durham, NC; London: Duke Univ. Press, 1996.

Brady, Mary Pat. *Extinct Lands, Temporal Geographies: Chicana Literature and the Urgency of Space.* Durham, NC; London: Duke Univ. Press, 2002.

Breckenridge, Carol A., Sheldon Pollock, Homi K. Bhabha, and Dipesh Chakrabarty (eds.). *Cosmopolitanism.* Durham, NC; London: Duke Univ. Press, 2002.

Brennan, Teresa. *Exhausting Modernity: Grounds for a New Economy.* London; New York: Routledge, 2000.

———. *Globalization and Its Terrors: Daily Life in the West.* London; New York: Routledge, 2003.

———. *The Transmission of Affect.* Ithaca, NY; London: Cornell Univ. Press, 2004.

Brooks, Peter. *The Melodramatic Imagination: Balzac, Henry James, Melodrama, and the Mode of Excess.* New Haven, CT; London: Yale Univ. Press, 1995.

Brown, Norman O. *Life against Death: The Psychoanalytical Meaning of History.* Middletown, CT: Wesleyan Univ. Press, 1985.

Brunotte, Ulrike. *Zwischen Eros und Krieg: Männerbund und Ritual in der Moderne.* Berlin: Klaus Wagenbach, 2004.

Bruzual, Alejandro. "El espectador asesinado: La incomunicación como estrategia discursiva." In Luis Duno. *Imagen y subalternidad: El cine de Víctor Gaviria.* Caracas: Fundación Cinemateca Nacional, 2003.

Buck-Morss, Susan. *The Dialectics of Seeing: Walter Benjamin and the Arcades Project.* Cambridge, MA; London: MIT Press, 1989.

———. *Thinking Past Terror: Islamism and Critical Theory on the Left.* London: Verso, 2003.

Buendía, Rafael. *El contrabando del muerto* (corrido). In José Manuel Valenzuela. *Jefe de Jefes: Corridos y narcocultura en México.* Barcelona; Mexico City: Plaza & Janés Editores, 2002.

Butler, Judith. *Excitable Speech: A Politics of the Performative.* New York: Routledge, 1997.

———. *Precarious Life: The Powers of Mourning and Violence.* London; New York: Verso, 2004.

———. *The Psychic Life of Power: Theories in Subjection.* Stanford: Stanford Univ. Press, 1997.

Calderón, Héctor and J. D. Saldívar (eds.). *Criticism in the Borderlands.* Durham, NC; London: Duke Univ. Press, 1991.

Canguilhelm, Georges. *The Normal and the Pathological.* Trans. Carolyn R. Fawcett. New York: Zone Books, 1989.

Carpenter, Ted Galen. *Bad Neighbor Policy: Washington's Futile War on Drugs in Latin America.* New York: Palgrave Macmillan, 2003.

Carpentier, Alejo. *La novela latinoamericana en vísperas de un nuevo siglo y otros ensayos.* Mexico City: Siglo XXI, 1981.

Castañeda Naranjo, Luz Stella, and José Ignacio Henao Salazar (eds.). *Diccionario de Parlache.* Medellín: La Carreta Editores, 2006.

Castillo, Ana. *Massacre of the Dreamers: Essays on Xicanisma.* New York: Plume/ Penguin Books, 1995.

Cavarero, Adriana. *Relating Narratives: Storytelling and Selfhood.* Trans. Paul A. Kottman. London; New York: Routledge, 2000.

Certeau, Michel de. *The Practice of Everyday Life.* Trans. Steven Rendall. Berkeley; Los Angeles: Univ. of California Press, 1988.

Chartier, Roger. *Cultural History: Between Practices and Representations.* Trans. Lydia G. Cochrane. Ithaca, NY: Cornell Univ. Press, 1988.

Clayton, Martin, Trevor Herbert, and Richard Middleton (eds.). *The Cultural Study of Music.* New York; London, 2003.

Colebrook, Claire. *Deleuze: A Guide for the Perplexed.* London; New York: Continuum, 2006.

Connolly, William E. *Political Theory and Modernity.* Oxford: Basil Blackwell, 1988.

Contreras, Manuel. *El Hijo de Camelia* (corrido). Mexico 1977 (in Astorga, *Mitología,* 128).

Cornell, Drucilla. "The Philosophy of the Limit: Systems Theory and Feminist Legal Reform." In D. C., Michel Rosenfeld and David G. Carlson (eds.). *Deconstruction and the Possibility of Justice.* New York; London: Routledge, 1992.

Costa Lima, Luiz. "Zwischen Realismus und Figuration: Auerbachs dezentrierter Realismus". In Karlheinz Barck and Martin Treml. *Erich Auerbach: Geschichte und Aktualität eines europäischen Philologen.* Berlin: Kulturverlag Kadmos, 2006.

Courtwright, David T. *Forces of Habit: Drugs and the Making of the Modern World.* Cambridge; London: Harvard Univ. Press, 2000.

Cuddon, J. A. *A Dictionary of Literary Terms.* Middlesex; New York: Penguin Books, 1979.

Cumbides, Humberto J., María Cristina Laverde Toscano, and Carlos Eduardo Valderrama (eds.). *Viviendo a toda: Jóvenes, territorios culturales y nuevas sensibilidades*. Bogotá: Fundación Universidad Central/Siglo del Hombre, 2002.

D'Arcais, Paolo Flores. *Libertärer Existentialismus: Zur Aktualität der Theorie von Hannah Arendt*. Frankfurt Main: Suhrkamp, 1993.

Damasio, Antonio. *Looking for Spinoza: Joy, Sorrow, and the Feeling Brain*. Orlando; Austin: Harcourt, 2003.

Davis, Mike. *In Praise of Barbarians: Essays against Empire*. Chicago: Haymarket Books, 2007.

———. *Planet of Slums*. London; New York: Verso, 2006.

de Man, Paul. *Allegories of Reading: Figural Language in Rousseau, Nietzsche, Rilke, and Proust*, New Haven, CT; London: Yale Univ. Press, 1979.

———. "The Epistemology of Metaphor." In Paul de Man. *Aesthetic Ideology*. Ed. by Andrzej Warminski. Minneapolis; London: Univ. of Minnesota Press, 1996.

Debord, Guy. *The Society of the Spectacle*. Trans. Donald Nicholson-Smith. New York: Zone Books, 1995.

DeGrandpre, Richard. *The Cult of Pharmacology: How America Became the World's Most Troubled Drug Culture*. Durham, NC; London: Duke Univ. Press, 2006.

Deleuze, Gilles. *Cinema 1: The Movement-Image*. Trans. Hugh Tomlinson and Robert Galeta. Minneapolis: Univ. of Minnesota Press, 1986.

———. *Cinema 2: The Time-Image*. Trans. Hugh Tomlinson and Robert Galeta. Minneapolis: Univ. of Minnesota Press, 1989.

———. *Nietzsche and Philosophy*. Trans. Hugh Tomlinson. New York: Columbia Univ. Press, 1983.

———. *Pure Immanence. Essays on a Life*. Trans. Anne Boyman. New York: Zone Books, 2001.

Deleuze, Gilles and Félix Guattari. *Anti-Oedipus: Capitalism and Schizophrenia*. Trans. Robert Hurle, Mark Seem, and Helen R. Lane. Minneapolis: Univ. of Minnesota Press, 1983.

———. "The Plane of Immanence." In G. Deleuze and Félix Guattari. *What Is Philosophy?* New York: Columbia Univ. Press, 1994.

Derrida, Jacques. "Force of Law." In Gil Anidjar. *Acts of Religion*. New York; London: Routledge, 2002.

———. *Margins of Philosophy*. Trans. Alan Bass. Chicago: Univ. of Chicago Press, 1986.

Derrida, Jacques and Gianni Vattimo (eds.). *Religion*. Stanford: Stanford Univ. Press, 1998.

Domínguez Cataño, Edgar. *Leidy Tabares: La niña que vendía rosas*. Bogotá: Intermedio, 2003.

Drury, Shadia. *Terror and Civilization: Christianity, Politics, and the Western Psyche*. New York: Palgrave Macmillan, 2004.

Duno, Luis (ed.). *Imagen y subalternidad: El cine de Víctor Gaviria*. Caracas: Fundación Cinemateca Nacional, 2003.

Durkheim, Émile. *The Elementary Forms of Religious Life*. Trans. Carol Cosman. Oxford: Oxford Univ. Press, 2001.

Eagleton, Terry. *The Idea of Culture*. Oxford; Malden: Blackwell, 2000.

———. *Sweet Violence: The Idea of the Tragic*. Malden; Oxford: Blackwell, 2003.

Edberg, Mark Cameron. *El Narcotraficante: Narcocorridos and the Construction of a Cultural Persona on the U.S.-Mexican Border*. Austin: Univ. of Texas Press, 2004.

Faciolince, Héctor Abad. "Entrevista con Héctor Abad Faciolince" by Jaime A. Orrego. In http://www.escritoresyperiodistas.com.Numero27/jaime.htm.

———. *Las formas de la pereza.* Bogotá: Aguilar, 2007.

Foucault, Michel. *The History of Sexuality: An Introduction.* Vol. 1. New York: Vintage Books, 1990.

———. *The History of Sexuality: The Use of Pleasure.* Vol. 2. New York: Vintage Books, 1990.

———. *The History of Sexuality: Care of Self.* Vol. 3. New York: Vintage Books, 1988.

———. "Introduction." In Georges Canguilhem. *The Normal and the Pathological.* New York: Zone Books, 1989.

———. *Surveiller et punir: naissance de la prison.* Paris: Gallimard, 1975.

Franco, Jean. *The Decline and Fall of the Lettered City: Latin America in the Cold War.* Cambridge, MA; London, England: Harvard Univ. Press, 2002.

Franco Ramos, Jorge. *Rosario Tijeras.* [1999] Trans. Gregory Rabassa. New York; London: Seven Stories Press, 2005.

Freud, Sigmund. *Civilization and Its Discontents.* Trans. James Strachey. New York; London: W. W. Norton, 2005.

———. *Moses and Monotheism.* Trans. Katherine Jones. New York: Vintage, 1967.

Friedman, Jonathan (ed.). *Globalization, the State, and Violence.* Walnut Creek; Lanham: Rowman & Littlefield, 2003.

García Canclini, Néstor. *Culturas híbridas: Estrategias para entrar y salir de la modernidad.* Mexico City: Grijalbo, 1990.

Gaviria, Víctor. *El pelaíto que no duró nada.* Bogotá: Planeta, 1991.

Geertz, Clifford. *The Interpretation of Cultures.* New York: Fontana Press, 1993.

Genet, Jean. *Our Lady of the Flowers* (1943). Trans. Bernard Frechtman. London: Paladin, 1988.

Gilroy, Paul. *Postcolonial Melancholia.* New York: Columbia Univ. Press, 2005.

Ginzburg, Carlo. *The Cheese and the Worms: The Cosmos of a Sixteenth-Century Miller.* Trans. John and Anne Tedeschi. Baltimore, MD: Johns Hopkins Univ. Press, 1980.

Girard, René. *Violence and the Sacred.* Trans. Patrick Gregory. Baltimore, MD: Johns Hopkins Univ. Press, 1977.

Goetschel, Willi. *Spinoza's Modernity.* Madison: Univ. of Wisconsin Press, 2004.

González, Angel and Estanislao Rivera. *Contrabando y Traición* (corrido). Mexico 1975 (in Astorga, *Mitología,* 127).

———. *Ya encontraron a Camelia* (corrido). Mexico 1980 (in Astorga, *Mitología,* 128).

Goodman-Thau, Eveline. "Auf der Kreuzung von Geschichte und Freiheit – Abendländische Eschatologie an der Jahrtausendwende." In Richard Faber, E. Goodman-Thau, and Thomas Macho (eds.). *Abendländische Eschatologie. Ad Jacob Taubes.* Würzburg: Königshausen & Neumann, 2001.

Grandin, Greg. *Empire's Workshop: Latin America, the United States, and the Rise of the New Imperialism.* New York: Henry Holt, 2007.

Greenblatt, Steven. *Renaissance Self-Fashioning: From More to Shakespeare.* Chicago; London: Univ. of Chicago Press, 1980.

Guillory, John. *Cultural Capital: The Problem of Literary Canon Formation.* Chicago; London: Univ. of Chicago Press, 1993.

Gumbrecht, Hans Ulrich. "Cosmological Time and the Impossibility of Closure: A Structural Element in Spanish Golden Age Narratives." In Marina Brownlee and

H. U. Gumbrecht (eds.). *Cultural Authority in Golden Age Spain*. Baltimore, MD; London: Johns Hopkins Univ. Press, 1995.

———. *Production of Presence: What Meaning Cannot Convey*. Stanford: Stanford Univ. Press, 2004.

Hallward, Peter. *Absolutely Postcolonial: Writing between the Singular and the Specific*. Manchester; New York: Manchester Univ. Press, 2001.

———. "Translator's Introduction" to Alain Badiou. *Ethics: An Essay on the Understanding of Evil*. London; New York: Verso, 2001.

Hamacher, Werner. "Schuldgeschichte: Benjamins Skizze 'Kapitalismus als Religion.'" In Dirk Baecker (ed.). *Kapitalismus als Religion*. Berlin: Kulturverlag Kadmos, 2003.

Hamnett, Brian. *A Concise History of Mexico*. Cambridge: Cambridge Univ. Press, 1999.

Hardt, Michael and Antonio Negri. *Empire*. Cambridge, MA: Harvard Univ. Press, 2000.

Hartwich, Wolf-Daniel, Aleida Assmann, and Jan Assmann. "Afterword." In Jacob Taubes. The Political Thelogy of Paul.

Harvey, David. *A Brief History of Neoliberalism*. Oxford: Oxford Univ. Press, 2005.

———. *The Condition of Postmodernity: An Enquiry into the Origins of Cultural Change*. Oxford: Basil Blackwell, 1990.

———. *The Limits to Capital*. London; New York: Verso, 2006.

———. *The New Imperialism*. Oxford: Oxford Univ. Press, 2003.

———. *Spaces of Hope*. Berkeley; Los Angeles: Univ. of California Press, 2000.

———. "Spaces of Insurgency." In John Beverley, Phil Cohen, and David Harvey. *Subculture and Homogenization*, Barcelona: Fundació Antoni Tàpies, 1998.

Haverkamp, Anselm. "Allegorie." In Karlheinz Barck, Martin Fontius, Dieter Schlenstedt, Burkhardt Steinwachs, and Friedrich Wolfzettel (eds.). *Ästhetische Grundbegriffe*. Vol 1.

———. "Kritik der Gewalt und die Möglichkeit von Gerechtigkeit: Benjamin in Deconstruction." In A. Haverkamp (ed.). *Gewalt und Gerechtigkeit*. Frankfurt Main: Suhrkamp, 1994.

Hegel, G. W. F. "Aesthetics: Tragedy, Comedy and Drama." In Stephen Houlgate. *The Hegel Reader*. Malden; Oxford: Blackwell, 1998.

———. *Elements of the Philosophy of Right*. Trans. H. B. Nisbet. Cambridge: Cambridge Univ. Press, 1991.

Heidegger, Martin. *Being and Time*. Trans. Joan Stambaugh. Albany: State Univ. of New York Press, 1996.

Herlinghaus, Hermann. *Renarración y descentramiento: Mapas alternativos de la imaginación en América Latina*. Madrid; Frankfurt: Iberoamericana, 2005.

——— (ed.). *Narraciones anacrónicas de la modernidad: Melodrama e intermediali-dad en América Latina*. Santiago de Chile: Cuarto Propio, 2002.

———. "Walter Benjamins Begriff des Rausches zwischen Surrealismus und Drogenkrieg." In Reinhard Krüger. *Grenzgänge, Hybride und Fusionen: Romanistische Beiträge zu polykulturellen Kommunikationsprozessen*. Berlin: Weidler Buchverlag, 2007.

———. "Zur neuen Krise der kosmopolitischen Imagination." In Walter Fähnders, Nils Plath, and Hendrik Weber (eds.). *Berlin, Paris, Moskau: Reiseliteratur und die Metropolen*. Bielefeld: Aisthesis Verlag, 2005.

Herrera-Sobek, María. *The Mexican Corrido: A Feminist Analysis*. Bloomington; Indianapolis: Indiana Univ. Press, 1990.

————. *Northward Bound: The Mexican Immigrant Experience in Ballad and Song.* Bloomington; Indianapolis: Indiana Univ. Press, 1993.

Higgins, Dick. *Horizons: The Poetic and Theory of the Intermedia.* Carbondale; Edwardsville: Southern Illinois Univ. Press, 1984.

————. *Modernism since Postmodernism: Essays on Intermedia.* Calexico, CA; San Diego: San Diego State Univ. Press, 1997.

Hiller, Kurt. "Linkspazifismus" [1920]. In K. Hiller. *Radioaktiv. Reden 1914–1964.* Wiesbaden: Limes Verlag, 1966.

Hobsbawm, Eric. *Primitive Rebels: Studies in Archaic Forms of Social Movement in the 19th and 20th Centuries.* New York: Norton Library, 1965.

Holy Bible (*The New Scofield Reference Bible*, ed. C. I. Scofield). New York: Oxford Univ. Press, 1967.

Hondagneu-Sotelo, Pierette. "The History of Mexican Undocumented Settlement in the United States." In Mary Romero, Pierrette Hondagneu-Sotelo, and Vilma Ortiz (eds.). *Challenging Fronteras: Structuring Latina and Latino Lifes in the U.S.* New York; London: Routledge, 1997.

Horkheimer, Max and Theodor W. Adorno. *Dialectic of Enlightenment.* Trans. John Cumming. New York: Herder and Herder, 1972.

Huntington, Samuel P. *Who Are We? The Challenges to America's National Identity.* New York; London: Simon & Schuster, 2004.

Hutcheon, Linda. *Narcissistic Narrative: The Metafictional Paradox.* New York; London: Methuen, 1984.

Hylton, Forrest. "Colombia: An Evil Hour." *New Left Review,* 23. Sept.–Oct. 2003.

————. *Evil Hour in Colombia.* London; New York: Verso, 2006.

————. "Extreme Makeover." In Mike Davis and Daniel Bertrand Monk (eds.). *Evil Paradises: Dreamworlds of Neoliberalism.* New York; London: New Press, 2007.

————. "*Rodrigo D. No Futuro* y la política (trans)cultural de la desesperación." In Luis Duno. *Imagen y subalternidad: El cine de Víctor Gaviria.* Caracas: Fundación Cinemateca Nacional, 2003.

Inwood, Michael. *A Heidegger Dictionary.* Oxford: Blackwell, 1999.

Jaramillo Morales, Alejandra. *Nación y melancolía: Narrativas de la violencia en Colombia (1995–2005).* Bogota: Instituto Distrital de Cultura y Turismo, 2006.

Jaspers, Karl. *Nietzsche und das Christentum.* Hameln: Verlag der Bücherstube Fritz Seifert, 1946.

Jáuregui Carlos. "Entrevista con Víctor Gaviria: Violencia, representación y voluntad realista." In Luis Duno. *Imagen y subalternidad: El cine de Víctor Gaviria.*

Jauss, Hans Robert. *Ästhetische Erfahrung und literarische Hermeneutik.* München: Wilhelm Fink, 1977.

Jewett, Robert. "Romans." In James D. G. Dunn. The Cambridge Companion to St. Paul. Cambridge; New York: Cambridge Univ. Press, 2003.

Judy, Ronald. "America and Powerless Potentialities." In REAL. Yearbook of Research in English and American Literature. No. 19 (*Thories of American Culture.* Eds. Winfried Fluck and Thomas Claviez). Tübingen: Gunter Narr, 2003.

Kadir, Djelal. *The Other Writing: Postcolonial Essays in Latin America's Writing Culture.* West Lafayette: Purdue Univ. Press, 1993.

Kaminski, Gregorio, Darío Kosovsky, and Gabriel Kessler. *El delito en la Argentina post-crisis.* Buenos Aires: Univ. Nacional de Lanus, 2007.

Kantaris. Geoffrey. "Allegorical Cities: Bodies and Visions in Colombian Urban Cinema." In *Estudios Interdisciplinarios de América Latina y el Caribe.* 9 (2), July–Dec. 1998.

Kantaris. Geoffrey. "Peripheries of Globalization: Fredric Jameson's *The Seeds of Time* and Víctor Gaviria's *The Rose Seller.*" Paper given at the Univ. of Cambridge, Feb. 13, 2001.

Kantorowicz, Ernst. *The King's Two Bodies: A Study in Mediaeval Political Theology.* Princeton, NJ: Princeton Univ. Press, 1957.

Kaufman, Eleanor and Kevin Jon Heller (eds.). *Deleuze&Guattari: New Mappings in Politics, Philosophy, and Culture.* Minneapolis; London: Univ. of Minnesota Press, 1998.

Kessler, Gabriel. *Sociología del delito amateur.* Buenos Aires: Paidós, 2006.

Kipp, Jeremiah. "Amores Perros." (Film Review). In *Filmcritic.com,* 2001.

Kirk, Robin. *More Terrible than Death: Massacres, Drugs, and America's War in Colombia.* New York: Public Affairs, 2003.

Kittredge, George Lyman. "Introduction." In Helen Child Sargent and George Lyman Kittredge. *English and Scottish Popular Ballads.* (From the Collection of Francis James Child). Boston; New York: Houghton Mifflin, 1904.

Klein, Naomi. *The Shock Doctrine: The Rise of Disaster Capitalism.* New York: Metropolitan Books/Henry Holt, 2007.

Kraniauskas, John. "Beware Mexican Ruins! 'One-Way Street' and the Colonial Unconscious." In Peter Osborne (ed.). *Walter Benjamin: Critical Evaluations in Cultural Theory.* Vol. 1. London; New York: Routledge, 2005 (originally published in Andrew Benjamin and P. Osborne (eds.). *Walter Benjamin's Philosophy: Destruction and Experience,* Routledge, 1994).

———. "*Cronos* and the Political Economy of Vampirism." In Francis Barker, Peter Hulme, and Margaret Iverson (eds.). *Cannibalism and the Colonial Order.* Cambridge: Cambridge Univ. Press, 1998.

Kristeva, Julia. *Powers of Horror: An Essay on Abjection.* New York: Columbia Univ. Press, 1982.

Kuhn, Cynthia, Scott Swartzwelder, and Wilkie Wilson. *Buzzed: The Straight Facts about the Most Used and Abused Drugs from Alcohol to Ecstasy.* New York; London: W. W. Norton, 2003.

Lambert, Malcolm D. *Franciscan Poverty: The Doctrine of the Absolute Poverty of Christ and the Apostles in the Franciscan Order 1210–1323.* St. Bonaventure, NY: Franciscan Institute, 1998.

Latour, Bruno. *Politics of Nature: How to Bring the Sciences into Democracy.* Trans. Catherine Porter. Cambridge, MA; London: Harvard Univ. Press, 2004.

———. *We Have Never Been Modern.* Trans. Catherine Porter. Cambridge: Harvard Univ. Press, 1993.

Leech, Gary. *Killing Peace: Colombia's Conflict and the Failure of U.S. Intervention.* New York: Information Network of the Americas, 2002.

Liera, Óscar. *El jinete de la divina providencia* (The Horseman of Divine Providence, 1984). In Vicente Leñero (ed.). *La nueva dramaturgia mexicana.* Mexico: Ediciones el Milagro, 1996.

Lindemann Nelson, Hilde. *Damaged Identities, Narrative Repair.* Ithaca, NY; London: Cornell Univ. Press, 2001.

Lindner, Burkhardt (ed.). *Benjamin Handbuch. Leben – Werk – Wirkung.* Stuttgart; Weimar: J. B. Metzler, 2006.

Löwith, Karl. *Weltgeschichte und Heilsgeschehen: Die theologischen Voraussetzungen der Geschichtsphilosophie.* Stuttgart; Berlin: Verlag W. Kohlhammer, 1979.

Lorey, David E. *The U.S.-Mexican Border in the Twentieth Century: A History of Economic and Social Transformation.* Wilmington: Scholarly Resources, 1999.

Lyotard, Jean-François. *The Postmodern Condition: A Report on Knowledge.* Minneapolis: Univ. of Minnesota Press, 1984.

Marez, Curtis. *Drug Wars: The Political Economy of Narcotics.* Minneapolis; London: Univ. of Minnesota Press, 2004.

Margulis, Mario and Marcelo Urresti. "La construcción social de la condición de juventud." In Humberto J. Cumbides, María Cristina Laverde Toscano, and Carlos Eduardo Valderrama (eds.). *Viviendo a toda: Jóvenes, territorios culturales y nuevas sensibilidades.* Bogotá: Fundación Universidad Central/Siglo del Hombre, 2002.

Marramao, Giacomo. *Cielo e terra. Genealogia della secolarizzazione.* Rom; Bari: Gius. Laterza & Figli, 1994.

Martín-Barbero, Jesús. "Jóvenes: Des-orden cultural y palimpsestos de identidad." In Humberto J. Cumbides, María Cristina Laverde Toscano, and Carlos Eduardo Valderrama (eds.). *Viviendo a toda: Jóvenes, territorios culturales y nuevas sensibilidades.* Bogotá: Fundación Universidad Central/Siglo del Hombre, 2002.

———. "Materiales para una nueva agenda desde la encrucijada de las urbanías y las ciudadanías." Manuscript. Bogotá, Aug. 2007.

Marx Karl. *Capital: A Critique of Political Economy.* Vol. I. Trans. Ben Fowkes. London; New York: Penguin Books/New Left Review, 1990.

Massumi, Brian (ed.). *The Politics of Everyday Fear.* Minneapolis; London: Univ. of Minnesota Press, 1993.

McDowell, John H. *Poetry and Violence: The Ballad Tradition of Mexico's Costa Chica.* Urbana; Chicago: Univ. of Illinois Press, 2000.

McKenna, Teresa. "On Chicano Poetry and the Political Age: Corridos as Social Drama." In Héctor Calderón and J. D. Saldívar (eds.). *Criticism in the Borderlands.* Durham, NC; London: Duke Univ. Press, 1991.

Medina, Javier. *El trueno sobre los cocales: Coca, cultura y democracia participativa municipal.* La Paz: Hisbol, 1995.

Mendoza, Elmer. *Cada respiro que tomas.* Culiacán, Mexico: Dirección de Investigación y Fomento de Cultura Regional del Gobierno del Estado de Sinaloa, 1991.

Mendoza, Vicente T. *El Romance Español y el Corrido Mexicano: Estudio Comparativo.* Mexico: Univ. Nacional Autonoma, 1997.

Menéndez-Pidal. Ramón. *Romancero Hispánico. Teoría e Historia.* Vol. I. Madrid, 1953.

Menke, Christoph. *Tragödie im Sittlichen: Gerechtigkeit und Freiheit nach Hegel.* Frankfurt Main: Suhrkamp, 1996.

Mignolo, Walter D. *The Idea of Latin America.* Oxford: Blackwell, 2005.

———. *Local Histories/Global Designs: Coloniality, Subaltern Knowledges, and Border Thinking.* Princeton, NJ; Oxford: Princeton Univ. Press, 2000.

Millán, Francisco. *Las huellas de Buñuel.* Teruel: Instituto de Estudios Turolenses, 2004.

Mitchell, Margaret M. "1 and 2 Thessalonians." In James D. G. Dunn. *The Cambridge Companion to St. Paul.* Cambridge; New York: Cambridge Univ. Press, 2003.

Mitschein, Thomas, Henrique R. Miranda, and Mariceli C. Paraense. *Urbanização, selvagem e proletarização na Amazonia.* Belém: CEJUP, 1989.

Mondaca Cota, Anajilda. *Las mujeres también pueden: Género y narcocorrido.* Culiacán: Universidad de Occidente, 2004.

Monsiváis, Carlos. "Citizenship and Urban Violence." In Susana Rotker. *Citizens of Fear: Urban Violence in Latin America.* New Brunswick; London: Rutgers Univ. Press, 2002.

Monsiváis, Carlos. "De la frontera y el centro." In J. M. Valenzuela (ed.). *Procesos culturales de fin de milenio.* Tijuana: Centro Cultural Tijuana, 1998.

———. "En los albores de la indústria heterodoxa." In C. Monsiváis. (ed.). *Viento Rojo. Diez historias del narco en México.* Mexico: Plaza & Janés, 2004.

———. *Los mil y un velorios: Crónica de la nota roja,* Mexico: Alianza Editorial, 1994.

Montemayor, Carlos. *Chiapas, la rebelión indígena en México.* Mexico City: Joaquín Mortiz, 1997.

Morandé, Pedro. *Cultura y modernización en América Latina.* Santiago de Chile: Encuentro, 1984.

Müller. Ernst. "Auerbach's Realismus." In Karlheinz Barck and Martin Treml. *Erich Auerbach: Geschichte und Aktualität eines europäischen Philologen.* Berlin: Kulturverlag Kadmos, 2006.

———. "Hannah Arendts Marxkritik." *Berliner Debatte Initial,* 14 (2), 2003.

Müller, Heiner. *Jenseits der Nation.* Nördlingen: Rotbuch Verlag, 1997.

MV Bill. *Traficando informação.* (music CD), São Paulo, 1999.

———. *Declaração de guerra.* (music CD), São Paulo, 2002.

Negri, Antonio. "The Political Subject and Absolute Immanence." In Creston Davis, John Milbank, and Slavoj Žižek (eds.). *Theology and the Political:* The New Debate. Durham, NC; London: Duke Univ. Press, 2005.

———. *The Savage Anomaly: The Power of Spinoza's Metaphysics and Politics.* Trans. Michael Hardt. Minneapolis; Oxford: Univ. of Minnesota Press, 1991.

———. *Time for Revolution.* Trans. Matteo Mandarini. New York; London: Continuum, 2003.

Nietzsche, Friedrich. *On the Genealogy of Morality.* Ed. Keith Ansell-Pearson. Trans. Carol Diethe. Cambridge; New York: Cambridge Univ. Press, 2007.

Nold, Patrick. *Pope John XII and His Franciscan Cardinal: Bertrand de la Tour and the Apostolic Poverty Controversy.* Oxford: Clarendon Press, 2003.

O'Bryan, Rory. "Representations of the City in the Narrative of Fernando Vallejo." *Journal of Latin American Cultural Studies,* 13 (2), Aug. 2004.

Ong, Aihwa. *Neoliberalism as Exception: Mutations in Citizenship and Sovereignty.* Durham, NC; London: Duke Univ. Press, 2006.

Orrego, Jaime A. "Entrevista con Héctor Abad Faciolince." (July 4, 2006). In La Hojarasca. Alianza de Escritores y Periodistas (http://www.escritoresyperiodistas.com.Numero27/jaime.htm).

Ortiz, Fernando. *Cuban Counterpoint: Tobacco and Sugar.* Trans. Harriet de Onis. Durham, NC; London: Duke Univ. Press, 1995.

Orwell, George. "Looking Back on the Spanish War." In G. Orwell. *A Collection of Essays.* Garden City, New York: Doubleday, 1954.

Osborne, Peter. *The Politics of Time: Modernity and Avant-Garde.* London: Verso, 1995.

Oubiña, David. "El espectáculo y sus márgenes. Sobre Adrián Caetano y el nuevo cine argentino." *Punto de Vista,* 76, Aug. 2003.

Paredes, Américo. *Folklore and Culture on the Texas-Mexican Border.* Austin: Univ. of Texas at Austin, 1993.

Parker, Patricia. "Metaphor and Catachresis." In John Bender and David E. Wellbery (eds.). *The Ends of Rhetoric: History, Theory, Practice.* Stanford: Stanford Univ. Press, 1990.

Perelman, Michael. *The Invention of Capitalism: Classical Political Economy and the Secret of Primitive Accumulation.* Durham, NC; London: Duke Univ. Press, 2000.

Pérez Ramírez, Marcos. "La narcoliteratura y sus fieros caminos," *El Nuevo Día/ Letras*, San Juan (Puerto Rico), Nov. 27, 2005.

Pérez-Reverte, Arturo. *La Reina del Sur.* Madrid: Alfaguara, 2002.

Piglia, Ricardo. *Plata quemada.* Buenos Aires: Planeta, 1997.

Pisters, Patricia. *The Matrix of Visual Culture: Working with Deleuze in Film Theory.* Stanford: Stanford Univ. Press, 2003.

Plato. *The Republic.* Oxford: Oxford Univ. Press, 1941.

Pollock, Sheldon, Homi K. Bhabha, Carol A. Breckenridge, and Dipesh Chakrabarty. "Cosmopolitan and Vernacular in History." In Carol A. Breckenridge, Sheldon Pollock, Homi K. Bhabha, and Dipesh Chakrabarty (eds.). *Cosmopolitanism.* Durham, NC; London: Duke Univ. Press, 2002.

———. "Cosmopolitanisms." In Carol A. Breckenridge, Sheldon Pollock, Homi K. Bhabha, and Dipesh Chakrabarty (eds.). *Cosmopolitanism.* Durham, NC; London: Duke Univ. Press, 2002.

Ponce, Mary Helen. "The Marijuana Party." In Ray González (ed.). *Mirrors Beneath the Earth.* Willimantic, CT: Curbstone Press, 1992.

Quijano, Aníbal. "Coloniality of Power, Eurocentrism, and Latin America." *Nepantla: Views from the South,* 1 (3), 2000.

Quijano, Aníbal and Immanuel Wallerstein. "Americanity as a Concept or the Americas in the Modern World System." *International Journal of Social Sciences,* 134, Nov. 1992.

Quinn, Eithne. *Nuthin' but a "G" Thang: The Culture and Commerce of Gangsta Rap.* New York: Columbia Univ. Press, 2004.

Quiñones, Sam. "San Jose's Los Tigres del Norte Have Remade Mexican Pop Music Twice Over." In *Metroactive,* Dec. 31, 1997–Jan. 7, 1998.

———. *True Tales from another Mexico: The Lynch Mob, the Popsicle Kings, Chalino, and the Bronx.* Albuquerque: Univ. of New Mexico Press, 2001.

Ranciére, Jacques. *The Politics of Aesthetics: The Distribution of the Sensible.* Trans. Gabriel Rockhill. London; New York: Continuum, 2004.

Rasch, William. *Niklas Luhmann's Modernity: The Paradoxes of Differentiation.* Stanford: Stanford Univ. Press, 2000.

———. *Sovereignty and Its Discontents: On the Primacy of Conflict and the Structure of the Political.* London: Birkbeck Law Press, 2004.

Reguillo, Rossana. "The Social Construction of Fear." In Susana Rotker. *Citizens of Fear: Urban Violence in Latin America.* New Brunswick, NJ; London: Rutgers Univ. Press, 2002.

Ricoeur, Paul. "The Human Experience of Time and Narrative." In Mario J. Valdés (ed.). *A Ricoeur Reader.* Toronto; Buffalo: Univ. of Toronto Press, 1991.

———. *Time and Narrative.* Vol. 3. Trans. Kathleen McLaughlin and David Pellauer. Chicago: Univ. of Chicago Press, 1988.

Riley, Kevin Jack. *Snow Job? The War against International Cocaine Trafficking.* New Brunswick, NJ; London: Transaction, 1996.

Rivera Cusicanqui, Silvia. *Las fronteras de la coca: Epistemologías coloniales y circuitos alternativos de la hoja de coca. El caso de la frontera boliviano-argentino.* La Paz: Universidad Mayor de San Andrés / Ediciones Aruwiyiri, 2003.

Rosen, Philip. *Change Mummified: Cinema, History, Theory.* Minneapolis; London: Univ. of Minnesota Press, 2001.

Rotker, Susana (ed.). *Citizens of Fear: Urban Violence in Latin America.* New Brunswick; London: Rutgers Univ. Press, 2002.

Rozitchner, León. *La cosa y la cruz: Cristianismo y capitalismo. En torno a las 'Confesiones' de San Agustín.* Buenos Aires: Losada, 2001.

Russel, Lawrence. "Our Lady of the Assassins." In *Filmcourt*, 6/2002 (http://www.culturecourt.com/F/Voyeur/OLA.htm).

Said, Edward. *Beginnings: Intention and Method*. New York: Columbia Univ. Press, 1985.

———. "Introduction" to Auerbach. *Mimesis*. Princeton, NJ; Oxford: Princeton Univ. Press, 2003.

———. *Orientalism*. New York: Pantheon Books, 1978.

Salazar J., Alonso. *Mujeres de fuego*. Medellín: Corporación Región, 1993.

———. *No nacimos pa' semilla: La cultura de las bandas juveniles en Medellín*. [1990] Bogotá: Planeta, 2002. (Engl. *Born to Die in Medellin*. Trans. Nick Caistor. London: Latin American Bureau, 1993).

Salazar J., Alonso and Ana María Jaramillo. *Medellín: Las subculturas del narcotráfico*. Bogotá: Cinep, 1992.

Saldívar, José David. *Border Matters: Remapping American Cultural Studies*. Berkeley; Los Angeles: Univ. of California Press, 1997.

———. *The Dialectics of Our America: Genealogy, Cultural Critique, and Literary History*. Durham, NC; London: Duke Univ. Press, 1991.

Sánchez-Prado, Ignacio. "Amores Perros: Exotic Violence and Neoliberal Fear." *Journal of Latin American Cultural Studies*, 15 (1), March 2006.

Sander, Sheila Rebecca. "Tropes and Trojan Horses: An Essay on Catachresis." *Literary Research/Recherche Littéraire*, 19, 37–38, 2002.

Santner, Eric L. *On the Psychotheology of Everyday Life: Reflections on Freud and Rosenzweig*. Chicago: Univ. of Chicago Press, 2001.

———. *On Creaturely Life: Rilke, Benjamin, Sebald*. Chicago; London: Univ. of Chicago Press, 2006.

Sartre, Jean-Paul. *Saint Genet: Actor and Martyr*. New York: Mentor/New American Library, 1963.

Sassen, Saskia, "Globalization after September 11." *Chronicle of Higher Education*, Jan. 18, 2002.

———. "Economic Globalization and the Redrawing of Citizenship." In Jonathan Friedman. *Globalization, the State, and Violence*. Walnut Creek; Lanham: Rowman & Littlefield, 2003.

———. *Territory – Authority – Rights: From Medieval to Global Assemblages*. Princeton, NJ: Princeton Univ. Press, 2006.

Schmitt, Carl. *Political Theology: Four Chapters on the Concept of Sovereignty*. Trans. George Schwab. Cambridge, MA; London: MIT Press, 1985.

Scholem, Gershom. *Major Trends in Jewish Mysticism*. New York: Schocken, 1995.

Sieber, Harry. "Literary Continuity, Social Order, and the Invention of the Picaresque." In M. S. Brownlee and H. U. Gumbrecht (eds.). *Cultural Authority in Golden Age Spain*. Baltimore, MD; London: Johns Hopkins Univ. Press, 1995.

Simonett, Helena. *Banda. Mexican Musical Life across Borders*. Middletown, CT: Wesleyan Univ. Press, 2001.

Sloterdijk, Peter. *Critique of Cynical Reason*. Trans. Michael Eldred. Minneapolis: Univ. of Minnesota Press, 1987.

Smith, Daniel W. "The Place of Ethics in Deleuze's Philosophy: Three Questions of Immanence." In Eleanor Kaufman and Kevin Jon Heller. *Deleuze & Guattari: New Mappings in Politics, Philosophy, and Culture*. Minneapolis; London: Univ. of Minnesota Press, 1998.

Smith, Paul Julian. "Homographesis in Salicio's Song." In M. S. Brownlee and H. U. Gumbrecht. *Cultural Authority in Golden Age Spain*. Baltimore, MD; London: Johns Hopkins Univ. Press, 1995.

Sontag, Susan. *Against Interpretation*. New York: Dell, 1966.

Sorel, Georges. *Reflections on Violence*. Trans. T. E. Hulme and J. Roth. Glencoe, IL: Free Press, 1950.

Spedding, Alison and Abraham Colque (eds.). *Nosotros los Yungueños: Testimonios de los Yungueños del siglo XX*. La Paz: Instituto Mama Huaco, 2003.

Spinoza. *Ethics*. Trans. G. H. R. Parkinson. Oxford: Oxford Univ. Press, 2000.

Steiner, Uwe. "Kapitalismus als Religion." In Burkhardt Lindner (ed.). *Benjamin Handbuch: Leben—Werk—Wirkung*. Stuttgart; Weimar: J. B. Metzler, 2006.

———. *Walter Benjamin*. Stuttgart; Weimar: Verlag J. B. Metzler, 2004.

Sterne. Jonathan. *The Audible Past: Cultural Origins of Sound Reproduction*. Durham, NC; London: Duke Univ. Press, 2003.

Stokes, Doug. *America's Other War*. London; New York: Zed Books, 2005.

St. Paul. "The Letter to the Romans." In Wayne A. Meeks (ed.). *The Writings of St. Paul*. New York; London: W. W. Norton, 1972.

Suárez, Juana. "Los estragos de la euforia: Dinámicas urbanas en *Rodrigo D, La vendedora de rosas* y *Sumas y Restas*." In Luis Duno. *Imagen y subalternidad: El cine de Víctor Gaviria*. Caracas: Fundación Cinemateca Nacional, 2003.

Taubes, Jacob. "Der dogmatische Mythos der Gnosis." In Manfred Fuhrmann (ed.). *Terror und Spiel*. München: Wilhelm Fink, 1971.

———. *The Political Theology of Paul*. Trans. Dana Hollander. Stanford: Stanford Univ. Press, 2004.

Taussig, Michael. *Defacement: Public Secrecy and the Labor of the Negative*. Stanford: Stanford Univ. Press, 1999.

———. *Mimesis and Alterity: A Particular History of the Senses*. New York; London: Routledge, 1993.

———. *Shamanism, Colonialism, and the Wild Man: A Study in Terror and Healing*. Chicago; London: Univ. of Chicago Press, 1987.

———. "Transgression." In Mark C. Taylor (ed.). *Critical Terms for Religious Studies*. Chicago; London: Univ. of Chicago Press, 1998.

Taylor, Diana. *The Archive and the Repertoire: Performing Cultural Memory in the Americas*. Durham, NC; London: Duke Univ. Press, 2003.

Topik, Steven, Carlos Marichal, and Zephyr Frank (eds.). *From Silver to Cocaine: Latin American Commodity Chains and the Building of the World Economy, 1500–2000*. Durham, NC; London: Duke Univ. Press, 2006.

Toro, María Celia. *Mexico's War on Drugs: Causes and Consequences*. Boulder, CO; London: Lynne Rienner, 1995.

Uribe, María Teresa. "Presentacion." In Alonso Salazar J. *Mujeres de fuego*. Medellín: Corporación Región, 1993.

Valenzuela, José Manuel. *Jefe de Jefes: Corridos y narcocultura en México*. Barcelona; México City: Plaza & Janés Editores, 2002.

———. "Recreación del melodrama en el narcocorrido y la canción ranchera." In Hermann Herlinghaus (ed.). *Narraciones anacrónicas de la modernidad: melodrama e intermedialidad en América Latina*. Santiago de Chile: Cuarto Propio, 2002.

Vallejo, Fernando. "Electricidad apocalíptica." In *Con-Fabulación*. Periódico Virtual, May 7, 2008.

———. *La puta de Babilonia*. Mexico City: Planeta, 2007.

———. *La virgen de los sicarios* [1994]. Bogotá: Alfaguara, 1998. (Engl. *Our Lady of the Assassins*. Trans. Paul Hammond. London: Serpent's Tail, 2001.)

Vanderwood, Paul J. *Juan Soldado: Rapist, Murderer, Martyr, Saint*. Durham NC; London: Duke Univ. Press, 2004.

Van Schendel, Willem and Itty Abraham (eds.). *Illicit Flows and Criminal Things: States, Borders, and the Other Side of Globalization.* Bloomington; Indianapolis: Indiana Univ. Press, 2005.

Varella, Drauzio. *Estação Carandiru.* São Paulo: Companhia das Letras, 1999.

Vargas, Paulino. *La Banda del Carro Rojo* (corrido). Mexico 1975 (in Astorga, *Mitología*, 126).

Vico, Giambattista. *New Science.* Third Edition. Ed. Anthony Grafton. Trans. David Marsh. London; New York: Penguin Books, 2001.

Villegas, Daniel Cosío (ed.). *Historia General de México.* Vol. 2. Mexico City: El Colegio de México, 1999.

Wald, Elijah. *Narcocorrido: A Journey into the Music of Drugs, Guns, and Guerrillas,* New York: HarperCollins, 2001.

Walde, Erna von der. "La novela de sicarios y la violencia en Colombia." *Iberoamericana,* 1 (3), 2001.

Weber, Max. *The Protestant Ethic and the Spirit of Capitalism.* Trans. Talcott Parsons. Mineola, NY: Dover, 2003.

Weigel, Sigrid. *Literatur als Voraussetzung der Kulturgeschichte. Schauplätze von Shakespeare bis Benjamin.* München: Wilhelm Fink, 2004.

———. "Warum Walter Benjamin Now?" In "Now—das Jetzt der Erkennbarkeit: Orte Walter Benjamins in Kultur, Kunst und Wissenschaft." Benjamin Festival (Program). Berlin: Zentrum für Literatur- und Kulturforschung (ZfL), Oct. 17–22, 2006.

White, Hayden. *The Content of the Form: Narrative Discourse and Historical Representation.* Baltimore, MD; London: Johns Hopkins Univ. Press, 1987.

———. *Figural Realism: Studies in the Mimesis Effect.* Baltimore, MD; London: Johns Hopkins Univ. Press, 1999.

Witte, Bernd. *Walter Benjamin: An Intellectual Biography.* Trans. James Rolleston. Detroit: Wayne State Univ. Press, 1991.

Wolin, Richard. "Experience and Materialism in Benjamin's *Passagenwerk.*" In Gary Smith (ed.). *Benjamin: Philosophy, Aesthetics, History.* Chicago; London: Univ. of Chicago Press, 1989.

Young, Julian. *Heidegger's Later Philosophy.* Cambridge: Cambridge Univ. Press, 2002.

Žižek, Slavoj. *The Fragile Absolute or: Why Is the Christian Legacy Worth Fighting For?* London; New York: Verso, 2000.

———. "Pure Gewalt: Unkorrekte Reflexionen zu New Orleans, Frankreich und Verwandtem." *Lettre International.* Vol. 71. Berlin, Winter 2005.

———. Welcome to the Desert of the Real. London; New York: Verso, 2002.

INDEX